Nikolaus Koenig, Natalie Denk,
Alexander Pfeiffer, Thomas Wernbacher (Editors)

THE MAGIC OF GAMES

Editors: Nikolaus Koenig, Natalie Denk, Alexander Pfeiffer, Thomas Wernbacher

Cover, Illustration: Constantin Kraus

Publisher: Edition Donau-Universität Krems

Print: tredition GmbH, Halenreie 40-44, 22359 Hamburg

ISBN Paperback: 978-3-903150-72-0
ISBN e-Book: 978-3-903150-73-7

Contact:
Center for Applied Game Studies
Department for Arts and Cultural Studies
University for Continuing Education Krems
www.donau-uni.ac.at/ags
ags@donau-uni.ac.at

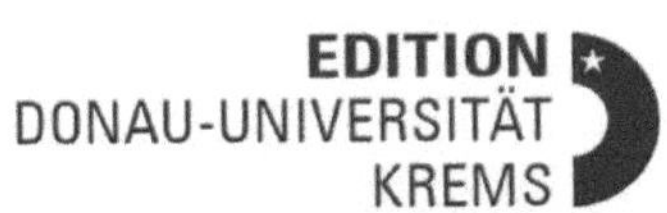

CONTENTS

Introduction

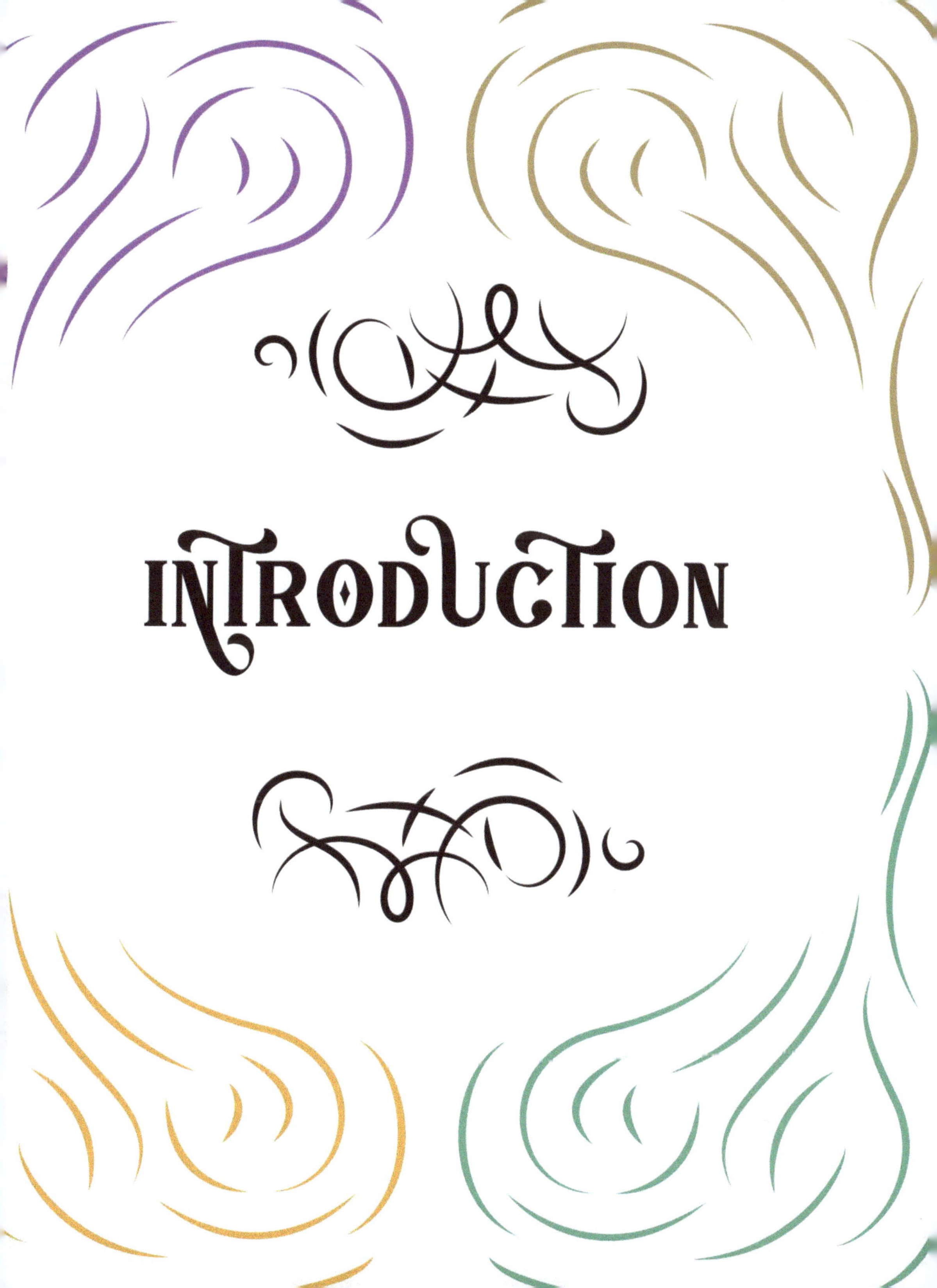

INTRODUCTION

THE MAGIC OF GAMES

Magic, while usually considered not entirely real, affects our lives in many ways. It can be a soothing fantasy, a useful and potent metaphor, or at the very least a void we desire to be filled, the universal placeholder for all the voids that make up the human condition. So, we chase those magic moments and wait to feel the magic in the air; we aspire to create at least a modicum of magic in our crafts, and when we are at the end of our wits and abilities, more often than we'd like to admit, we give into a little bit of magical thinking.

Magic in its most general form (as acknowledged by the ancient tomes of Merriam-Webster) is "a power that allows people [...]to do impossible things". It is the absolute (and thereby almost divine) ability to create, sometimes counter-intuitive, sometimes seemingly more intuitive than the strict, mechanical and demanding workings of the natural world. *Magic* promises freedom from the laws of physics and society, it represents power through knowledge and the skill to apply this knowledge to the world.

But by the same account, *Magic* is also "the art of producing illusions by sleight of hand": it is the dazzler's deceit, the tricks played on our mind (and our mind playing tricks), the deceptive gleam that diverts our gaze from the truth. *Magic* in this sense is something we need to beware of, lest it make fools of us. But it can also be something quite liberating, an escape from the cold hard truths of our daily routines, the welcome fantasy that things may, for a while, be a little more interesting than they usually appear.

Between these two understandings of *Magic*, it quickly becomes clear that there is more than one connection between *Magic* and *Games*. In making games, we also exert the power to create otherwise impossible worlds; in playing games, we make experiences or gain abilities that are inaccessible in the real world (especially in times of a pandemic, when even access to the mundane aspects of the real world is often denied); in playing together, we make connections on a level that we can hardly achieve in daily live; when it comes to *Magic* itself, it is rarely so tangible as when represented in games; and finally, there is Johan Huizinga and his *Magic Circle* – the gift that almost magically keeps on giving by providing generations of game scholars with cause for debate and controversy, ranging from discussions of its general usefulness to the burning of argumentative strawmen and the not so basic question why Huizinga chose to put his concept in the context of *Magic* in the first place.

The 15th Vienna Games Conference "Future and Reality of Gaming" (FROG) 2021 - hosted by the University of Krems' Center for Applied Game Studies in cooperation with the Austrian Federal Chancellery - has gathered game scholars, creators, educators and activists to come together and address the Magic of Games in its many forms. The results of these stimulating, thought-provoking and often controversial discussions can be found in this anthology, which we have divided into four parts that reflect the primary focal points of the conference.

The first part ("Representations of Magic in Games") looks at how (and why) magic is represented in games as a subject, as a narrative device, as a game mechanic and as a metaphor. What can representations of magic in games tell us about our real-life desires and perceived limitations? How is magic idealized and how do its representations naturalize the superiority of the few, the (super)natural order of power and the false equivalence of spirituality and science? In this part, *Katarzyna Marak* takes a culture-conscious look at how magic is employed as a game mechanic and as a narrative element in independent horror games, and how it relates to immersion and agency, and along the way explores the medium-specific ways in which digital games shift our expectations of horror experiences in general; *Miłosz Markocki* pinpoints the intersection of game mechanics and narrativity by examining how different kinds of magic can influence and shape the identity of a game world's characters, communities or classes, employing examples from digital games as well as tabletop role-playing games; *Doris C. Rusch* and

Andrew M. Phelps discuss how, in their game The Witch's Way, they have conceptualized magic as a "resource of the Earth", and how such a kind of magic may help us address the individual and collective issues we face today; and *Hossein Mohammadzade* and *Atefe Najjar Mansoor* argue that magic in games is often used as a metaphor for science that can help us understand how science is often instrumentalized and mystified in real life and avoid the dangerous illusion of an apolitical science.

In the second Part ("The Magic of Creating through Games"), we deal with the question how to harness the power of game design to create impossible worlds, to examine new ideas, to test new solutions and to conquer otherwise mortifying challenges of life; but also how this power can be used to manipulate and to make false arguments deceptively convincing (not only, but also in regard to COVID-19). Here, *Clio Montrey* examines the magic of fantasy worldbuilding through music, exploring music as an atmospheric, dramatic and immersive device, and drawing a line from classical music to today's videogames. *Benjamin Hanussek* and *Tom Tucek* argue how moral complexity can be used as a game design element that can transform our play experiences, and how moral choice can be implemented as an engaging challenge in games; *Alexander K. Seewald* and *Alexander Pfeiffer* showcase a Magic Mirror they have created based on augmented reality technologies, which lets users take on a potentially unlimited number of appearances -they discuss potential applications of their creation, and consider privacy issues related to such uses; and *Frank Pourvoyeur* presents his reflections on randomness in games, the advantages that an "intention-based luck modifier" might have over the use of simple random number generators, and what game designers can learn from real practitioners of Chaos Magick.

The third part ("Magics of Immersion and Transformation in Games") considers how can the joy of suspending disbelief and creating belief in games can give meaning not only to our play, but to the rest of our lives? How is it that games let us grow beyond our everyday personas by putting us in artificial situations, but still let us connect to each other on a level much more personal than most real-life encounters can provide? Has COVID-19 changed our desire, ability and necessity to immerse in virtual worlds? And how does this immersive quality of games sometimes keep us from seeing beyond the game where we should? Addressing these questions, *Josephine Baird*, *Sarah Lynne Bowman* and *Kjell Hedgard Hugaas* approach role-playing groups as transformational containers, which offer players opportunities to safely explore new aspects of their identities, and discuss how new relationship frames opened up through role playing games can not only let players experience intimacy within games, but also allow them to transform intimacy in real life – not without considering how these explorations can take place safely, consensually, and on a basis of trust; *Christin Reisenhofer* and *Andreas Gruber* show how digital games have helped adolescents through the COVID-19 crisis by providing experiences of agency, relationship building and an opportunity to escape from the pandemic's dire social consequences – all based on the findings of a qualitative study conducted in Austria and Germany; *Markus Meschik* presents and discusses a qualitative survey which highlights the mechanisms and dangers of "dark patterns" in digital game financing, which can put especially adolescents under their spell and, at worst, cause serious cognitive distortions; and *Sonja Gabriel* asks how educational games can draw on the magic of fairy tales, either by using narrative elements borrowed from fairy tales, by integrating fairy tale logics into the game mechanics, or by becoming modern, interactive fairy tales in their own right.

The fourth part ("Magic Circles in the Games Discourse") turns the gaze inward, to those who think about games, and to the *magic circles* that determine the form of the discourse on games: how can we, as game scholars, creators, and activists, make the magic of games tangible beyond our own circles, magic or otherwise? What are the roots of today's games discourse, and how deeply are we still entangled in obsolete concepts? What *is* a *Magic Circle* in the first place? And what are the enchantments that we find ourselves under, which make us see some things about games (and about ourselves), while obscuring the view of others? In this final part, *Alexis Ibarra Ibarra* examines how videogame exhibitions can capture the magic of videogames, and how the aesthetic qualities of videogames can be remediated in physical spaces; *Damiano Gerli* takes a closer look at the first "magic word" in the history of digital games – leading to a discussion of cheat codes as magic tricks; using the crowdfunded board-game World Control as a starting point, *Ivo Antunic* presents the idea of "Playerism" – a form of populism that relies on an inability to distinguish between play-worlds and ordinary life – as well as the presence (or absence) of physical magic circles throughout history; *Nikolaus Koenig* and *Gabrielle Trépanier-Jobin* take a close look at Huizinga's magic circle metaphor, and – by digging out its magical aspects – show how its use within today's game studies discourse might actually conceal its potential as an empowering and liberating concept that, while being firmly rooted in history, would well befit today's social and political discourse; and finally, *Tobias Unterhuber* draws back the curtains to unveil the workings of a remarkable magic trick - the Fountain of Youth that, even after two decades, still gives Game Studies the appearance of being a young discipline – and sheds a light on the functions, implications and often not so desirable effects of a cloaking spell that might put Dorian Gray to shame.

This publication, as well as the conference that has spawned it, would not have been possible without the help of the fabulous contributors who have acted as speakers, authors and reviewers, and who have once again pushed the boundaries of our field. Special thanks go out to Herbert Rosenstingl, whose patronage over the event has, once again, been invaluable. And finally, we are grateful to the greater FROG community, for continuously providing an environment in which critical reflection, bold ideas, and friendly cooperation can thrive. You create real life magic, and we are thankful for that!

Nikolaus Koenig
Natalie Denk
Alexander Pfeiffer
Thomas Wernbacher

Representations
of
MAGIC *in* GaMes

PLAYER'S POWERS: MAGIC AS MECHANICS AND AS NARRATIVE IN INDEPENDENT HORROR GAMES

Katarzyna Marak

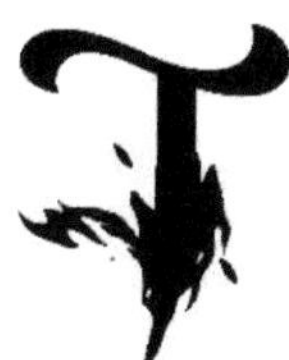 he paper discusses the medium-specific ways in which magic is portrayed and used in independent digital horror games. The two most important factors taken into consideration are the practical employment of magic, examined in terms of mechanics, and the fantastical employment of magic, discussed in terms of the narrative. Both these components are significant in horror fiction as a genre, where magic is primarily depicted as a source of threat, and only occasionally as the means to defend oneself - depending on the culture-related politics of magic. Such portrayal of magic does conform to the medium of digital games, but also breaks with the strict long-established convention of typical literary and film horror narratives in a medium-dependent way. Using a number of selected examples, the paper will examine specific representations of magic in game texts, with particular emphasis placed on the relationship between magic and immersion, as well as magic and agency.

Keywords: magic, immersion, agency, independent horror games

Introduction: Magic in Fiction

The presence of magic[1] in fiction goes far back in time, with magic itself being defined, portrayed, and represented in numerous ways. In everyday life, magic is not something that can be empirically observed or proven. There are people who believe in magic, and there are many people who disregard the very concept. Therefore, texts of popular media which concern magic require suspension of disbelief, which needs to be created and maintained. The rules according to which magic functions in fiction should be coherent and clear to "optimally/efficiently maintain" that suspension (Howard, 2014). In the imaginary worlds emerging from popular fiction, home to powerful entities, dangerous creatures, intimidating spell-casters and mystical places, the fantastic scale and ingenuity can occasionally make an odd demand on the audience's suspension of disbelief, but not that often; as J. R. R. Tolkien argued, this is due to the fact that the audience, when giving fantasy fiction credence, do more than just suspend disbelief (by willingly abandoning critical thinking in examining fictional texts for the sake of enjoying the text). While he does not go into detail about what this "more" is, he refers to it as "poetic faith" (Martin, 2019).

An honest examination of any aspect of horror games requires placing them in a broader context of other horror texts. The same poetic faith attitude observed in readers and viewers extends to horror game players, especially when the game places emphasis on lore; this focus on lore, as Joshua Bycer points out, can make it difficult for the player to "resonate with the character or become interested in the story", especially taking into consideration that "[m]any modern horror games are all about dealing with situations and events that have already happened" (Bycer, 2022). However, independent horror games tend to be small in scope, ranging from several minutes to several hours of gameplay time; as such, they are "meant to be a limited experience and too short to grow [a meaningful emotional] connection" with the avatar

---

[1] "Magic(al)" and "(the) supernatural" are complex as well as ephemeral concepts, and they are even harder to define and distinguish at the intersection between fantasy and horror fiction, which again use these concepts in different ways. In this chapter I will aim to use these terms as the context demands rather than clinging to all too strict, but misleading consistencies.

(Bycer, 2022). Therefore, engaging fantastic settings and challenges are even more welcome and readily accepted by the players of independent horror games.

This paper is devoted to horror games featuring magic and the way the use of magic in those texts affects the player experience. The two most important factors taken into consideration are the practical employment of magic, discussed in terms of mechanics, and the fantastical employment of magic, discussed in terms of the narrative. Both these components are particularly significant in horror fiction in general, where magic is primarily depicted as a source of harm and peril, and only occasionally as the means to defend oneself - often depending on the culture-related politics of magic of the culture depicted in the game text itself.

There are numerous perspectives on and definitions of magic. As a point of reference for this paper, "magic" can be characterized as calling upon invisible sources that would make it possible for a person or persons to influence events and affect change in the material world. While discussing magic in games, Jeff Howard situates its representation in a broader context suggesting that there are

> two major traditions as potential influences for game magic through which the human imagination has represented and theorized magic - fictive magic and occult magic. Fictive magic refers to sorcery as represented in the literature of the fantastic, broadly conceived to include ancient mythology, medieval romance, and especially modern fantasy. Fictive magic is one of the richest and most direct potential sources of inspiration for game magic. (Howard, 2014).

The other kind of magic described by Howard - "occult magic" - is, on the other hand, any magic in fiction that is or is not related to actual, real-life mythologies, rituals, spells or practices (Howard, 2014). It refers to existing mystical practices among people who believe the veracity of (Howard, 2014) magico-religious complexes (Pyysiäinen, 2004). For the purpose of this paper, there will be no distinction drawn between religious and non-religious magic, and both of them are discussed as belonging to the same category of magico-religious complexes, seeing as it is not possible to "meaningfully differentiate between magic and religion" (Pyysiäinen, 2014).

The genres most commonly associated with employing magic are primarily fantasy and, to a lesser extent, horror, specifically supernatural horror. As far as the fantasy genre is concerned, magic in a variety of forms tends to be embedded in the depicted world in one way or another, whereas in the case of horror fiction it more often than not constitutes some sort of supernatural intrusion into the natural order of things (Marak, 2014). Additionally, in contrast to fantasy fiction, which can introduce terror or horror elements but rarely lays particular emphasis on scaring its audience, horror fiction does strive to frighten the audience. Texts of both genres can feature a dangerous werewolf, for example, and the reader or viewer of either remains aware that the werewolf, while presenting a danger to the characters of the fictional world, poses no real threat to them; however, the horror genre aims to create a situation in which emotional responses of the audience will mirror to a certain degree responses of the protagonists of horror texts, thus provoking an emotion which Noël Carroll identifies as art-horror (Carroll, 1990). Curiously, whether or not the threat is realistic (e.g., a human attacker with a knife) or fictitious (a werewolf) makes little difference as far as evoking art-horror is concerned - presumably because not only younger audiences, but also many adults regard supernatural entities such as werewolves, mermaids, or zombies as frightening (Coelho et al., 2021). These characters hold an important place in horror texts belonging to a variety of media (Coelho et al., 2021), such as literature, film, comics, or games. Suspension of disbelief does not seem to be affected by the nature of the threat, since horror texts featuring supernatural elements "tend to trigger the same networks as real-life stimuli" as far as experiencing fear is concerned, "suggesting that supernatural fears recruit the same evolved brain mechanisms as natural fears" (Coelho et al., 2021).

For the most part, magic in horror fiction tends to be depicted primarily as a menacing threat to human characters - either innocent or otherwise. Making magic available as a means of attack or protection for the protagonists would counter the core of horror fiction, which requires protagonist to be in a position of helplessness and frailty. Although not unheard-of, magic in horror rarely is or even can be used for defensive purposes; such application is by no means absent in horror texts, merely scarce, and is usually presented as a character handling a magic object or creature (as can be seen in *The Harbor* by John Ajvide Lindqvist). Additionally - and, one might argue, more importantly in certain cases - magic in horror fiction tends to be portrayed according to the culture-related politics of magic. In other words, the manner in which magic is portrayed is connected with arbitrary values and relationships of power understood as the given supernatural phenomenon being perceived as morally charged and either granted or denied a place within sacrum. Due to the fact that the global horror fiction market, especially popular culture, appears to be heavily influenced by the American market - mostly owing to the sheer number of available texts and the relative linguistic accessibility of the English language - mystical practices tend to be portrayed with little care for cultural accuracy; there exist texts which attempt to provide accurate context, such as the more recent film *The Old Ways* (2020), but they remain a minority. The dominant perception and portrayal of magic in horror fiction, especially mainstream horror fiction, is oftentimes based on a division between the Western Judeo-Christian religion and the "alternative spiritual paths," which tend to include within and overlap with the label of "occult" (Fry, 2008) "Occult" is a nebulous descriptor with no single, agreed upon definition. As mentioned before, according to Howard, "occult magic refers to human mystical practices amongst people who on some level believe that magic is real (such as voodoo or Western ceremonial magick)" (Howard, 2014), a definition which in itself points to this stereotypical division. For example, Carrol Lee Fry uses the term "occult" in the following way:

> Belief in the literal truth of the Bible and atheism are opposite extremes in the national discourse on religion. ... A goodly part of those classified in the latter category are among the millions of people who have totally opted out of traditional Christianity and Judaism to follow alternative spiritual paths called New Religious Movements... . They include world religions that are hardly new but are at least new to the United States, brought by the waves of immigration following World War II. ... A significant number of these religious paths can only be categorized under the heading of occult. (Fry, 2008).

Such interpretation of what occult is and the assumption that Judeo-Christian practices are somehow fundamentally separate from any other magico-religious ones, results in a portrayal of magic in horror texts which presents any practice outside the Judeo-Christian context as associated with danger and evil - from narratives like *Rosemary's Baby* (1968), *The Craft* (1996), through *The Curse of La Llorona* (2019). As permeating as it is, this portrayal offers the audience a very reductive perspective on magic. It overlooks mystical practices belonging to other world religions (e.g., Buddhism, Ifá, Shinto etc.), excluding concepts, practitioners, and technicians of the sacred, including medicine people, priests/priestesses, or monks/nuns, as well as artifacts and objects of magic significance.

This dimension of culture-related politics of magic is almost non-existent in games, and as a result a variety of mystical practices of various origins is depicted. This might be related to the fact that there exist numerous American Hollywood remakes of works of international cinema, making them available to wider audiences while simultaneously restructuring the original supernatural concept; examples of this include *The Ring* (2002), *Shutter* (2008), *Quarantine* (2008), or *Mirrors* (2008). A similar effect can be noticed in American film adaptations of games, as it is the case with the 2006 film *Silent Hill*. In the case of the game industry, by contrast, both localizations of AAA games as well as the availability of independent titles with English subtitles translates into the players being exposed to a greater variety of portrayals and explanations of magic. While playing games such as *Stigmatized Property* (2020), *Unforgiving: A Northern Hymn* (2017), *Through the Woods* (2016), or *Detention* (2017), the player will encounter, respectively, Shinto shrines, objects and gods from Nordic mythology, rune stones, and all manner of rituals and artifacts meant to seek the guidance of boddhisatvas and ancestors. However, titles like *Faith* (2017) or *Evil Possession* (2017) offer the player little to no backstory or means of seeking advice or help.

Engagement: Magic and Immersion

Audiences open to fantastic and magical settings and elements tend to be imaginative and flexible, "happy to suspend disbelief in aid of a good tale and eager to enter a wide array of invented worlds," and to "appreciate magic of all kinds, from magical creatures to magical spells to magical places" (Wyatt and Saricks, 2019). In games, the representation of magic is diverse, showcasing both the relationship between magic and immersion as well as, more importantly, the relationship between magic and agency through actions and objects. These actions and objects correspond to those generally associated with actual mystical practices; actions constitute spells and rituals, namely the use of words or numbers possessing innate power, and ritual actions allowing to manipulate supernatural beings and forces. Objects, on the other hand, include artifacts and talismans, which are potent or sacred in the nature of their power.

This paper is devoted to the way the use of magic in games affects the player experience specifically in horror games. Due to the limited scope of the text, for the purpose of this paper the games discussed will be limited to horror games featuring magic, and not all supernatural horror games. To clarify, supernatural horror games are, in this context, games where the characters are powerless against the supernatural, or games that present a depicted world that features no explicit explanation as to the nature of the supernatural character of that world. Horror games featuring magic, on the other hand, not only make it possible, but actually require the player to perform magic-related tasks, such as spellcasting, ritual preparation or warding in order to proceed. With the subject of analysis narrowed down to these constrains, titles such as *Plead with the Mountain God* (2020), *The Night Way Home* (2021), *Pamali: Indonesian Folklore Horror* (2019), *Prognostic* (2021) and *Colina: Legacy* (2018) would fall into the category of horror games featuring magic, while *The Shore* (2021), *Dispatch* (2020), *Post-Trauma Demo* (2021), *Timore 6* (2018) or *Balavour* (2020) would not, being supernatural horror games.

Since horror games are still horror texts, the player experiences magic most often as the source of threat and terror: curses and spells cast on characters, or instances of summoning demons, various Antichrist characters, or other destructive entities. Sometimes the magic is vaguely familiar even if the entities themselves are fictional, but such arrangement is rather rare. It does, however, occur in a few games, examples being God in *Silent*

Hill (1999) or the Hunter in *The Ritual on Weylyn Island* (2015). In both cases, magic is the main cause of the threat in the game, but it is not the source of immediate danger; this role is fulfilled instead by the worshipers, and to a certain degree by the creatures related to the magic.

Horror games featuring magic portray it as unambiguously capable of influencing events and effecting change in the depicted world. Therefore, the use of magic has the potential to facilitate immersion. In order to do so, the game magic must work according to a system conforming to clear rules and must empower the protagonist. As the player's immersion and engagement with the magic system are established, enhanced, and maintained, the gap between the player's decision and actions and the avatar's performance becomes narrower.

A closer examination of how immersion can be created and maintained in horror games featuring magic can aid in understanding the game features involved, as well as the contribution of some creative choices. For example, *Pamali: Indonesian Folklore Horror* (2019) gives the player control over a character who has just inherited a run-down house after his parents' death. The task of the avatar is to prepare the house for sale by cleaning it and sorting through the family belongings. The player can interact with numerous items, from household objects such as scissors or combs, to fetishes, ceremonial objects, and personal belongings. Some of the items, such as the wedding memorabilia, appear to be regular items, while others can be immediately recognized as culturally charged, such as the *jenglot* (Marak, 2021b). Since the avatar starts out with virtually no magic-related knowledge, any and every element of the visual environment can have potential magic significance. The game world of *Pamali* is actually one of the better examples illustrating how magic can be effectively and unobtrusively incorporated into the game text.

A game comparable in its incorporation of magic into the virtual environment is *Detention* (2017). While the depicted world of the game is set in 1960s Taiwan under martial law, the virtual environment represents the hell realm in which the protagonist remains trapped, unable to resolve her evil deeds and guilt. The hell realm appears to her - and, consequently, the player - as her high-school building falling into darkness and ruin, where dangerous hungry spirits and other entities now roam the halls. The game world integrates both objects and interactions that affect the gameplay directly (divination packets, offerings) as well as elements which are significant to the overall experience, but not crucial for progression (e.g., praying, examining certain items). Adding ritual practice to the narrative allows to transfer selected cultural aspects to the in-game experience.

Other examples include *Project Nightmares Case 36: Henrietta Kedward* (2021) or *The Conjuring House* (2018), in which there are game world elements which affect the avatar's - and, once again, the player's - perception and comprehension of the depicted world, such as the special glass which allows the player to see what is normally hidden in *Project Nightmares* or magic artifacts in *The Conjuring House*. In *Curse* (2016), on the other hand, the avatar has at their disposal a variety of magic objects as well as the knowledge of effective actions and rituals which allow the player to both gather information and progress through the game. This kind of integration of magic into the depicted world, the virtual environment, and therefore into the very fabric of the gameplay experience leads to a greater level of immersion; such incorporation, additionally, works especially well in the medium of a game.

Empowerment: Magic as Agency

In the context of works of fiction, art-horror is more directly related to the way the characters' reaction to threat is portrayed than a truly subjective response of the viewer or reader. Specifically, outside of games, the audience is supposed to resonate with "emotional features that authors and directors attribute to characters molested by monsters" (Carroll, 1990). Game texts create space for the horror fiction to continuously evolve and explore the "dark corners of humanity in ways that no other medium can," moving "away from just emulating horror in other media" (Rouse III, 2006). The crucial difference and, simultaneously, key feature a horror scholar has to keep in mind while studying the potential and mechanisms of action of horror game texts is the player's agency, understood here as their ability to respond to the call of the machine (Murray, 2017), and also as their control over the avatar's action (how to move, when etc.). Horror games can employ adequate and unique mechanics fitting the game world reality (Rouse III, 2006), as well as the expectations of the audience. The player can be granted power through which they can actually influence the depicted world. Magic in game texts not only contributes to enjoyable world building for those players who appreciate such themes, but also makes it possible for them to explore concepts such as bravery, sacrifice, revenge, or power (Wyatt and Saricks, 2019) in a way more meaningful than it is possible in other media. The reason for this is that magic can be employed in game texts as player actions understood as anything from player verbs and mechanics to the overall gameplay experience. Especially independent digital horror games employ magic according to the medium-specific logic. One method is the storytelling and world-building employment of magic in the narrative; the other is the ludic representation - the active use of magic in the form of mechanics.

The idea of magic as an action available to the player is especially important in the context of horror games. Many independent horror games include supernatural enemies and magical objects or entities, while at the same time giving the player little to no means of defending themselves or attacking. In numerous titles, the avatar will confront the supernatural enemy with regular weapons (as can be seen in *Silent Hill*, *The Boogeyman* or *Perception* (2017)); even more often they will be offered no weapon at all (like in *Song of Horror* (2020), *Timore 6* or *Dispatch*). Consequently, the player is aware of the presence of the enemy, which constitutes an embodied threat, thus making the player's experience of the game as a text belonging to the horror genre more subjective and direct (Marak, 2021c). In this sense, magic can be interpreted as an instance of embodied agency since the player is offered a chance to confront the monster on a more or less equal footing. Additionally, seeing that "[f]ear of supernatural agents differs from common phobic objects … as they have no referents in the empirical world" (Coelho et al., 2021) it stands to reason that the player, in order to both experience the agency to the fullest and battle such threats, needs "weapons" whose power cannot be measured or visually observed in the empirical world as well.

From this perspective, magic makes it possible for the player to exercise agency in a meaningful way; the previously mentioned potent objects and sacred places actually affect, directly and immediately, the gameplay results. For example, in the symbolic oneiric sequences of *Detention*, the player can use the food offerings[2] to distract the ghost at the time and spot of their choice in order to get away. In *Night Way Home* (2021), the player can obtain an ōnusa, a wand of purification (mistranslated in the game as "harae", which is the action of using the wand) normally used to purify evil[3]. The wand works reliably every time, just like food offerings in *Detention*, but in both cases the player must rely on their reflexes and strategizing to make the most of the defensive capacity of those items.

In *Project Nightmares*, the player can create a salt barrier by pouring a line of salt to obstruct the enemy's route; if successful, the barrier will stop the phantom pursuing the avatar, allowing them to escape. The barrier, like the food offerings in *Detention* and wand of purification in *Night Way Home*, is reliable, allowing the player a sense of safety. In *Evil Possession* (2017), the player's quest is to set up a ritual to exorcise a demon out of a possessed girl; while the gameplay involves other mechanics and elements, there are stages to preparing the ritual, which - once all the steps have been completed - works without fail.

Sometimes the blend of ludic employment of magic with the narrative incorporation of magic might result in a slightly confusing gameplay - in *Detention*, for instance, some magic objects prove effective, while others do not; this, however, does not mean that the magic itself is unreliable. For example, the wooden moon blocks[4], meant to call upon divine assistance, may

---

[2] There is a tradition – e.g., in China or Taiwan - of presenting food offerings and sacrifices for uncared-for spirits known as hungry ghosts; the hungry ghosts can be extremely dangerous if they happen to be souls of those who died unnatural deaths, such as suicide or murder. Such spirits are trapped in a purgatory-like realm. (Bryant, 2003, p. 84-85) All these elements are logically incorporated into both story and gameplay of *Detention*.

[3] The wand of purification is usually a thin piece of wood, with a "paper or hemp-fiber streamer (onusa) attached to one end" (Nelson 2000, p. 179).

[4] Moon blocks, here represented as two shell-shaped wooden tools used for divination, are thrown after asking a yes or no question in search for divine guidance.

be seen by the players as ineffective, since they do not receive any noticeable or meaningful help; however, in the context of the story this lack of response makes sense, since the protagonist is trapped in a hell realm until she resolves her guilt and karma. This cannot be done for her by gods. The items and actions are available to the player, but do not affect the game outcome; even if the avatar performs those actions, she herself is unaware of the fact that they will not work or the reason for which they will not work.

A similar experience - in the sense that the final game outcome is unalterable due to circumstances unknown to the player during their first playthrough - is offered by another game, *Curse*, which employs its magic in a completely different manner. Throughout the game and until the very end, the player has at their disposal all the items and mechanics which are, at that time, dependable and effective (e.g., gaining information by using the ouija board, performing rituals to banish spirits, or opting for psychic reading to see that which is hidden). However, at the very end, when the player uses all the skills, objects, and spells - seemingly successfully - to defeat the evil spirits, the ending of the game reveals a twist, whereupon the player learns that the protagonist had been sent to the Atherton mansion as a sacrifice for the haunted house. It could be speculated that the difference between *Detention* and *Curse* lies in the protagonists themselves; in *Detention*, the player can learn the protagonist's story and develop some opinion regarding her situation and whether or not she deserves her fate. In *Curse*, the protagonist carries no dark past into the story, so the affective identification might actually come easier, and the ultimate fate of the character might be perceived as undeserved.

An additional issue worth mentioning at this point is the fact that the profound effect of combining digital gameplay with magic results in transcending the initial realism simulation; experiencing (as a player) something that is commonly outside of human experience projects the player into the realm of magic realism, the opposite of the realm of fantasy. Many horror games (and horror texts of other media) build around the concept of an abnormal, perverse invasion of the supernatural into the natural world, this violation being the primary vehicle for achieving the desired effect in the text of the genre. In the case of such games - like, for example, *Song of Horror* or *COLINA: Legacy* - the characters do indeed perceive the threat as something extraordinary. This aspect is additionally related to the culture of origin of the given game text - for example, in some games published by smaller Asian developers, such as all four Acts of the Indonesian game *Pamali: Indonesian Folklore Horror* or any of the titles released by the Japanese Chilla's Art, the characters perceive the "intrusion" (e.g. the ghost of the sister in *Pamali* Act 1, *The White Lady,* or the curse in *Stigmatized Property*) not as an intrusion at all, but as a natural part of reality. Similarly, a game revolving around magic already builds a world in which magic should be expected. As strange as it may initially seem, as far as the player experience is concerned the - usually rather crucial - difference between "invasive horror" and magic realism is, for all practical purposes, insignificant. The player expects being subjected to being hunted and attacked by magical or supernatural entities in any case. Additionally, in both scenarios the end result of failing at the game is the same - the avatar dies or is in some other way rendered impotent, and the player cannot continue. The supernatural nature of the enemy being a sudden revelation or, on the contrary, a fact known from the start is therefore secondary. In other words, the horror game might be intended as a conventional, complete-surprise horror text, but the player will most probably still experience it as magic realism. What *does* make a difference is making magic not just simply present in the game, but available to the player in the form of practical employment in ludic terms.

Application: Magic in games

In games, the player is responsible for a character who can both interact with the enchanted world and be affected by magic - which makes immersion in games different from immersion in literature or film. Depending on the fate of the avatar, the player may experience guilt or pride (Isbister, 2016). It is therefore interesting to note that a large number of independent horror games tend to be non-combat as far as mechanics are concerned. Some players believe this benefits the horror atmosphere, but many are of the opinion that it simultaneously removes the strategic dilemma of whether to avoid the enemy or to confront it

- the fight-or-flight dilemma (in analogy to the "fight-or-flight response" - which hinders player's agency (Marak and Markocki, 2016), together with the potential adrenaline rush and the perceived consequences related to it.

Two games by the same developer, Chilla's Art - *Night Way Home* and *Walk* (2021) - provide an excellent example of this effect. *Walk* is a game with tense atmosphere, memorable for its stylized camera angles, but using a very simple premise and mechanics. A girl on her way home is suddenly ambushed and chased by a monster; the only way for the player to guide her safely to her destination is to hide from the creature or run from it. There is no fight-or-flight dilemma, and the gameplay experience, even if satisfactorily stressful, is rather straightforward. In comparison, in *Night Way Home*, the moment the player is given the opportunity to use a magic object - one that belongs to the same realm as the enemy and is therefore reliable - the situation changes, as the gameplay switches from a non-combat stressful hide-and-seek simulation to a new, strategy-based sequence of confrontations. Interestingly, the wand of purification gives the player a feeling of safety while requiring neither precision - like the weapon in *The Fruit* (2021) - nor resource management - like the flashlight in *The Boogeyman* (2015); this lends the wand certain reliability - unlike in *Curse*, where the protagonist seemingly successfully banishes the ghosts of Athertons only to be claimed by them at the very end of the game. With the introduction of the wand of purification, the dynamics of the gameplay and the player experience changes - an immersive horror experience shifts towards an immersive unnerving magic realism experience.

Another game worth mentioning is the aforementioned independent title *The Fruit*, featuring a depicted world which allows for the mystical practices meant to harness the assistance of a specific magico-religious complex. In the small hamlet of Ravenhollow, an old, withered tree comes to blossom and bears fruit which bestows momentary access to irresistibly tempting knowledge beyond human comprehension. The player's character is deprived of the opportunity to partake in the fruit, but he learns that with the consumption of the fruit the villagers grasped a new language, in spoken and written form, where just five words are enough to express "every thought and feeling that has ever been and ever will be" (*The Fruit* 2021). The words carry "the knowledge of all the cosmos whispered on the wind" (the word "ku") or allow to run "fingers through the flowing state of things" (the word "xo") (*The Fruit* 2021). The villagers corrupted by the fruit attack the protagonist on sight, but the divine language does not translate into any advantage over the human protagonist - who, similarly, can learn the language as he wanders the vicinity, but cannot use the words against corrupted villagers to any effect (on the contrary, the player needs to make clever use of one melee weapon and one ranged weapon). The magic comes into play as a mechanic during puzzles and supernatural fights. In contrast, another game revolving around ritual magic, *Veiled* (2019), never makes magic available as a supernatural tool to the player. Instead, the player uses very basic mechanics - moving, and picking up or activating items - to actually perform all the steps of the ritual through the avatar's body within the depicted world. The player is tasked with resurrecting the protagonist's dead daughter by completing complex, elaborate rituals and summonings, which requires potent items and remembering the particular order in which some steps must be performed. In this way the game combines action and mechanics to represent magic rituals through puzzles (Howard, 2014).

Pamali: Indonesian Folklore Horror is another game which empowers the player with magic. Apart from the depicted world being permeated with magic, nearly all the gameplay elements - available items, interaction options, and choices - affect the gameplay experience and the final outcome (a variety of endings ranging in number depending on the Act) (Marak, 2021b). In Act 1, *The White Lady*, inspecting and using specific items can allow the player to either doom the avatar to a horrible curse or tragic death - if they attempt to mock the sister's ghost or cut a sacred tree, respectively - or help him find great power or fortune if they pursue the necessary path to feed the *jenglot* or succeed in locating documents of inheritance. The avatar can also perform a ritual that will release his sister's spirit, so that she can find peace. In Act 3, *The Little Devil*, the same gameplay elements make it possible for the player to find a material, pragmatic solution for the avatar's problem - collecting and selling objects from the inherited manor in order to raise money for her father's operation - or a more extraordinary one: the player can help the avatar to heal her father with the aid of a magic artifact - a sacred spear, if they manage to locate it - or have her perform a ritual that allows her to take control of the *tuyul*, thus making sure that money will not be a problem for her and her father ever again. However, idling and exploring for too long, or allowing the avatar to be tricked by the *tuyul* in the maze in one part of the huge house, will result in dooming her.

The examples discussed above are worth considering - and will hopefully be examined in greater detail in other scholarly texts – in as much as they all employ magic by adopting different techniques, but equally convincing approaches. Such portrayal of magic does conform to the medium of digital games, but it also breaks with the strict long-established conventions the audiences have been encountering in literary and film horror narratives by empowering the protagonist, and - by proxy - the player themself.

Conclusion: Empowerment

Using several selected examples, this paper has explored a number of varied representations of magic in games, with particular emphasis placed on the relationship between magic and immersion, as well as magic and agency. These two aspects are especially important in the case of independent horror games, which are smaller in scope and, as such, intended as limited experiences; the emotional connection between the player and the avatar, consequently, depends on the subjective attitude of the person playing (Bycer, 2022). This emotional connection to what is happening on screen is crucial for the game to effectively function as a text of its medium, capable of evoking a sense of responsibility, a feeling of pride, or the burden of guilt (Isbister, 2016). Additionally, the player should, optimally, experience affective engagement regarding their avatar, which ought to be both intense and emotionally immersive, but also based on strategy and calculated risk-taking, since the game protagonist is a vehicle for the player to enjoy the game world and to manipulate it (Marak, 2021a). Supernatural horror games based on the non-combat premise affect that identification in an adverse manner. However, horror games featuring magic, which offer a way in which the player can defend the avatar, or even attack or possibly defeat the monsters, provide the player with a greater sense of empowerment. The player can enforce their agency in a meaningful manner while being immersed in cohesive worlds, feeling that they are more than a passive witness to the events.

Horror games featuring magic present the players with an opportunity not all other games can offer, enabling them to savor brief but precious moments of experiencing the sensation of power coming from not only encountering, but also affecting a magical world. Having examined the selected independent titles, it was possible to outline certain critical aspects of the complex interplay of mechanics, narrative, and gameplay experience, which, when combined, allow independent digital horror games to grant their audiences the chance to obtain and use the power to make impossible things occur in and impact the game world, thus fully engaging and - most importantly - empowering the player.

References

Ajvide Lindqvist, J. (2011). *Harbor*. New York: Thomas Dunne Books.

Beil, B., Freyermuth, G. S., & Schmidt, H. C. (Eds.).(2021). *Paratextualizing Games: Investigations on the Paraphernalia and Peripheries of Play*. transcript Verlag.

Bell, A., & Ryan, M. L. (Eds.). (2019). *Possible worlds theory and contemporary narratology*. University of Nebraska Press.

Bryant, C. D. (Ed.). (2003). *Handbook of death and dying* (Vol. 1). Sage.

Bryant, C. D. (2003). Hosts and Ghosts: The Dead as Visitors in *Cross-Cultural Perspective. Handbook of death and dying*, 1, 77-86.

Bycer, J. (2021). *Game Design Deep Dive: Horror*. CRC Press.

Carroll, N. (1990). *The Philosophy of Horror: Or, Paradoxes of the Heart*. Routledge.

Coelho, C. M., Zsido, A. N., Suttiwan, P., & Clasen, M. (2021). Super-natural fears. *Neuroscience & Biobehavioral Reviews, 128*, 406-414.

The Craft (1996), dir. Andrew Fleming

The Curse of La Llorona (2019), dir. Michael Chaves

Fry, C. L. (2008). *Cinema of the occult: New age, Satanism, Wicca, and spiritualism in film*. Associated University Presse.

Gregory, R., Wagner, R., Luft, S., Schut, K., Waltemathe, M., Sisler, V., ... & Campbell, H. A. (Eds.). (2014). *Playing with Religion in Digital Games*. Indiana University Press.

Howard, J. (2014). *Game Magic: A Designer's Guide to Magic Systems in Theory and Practice*. CRC Press.

Isbister, K. (2016). *How games move us: Emotion by design*. MIT Press.

Marak, K. (2014). *Japanese and American Horror: A comparative study of film, fiction, graphic novels and video games*. McFarland.

Marak, K., & Markocki, M. (2016). *Aspekty funkcjonowania gier cyfrowych we współczesnej kulturze. Studia przypadków.* Wydawnictwo Naukowe Uniwersytetu Mikołaja Kopernika.

Marak, K. (2021a). "If the dog dies, I quit": Blair Witch and the problems of contemporary psychological horror games. *Studia Humanistyczne AGH (od 2012), 20* (2), 57-70.

Marak, K. (2021b). Benefits of Including Let's Play Recordings in Close Readings of Digital Game Texts. Discussing Multiple Player Competences in Selected Game Texts. *Paratextualizing Games: Investigations on the Paraphernalia and Peripheries of Play*, 213-236.

Marak, K. (2021c). Independent horror games between 2010 and 2020: Selected characteristic features and discernible trends. *Images. The International Journal of European Film, Performing Arts and Audiovisual Communication, 29* (38), 175-190.

Martin, T. L. (2019). "As Many Worlds as Original Artists". Possible Worlds Theory and the Literature of Fantasy. In Bell, Alice and Ryan, Marie-Laure (eds.) *Possible Worlds Theory and Contemporary Narratology* (pp. 201-224). University of Nebraska Press.

Mirrors (2008), dir. Alexandre Aja

Murray, J. H. (2017). *Hamlet on the Holodeck, updated edition: The Future of Narrative in Cyberspace.* MIT press.

Nelson, J. K. (2000). *Enduring Identities: The Guise of Shinto in Contemporary Japan.* Honolulu, HI: University of Hawaii Press.

The Old Ways (2020), dir. Christopher Alender

Perron, B. (Ed.). (2009). *Horror video games: Essays on the fusion of fear and play.* Jefferson, NC: McFarland.

Pyysiäinen, I. (2021). *How religion works: Towards a new cognitive science of religion.* Brill.

Quarantine (2008), dir. John Erick Dowdle

The Ring (2002), dir. Gore Verbinski

Rosemary's Baby (1968), dir. Roman Polanski

Rouse III, R. (2009). Match Made in Hell: The inevitable success of the horror genre in video games. *Horror video games: Essays on the fusion of fear and play*, 15-25.

Shutter (2008), dir. Masayuki Ochiai

Wagner, R. (2014) The Importance of Playing in Earnest. *Playing with Religion in digital games* (2014): 192-213.

Wyatt, N., & Saricks, J. G. (2001). *The Readers' Advisory Guide to Genre Fiction.* American Library Association.

Games cited

Balavour. (PC version) [Video game]. (2020). Vidas Games.

The Boogeyman. (PC version) [Video game]. (2015). Clockwork Wolf.

COLINA: Legacy. (PC version) [Video game]. (2018). Chance6 Studios.

The Conjuring House. (PC version) [Video game]. (2018). RYM GAMES.

Curse. (PC version) [Video game]. (2016). Stormlord Games.

Dispatch. (PC version) [Video game]. (Justin Kirkwood 2020)

Detention. (PC version) [Video game]. (2017). Red Candle Games

DreadOut. (PC version) [Video game]. (Digital Happiness 2014)

Evil Possession. (PC version) [Video game]. (2017). 2DragonsGames.

Faith. (PC version) [Video game]. (2017). Airdorf Games.

The Fruit. (PC version) [Video game]. (2021) Christopher Yabsley.

Home Sweet Home (PC version) [Video game]. (2017). Yggdrazil Group.

The Night Way Home. (PC version) [Video game]. (2021). Chilla's Art.

Pamali: Indonesian Folklore Horror. (PC version) [Video game]. (2020). StoryTale Studios.

Pamali: Indonesian Folklore Horror. Act 1: The White Lady. (PC version) [Video game]. (2020). StoryTale Studios.

Pamali: Indonesian Folklore Horror. Act 3: The Little Devil. (PC version) [Video game]. (2020). StoryTale Studios.

Perception. (PC version) [Video game]. (2017). The Deep End Games.

Plead with the Mountain God (PC version) [Video game]. (2020). Potentially Odd.

Post-Trauma Demo. (PC version) [Video game]. (2021). RobertoSerraG.

Prognostic. (PC version) [Video game]. (2021). Steppe Hare Studio.

Project Nightmares Case 36: Henrietta Kedward. (PC version) [Video game]. (2021). NC Studio.

The Ritual on Weylyn Island (PC version) [Video game]. (2015). zigmaGamez.

The Shore. (PC version) [Video game]. (2021). Ares Dragonis.

Silent Hill (Konami 1999)

Silver Chains. (PC version) [Video game]. (2019). Headup.

Song Of Horror. (PC version) [Video game]. (2020). Protocol Games.

Stigmatized Property. (PC version) [Video game]. (2021). Chilla's Art.

Timore 6. (PC version) [Video game]. (2018). Vidas Games.

Through the Woods. (PC version) [Video game]. (2016). 1C Entertainment.

Unforgiving: A Northern Hymn (PC version) [Video game]. (2017). Angry Demon Studio.

Veiled. (PC version) [Video game]. (2019). RSPgamesInc.

Walk. (PC version) [Video game]. (2021). Chilla's Art.

MAGICAL AND MAGIC IDENTITIES IN GAMES

Miłosz Markocki

agic, magical qualities and phenomena, and magical items are often featured in various types of games. They can be depicted in a plethora of different ways, and be used as narrative or world building tools in game texts. Magic in games can be discussed and analysed as a game mechanic that influences the gameplay - for example when the player's avatar is brought back to life because resurrection magic exists in the game world - or as the main plot point around which the entire story of a game is based on - such as in the case where the player has to fulfil various tasks in the game to lift an evil curse. This paper will focus primarily on magic as an element that facilitates the creation and development of different identities in a variety of games, as well as on the different ways of depicting, defining and classifying magic and the manner in which they influence potential individual and group identities in specific games. Based on examples of tabletop role-playing games and digital games, the paper will explore and analyse the way in which games depict and define diverse types of magic influencing and shaping the identities of singular entities, as well as larger groups, communities, classes, and even entire races of beings.

Keywords: magic, identity, digital games, tabletop role-playing games

Introduction

Magic is depicted in many texts of various media for a long time. In many games - including digital ones - magic is also depicted in different ways. Both magic itself as well as its depiction can be used by game developers in various ways and for various purposes. This paper focuses specifically on the way in which game creators use magic to help establish identity[1] of individual characters, whole societies or factions in their games, as well as to help players create the identity of their character or avatar. In many books, movies and games there are examples of characters or races who are defined in the depicted world of the story by their ties to magic or by their magical skills. One of such examples is the race of elves from *Lord of the Rings* who can use magic - while dwarfs and humans, in comparison, cannot. With the development of culture, technology and new forms of media various types of games also depict magic or use magic to identify specific characters, factions or races. A variety of games, both tabletop role playing games and digital ones - especially fantasy role playing games - include not only magic not only in the form of magic items, effects or skills as part of the gameworld or game mechanics, but also as elements to be used by players during the character creation. Similarly, magic itself, as well as magical skills and characteristics, can be used by game creators as a defining element of the identity of an individual character, a faction, or a whole race of beings. Although the important fact is that, depending on the type of game the magic as part of identity of a character or a nation, it will be used in a different way. Often the use of magic by a character or a faction is also connected to the game mechanics. Because of that different games will depict magic differently; moreover, they may depict various types of magic and use those differences for creating the identity of a person or a race.

---

[1] In this paper I refer to identity in the context of the player's sense of who or what their character is, as well as in the context of identity of the non-player characters in the game as they are perceived by the player (Hedland et al., 2016).

Magic in Fantasy Texts

Many cultural texts since the beginning of writing and oral traditions have included manifold depictions of some type of magic. Magic in many narratives - regardless of the medium, be it book, movie or game - has many different functions, but one of the main ones is to indicate that something or someone is special (e.g., the chosen one or a child of a prophecy) and extraordinary. For example, in texts of most cultures it would be difficult to find a character of a hero or demigod who had no magical characteristics or could use neither magic spells nor magic items. This can be seen in case of Achilles, who had almost fully invulnerable body, which can be interpreted as magical characteristic. However, nowadays the main texts that include depictions of magic are primarily fantasy texts of various media. One of the reasons for the popularity of such texts is the continuous use of specific narratives, tropes, and magic - according to Wyatt and Saricks, the audiences of those texts are characterized by the imagination and flexibility of reception and participation, and ease of suspending their disbelief for the purpose of enjoying a variety of invented worlds. Furthermore, they expect and recognize "fundamental ideas (...), wishing to explore concepts such as bravery, redemption, sacrifice, justice, revenge, and power," as well as "magic of all kinds, from magical creatures to magical spells to magical places." (Wyatt and Saricks, 2019, p. 134).

Wyatt and Saricks's observation might point to the reason why magic or use of magic permeates texts belonging to genres other than only fantasy. That is also the reason why numerous academics refer to magic in the context of supernatural while analyzing horror texts, often pointing out that depictions of either magic, supernatural beliefs (including religious beliefs) or superstitions are similar in those texts. Additionally, they indicate that the idea of objects or locations having magical properties is not that different from the belief in many cultures that old objects or buildings can in fact have memory, especially related to people previously using or inhabiting them (Coelho, et al. 2021).

It is also important to point out that for many fantasy narratives the inclusion of supernatural or magic elements is fundamental, as Timmerman states that:

(...) the use of the supernatural is not simply a "possibility" in fantasy; it is the driving force in the story and takes a central role in the development and shaping of characters as well as plot. (Timmerman, 1983, p. 72).

In the context of digital games, the idea of including the magic - which is regarded as relatively difficult to explain and not particularly coherent element as it (in theory) allows characters to perform "impossible" actions - may seems risky, as digital games require the game narrative and game mechanics to work in tangent to create a coherent gaming experience. But the inclusion of an element that is - at the first glance - ill matched with the idea of the rigid set of rules and game mechanics that must work together in order to create a properly functioning game system is not that bad of an idea; as Fowkes (2010) points out, it is important to remember that in the fantasy genre, "the use of magic may subvert the normal circuits of cause and effect, but this in no way implies a lack of logic or coherence in the rest of the story." (p. 4). On the contrary, magic takes on the role of realistic causality, and this function serves as one of the constitutive traits of the genre (Fowkes, 2010).

That is why so many games of any types use magic, as it allows for inclusion of interesting and novel game mechanics that can be easily explained in the narrative and story of the game without influencing the experience of playing that game in negative way. Also, because many potential players are familiar with fantasy texts of different media, they expect that digital games will include many of the recognizable elements from those other texts. Manlove draws attention to the fact that the "supernatural or impossible in fantasy is not simply strange and wonderful, nor is it considered in terms only of distance" (Manlove, 1975). Therefore, just as the reader (or viewer) naturally and progressively "becomes partially familiar with or at home in the marvellous worlds presented", in the same way the player immerses in the gameworld and can establish what Manlove calls "relationships with beings or objects from the 'beyond'" (Manlove, 1975, p. 9).

The inclusion of magic as a part or the basis of the depicted world in many media texts also influences the way in which specific characters, nations, or races are depicted in those worlds. It is an important aspect of creating identity of a specific character, especially in tabletop and digital games; the way audiences perceive and think of the characters in a given text - known as affective engagement - is more complex, as Marak claims, in case of digital games (Marak, 2021), and tabletop games. Referring to Salen and Zimmerman's observations, Marak points out that emotional engagement with playable characters goes beyond simple direct identification, since the players experience "double-consciousness of play" while relating to those characters, regarding them simultaneously as individuals with backstories and motivations as well as puppets or objects to be manipulated (Salen and Zimmerman, 2003; Marak, 2021, p. 59f.).

Also, as mentioned previously, the existence of magic, the ability to use magic or magical skills not only are natural to fantasy narratives in various media texts but also constitute one of the defining characteristics of the hero of the story. That is why most of games - both digital and not - that are set in a fantasy world will include magic and magic abilities for the players' character; having these is expected by players for better identification with their avatar as "the hero of the game". The same can be said about magic and especially magical beasts and beings that the players face in the games, seeing as fighting those help to establish players' character as a heroic figure (Armitt, 2005). Connected to using magic by the character of hero and fighting magical beings or "evil" witches and warlocks in fantasy narratives is the fact that in many such texts "(t)he use of magic and supernatural powers inevitably turns actions to good or evil significance" (Timmerman, 1983). This specific fantasy trope is quite prevalent and because of that is often used in many games to indicate that some characters, nations or races are "good" or "evil," depending on what kind of magic they use. In many fantasy texts of any medium some types of magic are almost unitarily regarded as "bad" or "evil," as in the case of dark magic or necromancy, while, on the other hand, light or "holy" magic is universally regarded as "good" magic. Through connecting specific types of magic with generalized moral values - another previously mentioned element of fantasy narratives - the inclusion of various types of magic in games give the developers another tool to create the identity of beings depicted in their games.

Some scholars are also interested not only in the sheer inclusion of magic in various media texts - including digital games - but also in the sources or inspirations for the different kinds of magic depicted in them. Howard uses two terms to discuss magic in game texts, "fictive magic" and "occult magic." According to him,

[f]ictive magic refers to sorcery as represented in the literature of the fantastic, broadly conceived to include ancient mythology, medieval romance, and especially modern fantasy (such as the work of George R.R. Martin and Michael Moorcock). Fictive magic is one of the richest and most direct potential sources of inspiration for game magic. When discussing the literature of the fantastic, it is common to speak of the magic system of a given fantasy novel or series, referring to the techniques and metaphysical underpinnings of magic in a given fantasy universe. (Howard, 2014, p. 4)

However, it is important to remember that texts of different media "tell" their stories differently and the expectations of the target audience of each medium will be different. That might account for the ways in which magic exists in various depicted worlds, as well as for the introduction of magic into the specific mechanics and workings of diverse media. As Howard specifically points out, the potential of fictive magic as inspiration for the depiction of magic in a game might be limited by the fact that it tends to be used for narrative purposes rather than ludic ones. Regardless of "how coherent world-building in a given story, readers can passively observe magic-using characters casting spells without having to actively participate in sorcerous mechanics" (Howard, 2014). The readers (or viewers) can be entertained by "a fictive magic system," in Howard's words, and suspend their disbelief, but neither them nor the text creators need to wonder whether the audience could actually "perform the magic in the story as a system"; according to Howard this is the reason why in order to structure a coherent magic system in a game another type of magic is necessary, one he calls "occult magic" (Howard, 2014).

This specific observation stems from the simple fact that both in tabletop roleplaying games and digital games of many different types magic serves not only as a narrative element but also, if magic is depicted in the gameworld, it is an integral part of the game mechanics or be a specific game mechanic on its own. For better implementation and incorporation of any potential magic or magic system into the game story, narrative or mechanics the game, designers reach for what Howard calls "occult magic", due to the fact that it

(…) is useful for game designers because when a group of people believes in the reality of contacting and manipulating mystical forces, they often invest intense energy into assuring that their magical system is coherent and workable. Occult magic consists of systems of interactive practice in the real world, involving imaginative voyages and quests into other dimensions that parallel those of gamers into virtual worlds. Regardless of whether or not occult magic is real, its coherent systems of performance and practice make it a useful source of inspiration for game designers. Occult magic allows us as designers to invest our games with a deep sense of authenticity and internal coherence, allowing us to remain agnostic about the metaphysical content of our games as long as it deepens and enriches players' experiences. (Howard, 2014, p. 4)

The most significant purpose of the reflections mentioned until this point is to actually see the use of magic as an element of an identity of specific character, nation or race in practice. For this, multiple titles of several series of games were chosen for brief analysis in order to present the widest scope of possible uses of magic specifically for the purpose of identity creation in both tabletop role playing games and digital games.

Dungeons & Dragons

An excellent example of using the magic in all previously mentioned ways is present in a classic - and one of the most popular - tabletop role playing game *Dungeons & Dragons*. In this game players create their characters who are supposed to be adventurers exploring ancient ruins or dungeons and, fighting various monsters, so it is natural that the game designers want the players to feel like heroes of their own fantasy story. As with fantasy heroes from other media, one of the ways in which developers can make players feel special and heroic is to give them magical abilities (skills, spells, etc.) and items. That is why many mechanics and rules of *Dungeons & Dragons* revolve around the existence of magic in the gameworld. Since the premiere of the first edition of the game in 1974 many elements of the game and its mechanics have been changed, so this paper will focus mostly on the information and mechanics from the latest, fifth edition from the year 2014. The fifth edition of *Dungeons & Dragons* presents magic in its various forms such as spells, items, magical effects, skills, or characteristics specific to certain beings or races. The main part of the game that is mostly influenced by the inclusion of magic is the player's character creation. The two main choices for the players during the character creation that are closely connected to the presence of the magic in the game are choosing the character's race and class.

In the fifth edition of *Dungeons & Dragons*, many races have magical characteristics or special magical abilities available only to that specific race. Examples of such characteristics and skills are present among the primary choices of races for the players in *Dungeons & Dragons: Player's Handbook*. Among various races available to the player, each has a set of special abilities and characteristics. Some of them are either magical in nature or can influence working of specific kinds of magic on beings from that specific race. For example, if during the character creation players decide to choose a half-elf, then their character gains a characteristic called *fey ancestry*, which gives them immunity against sleep spells and resistance to charm abilities and spells (Cordell & Schwalb, 2014). Another example of magic spells or effects that players gain if they choose a specific race for their character is the race of tieflings. Choosing to create a character of a tiefling makes it possible to will gain two magic characteristics: *hellish resistance* and *infernal legacy. Hellish resistance* gives the character resistance to fire damage - both normal and magical, like fire-based spells e.g. fire ball - while *infernal legacy* gives them an ability to cast three specific spells when they reach a certain character level (Cordell & Schwalb, 2014). What is important is that the spells that tieflings can cast are useable to the players regardless of the character class choice, therefore the player is offered the power of magic even if they afterwards choose a non-magical or martial class.

Dungeons & Dragons offers players a wide variety of choice in regard to the character classes - basically character's specialisation fulfils many of traditional fantasy stereotypes, like warrior or mage for example. All of the classes in *Dungeons & Dragons* can be divided into two main categories: non-magical or martial, and magical or spell casters. The first category of classes are focused on giving players various abilities and tools to allow them to better fight their enemies with range or hand weapons. Many of these classes permit players to use special skills that have supernatural effects, but are nonetheless specifically categorized as non-magical effects. For example, the players who chose the monk class either gain a character ability of being immune to diseases and poisons, or running on the surface of water. Those are abilities specified as monk's innate abilities, and not as spells or magic effects - therefore they cannot be overcome by using spells or other magic. There is a magic spell in the game called *water walk*, which allows a being on whom the spell is cast to walk on water, but if some other character casts the spell *dispel magic*, that effect ends, and the being affected falls into the water. In the same scenario, if the entity walking on water is a monk, and they use their monk skills instead of a spell, then casting *dispel magic* on them will do nothing, and the monk can still run across water with no problems. This example depicts how much the magic is integrated into not only the game mechanics of *Dungeons & Dragons* but also the way in which the gameworld works and its rules. Magic allows for many different things in the world of *Dungeons & Dragons,* but at the same time that magic can be disrupted or influenced by other specific types of magic; however, if the player's character's skills and abilities are not magical, then the same spells and effects will not work on them.

The second category of classes available for players' characters commonly called spell casters are significantly more closely connected to the magic used and depicted in the game. These classes allow players' characters to cast various magic spells, which are divided into many different types. This way not only the ability of casting spells but also the nature or type of the spells the player's character may cast helps in creating the identity of that character. The game rules concerning the kind of spells that can be cast by specific characters are numerous, and further divide the magic wielded by the player's character into two subcategories: arcane magic and divine magic. Arcane magic is the most recognizable stereotypical type of magic depicted in many fantasy texts in various media. This category of spells available to players includes spells like *fire ball*, *fly* or *telekinesis*. This type of magic - according to the rules of the gameworld of *Dungeons & Dragons* - can be wielded by virtually anyone, and the only difference is in the source of the arcane magic that the player's character has.

Player may decide to choose the class of *sorcerer,* who is a type of a spell caster born with the magic. Their own blood and life force are the source of the magic they wield, and because of that in the reality of gameworld *sorcerers* - regardless of their race chosen by the player - are regarded to have magical beings, like demons, angels or dragons in their ancestry (Cordell & Schwalb, 2014). This naturally can greatly influence the identity of the character that player's try to create, or - for players well versed in game knowledge - the identity of the characters created by the game master in the gameworld. Different type of the spell caster classes gain their magic and ability to cast magic spells from knowledge. *Wizards* - and many sub-classes of martial classes - can learn magic and casting spells simply by studying at a magic academy. In this regard, in the context of most spell casting classes and sub-classes, magic is treated as just another skill, meaning that it can be practiced - the more the player's character studies magic, the more powerful spells they will be able to cast. The last type of source of arcane magic is available to the class of *warlocks,* who gain their magic through making a pact with a powerful entity that bestows a part of their power and magic on the character, so that they are able to cast spells (Cordell & Schwalb, 2014). The nature of the entity and the type of the pact that the players choose for their character will determine what spells and magic abilities their *warlock* gains access to. This is related to the fact that in the gameworld of *Dungeons & Dragons* the type of the pact determines if the character will be more focused on casting the arcane spells, or on magic spells and abilities available only to *warlocks*.

The other category of spell casting classes are characters who focus on divine spell casting. This type of magic is available to the classes of *cleric* and *paladin*. Both of these classes can cast spells and use magic abilities, but the source of their magic and the way in which they cast their spells is different from the rest of the spell casting classes. *Clerics* and *paladins* cast their spells by praying to their deities and it is those deities that are the source of magic for those classes (Cordell & Schwalb, 2014). This can naturally influence the identity of the character created by the player to a great degree, seeing as being a *cleric* or *paladin* in the reality of *Dungeons & Dragons* gameworld means that the player's character not only serves of a specific god but also has to act in certain way as not to provoke the ire of their patron deity. If the player decide to roleplay their character in breach of the articles of the faith they have chosen for their *cleric* or *paladin*, they do, in a way, defy their god; the character can lose all their magic abilities and spells, and their god may decide not to listen to the their prayers anymore.

There are also many other means of creating identity of single characters as well as of whole races through magic in *Dungeons & Dragons*, but they are very dependent on the game rules, and to try to present every single one of them in detail is not possible in a paper of this length. That is why the text focuses only on the fundamental and most obvious ways in which the magic in *Dungeons & Dragons* can influence the identity of any character or race in the game.

Warhammer Fantasy **and** *Total War: Warhammer*

Another example of games in which developers are using magic as a crucial element of identity of specific characters, factions, or races are titles from both the tabletop role playing games and turn-based strategic digital games. These are games that use the setting and the world established in the *Warhammer* franchise. In the gameworld of *Warhammer* there are many different races locked in never-ending conflict with each other. In this gameworld many aspects of identity of certain races are defined not only by the existence of magic, but also by the relationship of those specific races with magic. Titles from both series of games - the *Warhammer Fantasy* series tabletop roleplaying games and the digital games belonging to the *Total War: Warhammer* series - are used in this analysis, seeing as they use the same depiction of races based on their relationship and influence of magic.

One way in which creators use magic to establish the identity of specific races in the gameworld is by stating that certain races have closer affinity with magic than others. In the world of *Warhammer* various factions of elves are the most talented in most types of magic. Humans also can use the same magic and spells as elves, but their mages will never be as powerful is those of the elves. The main reason for which elves as a race are more proficient at magic than humans in the depicted world of *Warhammer* is the same as in the world of *Dungeons & Dragons* - the longer someone can study magic the more powerful they become. The simple fact that the lifespan of humans in the setting of *Warhammer* is one hundred years, while elves can live for thousands of years, makes elves naturally more knowledgeable and well-versed in magic, as they have at their disposal more time to master it. Except for making some of the races better at using of magic than others, the creators of *Warhammer* also included in their world races and factions that are defined by their relationship with magic.

The first example of a race in *Warhammer* setting whose identity is greatly determined by their relationship with magic are dwarves. Main characteristic that defines dwarves is the fact that they are completely incompatible with any of the main types of magic existing in the world of *Warhammer*. Because of the way this trait is described in the lore of the franchise, such incompatibility is in a way both a problem and a blessing for the dwarves. Dwarves are unable to cast any magic spells that other races can, but at the same time they are also dwarves highly resistant to being affected by that same magic. In both table top roleplaying games and digital games this characteristic translates into game mechanics, making dwarves resistant to some of the magic effects or simply causing them to take less damage from the offensive magic spells. The second example of races defined almost solely by their relationship with magic are various factions of vampires and *Tomb Kings*. The factions of both those races have their whole identity based on the use of the magic of necromancy. Both of them are comprised of undead beings - with the exception of few characters - and various types of skeleton- or zombie-like creatures comprise the bulk of these factions' armies. As in many fantasy texts from other media, in *Warhammer* games the undead are also regarded as predominantly mindless creatures who are bent to the will of their master - in this case, a powerful vampire, a necromancer or an influential king raised from the dead. The main mechanic included in all *Warhammer* games - be it tabletop or digital - regarding necromancy is allowing the beings wielding that particular magic to raise bodies of defeated foes from the dead and make them fight for the necromancer. In the case of the *Total War: Warhammer* series, various vampire and *Tomb King* factions having one additional mechanic for recruiting units to their armies. Except for being able to pay for additional units after having erected specific military buildings in the cities that faction owns, the undead factions can also raise new units from the necromancy panel. The game will calculate the number of units killed in a specific region in the last few turns of the game, and, depending on the number of beings killed there, the players playing the vampire or the *Tomb King* faction will be able to recruit a number of undead units of lower or better quality. Naturally, the more units die in one region, the more and better units the players can recruit through the magic of necromancy. Making the use of necromancy such an important and integral element of the faction identity and the army building mechanics of the vampire and *Tomb King* factions in the *Total War: Warhammer* by the developers has led to an interesting strategy devised by the players. The players would create vast armies of low-grade units and would send them against enemies to lose battles on purpose in such a way as to both inflict and suffer as high casualties as possible in both armies. In this way they would artificially increase the kill count for the region and later return to it with their main army to recruit through necromancy high level units they would not have been able to recruit otherwise in their cities for dozens of turns or more. Also, what is quite an interesting about this example is the fact that many players using that strategy argued that it was not "cheating" or "abusing" the game mechanic, but actually "embracing" or "role playing"[2] the faction that has access to the necromancy magic, which should make them perceive the dead as a mere resource to be used in war.

The last way in which the games depicting the world of *Warhammer* use the magic to help create the identity of factions or races is by including race-specific magic. This is a type of magic that can be used only by one particular race and no other. The best examples of this are again the dwarves and the greenskins - which in the world of *Warhammer* is the name that is given to orcs and goblins. As it was mentioned before, dwarves are incompatible with the most prevalent types of magic of the depicted world to a degree that they cannot use them at all. Because of this, dwarves developed their own type of magic: the "magic of runes". This magic does not work by casting spells, but by applying runes of power onto items, like armour or weapons. Unfortunately, because of the limitations of the game mechanics and programming in the *Total War: Warhammer* series, the rune magic mechanically works in the same way during battles as all other types of magic do. The main difference between runic magic and other types of magic while being translated into the digital game format is the focus of the available "spells" for the dwarves. Instead of focusing on spells that inflict direct damage or weaken the enemies, the dwarven runic magic focuses on raising the fighting capabilities of units in the armies of dwarves or their allies.

As far as the orcs and goblins are concerned, they are the only ones in the world of *Warhammer* that have access to the *Waaagh!* magic. The *Waaagh!* magic is a manifestation of the mental energy of all the greenskins in the given tribe or army that their shamans can gather and channel in the form of magic spells. In games this magic is similar to other types of magic giving the players access to spells that inflict direct damage, weaken enemies or increase the abilities of players' units. The main difference is that effects of the *Waaagh!* spells are specific only to greenskins, and other races cannot cast spells with the same - or often even similar -

---

[2] Those players refer to the whole faction, they still primarily thinking about faction identity, i.e. what the faction is, in essence - hence the use of the term „role-playing" in the context of a numerous individuals instead of one.

effects. Another aspect of the *Waaagh!* magic is that the players who choose to play greenskins in the *Total War: Warhammer* games have to deal with the *Waaagh!*-specific mechanic. This is also distinct to the greenskin races ability, or characteristic, that makes their armies fight better the longer and more often they battle their enemies. In the world of the *Warhammer* franchise the *Waaagh!* is a magical phenomenon that makes orcs and goblins subconsciously gather together when there is a great conflict or all-out war, even if it is dozens of kilometres away. Somehow, magically - literally in a magical fashion - all greenskins from a certain area will instinctually start to move in the direction of the fighting. In the *Total War: Warhammer* games this magic ability is translated into a mechanic that will spawn an additional army of greenskins next to the army that has just achieved their maximum level of *Waaagh!*; in other words, a new army magically appears in the vicinity an army that is strong in *Waaagh!*.

Conclusion

The goal of presenting all of the aspects of fantasy narratives, depictions of magic in media texts, expectations regarding magic in texts - specifically digital games - or the potential problems and consequences of including magic or magic system in a game mentioned in the introduction was to give the readers an approximation of just how intricate and complex the subject of magic in games, or in fantasy texts in general, is. Also, the examples of academic texts and games were chosen specifically to present the possibly wide scope of different ways of using magic as a part of creating identities of specific characters, nations or races of beings in games - even if only in broad strokes, and within the limits of the format of a paper. Naturally, there are more examples of well-known game titles and series in which magic or various types of magic is one of the main elements constituting an identity of specific faction or race. A few examples worth mentioning, in which this dependency on magic in regard to faction or race identity is clearly visible - even if only by name - are: the *Heroes of Might and Magic* series of digital games, the *Legend of the Five Rings* tabletop role playing game, and the digital game *Endless Legend*. Of course, this paper only barely touched upon that subject, nonetheless it can provide any scholar interested in exploring it further with a starting point of more advanced research.

References

Armitt L. (2005). Fantasy fiction: an introduction. New York: The Continuum International Publishing Group INC

Coelho, C. M., Zsido, A. N., Suttiwan, P., & Clasen, M. (2021). Super-natural fears. Neuroscience & Biobehavioral Reviews, 128, 406-414.

Cordell B., and Schwalb R. J. (2014). Player's Handbook. 5th Edition. Renton: Wizards RPG Team

Headleand, C. J., Jackson, J., Williams, B., Priday, L., Teahan, W. J., & Ap Cenydd, L. (2016). How the perceived identity of a npc companion influences player behavior. In Transactions on Computational Science XXVIII (pp. 88-107). Springer, Berlin, Heidelberg.

Howard, J. (2014). Game Magic: A Designer's Guide to Magic Systems in Theory and Practice. CRC Press

Fowkes K. A. (2010). The Fantasy Film. Malden: Wiley – Blackwell

Manlove C. N. (1975). Modern fantasy: five studies. New York: Cambridge University Press

Marak, K. (2021). "If the dog dies, I quit": Blair Witch and the problems of contemporary psychological horror games. Studia Humanistyczne AGH (od 2012), 20(2), 57-70.

Salen, K. & Zimmerman, E. (2003). Rules of play: Game design fundamentals. MIT press.

Timmerman J. H. (1983). Other worlds: the fantasy genre. Bowling Green: Bowling Green University Popular Press

Wyatt, N., & Saricks, J. G. (2001). The Readers' Advisory Guide to Genre Fiction. American Library Association.

Games cited

Advanced Dungeons & Dragons (TRS 1977-1979)

Advanced Dungeons & Dragons 2nd edition (TRS 1989-1995)

Dungeons & Dragons (TSR 1974)

Dungeons & Dragons 3rd edition (Wizards of the Coast 2000)

Dungeons & Dragons v3.5 (Wizards of the Coast 2003)

Dungeons & Dragons 4th edition (Wizards of the Coast 2007)

Dungeons & Dragons 5th edition (Wizards of the Coast 2010)

Endless Legend (Sega 2014)

Heroes of Might and Magic (New World Computing 1995)

Heroes of Might and Magic II (The 3DO Company 1996)

Heroes of Might and Magic III (The 3DO Company 1999)

Heroes of Might and Magic IV (The 3DO Company 2002)

Heroes of Might and Magic V (Ubisoft 2006)

Legend of the Five Rings Roleplaying Game (Alderac Entertainment Group 1997–2010)
Warhammer Fantasy Battle (Games Workshop 1983-2015)
Warhammer Fantasy Roleplay (Games Workshop 1986)
Warhammer Fantasy Roleplay Second Edition (Black Industries 2005)
Warhammer Fantasy Roleplay Third Edition (Fantasy Flight Games 2009)
Total War: Warhammer (Sega 2016)
Total War: Warhammer II (Sega 2017)
Total War: Warhammer III (Sega 2022)

THE MAGIC OF THE WITCH'S WAY

Doris C. Rusch

Andrew M. Phelps

This paper discusses the influences and inspirations behind the design of the interactive text adventure game The Witch's Way, focusing on its conceptualization of magic. Looking at the global context within which this work happens – climate change, war, post-pandemic social and economic challenges, mental health crisis – the world could definitely use some magic. But what kind of magic exactly are we talking about and how is it going to help us address the big challenges we face individually and collectively, inwardly and outwardly? Coupled with these individual and existential concerns are the ways that we connect to each other and, importantly, to the planet: magic in The Witch's Way functions not as a mystical force from beyond, but as a resource of the Earth, one that must be tended and cared for in ways that are environmental and sustainable. The Witch's Way is part of a bigger research endeavor that aims to articulate a theoretical framework for existential, transformative game design. The main pillars of this framework so far have been existential psychotherapy, and myth and ritual as psychologically resonant modalities to access and engage our deeper selves for personal change. The Witch's Way serves as an example for the application of the theory to design practice and harnesses the symbolic language of myth and ritual to facilitate a transformative process for players that is self-directed and uncoerced. Explorations into neuroscience have greatly informed our understanding and creative rendering of magic as metaphor. This paper presents some key ideas from neuroscience and how they can inspire different kinds of games that can make a difference for a more whole, aligned life and a more whole, sustainable relationship with our environment.

Keywords: transformative game design, myth, metaphor, magic, sustainability

Introduction

Disclaimer: this is an opinionated paper that – while drawing on research from myth and ritual studies, psychology and neuroscience – does not aim to make a contribution to these fields. It does not aim to preach any spiritual ideas, nor to convince others to follow them. Much as the author's approach to existential transformative game design is that of an invitation – to make games that facilitate self-directed change – this paper is an invitation as well: to open one's mind to ideas that connect myth, meaning and magic in ways that might feel bold, maybe even outrageous, but also different and hopefully inspiring to create different kinds of games. Its language reflects this approach and is deliberately playful, personal and poetic rather than academic. The game that is being discussed by way of example – *The Witch's Way* – has been created by the authors. The ideas presented here have informed the design but the design process itself has also promoted the reflection and deepening of the ideas. The first part of the game – chapter 1: Spring – has been released two years ago and presented at various festivals and conferences where it received much positive feedback, e.g. it won second place in best of show at Foundations of Digital Games (FDG) 2021 and was presented in the juried venues of International Conference on Interactive Digital Storytelling (ICIDS) 2021 and International Communication Association (ICA) 2022. While designing the game and in preparation for its second chapter, the authors have been in close exchange with neuroanatomist Jill Bolte Taylor, who is also a collaborator on a research project on Whole Brain Games for Transformative Futures, housed at Uppsala University. Another close advisor to the design and the bigger research context it happened in has been Erik Goodwyn, MD, Psychiatrist and faculty at University of Louisville, School of Medicine.

After two years of living through a pandemic, we went straight into a war in Europe, and all of this is happening before the backdrop of ongoing climate change and significant social and environmental issues. It's not like there haven't been challenges before, but boy, are we in need of some magic these days! Not the kind of syrupy, fairy dust magic, though, that enchants us and takes us away from our troubles. No, we need the kind of magic that allows us to face them with honor, dignity and grace. As mythologist and storyteller Martin Shaw (2020) put it: "bad storytellers make spells. Great storytellers break them." (p.4) Games are more often associated with the enchantment of escapism than "breaking the spell". We, however, ask: *how can we develop games that help break the spells we as individuals, communities and society are under and contribute to a meaningful life, to inner alignment, peace and compassion with self and others?*

The Witch's Way aims to be an example of these kinds of games - games that facilitate players to "wake up" from what Martha Beck has referred to as the "social self", to the reality of their "essential self" (Beck, 2001), which is also often called true, deep or authentic self in various psychology (and spiritual) literature, or quite simply "soul" (Hillman, 1996) or "home" (Estes-Pinkola, 1992). How does this play out in the game? You might want to judge for yourself and play it first: https://andrewphelps.itch.io/the-witchs-way.

Written by Doris and illustrated by Andy, *The Witch's Way* takes the form of an interactive text adventure game. You play a middle-aged woman named Lou, who decides to take a time out from her busy and outwardly successful but inwardly unfulfilled life, and move to the cottage in the woods her aunt – who happened to be a competent witch – has left her. There, Lou establishes contact with nature, explores the Unknown Forest behind the cottage, and the mysterious beings that dwell within it. Guided by animal spirits, a wise and quirky bookshelf and her aunt's magical clues, Lou learns about the Witch's Way: how to live in greater alignment with herself and the world around her, tapping into the pervasive and powerful magic of the energy web – the energy that flows through and between all living beings in a great web of connected perceptions – that changes her and her life forever.

The game is made in the Twine engine, a tool to create mainly text-based, game-like interactive experiences, for which Andy has conjured up some extra snazzy tech features, e.g. a save-game option (which may not sound impressive, but since Twine does not come with a save game option, this is an important addition when creating a game that takes ca. 3hrs to experience). The full version of the game is planned to have four parts: Spring, Summer, Fall, Winter. For now, there is only Spring. (Summer is a work in progress.) The outlines of Fall and Winter are visible through the haze in the distance. It will take a few more years to finish it all. Magic (and witches) cannot be forced into the conventional corset of time and timing, after all.

Spring was written during the literal Spring, and Doris intends to continue writing the other seasons in sync with the actual time of the year, too, because *The Witch's Way* is very real where she lives – a little Swedish island in the Baltic sea – and the process of writing is more a process of beholding and communicating with the environment (inner and outer) than "making things up". It is a form of meditation and "wayfinding" (Beck, 2012; Davis, 2009) through writing, attunement and quiet, open awareness. Of course, the background research and the development of the existential transformative game design framework acted as fertilizer to the creative process, but so did life itself. We accounted for this important intertwining of these different ways of knowing – intellectual and embodied, emotional and spiritual – in the design framework itself (Phelps & Rusch, 2020; Rusch & Phelps, 2020; 2021) when we discuss how designers can harness the tools of "inner work" – e.g. active imagination and dreamwork – to mine their own unconscious as sources (Rusch, 2020) for potentially psychological resonant (Goodwyn, 2016; 2018), creative mythology (Campbell, 1991).

The Witch's Way hopes to provide players with evocative imagery and symbolism that resonate on a deep level, opening a communication channel to the unconscious, bringing to consciousness whatever they may have disowned about themselves for the sake of conforming to society (allowing the social self to dominate) and thus sacrificed their own inner integrity. By integrity we mean "wholeness", a smooth working together of all our parts so that we experience inner peace and balance and are able to respond to life ("response-ability") rather than merely react (Beck, 2021). When we become aware of the external, social, cultural expectations and norms that have ensnared and shaped us since childhood – that have (to use the imagery of the game) wrapped our unique, individual creativity and playfulness in the cloth of expectations and tied them with the belt of physical or emotional punishment in case of disobedience – we can bring our attention to a deeper inner truth, one that allows us to identify inner and outer areas of misalignment and incongruency and bring them into integrity.

This paper, which is part of the existential, transformative game design framework, takes a very focused look on the technologies of magic – informed by neuroscience – that promote inner alignment as well as an experience of oneness and connectedness with everything alive. After briefly contextualizing the work in the bigger framework, it discusses the technologies of magic and their scientific sources and then trace how they are applied to game design in *The Witch's Way*.

The existential, transformative game design framework

The existential, transformative game design framework sketches out a 'design triangle', mapping three key elements of existential design: First, that the game engage itself with existential themes (i.e. death, isolation, meaning, freedom of choice (Yalom, 1980); Second, that it engage myth and ritual in such fashion as to extend beyond the conscious act of play and to tug at the unconscious roots of these elements that inform our inner resonance with these kinds of acts; and Third, that these games operate in a direct experiential fashion, which is to say that the acts that the player performs in the game are directly mappable to the kinds of individual change(s) desired.

This is in direct contrast to a more traditional 'games for change' agenda which often seeks to view games as catalysts for a prescribed, outer change such as performance on a standardized measure examining a specific skill or specific knowledge about a topic (Culyba, 2018). Games that fall into the existential transformative design space are, by design, non-prescriptive and highly personal to both their creators and their players, but this does not make the kinds of change(s) they aspire to create less meaningful, in fact quite the opposite. The role of games in this context is to position players for their own transformations, recognizing that change happens not in the game, but in the player themselves.

Based on existential psychotherapy, existential transformative games would not only help players ponder the givens of existence but would further promote inner alignment and balance between feeling and thinking self. As existential psychotherapist James Bugental (1990) notes: "viewed from an existential perspective, the good life is an authentic life, a life in which we are as fully in harmony as we can be. Inauthenticity is illness, is living in distorted relationship with our true being." (p.246). As we will expand upon later, note that in our conception of magic, this authentic relationship goes beyond the individual and extends to nature as a whole. How can we cultivate harmony and alignment between all living beings?

How can this alignment be facilitated? Existential psychotherapy is not characterized by many tools or strategies, but it has an affinity towards myth, seeing in it a roadmap to the human psyche and its development towards personal meaning. As Rollo May states: "a myth is a way of making sense in a senseless world." (1991, p.15). Myth is thus viewed as patterns of the human psyche that can bring areas of ourselves to our attention that want to be developed, lived, and infused with soul. In the existential transformative game design framework, we aim to facilitate game design that taps into myth, symbolism and imagery to establish connection between the feeling and the thinking self, the conscious and the unconscious mind and set uncoerced transformative processes in motion that work through what Jungian psychiatrist Erik Goodwyn (2012, 2016) calls 'psychological resonance'. We argued for the role of myth in this process of finding meaning and bliss, personal alignment and authenticity in previous publications, including guidelines for designers on how to birth new mythologies through inner work e.g. dreamwork and active imagination (see our references above for previous work).

This current paper ties directly to representation of magic in that in this instance magic is both the myth that engages the player in the world, and interacting with it is the ritual that grounds them in that engagement. In many games, magic is represented primarily as a system, be it through points, ingredients, potions, recipes, etc. But in *The Witch's Way* we take a much older, mythical look at magic and its representation as a force of Nature, of the world, one that must be both carefully engaged with and yet at the same time tended and nurtured. This view on myth and magic as deeply connected to nature owes a great deal to the work of David Abram (2017) as well as Martin Shaw, as will be unpacked in the following (2020, 2016, 2011).

This intersection of the existing existential framework and its roots in psychotherapy, combined with the mythology and symbolism of magic and witches, is used to significant effect as a way to guide a careful self-examination and reflective process throughout the narrative of the game.

The Season of the Witch

There are many scholarly as well as spiritual perspectives on witches and magic. We are not going to dive into that background as it did not (consciously) inform our work. Instead, we focus on the sources that did inform it. We view both concepts – 'witch' and 'magic' – as metaphors for ways of being and acting that promote transformation towards inner and outer alignment and harmony. What is important about our notion of the witch, is their sovereignty over themselves and their deep alignment with their inner truth as well as the energy web that surrounds them. 'Energy web' is a term used by Martha Beck (2012) meaning the entanglement of all living matter. 'Entanglement' is a term borrowed from quantum physics and introduced into sustainability and climate change research by Karen O'Brien (2021) as part of her quantum social change approach. It is based on the understanding that we are all parts of systems and that system elements can be entangled with each other in such a way that they are "non-locally correlated to predictably and instantaneously interact with each other, regardless of the distance between them." (O'Brien, 2021, p.21). On a metaphysical level this means that "we are part of the nature that we seek to understand" (Barad, 2007, p.67) and our being-in-it is entangled with what we manifest, both in the here and now and non-locally. We are not separate. We are one. This crucially relates to the existential theme of "isolation" and is key to our concept of magic in *The Witch's Way*.

Witches are – in our interpretation – the epitome of authenticity and personal integrity, from which flows their magic. This is in part inspired by Maya Deren's account of witches as "successful deviants". Maya Deren (1947) writes in her notebook, which she kept while doing field studies in Bali:

> A witch is, actually, a successful (in the sense of surviving) deviant. You have a cultural, ideological, social, what-not pattern which is, for that society in question, normal (and, importantly, that is understood as a synonym for *natural*.) Most people survive because they conform to these patterns – because they behave normally. Then suddenly you have someone not behaving "normally," and usually they cannot survive, since having rejected the system and its support they go under, so to speak, and are referred to as "subnormal," "maladjusted," and other such terms which have a negative relation to the standard norm. But then suddenly you get a deviant which survives, and since it does not draw its support from the normal pattern – and since the normal people only consider themselves as natural – that deviant is understood as drawing its support from "unknown," "supernatural" sources. This "independence" of the accepted, natural pattern upon which the normals are dependent jibes, of course, with the universal attributes of witches as being "solitary," owning cats (since cats share this independence), etc. (p.33)

As alluded to before, there is also a strong connectedness to nature in our interpretation of "witch", which has been inspired by the work of David Abram (2017) as well as Wade Davis (2009). Both authors have studied the magic indigenous sorcerers (Abrams) or e.g. Polynesian Wayfinders (Davis) tap into, to connect to the energy web of the living world around them. Taking an ecological perspective, Abram explains what characterizes a sorcerer.

The ability to readily slip out of the perceptual boundaries that

demarcate his or her particular culture – boundaries reinforced by social customs, taboos, and most importantly, the
common speech or language – in order to make contact with,
and learn from, the other powers in the land. His magic is precisely this heightened receptivity to the meaningful solicita-
tions – songs, cries, gestures – of the larger, more-than-human
field. (Abram, 2017, p.9)

Again, we come across this transcendent / transgressive,
boundary crossing quality of the sorcerer / witch, the ability to
break out of social norms and perceptual limitations into the
wider energy web. The witch's way of acting and being is holistic
and embodied. It is a way of engaging with the world that requires
ways of knowing western culture has pushed far into the
background: an open awareness / open focus attention (Fehmi &
Robbins 2007) for one's surroundings, that simultaneously
captures the subtlest nuances and integrates it all into a big,
sensual picture or system of entangled elements.

This is similar in many respects to depictions of magic, sorcery,
and the occult not through the lens of paganism, but rather
through much older roots in Druidism (meaning, namely, the
original Druids of the 4th C. B.C. to 1st C. A.D.).

So who were the Druids? The Classical texts ascribe to them a
formidable variety of functions: they were philosophers, teachers, judges, the repository of communal wisdoms about the
natural world and the traditions of the people, and the media-
tors between humans and the gods. (Cunliffe, 2010 p.3)

It is in this context that the magic of *The Witch's Way* grounds
itself: witches in the context of the game are menders (who bring
inner and outer things that are out of whack back into alignment),
are keepers of wisdom, are the knowers of secrets and act as the
communal forces with nature. Interestingly, it was not until the
Imperial age that Druids were associated with human sacrifice,
the occult, and other such paradigms that had less to do with
actual practice and much more to do with providing justifications
for conquest (Cunliffe, 2010, p. 7). Or, as noted by Ellis (1995),
they were 'no simple barbaric priests' but rather represented the
intellectual or learned caste within their societies across a wide

variety of professions and functions ranging from art and music to astronomers, philosophers, and physicians. (p.14)

The game draws directly from these older, more naturalistic views of magic, and importantly draws from the concept of harmony and oneness with nature, and the idea that myth helps us explain our place in the world and our situated human experience. The role of the Druid was not as magician, but rather as a spiritual guide, as learned councilor, as community leader, and it is in this role that Lou is cast as well. But first, she needs to get ready for it and this constitutes the transformative journey of the game.

Of Magic and Sustainability

To step into this role, to become part of the mender "team", as Martha Beck (2012) calls it, she needs to heal herself. It is part of initiation to go through a crisis, a dark night of the soul, and to return with the boon: a broader, connected, entangled, ego-transcendent perspective. This is the archetypal, mythical pattern that is also reflected in the hero's journey (Campbell, 2008) and which interestingly Jill Bolte Taylor (2021) also refers to in regards to *Whole Brain Living:*

> In the language of the brain, the hero must step out of his own ego-based left-brain consciousness into the realm of his right brain's consciousness. At this point the hero feels connected to all that is, and is enveloped by a sense of deep inner peace. (p.11)

Healing happens when you do not get stuck dwelling on the wound, taking apart one's personal story indefinitely. It is about finding the gold in the muck, about returning with the claw marks of Baba Yaga on our bodies (Shaw, 2011). We had a scrap, we carry the scars, we live on and we encounter life with more zest, openness and compassion. This is deep soul work and Lou does it by confronting what freezes her garden – that part of herself, that has gotten hung up on the wound, unable to move on and thrive.

The journey, however, does not just lead within. It leads within and without – towards the personal and the universal. Modern life has, in many respects, fragmented and stunted our engagement with our true selves: we burrow inward, focusing on small interactions such as those on social media or email rather than deep and sustained conversations and friendships. We go blind to those around us. Or we numb our pain by only going outwards, which can either manifest in excessive consumption of goods, food, substances, people or a kind of care that is to distract from oneself. This has led, in part, to a resurgence and growth of people engaged in various forms of mediation and mindfulness, as an inwardly grounding activity of contemplation and mental cleansing, but how can we address the larger frame of our existence in harmony not just with ourselves, but with others and with our world?

What we try to communicate with *The Witch's Way,* and Lou's journey of personal development is that it's about building a bridge, about seeing that we are but a fractal in the big picture of life. The soul work is being done both within – the metaphorical inner landscape: the garden that needs unfreezing, tending, the Unknown forest that needs consulting, the private dungeon, whose self-made walls need to be transcended – and without: our literal gardens and forests are in trouble.

That what ails us, ails our environment also. If we are stuck, inauthentic and removed from our essential selves, we lack the basis for deep and true connection, empathy and compassion with other living creatures, the soil itself. We need our right brain hemisphere and particularly our character 4, as Bolte Taylor (2021) calls it, to go beyond the ego and acknowledge our entanglement. A systemic view of earth does not allow for contained problems. The ice spreads outwards. As alluded to before, sustainability researcher Karen O'Brien unpacks this idea of quantum social change in her book *You Matter Than You Think* (2021). This is a message of hope, because it means we can DO something. We are not powerless in the face of climate change, at the mercy of politicians and other big players who make the decisions for us and are the only ones with REAL influence. What we do, little by little, daily, matters. Because we are all tapped into the energy web and how we engage with ourselves and each other creates small ripples of transformational energy every second of every day. Some may argue that the reason the world is in trouble is not because people are not in touch with their feelings. We beg to differ. We absolutely must be in touch with ourselves and cultivate personal integrity and wholeness, to be able to love and do something about the bigger systemic issues and power dynamics that allow the inner disconnect to amplify. When we say "love" we mean a kind of unimposing beholding and "worth-ship" that is both deep and without selfish urgency, that gives and receives gracefully rather than greedily and anxiously to satisfy personal needs. This kind of love is key to a lived experience of morality, of holding dear rather than just paying lip service to values of equity, justice and dignity. If this sounds like mumbo jumbo and the wishful thinking of some dreaming, naïve academics / artists, let us just state that these universal values – equity, justice and dignity for all – are what underpins the radical transformational leadership for sustainability model created by Monica Sharma and *cChange*. They are – according to Sharma who has led impactful sustainability projects with measurable results for the UN over the last 25 years – the spiritual basis for lasting change (Sharma, 2017). In this sense, the kinds of games we make and play matter. Games that foster inner alignment, that aim to attune our attention to our true nature and thus nature in the more encompassing sense.

The multi-faceted and naturalistic role of the Druid also leads into the larger frame in which magic operates within the game as a metaphor not just for healing and rebirth, but also speaks to notions of global sustainability and climate. In the game, magic is a resource generated through the forests, the rivers, the land, the trees. It is the interconnectedness of all things, drawing from countless myths and stories that stretch back through time. Storyteller, mythologist and wilderness rites-of-passage facilitator Martin Shaw writes about the importance of place for myth. This sense of place, not as 'the land we are *from*', but as in 'the land we are *of*', is a particularly crucial theme in his book *Scatterlings* (Shaw, 2016) and by being *of* the land, he means a deeper way of being connected to and *claimed* by a specific locale. If we view myth only as the domain of psychology, if we emphasize the hero's journey as the journey of the individual only, we disregard that myth comes from a time when we as humans were but a part of the bigger picture, a bigger living context we were just a fractal of.

Our problems were not bigger or more important than the oak tree or the creek, or the hare. Stories were told to reflect nature back at itself. The human centered view of myth, as Shaw reminds us across all of his writings and stories, is a sign of modern times and a symptom of our skewed values. It is time we see myth in its natural context of origin again: as deeply rooted to a place that we admire and behold in a way that makes the thundercloud blush.

Having said that, yes, *The Witch's Way* emphasizes Lou's personal transformation. It starts with the individual layer in this first part of the game. However, we at least aimed to perforate the boundaries between inside and outside with our magical realism approach. Lou has been cut off from interaction with the (inner and outer) natural forces, and must rediscover how to awaken them. Yet, at the same time, these forces themselves are dwindling without careful care and attention from Lou and those like her that can sense and act on problems in this realm. They are under attack, and without intervention will likely no longer be viable in the long run: without the care of Lou's aunt they have already fallen into disarray, and neglect here is the silent, true killer. This is an obvious and direct metaphor for our own need to live with awareness of our impact on the Earth, both individually and collectively, and the idea that only through our own considered action are any of these systems sustainable.

The Technologies of Magic

It is not an accident that magic in this context is reachable through technology, i.e. the Thaum-Pump in the basement of Lou's cottage. This is a deliberate design choice, and one of the most powerful scenes in the game: Lou's first real awareness of magic, and its interconnectedness to the forest, is through the Thaum-Pump manual. That these connections are made not through outdoor ritual but through a glorified and complex furnace contraption reflects the notion that, in today's world, living without technology is not the answer – nowhere in the game is it suggested that Lou simply run off into the woods to live amongst nature and never return to civilization. Indeed, her role and connectedness to the town and its people are ever-present throughout much of the game. Instead, the game seeks to foreground the role of technology both as a gateway to understanding the world and its many interconnected functions, as well as a tool to better live in harmony with it. It is in essence using the idea of magic as a love-letter to Science, noting that, in fact, these two notions are not actually orthogonal. It also plays on Shaw's notion that to develop ourselves and to positively, sustainable transform our world, we need to bring the "village" and the "forest" together (Shaw, 2016, 2011).

The technologies of magic Lou has to learn in order to reconnect with her deeper self, unfreeze the garden and diffuse her inner dungeon walls of disconnect with (inner and outer) nature are technologies used by indigenous people that make their abilities seem like magic: through dropping into a wordless space, they open the attention to an experience of oneness, which gives rise to imagination and forming. This imagination is not wishful thinking, though. What is formed and manifested is not a result of throwing fairy dust or waving a magic wand. It is about bringing forth that which is already there, willing to be revealed if we only look, e.g. the water in the root buried deep in the desert sand, or the love for singing country songs in the successful lawyer. It is about dissolving a boundary, transcending disconnect from nature and overcoming a splintered view of the world / environment rather than making something appear artificially. For indigenous peoples this meant being able to track animals or survive in the desert or navigating towards the tiniest islands in vast stretches of open water as the Polynesian Wayfinders did (Davis, 2009). Social scientist and life coach Martha Beck recognized these technologies as something we in our modern, western world dearly lack to find our way to our own meaning and purpose (Beck, 2012). We may be able to pop into the local coffeeshop for a caramel latte rather than dig for roots in the Sahara, but that doesn't mean our souls aren't parched. Wayfinding in the modern western world has become a metaphor, but one just as key to our survival: the survival and thriving of our essential selves. The technologies of magic we need to learn to ensure it, though, remain the same: dropping into wordlessness, experiencing oneness, imagining and forming. But this magic, too, is a metaphor. Its results truly look magical. Jung (1973) has already spoken about it as 'synchronicity'. Julia Cameron points towards it in her seminal workbook to unblock creativity, *The Artist's Way* (2002) (the similarity in title to *The*

Witch's Way is an homage to this book, as well as a nod to the magic of wayfinding): that once we connect to the playful side in us – our inner artist / inner child – we come across the things we need to continue on our authentic journey. All the little and big coincidences that start to happen: meeting the right people, becoming aware of important opportunities and picking out helpful information from the daily noise. Tuning in to true north requires a kind of embodied presence that de-emphasizes language, our constantly chattering brain - so we can feel, sense and become much more open to all the clues, big and small, that point us towards the island in the ocean, the lion cubs hiding behind the shrub, the singing lessons we've been longing to take organized by a neighbor in her garage.

This "magic", though, is about how we pay attention. The true power is brain power – fully embodied brain power. *The Witch's Way* tries to illustrate that, give a taste of it through story, through letting the player "borrow" the cat named Ghost, and through the interactions with Dog, merging with his wordless, fully present dog consciousness. Ironically, our only means to afford players these opportunities in *The Witch's Way* is through language. It is, however, an imagery-rich language; one that aims to evoke feelings, sensations, the immediacy of embodied experience, rather than concepts or categorizations. It aims to create a mythical way of communicating. Exploring more deeply how to do so, is part of a future research project that focuses specifically on creating a bridge between game design and neuroscience, inspired by Jill Bolte Taylor's work on *Whole Brain Living* (2021), which in turn owes a great deal to Ian McGilchrist's research on the functions of the left and right brain hemisphere. (2019; 2009). Magic, connectedness, oneness, empathy, compassion, love – they all need the right hemisphere. Yet, it is the left hemisphere, as McGilchrist explains, that our western, modern world has come to value and nourish more. The left hemisphere is concerned with the parts, rather than the whole, clear distinctions, discernment, judgement. It puts things in boxes, labels them and thinks it is always right. It doesn't believe it is necessary to change its mind, because the system it creates out of its piecemeal way of making sense of the world is inherently logical and self-sufficient. It is a closed system.

We've seen where these closed systems of self-sufficient logic and partial views have brought our relationships with ourselves, others, and the planet. We are not arguing to abandon the left hemisphere. As Bolte-Taylor explained in *My Stroke of Insight* (2009) where she describes her experience of having a blood clot the size of a golf ball in her left hemisphere, sending this part of her brain effectively offline, she felt utterly blissful, expansive and connected to all off the universe, but was not a functional human being. She had the agency of an infant. We clearly do not want that. This is not the way to solve the world's problems. We argue instead for greater balance. For restoring some appreciation for the right hemisphere and the magic it helps make happen together with the left hemisphere and its executive functioning. Neither do we argue that we should all run off into the woods to live in cottages without running water or electricity. Even Martin Shaw, who spent four years living in a tent in the wilderness speaks of the importance of creating pathways between the forest (which we understand as a metaphor for perceiving reality through the right hemisphere) and the village (a metaphor we understand for perceiving reality through the left hemisphere). To remain in the forest (a fully present, uncategorized, connected, blissful state of being) is to run away and squander the boon that engaging in wilderness bestows upon us for the betterment of society. (Shaw, 2020; 2016). Technology can be a wonderful thing, but we must always recognize its role, and in many ways how it functions as a form of magic itself. As Arthur C. Clarke (1962) wrote: "Any sufficiently advanced technology is indistinguishable from magic."

Conclusion

In this paper we have explored various facets of magic as presented in our game, The Witch's Way, and how the game as an artefact ties to our larger framework on existential, transformation game design. Rather than drawing on typical frameworks for magic, and indeed presenting magic as a 'system' of balancing points, reagents, scrolls, ingredients, and similar systems based on levels or inventories, our work here seeks to consider deeply the myths of magic in the context that myth is our way of making sense of the world, of things we don't yet understand or comprehend. We draw from naturalistic representations of magic, from witches and warlocks and druids, that teach us that magic is of the Earth, that magic is of the air, that magic connects all things in harmony rather than through the occult. We connect these older, naturalistic notions to modern concepts of neuroscience, of balance and harmony with one's self, and ones lived experience on this planet both as an individual and as a society. Through these lenses, we use the game not just to comment on ideas of sustainability and harmony, but to transform our players in ways that are individual, but ideally congruent with these ideals.

References

Abram, David (2017): The Spell of the Sensuous, New York, NY: Vintage.

Barad, Karen (2007): Meeting the Universe Halfway, Durham, UM: Duke University Press Books.

Beck, Martha (2001): Finding Your Own North Star, London, UK: Piatkus.

Beck, Martha (2008): Steering by Starlight, London, UK: Piatkus.

Beck, Martha (2012): Finding Your Way in a Wild New World, London, UK: Piatkus.

Beck, Martha (2021): The Way of Integrity, London, UK: Piatkus.

Bolte-Taylor, Jill (2021): Whole Brain Living, New York, NY: Hay House.

Bolte-Taylor, Jill (2009): My Stroke of Insight, London, UK: Plume.

Bugental, James (1990): Intimate Journeys: Stories from Life-Changing Therapy, San Francisco, CA: Jossey-Bass.

Culyba, Sabrina (2018): The transformational framework. Pittsburgh,

PA: ETC Press.

Cameron, Julia (2002): The Artist's Way, New York, NY: Tarcher/Putnam.

Campbell, Joseph (2008): The hero with a thousand faces. Novato, CA: New World Library.

Campbell, Joseph (1991): Creative Mythology, New York, NY: Penguin Arkana.

Cunliffe, Barry W. (2010): Druids: A Very Short Introduction. Oxford University Press.

Davis, Wade (2009): The Wayfinders, Canada: Anansi.

Deren, Maya (1947): "From the Notebook of Maya Deren, 1947." In: October 14 (1980), Cambridge, MA: The MIT Press, pp. 21-46. https://doi.org/10.2307/778529

Ellis, Peter Berresford (1995): The Druids. W.B. Eerdmans Pub. Com.

Fehmi, Les and Robbins, Jim (2007): The Open Focus Brain. Boulder, CO: Trumpeter.

McGilchrist, Ian (2019): Ways of Attending, New York and London: Routledge.

McGilchrist, Ian (2009): The Master and His Emissary, New Haven, CT: Yale University Press.

May, Rollo (1991): The Cry for Myth, New York and London: W.W. Norton & Company.

Goodwyn, Erik (2012): The Neurobiology of the Gods: How Brain Physiology Shapes the Recurrent Imagery of Myth and Dreams, London and New York: Routledge.

Goodwyn, Erik (2016): Healing Symbols in Psychotherapy: Ritual Approach, London and New York: Routledge.

Hillman, James (1996): The Soul's Code, New York, NY: Ballantine Books.

Jung, Carl G. (1973): Synchronicity: An Acausal Connecting Principle, Princeton, NJ: Princeton University Press.

O'Brien, Karen (2021): You Matter More Than You Think. Oslo, Norway: cChange Press.

Phelps, Andrew/Rusch, Doris (2020): Navigating Existential, Transformative Game Design, Digital Games Research Association (DiGRA) 2020, Center of Excellence in Game Culture Studies, Tampere, Finland.

Pinkola-Estes, Clarissa (1992): Women Who Run With The Wolves, New York, NY: Ballantine Books.

Rusch, Doris C. (2020): "Existential, Transformative Game Design." In: Journal of Games, Self & Society 2/1, pp. 1-39. https://doi.org/10.1184/R1/12215417.v1

Rusch, Doris C./Phelps, Andrew (2020): "Existential Transformational Game Design: Harnessing the 'Psychomagic' of Symbolic Enactment." In: Frontiers in Psychology. Special Issue on Digital Games and Mental Health. DOI: 10.3389/fpsyg.2020.571522.

Rusch, Doris C./Phelps, Andrew (2021): "Games of the Soul." Proceedings of the 14th Vienna Games Conference

Sharma, Monica (2017): Radical Transformational Leadership, Berkley, CA: North Atlantic Books.

Shaw, Martin (2020): courting the wild twin, Devon, UK: Cista Mystica Press.

Shaw, Martin (2016): scatterlings, Devon, UK: Cista Mystica Press.

Shaw, Martin (2011): A branch from the lightning tree, Devon, UK: Cista Mystica Press.

Yalom, I. 1980. Existential Psychotherapy. New York, NY: Basic Books.

REVISTING SCHOOLS IN MAGIC GAMEWORLDS: POLITICAL MAGIC REPRESENTING POLITICIZED SCIENCE

Hossein Mohammadzade

Atefe Najjar Mansoor

he vocabulary used to describe the process of learning magic is often similar to what is used to describe science. This can be seen, for instance, in two major videogames examined in this paper: *The Elder Scrolls V: Skyrim (Special Edition)* and *The Witcher 3: Wild Hunt*. However, this is not the only similarity between science and magic in these gameworlds. For example, magic is often political and mages are used by politicians. There are characters that fear magic, associate it with the divine, and assume that some individuals are born with a talent for it, almost in the same way that people have perceived science and scientists at times. Therefore, this study argues that the resemblance between the two concepts hints at a symbolic meaning: magic can be considered a metaphor for science. The political magic in these gameworlds might represent politicized science in the physical world, and associating magic with science could have political implications, which will be addressed here through a close reading of the two games and a sociology of science. This paper also argues that studying how characters perceive or interact with magic in these videogames could lead to a better understanding of how people engage with science in modern societies, how they understand it, mystify it, possibly even fear it or distort it into a modern religion, and how they believe and spread misinformation. Moreover, doing so could also help understand the relationship between ideology and science, and challenge the notion of apolitical science.

Keywords: Magic, Science, Ideology, *The Elder Scrolls V: Skyrim (Special Edition)*, *The Witcher 3: Wild Hunt*

Introduction

Gameworlds often create experiences or occurrences which could be read as metaphors for aspects of the physical world. For instance, while magic and science are usually seen as unrelated or even opposites, magic could be a metaphor for science in videogames. This paper argues that this is the case in two major videogames, *The Elder Scrolls V: Skyrim (Special Edition)* and *The Witcher 3: Wild Hunt* because of the similarities between magic and science in these games. Through a close reading of illustrative examples from the games and a discussion of the social aspects of science, this study argues that due to the symbolic meaning of magic, its political aspects also represent the political aspects of science and how science influences and is influenced by politics. Consequently, the characters' understanding or perception of magic in these gameworlds is important because it could help discuss people's understanding and perception of science in the physical world. In modern societies, science is understood in various ways, and there is also a tendency to mystify science, pretend it exists in some sort of void, detached from the world, even from politics and the economy, and rather "pure." Such a concept rather resembles a modern-era religion. When this happens, people become prone to spreading misinformation. This study also argues that studying magic in these videogames could help understand the aforementioned problems; therefore, a discussion of such a metaphor could have political implications, especially by shedding some light on the relationship between ideology and science, thus discrediting a popular attempt at depoliticizing science. It also argues that to solve common problems regarding science, and to prevent future problems, the notion of apolitical science must be challenged, which this paper also tries to do here.

Bethesda's *The Elder Scrolls V: Skyrim* is an open-world action role-playing game in which the player-character – the

Dragonborn, who has magic abilities – is on a quest to defeat Alduin the World-Eater, a dragon trying to conquer the world. CD Projekt Red's *The Witcher 3: Wild Hunt* is also an open-world action role-playing game. The player-character, Geralt, is a witcher – a monster slayer whose abilities have been magically enhanced and who also has some magic powers – who tries to save his world and his adopted daughter, Ciri, from the Wild Hunt, whose leader has invaded their world because he needs Ciri's magic powers to save his own world.

In *The Elder Scrolls V: Skyrim* and *The Witcher 3: Wild Hunt*, magic is not simply something primitive which is only found in nature or strange creatures, or only associated with creepy witches whose behavior is far from civilized. The magic in these gameworlds is also associated with knowledgeable mages who usually study and learn magic in a school, college, or academy. Therefore, when magic is being discussed by the characters, terms and concepts normally associated with schools and science are often used. For instance, magic is "studied" and the mages usually seek more "knowledge." There are also mages who constantly do "research" to gain more knowledge. Moreover, magic plays a vital role in both videogames. In *The Witcher 3*, the eponymous Wild Hunt is only possible through magic, and the main characters are there mostly because of magic. In *Skyrim*, dragons and the Dragonborn are all born of magic. Magic is not detached from the world. Rather, it is often political and is even used by politicians. Further, different characters have different attitudes toward it. It is sometimes considered to be divine, and sometimes to be merely belonging to a certain talented or lucky elite. Some have mixed feelings about it, some avoid it, despise it, or fear it, while others are fascinated by it, study it, or even devote their whole lives to it.

Magic Representing Science

It is necessary to begin with a discussion of the relationship between magic and science, and how magic can be a metaphor for science. Brooke (1991) argued that the stereotypes used to distinguish science from magic are not always historically accurate; for instance, magic and medicine were often together in the same position (p. 64). Similarly, the herbalists are sometimes sorceresses in *The Witcher 3*. Even the sorceress Keira Metz's work in Velen – one of the regions in the game – mostly involved the tasks of a healer at some point. Walker (1922/2000) said "magic was always on the point of turning into art, science, practical psychology, or, above all, religion" (pp. 75-76). Walker's remarks bring to mind Corinne Tilly's abilities in interpreting dreams in *The Witcher 3*. Deciphering dreams is attempted by science, magic, and religion. All these three seem to have been people's ways of finding some answers or overcoming some obstacles; accordingly, it would only be natural to treat them as related.

In both games, there are many examples of elements borrowed from the scientific domain. In *The Witcher 3: Wild Hunt*, there are various "schools" of witchers. The Ban Ard Academy, which is a place to learn magic, is mentioned in the bestiary, and the Aretuza Academy for Sorceresses is mentioned in a journal entry about a sorceress called Margarita. Druids are scholars who constantly study nature; they are herbalists, alchemists, and many of them can do magic. An in-game book called *Introduction to Applied Magic* says "magic is the science of harnessing, subduing, and making use of the power of the elements." In *The Elder Scrolls V: Skyrim*, the mages and apprentices learn magic in the "College" of Winterhold by using spell "books" and "libraries," and doing "experiments." In order to enter the college, the player-characters have to prove their magic skills first, which is similar to applying to a university.

However, referring to magic and activities related to magic using such terms which are associated with schools and science is not the only similarity between science and magic in these gameworlds. For example, in *The Witcher 3*, Geralt creates potions using alchemy, and when he examines an area using his magically enhanced senses, he resembles a forensic scientist using advanced technology. Alexander's laboratory is also a good example of how the lines between magic, alchemy, and science blur in the game. He does research and performs experiments in order to study a disease, and his work (just like many scientific discoveries) can be used either as a weapon or remedy, thus highlighting its political aspect. In addition, Kiera Metz, a mage, intends to give his notes to Radovid, king of Redania, to possibly buy her freedom and safety in a world where mages are persecuted. In *Skyrim*, the Temple of Kynareth in Whiterun seems to be both a temple and an infirmary of some sort. Healing power is something that magic, divinity, and alchemy, have in common in this game. Moreover, in terms of the reward system, both games reward curiosity – another feature often associated with the scientific mindset. The player needs to be curious in order to find good spell books and learn magic in *Skyrim*, and in *The Witcher 3*, the player can find places of power and better gear by exploration, which is similar to the common notion that science rewards the curious.

Creations of mages also resemble those of science and technology, like when Geralt uses a magic device similar to a cell phone or walkie in a quest. Even Igni – one of the five magic signs that Geralt uses – in *The Witcher 3*, and fire magic in *Skyrim* work very much like a flamethrower, only using signs or magicka as fuel. Jameson (2005) has pointed out that in stories, magic should be treated as something that can help humans to boost their powers and overcome their limits, not a narrative tool to be used to easily manipulate the events – which is sometimes the case in some works (p. 66). In this sense, the role of magic is similar to that of science. Moreover, Malinowski (1948) said that magic requires strict conditions and technique; it is pseudo-science. He said magic and science are primarily for specialists to perform, but religion is for all (pp. 66-69). Weber (1922/1963) also noted that a small deviation from the strict process makes it doomed in magic (p. 77), which again brings to mind the strict scientific processes. In order to further establish this similarity, it should be noted that the magic in these gameworlds is not illogical, it is rather non-logical. According to Winch (1958/1990), an illogical act is one that defies logic, but a non-logical act is one that is not against logic because it is not defined by logic at all (p. 100). In this sense, when people with no expertise in a field watch experts do their job, they cannot say if every single step they take during the process of performing a task is logical or illogical, because they have no knowledge of it, so it is non-logical to them. Brown (2003) also wrote that to a lot of people, the work of scientists is like a mystery, and science is like some kind of magic which needs years of learning (p. 1). In the physical world, ordinary citizens who are not experts, do not usually know how everyday technology does what it does, and they often simply push a button and might not even care how it works as long as it works. It is very much magical to the untrained citizen, yet it does not make the technology illogical but non-logical. The same could be said about magic in these gameworlds – that magic is not illogical but non-logical, thus not losing its similarity with science simply because every step or element of it is not clear or explainable to the player; on the contrary, this aspect of magic makes it seem more technical and even more similar to science. This mysterious technicality of magic is reflected in a conversation in *The Witcher 3* between Geralt and Corinne Tilly, in which even Geralt cannot completely explain what Yennefer has told him about Ciri's magic abilities, due to her technical explanation. After explaining a bit, he continues, "[…] turns out I don't know how to talk about it. Didn't really understand much of what Yen told me."

The Political Aspect of Magic

In both games, magic has a political side. In *The Witcher 3*, the sorceress Fringilla's journal entry says, "Emperor Emhyr had once presented the mages of Nilfgaard with a simple choice: either serve their country unquestioningly or die in prison." The journal entry for Keira Metz says that she used to be the advisor of King Foltest, but then she lost his trust and joined the Lodge of Sorceresses which made the rulers of Redania and Nilfgaard dislike her too. Another in-game book titled *The Lodge of Sorceresses* says Radovid blames the lodge for plague and pox falling upon god-fearing folk. At the beginning of the story, Yennefer is trying to run out of a battlefield, which again shows a mage stuck because of politics, in this case both literally (because she is actually stuck between two approaching armies) and figuratively (because it is shown later in the game that she needs to work with Emperor Emhyr to find Ciri and defeat the Wild Hunt.) Supernatural creatures are also political in the game. For instance, fear of ghosts in people's own land does not let them enjoy it, unless there is a soldier there, or other representatives of the government. Even witchers, who are a product of magic and use magic to some extent, are soldiers who kill monsters. They are similar to the military products of scientists. Chalmers (1976/1999) has argued that science has a high position in society, but people sometimes despise it as well when they talk about things such as bombs (p. xix), which is similar to what is seen in the case of magic in these games. In addition, witchers are not welcome in the community and are called freaks and are disturbed. The mages are also blamed for creating them. Only three out of ten boys survive the procedure, and some witchers die trying to kill monsters and to save people, which again supports the warfare metaphor. Another in-game book called *Necromancy, the Forbidden Magic* says necromancy could be used to create re-usable soldiers and to revive or recycle them. Moreover, there are many moments in the game when people fear magic. Villagers think Yennefer's necromancy disrespects their customs. Freya's priestesses treat mages and sorceresses with caution. The priests of Eternal Fire are against magic and are witch hunters, and resemble religious groups that are afraid of science.

In *Skyrim*, the people of Winterhold blame the mages and the college for the collapse of the city. People are generally afraid of the consequences of magic also for other reasons such as the Oblivion Crisis. Interestingly, Styers (2004) has mentioned that magic has often been criticized for allegedly trying to disturb the material world (p. 73). However, characters seem to like Thu'um, or the Shout. They like restoration magic that heals them but not others labeled as destruction magic. This double standard is similar to how ideology treats science (which will be discussed in the section titled "Mystified Science as a Modern Religion"). In addition, in this game, some mages directly work for the Empire, some for their rivals, and many other mages directly or indirectly affect the political scenery of *Skyrim*. For instance, the Synod are a group of mages that work with the Empire. The player-characters can also use magic while interacting with their surroundings and deciding the storyline. Since magic is seen as a metaphor for science here, this political aspect of magic can reflect the political instrumentalization of science. For instance, military engineers developing advanced warfare, or scientists creating atom bombs or chemical weapons resemble the mages working with political groups in these games.

Magic and Religion

Etymologically, magic and religion are closely related. The term "magus" commonly refers to an ancient clan of Iranian priests often associated with Zoroastrianism, and according to De Jong (1997), Zoroaster was considered to have invented magic (p. 35). Weber (1922/1963) has also mentioned this Iranian origin of the term "magic" (p. 2). Weber then said that in some major religions, priesthood includes magic (p. 28). In addition, Jameson (2008) pointed out that for Weber, magic represents individuality while priesthood represents universality. Malinowski (1948) also explained that in magic, people and nature interact directly, but in religion people might achieve what they desire through the supernatural, a god or goddess (pp. 68-69). Yet, magic and religion have a lot in common. Lévi-Strauss (1962/1966) said, "there is no religion without magic any more than there is magic without at least a trace of religion" (p. 221).

In *The Witcher 3*, curses seem to be a common ground between magic and religion. Gods seem to be able to curse people, mages could curse people – or they could do research whose results would be identified as a curse by the people – and even raw human emotions could create curses. In *Skyrim*, the Greybeards, a group of monks who are masters of the Shout, are a good example of a close relationship between magic and religion. Another example would be amulets, which are both associated with the divine and magically enchanted. Daedra (singular: Daedroth) could also be a good example because they are godlike beings who possess magic abilities. Prophecy, as a magic element, is present in both games, predicting the Wild Hunt in one, and the Dragonborn in the other. Interestingly, prophecy is another thing that religion and magic have in common. In *The Witcher 3*, mages are burned at the pyre. It is mentioned in a dialogue that Radovid has made the people of Novigrad turn into extremists who want to get rid of the mages and follow the Eternal Fire, in order to weaken the city, because a city without mages is more vulnerable and easier to capture. In the physical world, consider the situation of researchers in the Middle East. Many are forced to move to other countries or escape as refugees, and as a result, the countries are easy to manipulate and exploit.

Otto and Stausberg (2013) have pointed out that magic has often been put in a triangle of magic, religion, and science, whose components have been defined in relation to each other, and in which magic has sometimes been considered to be easily distinguished from the other two or even their opposite, and sometimes not so distinct from or at least compatible with them (pp. 4-6). In both these games, magic and religion are present. Since magic is considered to be representing science here, a discussion of the relationship between magic and religion also helps better understand the relationship between science and religion, and see how mystified science could function like religion, thus considering studying magic in the triangle.

Mystified Science as a Modern Religion

Religion is not just about an afterlife; in fact, very much like magic and science, it has always been concerned with worldly issues. Weber (1922/1963) explained that the basic goal of religious or magical behavior is material. Even sacrifices were first done without hope of a reward in afterlife, but for an improvement of life in this world. He added that the work of a magician who tries to make rain fall from the sky is as magical as normal behavior which aims to achieve an end such as rubbing wood and creating sparks (p. 1). One distinction of religion and science has been that religion is unworldly and immaterial while science is worldly and material. However, considering Weber's argument, one could say that the two concepts do not always have different goals.

Mass media has a tendency to spread news of "research" or publish "scientific facts" without providing any valid scientific sources. For example, in a discussion of the quality of health information found online, Lindberg and Humphreys (1998) have noticed that "[m]any Web pages lack basic information about the origin, authorship, or age of the material they provide" (p. 1304). Moreover, journalists sometimes publish early research results, as also noted by Woloshin and Schwartz (2006). This is probably because they make good news and sound exciting. In addition, sometimes news outlets close to the government – or any other interest group – prefer to give publicity to research confirming the established ideology. For instance, if two studies on the advantages and disadvantages of fasting are done, one saying it is beneficial, the other saying it is dangerous, the latter is less likely to get media coverage in, for example, a religious Middle-Eastern country. Religion also has its own marketing techniques and strategies, and science is sometimes one of them. Chalmers (1976/1991) referred to a newspaper advertisement which was headed "Science speaks and says the Christian Bible is provedly true" and which said "even the scientists themselves believe it these days" (p. xix). Misinformation in the media seems to be turning into an ever more pressing issue. As a consequence, the consumers of misinformation gradually become so accustomed to reading and sharing it that the insistence on reputable sources or fact-checking seems increasingly outdated and futile. Moreover, Chalmers (1976/1999) said that in advertising, companies claim that their products have been scientifically approved, suggesting that therefore their quality is beyond dispute (p. xix). A case in point would be a wave of advertisement for copper cookware in Iran which, in a nostalgic tradition of praising ancient wisdom, quoted doctors and emphasized that many other cookware made with other materials might be toxic, while copper cookware was not only safe but also beneficial, which led to a copper rush in the market (Shargh Daily, 2001). However, after a while it was announced that copper cookware is harmful to the body (ISNA, 2018), which was again followed by advertising other products (Eghtesad News, 2019).

Further, the attempt to depoliticize what is already political or politicized, while claiming that it is not political or ideological, and accusing people or critics of politicizing it, can create serious problems. For instance, Demeritt (2001) has explained that science affects politics, but politics also affects science and shapes research questions, methods, and standards. He argued that ignoring the social aspects of science could lead to mistrust, such as when some people do not trust climate change science. However, politicians tend to try to depoliticize science. For example, U.S. president Joe Biden claimed in a tweet (2021) that under his administration, the CDC, NIH, and FDA would be free from politics. While Biden's claim was a reaction to Americans seeming concerned about the influence of US elections on the development of vaccines (Cohen, 2020; McCarthy, 2020), such claims ignore factors such as funding and social policies that make research possible. Science is often depicted as detached and existing in some kind of void or in isolation, not affected by anything, even the economy. Consequently, it is mystified, and almost anything with the word "science" attached to it, for instance on social media, could be accepted at once. Following such a fetishization of science, the sources spreading so-called scientific news become so many that those spreading misinformation are mixed and confused with those publishing facts or the findings of standard empirical research, at least in communities with more under-educated populations. The public is pushed by these reports not only toward certain habits of consumption that are beneficial to certain corporations, but also toward certain political parties or agendas. Moreover, sometimes what is published as scientific data is political from the start and is even used to satisfy religious groups at times, and to confirm the established ideology. In this way, science turns into a modern era religion that controls the public, with a clumsy holy book whose verses begin with the words "according to scientists."

A dialogue between Geralt and Keira Metz illustrates how easily people mystify science. When Geralt asks her if she finds "no joy in having the boundless respect and trust of the local peasantry," she answers, "They'd respect anyone who could produce hemorrhoid cream." Again, since magic is examined as a metaphor for science here, some examples of how magic turns into a religion in both games can also be helpful. In *Skyrim*, Miraak is a character with magic powers who literally has a temple being built for him through mind control, and in *The Witcher 3*, the Crones, who are three witches living in the swamps, are treated almost as gods by the people in Velen.

Gosden (2020) has said that magic encourages human participation, science encourages the individual to observe objectively, and religion channels human participation through a god. Based on this, magic might seem more chaotic at first, compared to religion which has a filter called God. However, experience suggests otherwise when the various interpretations of religious books create deadly and destructive wars. Yet, when science is mystified, it could be even worse than magic or religion. It could primarily be because science is seen as more civilized and the conqueror of the territory of magic and religion; consequently, its impact would be enormous. Whether the abusers of mystified and fetishized science are oppressive regimes, regressive political parties, or big corporations, science has to be demystified and the masses disillusioned. Malinowski (1948) said that magic and religion both answer emotional stress, and when there is no empirical way out, magic and religion offer one. They are both based on mythology and surrounded by taboos (pp. 67-68). Weber (1922/1963) explained how prayer is similar to magical rites and how religion has borrowed sacrifice from magic. He also explained that gods are comparable to earthly rulers (p. 25). If the similarity between gods and rulers means that religion or obeying the will of gods was training the masses to be obedient (which was probably very useful for the rulers in the absence of constant surveillance), then politicized and viral "scientific" content could serve the same purpose. Tylor (1871/1920) wrote that ordinary people did not understand science, so poets simplified the natural world, and the narrative then turned into myth (pp. 316-317). Therefore, one can assume that if science is transformed from empirical research and facts into a narrative without reliable sources, it could turn into myth, or something very similar to magic and religion, which also rely heavily on narrativity.

Conclusion

Through a sociology of science and an analysis of two major videogames, this study has tried to show that magic, religion, and science are related, and in both games, magic can be considered a metaphor for science – based on the similarities between the two concepts. Moreover, having explained how a discussion of the political aspects of magic in games (based on two illustrative examples) could reflect the political aspects of science, it is necessary to note that instead of trying to erroneously emphasize the notion of apolitical science, it is better to accept that everything in a society influences and is influenced by everything else in it, and if some political or ideological issues are creating false data, those issues should be addressed, not ignored. Claiming that science is beyond being influenced by those issues not only does not solve anything but can even create more serious problems. Such a reluctance to discuss the conditions in which scientific activity takes place seems to come from a false sense of safety about the present historical moment – that the age of science is different from the "old" barbaric world. However, in a rather similar situation while discussing the Enlightenment, Horkheimer and Adorno (1947/2002) warned that even an "enlightened" population could turn to new forms of barbarism and domination through instrumental reason. Now imagine domination through "scientific activity" which instead of just discovering facts, fabricates them. Latour and Woolgar (1979/1986) have argued that due to the nature of laboratory work, instead of merely discovering a reality that is out there, science can also construct reality, or in other words, accidentally produce an "artefact" instead of discovering a fact. So, what happens when a laboratory's funding, affiliation, and many other factors, push it toward certain results that serve certain groups? Only by acknowledging the political side of science can a society move toward educating people to avoid turning science into a new religion dictated to under-educated people who naively accept anything with the word "science" attached to it. Only then can a society even imagine conditions that might eliminate many of the factors that are possibly affecting research results or their publicity.

Acknowledgements

We would like to thank the paper's reviewers for their thoughtful and constructive suggestions.

References

Bethesda Game Studios. (2016). The Elder Scrolls V: Skyrim Special Edition (PC version) [Videogame]. Bethesda Softworks.

Biden, J. [@JoeBiden]. (2021, January 18). Our Administration will lead with science and scientists - with a CDC and NIH that are free from political influence [Tweet]. Twitter. Retrieved from
https://twitter.com/JoeBiden/status/1351228360123318272?t=KFgpeRxJNUoqXzAfnpuzNQ&s=19

Brooke J. H. (1991). Science and Religion: Some Historical Perspectives. Cambridge University Press.

Brown, T. L., (2003). Making Truth: Metaphor in Science. University of Illinois Press.

CD Projekt Red. (2015). The Witcher 3: Wild Hunt (PlayStation 4 version) [Videogame]. CD Projekt.

Chalmers, A. F. 1999. What is this thing called Science? (3rd ed.). Hackett Publishing Company, Inc. (Original work published 1976)

Cohen, J. (2020 August 28). Here's how the U.S. could release a COVID-19 vaccine before the election – and why that scares some. Science. Retrieved from https://www.science.org/content/article/here-s-how-us-could-release-covid-19-vaccine-election-and-why-scares-some

De Jong, A. (1997). Traditions of the Magi: Zoroastrianism in Greek and Latin Literature. Brill.

Demeritt, D. (2001). The Construction of Global Warming and the Politics of Science. Annals of the Association of American Geographers, 91/2, 307–37. https://doi.org/10.1111/0004-5608.00245

Eghtesad News. (2019 January 28). Behtarin zoroof baraye pokhtopaz [The best cookware]. Eghtesad News. Retrieved from https://www.eghtesadnews.com/%D8%A8%D8%AE%D8%B4-%D8%B3%D8%A7%DB%8C%D8%B1-%D8%B3%D8%A7%D9%86%D9%87-%D9%87%D8%A7-61/265246-%D8%A8%D9%87%D8%AA%D8%B1%DB%8C%D9%86-%D8%B8%D8%B1%D9%81-%D8%A8%D8%B1%D8%A7%DB%8C-%D9%BE%D8%AE%D8%AA-%D9%BE%D8%B2

Gosden, C. (2020 August 20). Magic was once seen as equal to science and religion – a bit of magical thinking could help the world now. The Conversation. Retrieved from https://theconversation.com/magic-was-once-seen-as-equal-to-science-and-religion-a-bit-of-magical-thinking-could-help-the-world-now-144241

Horkheimer, M. & Adorno, T. (2002). Dialectic of Enlightenment: Philosophical Fragments (E. Jephcott, Trans.). Stanford University Press. (Original Work Published 1947)

ISNA. (2018, December 5). Pokhtopaz dar zoroof-e mesi-e qadimi-e faqed-e loab mamnoo [Do not cook in old copper cookware with no coating]. Iranian Students' News Agency. Retrieved from https://www.isna.ir/news/97091407108/%D9%BE%D8%AE%D8%AA-%D9%88-%D9%BE%D8%B2-%D8%AF%D8%B1-%D8%B8%D8%B1%D9%88%D9%81-%D9%85%D8%B3%DB%8C-%D9%82%D8%AF%DB%8C%D9%85%DB%8C-%D9%81%D8%A7%D9%82%D8%AF-%D9%84%D8%B9%D8%A7%D8%A8-%D9%85%D9%85%D9%86%D9%88%D8%B9

Jameson, F. (2005). Archaeologies of the Future: The Desire Called Utopia and Other Science Fictions. Verso.

Jameson, F. (2008). The Ideologies of Theory. Verso.

Latour, B. & Woolgar, S. (with Salk, J.). (1986). Laboratory Life: The Construction of Scientific Facts. Princeton University Press. (Original work published 1979)

Lévi-Strauss, C. (1966). The Savage Mind. Weidenfeld and Nicolson. (Original work published 1962)

Lindberg, D. & Humphreys, B. (1998). Medicine and Health on the Internet: The Good, The Bad, and the Ugly. JAMA The Journal of the American Medical Association, 280/15, 1303-4. https://doi.org/10.1001/jama.280.15.1303

Malinowski, B. (with Redfield, R.). (1948). Magic, Science, and Religion, and Other Essays. The Free Press.

McCarthy, T. (2020, September 13). Trump's political play: can his Covid vaccine bet bring election success? The Guardian. Retrieved from https://www.theguardian.com/us-news/2020/sep/13/trump-political-play-vaccine-covid-election

Otto, B. & Stausberg, M. (Eds.). (2013). Defining Magic: A Reader. Routledge.

Shargh Daily. (2001, December 3). Ronaq-e mes dar bazar-e Seyed Esmaeel [Copper boom in Seyed Esmaeel bazaar]. Shargh Daily. Retrieved from https://www.sharghdaily.com/%D8%A8%D8%AE%D8%B4-%D8%B1%D9%88%D8%B2%D9%86%D8%A7%D9%85%D9%87-100/104041-%D8%B1%D9%88%D9%86%D9%82-%D9%85%D8%B3-%D8%AF%D8%B1-

%D8%A8%D8%A7%D8%B2%D8%A7%D8%B1-
%D8%B3%DB%8C%D8%AF%D8%A7%D8%B3%D9%85%D8%A7%D8%B9%DB%8C%D9%84

Styers, R. (2004). Making Magic: Religion, Magic, and Science in the Modern World. Oxford University Press.

Tylor, E. B. (1920). Primitive Culture: Researches into the Development of Mythology, Philosophy, Religion, Language, Art, and Custom (Vol. 1). John Murray. (Original work published 1871)

Walker, D. P. (2000). Spiritual & Demonic Magic: from Ficino to Campanella. The Pennsylvania State University Press. (Original work published 1922)

Weber, M. (with. Parsons, T.). (1963). The Sociology of Religion (E. Fischoff, Trans.). Beacon Press. (Original work published 1922)

Winch, P. (1990). The Idea of a Social Science and its Relation to Philosophy (2nd ed.). Routledge. (Original work published 1958)

Woloshin, S. & Schwartz, L. M. (2006). What's the Rush? The Dissemination and Adoption of Preliminary Research Results. Journal of the National Cancer Institute, 98/6, 372-373. https://doi.org/10.1093/jnci/djj115

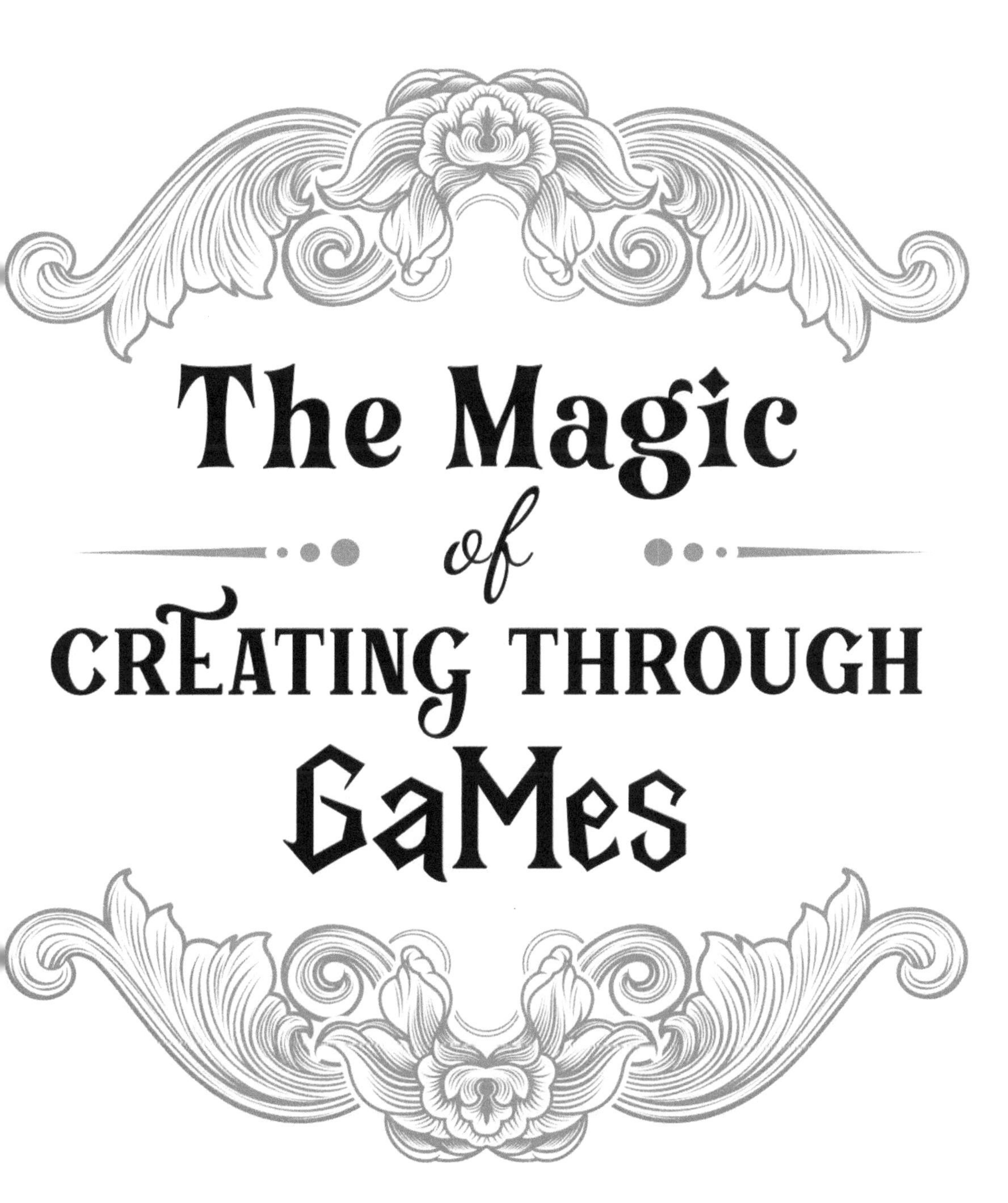

The Magic of CREATING THROUGH GAMES

BUILDING FANTASY WORLDS THROUGH MUSIC

Clio Montrey

usic and video games are symbiotic creatures. Nowhere is this more apparent than in the fantasy genre, with its magic-infused themes and tropes. Worldbuilding – the creation of imaginary worlds – is often perceived as a visual and narrative undertaking, but it can be accomplished through various other, complementary means – especially music. Whether in-world melodies performed by characters, as in Nintendo's *The Legend of Zelda* titles, or atmospheric soundscapes that provide a backdrop for the game's adventure, such as the stunning soundtracks of the *Final Fantasy* series, music renders gameplay more immersive and fosters a sense of escape from everyday life. Within the fantasy genre, it can even function as a narrative or descriptive device, acting as an aural representation of literal magical elements. In this paper, I introduce the concept of fantasy worldbuilding through music and explain key concepts of dramatic development through music. I then connect these concepts back to classical music in order to create parallels to earlier formats.

Keywords: fantasy, worldbuilding, music

Music for Worldbuilding

Games need worldbuilding. After all, what is a game if not a constructed world to sink into, to explore, to fight in, to live in, according to rules that may not entirely overlap with those in our physical universe?

According to Wikipedia, worldbuilding is "the process of constructing a world, originally an imaginary one, sometimes associated with a fictional universe"[1]. JRR Tolkien's works are a prime example of worldbuilding, where he even invented a variety of fictional cultures and languages (Tolkien, 1983).

In games, music creates a salient aural point for the player to grasp. Creating an aural soundscape or soundtrack is akin to building a physical or visual structure for a fictional world. Much as a writer builds up a fictional universe, a composer creates one through sound – in some cases, this may even be a standalone universe, as in programmatic music.[2]

With games, the storytelling necessarily relies primarily on the game narrative. With the exception of exclusively audio-driven games such as *A Blind Legend* (Dowino, 2015), the tonal and modal languages employed in game music underscore certain traits of the in-game universe that have usually already been established through the use of visuals. The instrumentation reflects the fictional environment of the instruments' story-world designers. It may even go as far as to reflect instruments seen in the game itself, such as the playable ocarina in *The Legend of Zelda: Ocarina of Time* (Nintendo, 1998.)

Music and sound can act as a device that represents magical elements. This can be the sounds magic makes: the sparkling of fairy dust, a dragon's roar. It can also be "descriptive": the kind of sound world where magic would naturally find itself at home, like a dark and mysterious cavern or a creaky and mysterious hut in the woods. The "characteristic sound" of magic can be portrayed more stereotypically, like John Williams' soundtrack for *Harry Potter and the Philosopher's Stone* (Columbus, 2001), with an orchestration focused heavily on celesta touches and "magical" accents. The "magic" can simply also be evocative of a fantasy setting, without showing any overt magical in-game phenomena,

---

[1] https://en.wikipedia.org/w/index.php?title=Worldbuilding&oldid=1103890924
[2] Programmatic music is a form of narrative music with roots in 19th century romanticism where a story was quite literally told through music alone. An example is Smetana's *Moldau* from his set of symphonic poems *Má Vlast*.

like the surreal beauty of Japanese Breakfast's soundtrack for the more subtly magical game *Sable* (Shedworks, 2021).

Classifying Game Music and Sound: a Few Definitions

Music in media can be classified in a variety of different ways, but for us it will be useful to look at the music that happens inside the fictional world, and that which takes place outside its confines, for the benefit of the player (or audience). In-world (diegetic) music is the music that takes place within the imaginary universe (van der Lek, 1991). An example would be the melodies on Link's Ocarina in *The Legend of Zelda: Ocarina of Time*. Playable character Link is well aware of the sound he is making on the ocarina, and the characters (and magic of the world) react to these melodies as if they perceived them.

In contrast, incidental music is heard by the player but not by the in-game characters (*ibid.*) Link and his fellow characters are not aware of the sweeping soundtrack that packages the game for the player's consumption. They do not react to the driving beats that take place during battles, nor do they hear ominous music in mysterious places they enter such as dungeons or caves. We use our suspension of disbelief because we know games are works of fiction, and in our role as the player, we accept the soundtrack as part of the experience, just as we accept the controller, the computer, the screen. It is part of the frame within which the fictional universe is positioned. In game studies, this definition is sometimes extended and reassembled into more specific layers, dependent on how much player interaction happens with the music/sounds (Sen, 2021; Whalen, 2004). However, in the interests of conciseness, I shall keep to simplified definitions.

Many composers cleverly unite diegetic music and the soundtrack, reflecting melodies that the characters are aware of or may even sing and play, and picking those up in the soundtrack, orchestrating musical textures around these melodies. This is termed trans-diegetic sound. Let's look again at our example from *The Legend of Zelda: Ocarina of Time*. Link's ocarina melodies are picked up and elaborated upon in the soundtrack and the incidental music, which extends and harmonizes these simple melodies, developing them into themes.

But what about those sounds that may or may not be termed music, or those that are clearly effects? They add to the worldbuilding as well. While these aspects are not the main focus of this paper, let's have a look at the different types of sound that will appear in a game. Sound effects and soundscapes reflect the auditory experiences of a fictional world, especially in relation to magic.

Sound effects are directly linked to worldbuilding: they populate the fictional universe with the type of things you'd hear in the moment: dripping drops in a cave, alarms, phone calls, and – in the case of fantasy games – sword whooshes, magical shimmers, and other in-game events. These will not be discussed in the paper, but they must be mentioned for context. Sound effects may be reflected in the music, much in the way trans-diegetic music is treated (e.g., a horn, klaxon or button sound may be picked up at the same pitch in the score, or vice versa). A prime example of this is Neo's alarm clock echoing the throbbing club music in the 1999 film *The Matrix* (Wachowski & Wachowski, 1999).

Sometimes considered sound design and at other times classified as music, **soundscapes** exist on a spectrum between effect and composition. An example would be the ambient music in a magical setting. Sen (2021) analyzes the battle between Link and a game enemy termed a "Guardian" in *The Legend of Zelda: Breath of the Wild* (Nintendo, 2017) in terms of sound layers, and concludes that "the diegetic and non-interactive sounds are always ambient noises that paint the soundscape of the story world" (Sen, 2021). In this particular scene, the sounds of nature (such as rain) overlap with the battle music with synths and piano – a hybrid consisting of a composed piece of music with identifiable melody, and background ambience, made possible by adaptive audio engines and audio implementation. Soundscapes are often more ambient. However, adaptive audio has brought new implementations and redefinitions of soundscapes: "video games make it possible to create incredibly complex sound structures that are able to explore sound's storytelling abilities" (*ibid.*).

There are many different types of sound in games, and music is crucial. It can act as a device that represents magical elements directly, as diegetic music for magic, or that supports the worldbuilding of a magical imaginary universe. Working a rich musical vein into game worldbuilding makes a game more magical, both figuratively and literally!

Basic Classical Music Concepts

Classical music has staying power. Its structures and forms have sustained generations of composers and reached countless audiences. Have you ever listened to a symphony by Mahler or Beethoven and thought these pieces would sound right at home in a cutscene? Most soundtracks in film and television are modeled on classical (western) music. Game soundtracks follow this pattern quite often.

Looking at the most basic and overarching forms omnipresent in classical music may help us not only to understand how the music in games is structured, but also how it may help elicit an emotional reaction in players, underscore an association with magic, or simply contribute to worldbuilding.

We can thus apply many of the elements we use for the analysis of classical music to soundtracks: the basic principles and structure are the same. Here we are looking, however, at larger-scale structures. For example, an opera, just like a game, possesses a dramatic arc that may be supported through a selection of suitable music. This music may either underscore the story or carry it. Finding operatic parallels to the overall structure of musical soundtracks and elements may unearth some interesting insights.

It is important to note that other music theory systems from around the world should likewise be studied. It is important to think critically about musical influences in games. For example, while they largely align with Western classical orchestration principles, the soundtracks of many Japanese games such as *Persona 5* (Atlus, 2015) are heavily influenced by local musical culture, and thus, whether directly or indirectly, traditional melodies, harmonies, and musical structures.

Themes and Motives

Music can also rely on melodic themes[3] and motives[4] to enhance or create dramatic development.

In classical music, there are many formal structures and sub-structures that, if one desires, one can analyze in detail and on several different levels. This includes analyzing the harmonies, melodies, chordal structure and texture, arrangement and orchestration, type of harmonies used, harmonic language, and so forth.

For the purposes of this paper, we will limit ourselves to a simplified form derived from sonata form, more concretely, the concept of **main theme** (in classical, referred to as the primary theme) and **secondary theme**. This nomenclature is most often applied to sonata form[5] but can be applied more loosely to any set of contrasting melodies that function together in a piece of music.

The primary (main) theme is the most recognizable melody you hear. It is the first melody stated, and it is this tune that you would hum when you recall the piece. Think of Beethoven's *Für Elise*. The tune you have in mind is the main theme.

---

[3] Recognizable tune that characterizes a melody. May be the entire melody, or the melody may run longer than the theme (which is its most important part - think of it as the opening statement of a musical essay). What you would hum or sing when recalling a piece of music.

[4] A short and recognizable bit of melody intended to be easily recognized, repeated and reused over the course of a musical work.

[5] An instrumental musical form popular in the classical and Romantic eras, consisting of an exposition with introduction of primary and secondary theme, development of these themes, and recapitulation. It is too strict for our discussion; therefore, the concepts of the primary and secondary themes have been extracted.

The secondary (or contrasting) theme is a second melody, one that is less commonly associated with the piece, but just as important in most cases. It is not always present in every composition, but is a common feature of longer, more developed pieces. For example, *Für Elise* contains a middle section that is not as recognized but just as important to the structure of the piece. Here arises musical conflict, a sense of contrast, and momentum due to moving onto a different (though complementary) idea.

This concept is illustrated well in the soundtrack to *The Legend of Zelda, Ocarina of Time*. Zelda's Lullaby begins with a particular theme (G Major) that leads into a contrasting statement in another key (C Major).

Zelda's Lullaby, main theme:

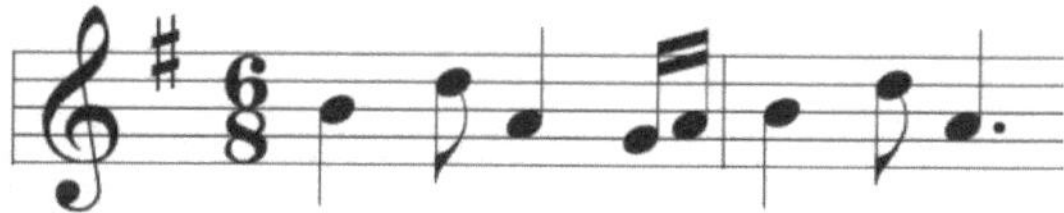

Zelda's Lullaby, contrasting theme (note the contrasting musical motion to the main theme):

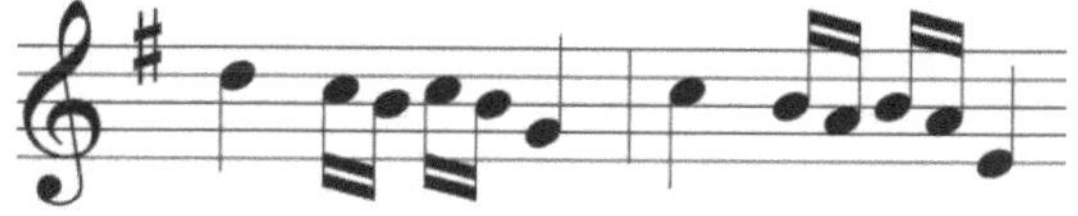

Figure 1. Notated approximation of the main and contrasting themes of Koji Kondo's piece Zelda's Lullaby from The Legend of Zelda: Ocarina of Time. Transcribed by paper author.

Leitmotifs

Leitmotifs (or *Leitmotivs*) are particular musical motives or themes that define a character or situation and keep returning along with that situation or character. In the *Star Wars* universe (Lucas et al., 1977 -), characters and concepts have a theme that composer John Williams has assigned them. When the audience hears this theme, they know that character or concept is being referenced (e.g. Luke, Leia, the Imperial March). These themes are woven into the soundtrack whenever certain characters appear or certain situations become relevant to the plot.

The term leitmotif (or *Leitmotiv*) is most often applied to the study of works by Richard Wagner, the composer of numerous late Romantic-era operas, including his famous Ring Cycle of operas based on Norse mythology, and Tristan und Isolde, whose works gave rise to the term in later analysis and critique[6].

In games, the concept of leitmotif is not only of tremendous importance but has the potential to gain new, interactive facets. In *Final Fantasy X* (Square, 2001) for example, the Zanarkand main game theme returns at important points, such as in a transformed form under the title *Movement in Green*. This is a treatment akin to one that would be undertaken for a film soundtrack. Yet many games take it several steps further in various ways. Within the fictional transmedia world focusing on the game *League of Legends* (Riot Games, 2009), characters are assigned their own thematic music. For popular champions and events, Riot has even created a set of music videos. Within the individual games, these musical motives can play a practical signaling role that underscores when a champion springs into action. In the online collectible card game *Legends of Runeterra* (Riot Games, 2020), for example, a distinct leitmotif sounds when each champion is brought into play on the board. This framing can render the leitmotif a useful vehicle for creating a magical atmosphere in games, as well as associating player actions with sound events: if a player plays a particular champion and the music is triggered, then the player associates this champion's magical abilities with their music.

---

[6] leitmotif | music | Britannica. (n.d.). Encyclopedia Britannica. Retrieved May 2, 2022, from https://www.britannica.com/art/leitmotif

Die Zauberflöte and Parallels to Magic in Game Worlds

There are few operas better known and loved than Mozart's *Die Zauberflöte* (The Magic Flute, Mozart, 1791)[7]. While Mozart's *Singspiel* has provided timeless entertainment for centuries, it also contains something more subtle: a magical prototype that may be considered a dramatic template for magical stories, and can be applied to storytelling (and music) in games.

I have chosen to have a look at because of its magical dramatic themes and relative accessibility to audiences who may otherwise be unfamiliar with opera. Many people who know no other opera have either seen or at least heard of *Die Zauberflöte*. It is easy to follow and understand, and the music is melodic, beautiful, and very catchy. It shares many characteristics with games in fantasy settings, and gives us a wonderful example from which to draw some parallels, especially on the subject of worldbuilding. And the best place to start is with an opera that focuses on magic, within a fictional fantasy world!

An opera has a libretto – a script akin to a screenplay in film – which makes it potentially quite useful as an object of study for game developers. A libretto fulfills the same function as a screenplay does for a film. It does not contain the musical aspects of the opera but covers the narrative bases, dialogue, and very often describes (possible) scenery, stage directions, actions of silent players, extras, and chorus. Often a libretto also gives certain technical or staging suggestions. The director, dramaturge, and entire leading team of the opera then make decisions on whether to accept or reject the dramatic groundwork laid out in the libretto, but it always begins with the librettist's written word.

Just as film analysis would make little sense when taking into account visuals without accounting for narrative content, it

---

[7] Denotes the premiere date of the opera. References allude to the publication of the Peters engraving (1875).

makes sense to consider opera as inextricably linked and dependent on the libretto. In opera, as in many genres where vocal music is employed, the text is intrinsic to the musical form and acts as a framework for the entire piece. In fact, when considering examples to compare with music in games, it may be more useful to focus on the narrative and dramatic elements conveyed through opera – even though this depends heavily on text – than to look at the harmonic and melodic structures and forms therein.

In opera, as in games, several musical forms can be used as devices to help us understand the characters, their motivations, and their place in the drama. An **aria** is a song in the context of an opera, sung by a solo character (in contrast to duets and ensemble numbers where there are multiple characters featured), often with orchestral accompaniment, that reflects what the character in question is feeling or doing and helps characterize this person: are they willful? Easily manipulated? The music directly reflects the character singing the work.

This can be likened in games to the various musical themes and songs applied to characters – also in additional content outside of the game world proper. For example, in the *League of Legends* (Riot Games, 2009) lore, *Get Jinxed* is a rock song that describes champion Jinx, performed by Agnete Kjølsrud with the explicit intent of portraying the character as a willful and violent personality who will stop at nothing to bring chaos into any situation she enters.[8] This is accomplished through a vocal line with intentional inclusion of some vocal fry[9] elements and metal-genre instrumentation: blaring guitars, driving beats. These same characteristics, incidentally, are used to represent the Jinx character within the game itself, when she levels up or attacks. In this way, the song creates a characterization of Jinx and

---

[8] While it is no longer considered main canon, this lore is a fantastic example of a song where a character explains motivations, much as an opera character would through an aria. It also happens to be more popular than ever due to the recent animated television series *Arcane* (Riot Games, 2021), despite its status as non-canon.

[9] Vocal fry refers to the vocal register where the voice sounds "gravelly". It is the range just slightly below normal speaking range. This range can be extended upwards in pitch somewhat, depending on the speaking or singing technique.

contextualizes the character as a powerful and chaotic figure, an archetype of the fantasy genre. Thus, Jinx provokes the imagination of players with her attitude illustrated thoroughly through music.

In *Die Zauberflöte*, Prince Tamino wakes up to find himself alone in a strange land populated by offbeat characters. (We could compare him to any playable character embarking on a quest.) As the audience follows his journey, they see this fictional universe through his eyes. Thus, for the purposes of this analysis, Tamino can be considered a template for a "playable character." His character is defined by his aria, *"Dies Bildnis ist bezaubernd schön,"* that shows his resolve to rescue the princess Pamina in the face of overwhelming odds.[10]

If we have our playable character cast, it won't be long until we cast around and find some non-playable characters (NPCs). The aforementioned Princess Pamina, much like Peach or Daisy in the Mario franchise, is in a terrible situation (as is the usual situation of princesses). Her aria, *"Ach, ich fühl's,"* expresses all the pain and hopelessness of her situation in a slow minor sarabande-like tempo.[11]

Papageno, the bird-catcher, and his love Papagena culminate their love story in a silly and jaunty duet (*"pa, pa, pa..."*) that reinforces these characters as our comic relief. Jaskier in *The Witcher* (CD Projekt, 2007) would be a good game analogy. A bard with a love of the bacchanal life and with an effusive fashion sense, yet with a tremendous sense of loyalty toward Geralt of Rivia (the Witcher of the game's title), Jaskier is a loyal (if sometimes annoying) companion to Geralt. In the opera, *Die*

---

[10] The operatic stereotypes of heroic prince and princess in a tower are of course best avoided when creating new games – reinforcing such stereotypes would only serve to perpetuate antiquated views of societal models. However, they persist, and so for the purposes of this analysis and to allow the drawing of parallels, this point is touched upon.

[11] A Baroque-era dance form. Not strictly the form employed by Mozart in this aria, but close enough in character to give an idea of how it should be sung: breathless and heavy with meaning but still with the momentum of a slow, inexorable dance.

Zauberflöte's Papageno is especially crucial to the plot of the opera, and just as Jaskier does in *The Witcher*, Papageno acts as a bard-like humorous character to whom situations just *happen*, and he is also a helper figure to the "playable character" figure (Tamino). Both Jaskier and Papageno are well versed in music and magic: they have seen magic consume and destroy (in Jaskier's case the monster the Witcher slays, in Papageno's the Queen of the Night and her dark forces) as well as provide hope and rescue in dark times and situations (the magic-wielders who protect cities in The Witcher; magical silver bells that Papageno must keep safe). Fantasy worldbuilding is most effective with small details like these bells – these are touches that strive to make the fictional world feel more relatable and real.

If we are to liken *Die Zauberflöte* to a game, we need enemies. The Queen of the Night (Die Königin der Nacht) is a strong contender. She wields strong magic, as alluded to in Schikaneder's libretto. Her wild aria, *"Der Hölle Rache,"* is sung in high and fantastic coloratura[12] and shows the audience just how much magical - and political - power she wields in this strange and fantastic land. A parallel in the world of games is a bit of dialogue offered in the digital card game *Legends of Runeterra* (Riot Games, 2020) – an assertion of power and strength. When any champion is played or levels up, a short musical clip plays, underscoring their bark[13] with a musical description of their power to back up their attack abilities. Yasuo, an important champion reminiscent of a Samurai warrior from a region called Ionia, has a folky flute line assigned to him that sings in a serene yet assertive upwards-tending line when his magical wind ability takes effect. Tryndamere, a battle-hardened Viking-like warrior, has a flash of ancient-sounding drone play when he announces his fearlessness in combat while leveling up. Gwen, a reanimated doll from the haunted Shadow Isles, speaks her line and springs into action while a tinkling melody over a hollow, haunted underlay plays; while the sweep of the melody is heroic, it also underscores her Pinocchio-like origin story and draws attention

---

[12] Extremely ornamented, fast and virtuosic runs of many notes, often sung on a single breath.
[13] A short and catchy line of dialogue.

to the wonder of her magical existence. Each of these little musical motives in Runeterra can be considered a leitmotif.

Much like Yasuo's flute theme in *Legends of Runeterra*, the flute mentioned in the title of the *Die Zauberflöte* has a magical motive, and the audience repeatedly hears it in various contexts. The libretto tells us this flute is supposed to turn sorrow into joy, and the music is a joyful, upbeat tune that is as catchy as it is evocative of its magical function. This flute can be considered a stand-in for a power-up or weapon that Tamino must wield in order to complete his quest. Here, the idea can transfer to games: if one has a particularly special or interesting item, one can assign it a special melody, or melodies. In fact, the entire concept of a magical musical instrument is transferred to the world of games rather effectively in *The Legend of Zelda: Ocarina of Time*, where the template of a magical flute is wielded to create one of the world's most celebrated games.

Princess Zelda, Link, and the Ocarina of Time

In *The Legend of Zelda: Ocarina of Time*, the in-game musical instrument Link wields, an ocarina, gives him the power to transcend time and realities. We can see many dramatic parallels to the previous example from opera: the conquering hero (Link, as Tamino), the princess (Zelda, as counterpart to Pamina), the terrifying and supernatural foe (Ganondorf/Ganon to the Queen of the Night). Musically speaking, the style is completely different, and to a point so is the function: while the opera above (unless you are a performer) creates a passive relationship between spectator and presentation, in *Ocarina of Time* "musical shifts in tempo or character motivate the player to perform the actions that connect the sequence of the game experience by rewarding successful behaviour and punish failure" (Whalen, 2004). This observation by Whalen offers strong support for the assertion that music renders fantasy game worlds more immersive and therefore strengthens their worldbuilding. However, useful parallels to non-interactive media such as film and theatre can still be drawn.

The tuning of Link's ocarina is D-F-A-B-D, a modal tuning. Pitch bending can be effectuated using the stick on the controller. This tuning outlines a D-minor 6th chord, which means a minor triad with an interval of a sixth from the tonic up top. In short, it is a very common chord employed both in classical and jazz music, as well as in other genres.

6 predominant pieces are featured in Ocarina of time, all based on the same 5-note pattern. As the controller stands in for the ocarina, this adds yet another level of participation for the player. This is especially effective in creating a magical architecture for the player in the game: the player knows that the music performed on the controller will directly result in a magical effect in the game.

The melodies were created by composer Koji Kondo to fit a very specific set of constraints, while remaining easy to recall and being playable after a small number of repetitions, even for those players who are not musicians (8-Bit Music Theory, 2021). These features render all the ocarina melodies highly memorable. The simplicity of the ocarina melodies belies their evocative qualities: each piece is a different take on the feature of the 5-note mode (scale), implying different (classical) musical key, harmonies, and moods. Thus, it is as effective an aural representation of magic that one could hope to find in the world of games.

In *Ocarina of Time*, there are many instances of trans-diegetic music, as well as rendering this in-game music an important gameplay element, as the controller "becomes" an ocarina. In this manner, the player is able to access a direct link to the game's magical spells through music. Link (and therefore, the player) learns and performs melodies on his ocarina that fulfill various specific magical functions, to travel through space and time, and to make the world react to these ocarina melodies, so that this music functions as a "heuristic device to further game play" (Whalen, 2004). An example is the melody for Saria's Song, which must be played on the ocarina, and which extends into the non-diegetic soundtrack in The Lost Woods, which contains the same melodic figure, along with an orchestrated accompaniment: "the looping theme music extends and elaborates Saria's Song in a straightforward 'theme and variations' structure" (*ibid.*)

Implementing Musical Magic as a Game Developer

In order to create a convincing, "living" fictional world for a fantasy game setting, the music must be not only captivating but meaningfully connected to the game world. This means taking into account the different types of sound that might be present in this fantastical setting, as well as finding salient points for the audience to connect with. Trans-diegetic music can be employed very effectively in games, with the player using some sort of notification chime tone perhaps (an alarm, a fragment of a song or melody) and then having this pick up in the underlying soundtrack.

Most importantly, developers should strive to work with audio professionals who offer uniquely qualified insight into the musical sound world creation for fantasy games. A fantastical setting is likely not so interesting when the tonal language employed is a purely "stereotypical" one, with tinkling sounds instruments, but some tropes may be necessary so that the player understands the game world more viscerally. For instance, a dragon who beeped instead of roaring might be viewed with some confusion by a player. Similarly, a mythical setting might find itself ill-supported by a score consisting of ukulele riffs. But who knows? Offbeat musical ideas can likewise find a home in worldbuilding, if framed effectively. Context is everything, and in a fantasy game, magic can make even the most surreal elements fit together cohesively.

While the code, design, narrative, and art are usually established when a composer or sound designer joins the project, teams may find it useful to consider what the music might sound like at an early stage of the project, at least to sketch out what ideas might fit where, and find suitable reference tracks. Worldbuilding through music works best when the sound has solid foundations.

Music is just as important to the inhabitants of that fictional game world as their language, their clothing, and their physical surroundings. It has the ability to make or break the impression of a fantasy world for players. As such, music is a crucial element of worldbuilding in fantasy games.

References

Games

A Blind Legend (R. Rascati, composer) [Computer game]. (2016). Dowino on Steam. https://store.steampowered.com/app/437530/A_Blind_Legend/

Fujibajashi, H. (2017). The Legend of Zelda: Breath of the Wild (H. Wakai, composer) [Video game]. Nintendo.

Hashino, K. (2016). Persona 5 (S. Meguro, composer) [Video game]. Atlus.

Kitase, Y. (2001). Final Fantasy X (N. Uematsu et al., composers.) [Video game]. Square.

Kythreotis, G. Sable (Japanese Breakfast, composer) [Video game]. (2021) Shedworks. Raw Fury.

Miyamoto, S. (1998). The Legend of Zelda: Ocarina of Time (K. Kondo, composer) [Video game]. Nintendo.

The Witcher [Video game series]. (2007) CD Projekt RED on Steam. https://store.steampowered.com/developer/CDPR/

Van Roon, A. League of Legends (Various composers) [Video game]. (2009). Riot Games. https://leagueoflegends.com

Yip, A. Legends of Runeterra (Various composers) [Video game]. (2020). Riot Games. https://playruneterra.com/

Films and Television

Columbus, C. (2001). Harry Potter and the Philosopher"s Stone (John Williams, composer) [Film]. Warner Bros.

Kirshner, I. (Director). (1980). Star Wars: The Empire Strikes Back [Film].

Linke, C., & Lee, A. (creators). (2021). Arcane [TV series]. Riot Games. https://www.netflix.com/at-en/title/81435684

Lucas, G. (Director). (1977). Star Wars [Film].

Marquand, R. (Director). (1983) Star Wars: Return of the Jedi (John Williams, composer) [Film].

Musical Scores

Beethoven, L. van. (1867). Bagatelle No. 25 in A minor (WoO 59, Bia 515) for solo piano("Für Elise") [musical score]. J. F. Cotta, Ed.; First edition.

Mozart, W. A. (1875). Die Zauberflöte [musical score]. Leipzig: C.F. Peters.

Smetana, B. (1879). Má Vlast [musical score]. Leipzig: Breitkopf und Härtel, n.d. (ca. 1930).

Books, Articles, Online Resources

Aria guides: Ach, ich fühl's. (2016, November 28). Schmopera. Retrieved May 2, 2022, from https://www.schmopera.com/aria-guides-ach-ich-fuhls/

Bruno, D. (n.d.). Ocarina music in The Legend of Zelda: Ocarina of Time. Dan Bruno. Retrieved May 2, 2022, from https://danbruno.net/writing/ocarina/

Diegetic Sound and Non-Diegetic Sound: What's the Difference? - 2022. (2021, September 3). MasterClass. Retrieved May 2, 2022, from https://www.masterclass.com/articles/diegetic-sound-and-non-diegetic-sound-whats-the-difference

How Creative Limitations Shaped Ocarina of Time's Best Music. (2021, September 29). YouTube. Retrieved May 2, 2022, from https://www.youtube.com/watch?v=_SeY_Gss2CY

Jacobson, B. (n.d.). sonata form | musical form | Britannica. Encyclopedia Britannica. Retrieved May 2, 2022, from https://www.britannica.com/art/sonata-form

Leitmotif | Music | Britannica. (n.d.). Encyclopedia Britannica. Retrieved May 2, 2022, from https://www.britannica.com/art/leitmotif

League of Legends, Kjølsrud, A., & Linke, C. ". (2013). Get Jinxed [Music video/song]. Youtube. https://www.youtube.com/watch?v=0nlJuwO0GDs

Lek, R. v. d. (1991). Diegetic Music in Opera and Film: A Similarity Between Two Genres of Drama Analysed in Works by Erich Wolfgang Korngold (1897-1957). Rodopi.

Motive | Music | Britannica. (n.d.). Encyclopedia Britannica. Retrieved May 2, 2022, from https://www.britannica.com/art/motive-music

Parkin, S. (2021, November 6). Sable review – go build yourself a future, girl. The Guardian. Retrieved May 2, 2022, from https://www.theguardian.com/games/2021/nov/06/sable-review-go-build-yourself-a-future-girl

Sen, M. (2021). Exploring the Narrative Aspect of Video Game Soundscapes. Klangschaften. Retrieved 7 August 2022, from https://blog.uni-koeln.de/klangschaften/2021/08/27/exploring-the-narrative-aspect-of-video-game-soundscapes/

Sonata form | Musical form | Britannica. (n.d.). Encyclopedia Britannica. Retrieved May 2, 2022, from https://www.britannica.com/art/sonata-form

Synopsis: The Magic Flute. The Metropolitan Opera. Retrieved May 2, 2022, from https://www.metopera.org/discover/synopses/the-magic-flute/

Tolkien, J. R. R. (1984). The monsters and the critics, and other essays (C. Tolkien, Ed.). Houghton Mifflin.

Whalen, Z. (2004). Play Along - An Approach to Videogame Music. Game Studies: the International Journal of Computer Game Research, 4(1). Retrieved August 3, 2022, from http://www.gamestudies.org/0401/whalen/

THE MAGIC OF MORAL ENGAGEMENT IN VIDEOGAMES: COMPLEXITY, CHALLENGE & COMPETENCE

Benjamin Hanussek

Tom Tucek

According to Csikszentmihalyi's concept of flow, enjoyment of an activity maximises when the challenge it presents matches one's skill level. Similarly, we think that to allow for an enjoyable moral experience in videogames, it requires manageable moral complexity, which corresponds to a distinct degree of players' moral competence. While morality in videogames is often seen as an opportunity for philosophical reflection, in this paper, we treat it as a deliberately implemented game design element, constructed to keep players engaged. We argue that the complexity in which morality appears in contemporary games follows a reproducible system, which we call moral complexity and it consists of the degree to which a game offers players alternatives and commentary to violent and deceitful actions. This system allows for a scale of low to high moral complexity, which establishes its manageability just like generic difficulty in games. We proceed with our argumentation that depending on the degree of moral complexity, some sort of player skill is demanded to enjoy dealing with moral encounters. This skill is moral competence and refers to one's ability to perform moral actions according to one's internal moral principles. Our hypothesis states that players with low moral competence prefer games with low moral complexity, and that players with high moral competence prefer games with high moral complexity. To test this, we have designed a survey study, and this work aims to serve as a work-in-progress report for this experiment, expanding on both the technical details of this project, while also discussing the pragmatic nature of morality within contemporary game design.

Keywords: moral complexity, moral competence, flow, game studies, videogame ethics

Introduction

Moral engagement in videogames has arguably become a new gold standard in videogames (Zagal, 2013; Groen et al., 2020). Moral choices in games can influence difficulty, relationships with other characters, or how the story develops, and thus allow for an elevated feeling of agency and add meaning to our actions (Egenfeldt-Nielsen et al., 2020, p. 216). Games like Frostpunk (11 bit studios, 2018) or Detroit Become Human (Quantic Dream, 2018) exemplify how moral economies are essential parts of a distinct gameplay experience, namely one that engages players beyond generic scores and item collection.

Now, from a psychological standpoint alone it may be argued that players' engagement is simply intensified by fulfilling their need for autonomy (Przybylski et al., 2010, p. 155). However, there is much more to it than giving players just a choice. In this paper, we argue that to allow for an optimal moral experience in videogames, it requires manageable moral complexity which corresponds to a distinct degree of players' moral competence. We treat morality, as it appears in videogames, as a deliberately implemented game design element, constructed to keep players engaged, or even in flow. It is important at this point to clarify that within this research, flow is treated as a game's optimal experience and that we assume, that moral encounters in games are usually constructed in a way to enable flow. For example, first-person shooter games will seldomly interrupt gameplay with moral dilemmas, while they are more common in roleplaying videogames. Therefore, we argue that the complexity in which morality appears in (most) contemporary games follows a reproducible system, which we call moral complexity. It consists of the degree to which a game offers players alternatives and commentary to violent and deceitful actions. This system allows for a scale of low to high moral complexity, which establishes its manageability just like generic difficulty (i.e., increasing or decreasing damage output of enemies). Low moral complexity games could be enjoyable because one does not have to consider one's moral principles while playing them, whereas high moral complexity games would be appreciated more by those that like to engage in the topics of ethics and morality. Thus, we hypothesize that depending on the degree of moral complexity, some sort of player skill is demanded to enjoy dealing with certain moral encounters. This skill would be moral competence, an empirical notion discovered by the psychologist Georg Lind, that refers to one's ability to perform moral actions according to one's internal moral principles (2019). Thus, our hypothesis states that players with low moral competence prefer games with low moral complexity, and that players with high moral competence prefer games with high moral complexity. The goal of this research is to show the pragmatic nature of morality in contemporary game design, which aims at flow, or some sort of moral challenge, rather than involving players solely based on the sublimity of morality. It does not mean, however, that one necessarily excludes the other.

Thus, this paper begins by introducing our notion of moral complexity to the reader. Understanding moral complexity requires a clarification of the term morality and what we mean by it in this research. A short discussion on how morality appears in contemporary games follows. Furthermore, the notion of flow is presented to underline the aspect of challenge in moral complexity. To complement this theoretical foundation with an empirical investigation, the concept of moral competence is explained. While moral complexity refers exclusively to content in videogames, moral competence refers to players' ability and serves as the basis on which we have designed an experiment to test our hypothesis. The experimental design, which at the time of authoring this paper entered its operation, but is still work-in-progress, is described, and explained in the subsequent section in form of a development report. Based on our theoretical foundation and experiment, we discuss our expected results in contrast to practical issues in setting up the experiment. At the end, a preliminary conclusion is drawn. Definite conclusions, drawn from the data acquired in the context of the experiment, will be available in later publications, as well as in our theses at the University of Klagenfurt, scheduled to be published in autumn of 2022.

Moral Complexity

To understand our notion of moral complexity, it is necessary to discuss the term morality and how this research utilizes it. Morality is usually understood as a metaphysical domain that imposes judgements of right and wrong on our decision-making process (Kant, 1998, pp. 48-49). Now whether morality exists a priori, so before and beyond human experience, or a posteriori, after and constituted by human experience, is just a question of the chicken and the egg for us (Hanussek et al., 2021). At any rate, what is crucial is that, wherever morality may come from, in videogames we encounter a mere representation of it. Whether we hurt an NPC in a videogame or not, whether we steal from an NPC or not, has on one side no real-world consequences for us. On the other side, we may simply dissociate from the game and its magic circle at our convenience. It limits our concern for how we decide. Morality in videogames is therefore incapable of rendering the totality of morality and an intimate confrontation with us as humans. What videogames do instead, is that they represent a simplified version of how we normatively think of morality. By which we refer to global player audiences. An essential concern for developers when constructing this kind of artificial morality is the use of generally accepted notions understood across cultural borders, such as love, hate, freedom, or right and wrong. These notions are woven into greater meta-narratives (i.e., The Heroes Journey, The American Dream) that address our collective emotions and expectations (Goldenberg et al 2020, p. 155). Studies indicate that the more a game fulfils preconstructed expectations of players, the more likely they are to be satisfied with the game (Polashenski, 2017). If we think then of morality in video games within the context of trying to address as many players as possible, we need to think about the most universal associations we have when thinking about morality, and these can be seen as violence and deceit (Lind, 2019, p. 37). It can be argued that no society on the planet has not developed a code of ethics that regards violence and deceit in themselves as wrong, although what constitutes such, might differ. Whether members of these societies act upon these principles remains a different matter, however, as we will see later.

It comes as no surprise that the dominant representation of morality in videogames is constituted by expositions to violence and deceit. By violence, we mean physical and emotional harm that is inflicted on another person. With deceit, we mean deception of another person that results in emotional harm or deprives them of any private property. It is argued that violence and deceit are the foundation for most moral encounters visible, not only in AAA games, but also in indie games. Exposition, however, is not enough to trigger a moral experience, otherwise, games like Grand Theft Auto V (Rockstar, 2013) or Call of Duty: Modern Warfare (Infinity Ward, 2019) would qualify for higher degrees of moral complexity. For a game to be considered to have moral complexity, it requires the very fabric of what makes morality such a struggle for humans, namely reflection and choice. A game such as Spec Ops: The Line (Yager Productions, 2019) provokes reflection through critical commentary on violence and deceit, while Frostpunk offers choice through practical alternatives to them. The degree to which a game offers commentary and/or alternatives constitutes the degree of moral complexity. While Grand Theft Auto V, offering little to no alternatives and commentary, qualifies for low moral complexity, Spec Ops: The Line contextualizes violence and deceit through critical commentary, which makes it have medium moral complexity. Lastly, Frostpunk offers frequent alternatives and commentary towards violence and deceit, making it a high-moral-complexity game.

Moral complexity manages to not only represent morality, but also to operationalize it. This means that, while in low-moral-complexity games moral decision-making does not contribute to the overall gameplay, in medium- and especially high-moral-complexity games, moral reflection and decision-making become an integral part of the gameplay experience. In Frostpunk, we can even speak of a well-designed moral economy (cp. Hayse, 2016). In that sense, the higher the moral complexity, the more morality becomes part of the gameplay experience for which it has to be playable. This means that morally complex games must be designed in a way that makes them challenging, manageable, and therefore rewarding. To understand how moral complexity operationalizes morality, it makes sense to take a look at the notion of flow, which is widely considered to be the optimal experience in gaming.

> "Experiencing flow means perceiving the challenges at hand and one's own skills as balanced, being highly concentrated and achieving clearly defined goals. As the experience of flow is usually inherently rewarding and pleasurable, the activity enabling it will likely be engaged in voluntarily and repeatedly. Accordingly, flow can be considered as a type of intrinsic motivation and as highly relevant for supporting learning processes." (Kiel, 2020, p. 220)

It can be argued that, whether consciously or not, many developers aim for flow when designing games, so as to increase the enjoyment that players experience. It is therefore crucial for games that have morality within their core gameplay (i.e., Frostpunk, Detroit: Become Human) to implement it as a form of manageable economy. This moral economy must provide feedback on our actions, and it needs to allow us to make some predictions. Otherwise, games of high moral complexity become frustrating. After all, moral complexity is a representation of morality made playable. With some exceptions, such as subversive games (Wilson & Sicart, 2010), designers usually do not intend to disengage players during gameplay. Morality as an unpredictable force with no direct feedback to our actions and no logical solutions would cause exactly that, whereas morality that we as players can follow and understand (which we think is based on moral competence) allows us to enjoy and engage with games even more. Following Juul's postulate of games being sets of rules (2005), we might understand that what we find enjoyable in playing games is its magic circle, not merely for it being a detached consecrated space (Huizinga, 1938, p. 10) but for its simplified imperatives that impose a pleasant order within our minds.

> "What makes these activities conducive to flow is that they were designed to make optimal experience easier to achieve. They have rules that require the learning of skills, they set up goals, they provide feedback, they make control possible. They facilitate concentration and involvement by making the activity as distinct as possible from the so-called 'paramount reality' of everyday existence." (Csikzentmihalyi, 2002, p. 74)

So, to sum it up, moral complexity is the degree to which a game provides commentary and alternatives to violence and deceit. Higher moral complexity ties the aspect of morality closer to the core gameplay experience of the game. Once morality is an essential part of the gameplay experience, it needs to take shape as a challenging yet manageable form of moral economy to allow for flow, or at least enjoyable gameplay.

But which skill is needed to manage moral challenges? Do we always struggle when dealing with moral choices in videogames or does it depend on how moral we are? We argue that moral competence is the skill players need to engage with moral complexity. Whether players experience moral challenges as frustrating or engaging depends on their moral competence.

Moral Competence

Moral competence is "the ability to solve problems and conflicts through deliberation and discussion based on moral principles" (Lind, 2019, p. 7). Besides being empirically assessable, moral competence is a unique way of looking at moral capabilities of human beings. Moral competence does not ask whether people are moral at all, how moral they are, or which specific moral system they have internalized, but "the ability to solve problems and conflicts solely through deliberation and discussion, without using violence and deceit, or submitting to an authority" (Lind, 2019, p. 20). Lind, who has developed the notion, states that regardless of cultural or social background, most people care for certain core principles, such as avoiding violence and deceit (2019, p. 10). Whether one believes in deontology, utilitarianism, or divine command, violence and deceit seem to be of principal concern for every social conglomerate (Gensler, 2018). Already Nietzsche observed that the origin of morals points at the regulation (and domination) of social groups that ensures their survival and eventual prosperity, a collective understanding of how to deal with violence and deceit has been developed and passed down from generation to generation (1998). How to deal with these aspects may differ from culture to culture, but it can be hardly argued that any culture would promote violence and deceit of being any good in themselves.

For Lind, it is important to understand that promoting these universal principles as imperatives (i.e., thou shalt not kill or thou shalt not steal) in society has little to do with the actual competence of being able to apply them (2019, p. 78). In short, having moral principles does not equal the skill to execute them. So, if moral principles are directed at avoiding violent and deceitful conduct, moral action is performed by democratic and honest deliberation. Lind argues that the lack of moral competence is the main reason for violent crimes, fraud and corruption (2019, p. 69). He is, however, convinced that moral competence can be trained like a muscle (2019, p. 82). The aspect of strengthening moral competence exceeds the scope of this research and has already been, in the context of game-based learning, discussed by one of the authors in a different paper (Hanussek, 2021). Important for this paper is that moral competence seems to exist in different degrees. Most people's proficiency and interest in solving conflicts non-violently and without deceit is limited, but some seem to be more confident and efficient in aligning their moral intuition with their actions.

In regard to our hypothesis, we are interested in finding out whether the degree of moral competence of players correlates in a significant way with the satisfaction they have when playing games of corresponding moral complexity. As we regard flow as the primary source of satisfaction when playing videogames, our research tries to link moral competence as a skill to moral complexity as a challenge. The question is thus: Can moral challenges only be satisfying to those who have the moral competence to solve them?

As mentioned earlier, moral competence is empirically measurable. This means that Lind developed a test to assess moral competence. The Moral Competence Test (MCT) consists of a questionnaire that presents two moral dilemmas to participants in which decisions by fictional characters have been made. A scale from -3 to +3 asks participants to rate the decisions. Furthermore, "after each story, the participants are confronted with six arguments for and six arguments against the third party's decision – and, therewith, also for and against their opinion on this decision [...]. They must mark their answers on a scale from -4 (completely reject) to +4 (completely agree)" (Lind 2019, p. 56). On basis of the answers, a numerical score (0-100) is assigned, which indicates participants' moral competence.

Moral competence and its test allow us to approach morality from a truly innovative perspective. Instead of trying to assess morality psychometrically, a simple competence is investigated. With this approach, we hope to avoid common problems of ambiguity in empirical moral research (Pereira-Santos, 2019, p. 104).

Experiment

The following report describes our experiment, which is still a work in progress. The experimental design has been fully conceptualised and set up online. While writing, the experiment is in operation, which means that data is being collected but has not been analysed yet. We deem it important to bridge the theoretical ideas expressed in this work with their practical implementation, thus we will go into details regarding technical aspects and problems encountered during our work-in-progress project as well. Note, that these points do not necessarily relate to the original argument and hypothesis, and this chapter can be skipped by those only interested in theory.

The goal of the experiment is to test the hypothesis, that people with high/low moral competence (in this report referred to as "MC") enjoy games with high/low moral complexity (in this report referred to as "MCx") more. If found out to be true, it would compare to Csikszentmihalyi's concept of flow, which states that challenging activities are enjoyed most by those with the skill that matches the challenge. MC is measured by using Lind's Moral Competence Test (MCT), giving a numerical value to an individual's ability to solve moral problems and conflicts. MCx is represented using a simplified three-level model, with high, medium, and low MCx. Games that offer alternatives to violence and deceit and provide commentary on players' moral decisions are considered high, those that do only one of both are medium, and those that do neither are low MCx.

To test the hypothesis, an experiment has been designed that utilises Lind's MCT, a limited-scope game in which two versions of moral complexity have been implemented, and the Game User

Satisfaction Scale (GUESS) (Phan et al, 2016) to produce data which can be correlated.

The experiment was implemented as a completely web-based user survey. Before the game is played, participants have to agree to terms and conditions, enter some personal data, and take the MCT, which should take a total of around ten to fifteen minutes. Playing through the game should take around five minutes, and rating one's satisfaction using GUESS should take around three minutes, for a total of around twenty minutes.

Although originally there were plans of implementing all three abstract levels of MCx into the prototype, in the end it was deemed more reasonable to work with two – low and high. As such, the prototype has an adjustable level of MCx, and the game experience will change depending on that level. For example, in the high-MCx version, choices that do not resort to violence and deceit will be available when faced with challenges, and players will be given feedback on their actions through commentary by the game. For the study, one of the two levels is randomly decided without the player's knowledge, so that their enjoyment of one of them can be measured and to ultimately be able to see if a correlation between MC, MCx, and game enjoyment exists. Although not used, the prototype would theoretically also allow for dynamic adjustment of the MCx level while playing the game.

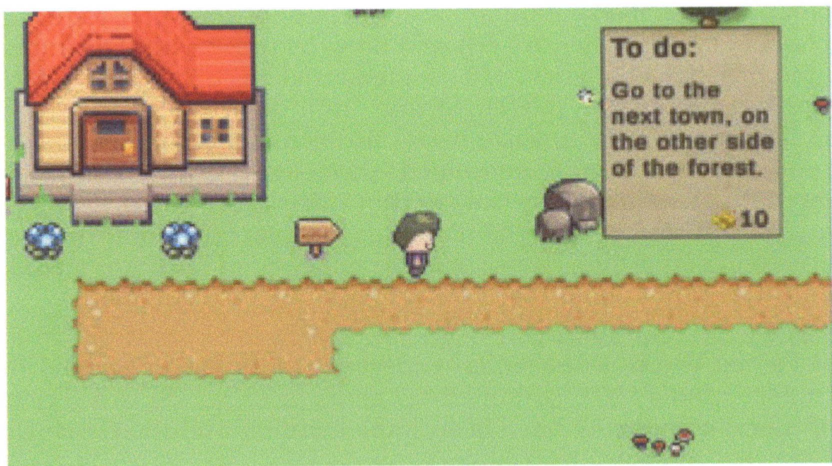

Figure 1: Screenshot from the game prototype

The game is implemented as a simple top-down 2D adventure game, similar to early Pokémon games. It was developed using the Unity Engine (version 2019.4.16f1) and exported to WebGL, using a secure web hosting service in order to ensure data protection. WebGL allows for a single build to run on every supported machine using the client's web browser, thus reducing the barrier to entry drastically, especially when considering the comparison to having to download a game before being able to play it.

The game was developed over the period of six months, through multiple iterations, including a completely scrapped first prototype, and underwent heavy playtesting and some pre-testing. Quantitative pre-testing using interviews showed that the final sequence of MCT-GAME-GUESS made little difference to an alternative order of GAME-GUESS-MCT. Although one would assume that taking the MCT before playing the game would influence participants' perception and maybe even satisfaction with the game, this does not necessarily seem to be the case. Instead, it has been argued that taking the MCT first increases participant retention, as people are less likely to stop midway through taking part in the survey when they have a game to look forward to. Testing also brought up problems with the wording of both in-game dialogue and the questionnaires, which were improved and clarified in response. Pre-testing also showed that most users would not read most of the instructions, or terms and conditions.

The main goal of the experiment development was to reduce "noise" for users when conducting the survey, thus allowing the measuring of the relevant data (satisfaction based on MC/MCx) without other factors (such as preference for certain kinds of gameplay, graphics, or story developments) interfering. For that reason, many aspects had to fall under the bland and not noticeable category. Licence-free background music and sound effects were used with great success in this regard, as testers reported barely noticing them. A retro-game-styled pixel-art look was also used for similar reasons, by employing free-to-use asset-packs, and although pixel-art can be argued to be a more contentious art-style, there are few alternatives for a game of this budget, and visual design is much harder to keep neutral than sound design anyway. Finally, the story development through the game was not allowed to change depending on the MCx-level, or choices made by the player, as differing results in a branching story would potentially influence enjoyment too much. As such, the game only offers the illusion of choice, as the story outcome is ultimately the same (see Figure 2). In the high-MCx version, however, choices made are still commented on, such as stealing money leading to the player character feeling remorse (communicated via a thought-bubble), or using violence to solve the encounter with the bandits showing the negative effects of such choices.

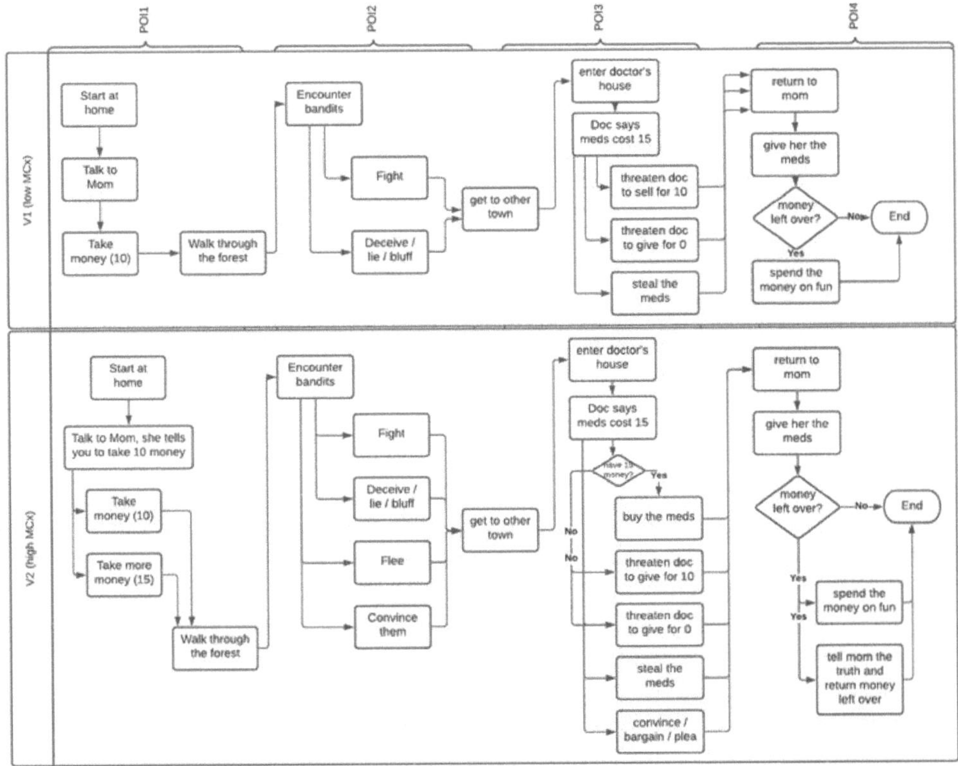

Figure 2: Story flowchart and available choices in the two versions of the prototype with different levels of moral complexity

Furthermore, the game was originally planned to run on all platforms capable of running WebGL via a browser. This included mobile terminals like smartphones and tablets, as well as various operating systems. For this purpose, touch and swipe controls were also implemented for both the game and the questionnaire, in addition to the baseline of using keyboard and mouse. To accommodate smaller screens, an internal resolution of 1280x720 pixels was chosen for the game.

However, pre-testing and playtesting showed that there were many problems with running the WebGL applet on various mobile terminals. Issues already started with mobile keyboard input being not inherently supported by Unity's WebGL export (as such, no keyboard would pop up on the screen when selecting an input form). This was solved by modifying a publicly available solution for input on Unity WebGL to suit our needs. Unfortunately, many problems, such as the applet unexpectedly crashing, randomly not displaying some of the graphics, or not being openable at all, forced us to abandon mobile support in the end. Instead, when opening the website, a warning is now displayed, recommending taking part in the survey on a desktop PC or laptop. Users are still allowed to take part using their mobile devices, but at their own risk, as crashing or exiting midway through entails the loss of all data.

Users are also required to give their explicit consent to sharing their data, which is done by having them read the terms of service and confirming having done so via checkbox at the very start of the survey. Data is then collected at two points of the survey (once before playing the game and once at the very end), temporarily stored on the EU-based server that also serves the WebGL applet and will be deleted after data analysis has been concluded, so as to conform with GDPR standards. Data provided via text forms is also checked for validity on the client-side, before being sent to the server. Communication occurs via SSL-secured connection, using JSON-data, serialized by a Unity C# script. In addition to personal data and survey data, choices made within the game, as well as overall time taken and time taken for just playing through the game are also measured and collected. Participants have the option of communicating any further thoughts via a free-form comment field at the end of the survey.

In the early phases of development, three different ways of publishing the study in combination with the prototype were sketched out. The first option (which was ultimately chosen) was to include everything, including the questionnaires, directly in the Unity WebGL applet. The second option would have been to create an HTML-based website, use standard form functionality for the questionnaire, and embed the game at a certain point during the survey. The biggest problem with this approach was the many interfacing components, and confirming that players actually played through the game before continuing with the experiment. The third option was to use pre-existing platforms to host the survey and game separately (such as soscisurvey.de and itch.io), but this would have only increased the problems of the previous approach, albeit potentially reducing development and hosting costs.

Ultimately, complete implementation using Unity WebGL was chosen, both for the interesting angle of creating a novel way of conducting studies, and the fact that a webserver was needed to collect the data for the experiment anyway. Conducting quantitative surveys by implementing them directly within a videogame executable is a novel approach to increase participation in such experiments, and will likely be further investigated and discussed in our upcoming works. The negative aspects of this approach – having to rebuild the entire project with every change, then upload it to the webserver before being able to test it – were taken into consideration. However, the lack of support for mobile WebGL applets was unexpected. It would have not made a difference for participants of the survey, as they would not have been able to play the game-part of the experiment with any of the other approaches either.

The experiment has been set online in mid-April 2022 and will be taken offline in July. Our goal is to reach at least 100 participants and favourably 200. Incentives for participation have been provided by a raffle of Steam vouchers that will be distributed among participants.

Discussion

At this point, it cannot be said whether our experiment will show that any sort of correlation between moral competence and moral complexity exists. However, what can be said, is that the concept of moral complexity and the experimental set-up are far from perfect. In regards to moral complexity, the concept at this point fails to account for the width of moral content in different kinds of games past and present. Restricting ourselves to violence and deceit, limits our contemporary understanding of morality in regard to newer branches of moral thinking, such as environmental ethics, which have already been thematised by games such as Civilization 6: Gathering Storm. Further, the notion of violence itself is problematic, as for example, self-defence seems to be an ambiguous form of violence, which can be interpreted as morally good or even bad, depending on one's ethical background. Also, our assessment of moral complexity seems to apply exclusively to single-player games with streamlined narration. Moral complexity can be therefore rightfully criticised as being reductionist. However, given the early stage of research, it was important for us to approach the topic of morality in videogames pragmatically and step by step. Our goal was to treat moral complexity in videogames as a representation of morality as it is found in most videogames. which can be rendered into reproducible rules that can be implemented in a game. Whether we managed to encapsulate the entirety of morality in videogames has not been our goal, but the operationalisation of that which can be operationalised in terms of morality as a game design element. The concept of moral complexity might however be a progressive way to categorise games according to their form of moral content, so as to inform for example rating agencies on their decisions, or platforms such as Steam on their suggestion and recommendation models for their players.

Regarding the experiment, it is difficult for us to anticipate technical issues such as bugs and errors which will have an influence on a participant's motivation to engage with the experiment. Also, on a, statistical level, the MCT remains statistically unverified. It can therefore mostly be regarded as an indicator of moral competence at the time a questionnaire was filled out. Further, our game is no state-of-the-art videogame production. It is difficult to claim equivalency in moral engagement between games that are produced with higher budgets, and our game. So, the question is how far do refined game aesthetics influence moral experience in regard to moral challenge, as an opportunity to experience a form of moral flow. Also, it may be possible that GUESS does not provide the right metric for assessing UX appropriately to be then correlated to moral competence. In short, regardless of our intense research and preparation for the experiment, it remains to be seen whether our experiment is fully capable of measuring what it is supposed to measure. This will have to be judged on basis of our analysis after the experiment is completed. In any case, we argue that our approach provides a novel way of measuring some form of players' moral activity that is not based on ambiguous questions of moral psychometry but on moral competence, the mere skill of being able to apply basic moral intuitions.

Conclusion

Our research has utilised the notion of moral complexity to assess the degree to which moral content as a form of manageable challenge is implemented in contemporary game design. Further, moral competence has been presented as a skill that allows for solving moral challenges. On basis of these insights, we have formulated our hypothesis which argues for a correlation between the satisfaction of players with distinct moral competence to corresponding degrees of moral complexity in a game. To test our hypothesis, we have designed an experiment that makes use of the MCT, a self-developed game with two degrees of moral complexity, and GUESS. The experiment is currently in operation and its results are expected to be analysed by September 2022.

A positive correlation would strengthen our hypothesis and indicate that the enjoyment of players when encountering moral challenges depends on their degree of moral competence. This insight could help developers to inform future game design tactics by implementing different degrees of moral complexity, just like generic difficulty, in order to allow a widening of their player audiences and diversify their gameplay experience. Also, moral complexity might help game platforms to create a metric that tracks players' interest in games with specific degrees of moral complexity to improve their suggestion modelling for their users. Regardless of whether a correlation between moral complexity and moral competence exists, rating agencies might find an interest in it, so as to improve their rating procedures by re-evaluating their understanding of violent content by contextualizing it by assessing moral complexity. This could lead to lower age ratings for games with violent content, as long as violence receives critical commentary and non-violent alternatives. This could be then again of interest to game developers that are interested in increasing their player outreach in general.

All in all, this research taps on a practical and new way to make use of morality in regard to videogames. It can help to improve moral experiences in games, our understanding of it and its operationalisation in terms of game design and e-commerce. However, this kind of research is at a very early stage and requires further research in theoretical aspects as well as empirical procedures to allow for more reliable application and results.

Acknowledgments

We would like to thank the University of Klagenfurt for funding this research and everyone who has helped us in improving our experimental design through pre-testing and critical feedback.

References

Csikszentmihalyi, M. (2002). Flow: The Classic Work on How to Achieve Happiness. London: Rider .

Egenfeldt-Nielsen, S., Smith, J. H., & Tosca, S. P. (2020). Understanding Video Games: The Essential Introduction (4th Edition ed.). Oxon: Routledge.

Firaxis Games. (2019). Civilization VI: Gathering Storm. 2K Games.

Gensler, H. J. (2018). Ethics: A Contemporary Introduction. Oxon: Routledge.

Goldenberg, A., Garcia, D., Halperin, E., & Gross, J. J. (2020). Collective Emotions. Current Directions in Psychological Science, 29(2), 154-160.

Groen, M., Kiel, N., Tillmann, A., & Weßel, A. (Eds.). (2020). Theoretical and Empirical Approaches to Ethical Questions in Digital Game Cultures. Wiesbaden: Springer VS.

Hanussek, B. (2021). Strengthening Moral Competence with Commercial Videogames: Integrating Papers Please into Lind's Konstanz Method of Dilemma Discussion. International Journal of TESOL & Education, 1(3), 192-208.

Hanussek, B., Reuscher, T., & Tucek, T. (2021). Tweaking Moral Complexity in Videogames? Optimising Player Experiences on Basis of Moral Competence. 14th International Conference on Game and Entertainment Technologies. Portugal.

Hayse, M. (2016). Ethics. In J. P. Wolf, & B. Perron (Eds.), The Routledge Companion to Video Game Studies (pp. 466-474). Oxon: Routledge.

Infinity Ward. (2019). Call of Duty: Modern Warfare. Activision.

Juul, J. (2005). Half-Real: Video Games between Real Rules and Fictional Worlds . Cambridge: MIT Press.

Kant, I. (1998). Groundwork of the Metaphysics of Morals. (M. Gregor, Trans.) Cambridge: Cambridge University Press.

Kiel, N. (2020). Using Digital Games for Sexual Education: Design Rules, Issues, and Applications. In M. Groen, N. Kiel, A. Tillmann, & A. Weßel (Eds.), Theoretical and Empirical Approaches to Ethical Questions in Digital Game Cultures (pp. 215-238). Wiesbaden: Springer VS.

Lind, G. (2019). How to teach moral competence. Berlin: Logos Verlag.

Pereira-Santos, C. (2019). Understanding people through games. Technische Universiteit Eindhoven.

Phan, M., Keebler, J. R., & Chaparro, B. S. (2016). The Development and Validation of the Game User Experience Satisfaction Scale (GUESS). Human Factors The Journal of the Human Factors and Ergonomics Society, 58(8), 1217-1247.

Polashenski, T. (2017, December 12). The Effect of Emotions and Expectations on Video Game Play: A Research Study. Retrieved April 19, 2022, from Medium: https://medium.com/@tpolashe/the-effect-of-emotions-and-expectations-on-video-game-play-a-research-study-968b406b3e

Przybylski, A. K., Rigby, C. S., & Ryan, R. M. (2010). A Motivational Model of Video Game Engagement. Review of General Psychology, 14(2), 154-166.

Wilson, D., & Sicart, M. (2010). Now It's Personal: On Abusive Game Design. Futureplay '10: Proceedings of the International Academic Conference on the Future of Game Design and Technology, (pp. 40-47).

Yager Productions. (2013). Spec Ops: The Line. 2K Games.

Zagal, J. P. (2013). Encouraging Ethical Reflection with Videogames. In J. P. Zagal (Ed.), The Videogame Ethics Reader (pp. 67-82). Cognella.

TEN YEARS OF MAGIC MIRROR: I AND MY AVATAR

Alexander K. Seewald

Alexander Pfeiffer

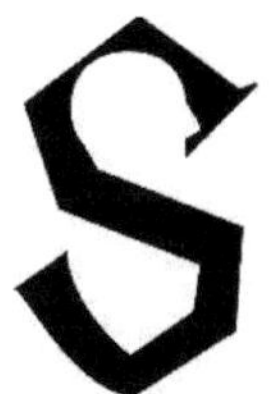ince 2012 we have been building the augmented reality system Magic Mirror based on Kinect V1 and V2's native API. It relies on the magic mirror metaphor, where a large screen shows a mirrored camera view with overlaid graphical elements. In our case, it shows a different face mesh over the person's face which reliably tracks face poses in real time while leaving the eyes and mouth of the person visible for interaction and to improve immersion; replaces the background with images that may be changed, smoothly zoomed and dragged; and allows to take screenshots which are automatically printed out on photo cards with an unique QR code linking to its digital twin. Control of the system is primarily via easily learned hand gestures very similar to multitouch screen gestures known from mobile phones and tablets. We have demonstrated the system to the public as well as in private over a wide variety of settings, faces and backgrounds. Here, we explain the challenges inherent in creating high- quality face meshes and textures from 2D images, and how we solved them; describe the different versions of the system, how they differ and their limitations; and demonstrate the usefulness of our system in several applications from people counting and tracking to obtaining height measurements without storing or processing personal data.

Keywords: Augmented Reality, Hand Gesture Recognition, Gaze Direction Heat Map, Shopping Window Rating, People Counting

In 2012 – when Microsoft's Kinect for Windows, which enabled using their XBOX depth camera on PCs, finally became available in Europe – my co-author Alex P. dropped a unit on my desk and challenged me to build a hand gesture control for his presentations using its – at that time – unprecedented body pose tracking. The Kinect V1 used an active sensor and was one of the first commercially available low-cost depth cameras. It also included a state-of-the-art face tracker as well as a pretrained random-forest-based classifier to automatically detect 3D body positions and poses (Shotton et al., 2011) – including a reasonably accurate position of both hands – so initial tests indicated that it should be quite feasible.

We implemented a first prototype in about two weeks. We were then invited by Microsoft to the Pioneers Festival 2012 in Vienna and presented a keynote on our gesture control app – of course using the same app.[1] There were many newspapers and magazine reports, and even an interview with a local TV station, W24.[2] We built a downloadable version, *Universal Remote*, in another few weeks and it sold reasonably well. However, the customer base of professional presenters was quite small, so we also wanted to build something for everyone to use and to show other uses of our gesture module and the Kinect itself. We additionally believed that the potential of this technology was far beyond our simple first application.

Our main inspiration for Magic Mirror came from game studies and especially the book *Man, Play and Games* by Caillois (1961) who extended the theories by Huizinga (1938) with four universal game types. One of these is Mimicry. Mimicry means *becoming someone else* and participating in an *illusionary world*. This can occur between the free game type (paida) and the rule-based game type (ludus). Here, the gamer is inside a virtual character that is an Avatar – a concept mentioned for example in Neal Stephenson's Science Fiction novel *Snow Crash* (Stephenson, 1992), where it has been introduced to the public in the context

---

[1] After the festival, we were invited by Microsoft Austria and told that we would get funding if only we could find a way to use Microsoft Azure, the cloud solution by Microsoft, which of course was completely nonsensical for this app. We declined and never heard from them again.
[2] Full interview is available at https://w24.k4w.at (archived).

of computer gaming. However already in the 80ies the computer game series Ultima introduced the concept of an *Avatar* – especially in part IV *Quest for the Avatar* where the gamer takes over the role of an Avatar as virtual image. (Gee, 2003) considers the different identities. For him there is the identity of the gamer, the identity of the avatar in the game, and the projected identity. By this he describes transfer effects between gamers and their Avatars.

This naturally led to a *face changer*, which allowed to replace the background as well as wearing a flexible mask which could show facial expressions – basically an avatar – all rendered in real-time and instantly responsive to changes in face and body pose. And so we called the system *Magic Mirror: I and my Avatar*, and defined it as an Autonomous Augmented Reality Art installation where AI and machine learning techniques for gesture control, body segmentation and face tracking (such as Random Forest, Active Appearance Models, Support Vector Machines and Dynamic Programming) are utilized to allow users to wear and intuitively change – by hand gestures – a dynamic virtual carnival mask which tracks detailed face expressions, and also replace their background with other scenes, real and imagined.

Within *Magic Mirror: I and my Avatar* we initially provided a mixture of characters from the well-known Massively Multiplayer Online Role-Playing Game *World of Warcraft*™ and contemporary Austrian politicians and presented it at a Future and Reality of Gaming conference (FROG 2012).

Even the first primitive version was instantly successful. It was very popular and we had long queues of people – so many that we needed to make it more robust against people in the background. People almost immediately started testing the limits of the system, for example walking back until they vanished and then putting just the head forward to create a floating head effect. We also observed people adapting body pose and facial expressions to the shown character (e.g. martial poses for male WoW characters, demure poses for female WoW characters, and meaningless smiles for politicians), and a clear preference for same-sex characters was observed indicating an identification with the shown characters. With later versions, handshakes between politicians or e.g. Snowden and Obama as well as more complex scenes involving interaction between multiple users was observed. More examples of such playful behaviours can be found in Section *Discussion*.

Afterwards, to make the installation more accessible to the general public, we successively extended the mask set. At present we have many different masks based on seasonal variations (Easter Bunny, Santa Claus and Christkind, Halloween Characters), European politicians and other persons of interest (such as the Pope and Edward Snowden). Our installation allows up to six users to each take over the role of a virtual figure or a politician in parallel and enables each one to change his face, reposition and resize the background, and make a snapshot, by simple hand gestures.

Related Research

Osokin (2018) describes a system for body pose estimation from RGB cameras that works bottom-up and therefore scales to a high number of persons – contrary to the Kinect with its top-down approach that restricts the number of tracked persons to at most six. It reconstructs roughly the same number and types of body parts as the Kinect. It works reasonably well according to real-life tests[3] and needs low computational resources comparable to the Kinect V1 itself. However no 3D positions of body parts are obtained, therefore our current hand gesture system cannot be applied directly to its output.[4]

Castro-Vargas et al. (2019) describe a system to directly learn four hand gestures (down, up, left, right) via 3D convolutional neural networks trained directly on depth camera images. While

---

[3] We tested it ourselves at ICAART 2019, together with all the other participants of the session.
[4] It may be feasible with stereo cameras, provided the replicability of body part keypoint detection over both cameras is sufficiently high.

an interesting idea, their quoted accuracy of 73% is not high enough for a practical system.[5]

Ferrari et al. (2019) describe a system for 3D face reconstruction from combined color and depth camera (RGB-D) data. While the quality of the 3D face construction is very good and comparable to Smolyanskiy et al. (2014), it has the disadvantage of needing a sequence of RGB-D frames to work with – rather than a single frame – and has not been tested with a single frame at all. So it is likely an application would not track face expressions sufficiently fast to be considered real-time which is however a primary constraint of our system.

Lastly, we note that this paper should be considered an augmented and extended version of Seewald and Pfeiffer (2022).

History

In this section we give an overview of the different releases as well as important components of Magic Mirror. Our claim that it is a single system is supported by the fact that all described variants can be created with different preprocessor defines from a single C/C++ source code project. A list of events where Magic Mirror was publicly presented can be found in Table 1.

---

[5] Although we do not have truly quantitative estimates, long-time experience indicates that after a short training phase by the human user, our system can recognize hand gestures at more than 98% of accuracy, corresponding to approximately one error every 50 gestures at most.

Table 1: List of public events where Magic Mirror was presented.

Date	Location	Vers.	Faces	Comments
2012/ 10/12-13	Future and Reality of Gaming (FROG 2012), Vienna City Hall, Austria	V1.0		One-face version
2013/ 09/27-28	FROG 2013, Vienna City Hall, Austria	V1.1		Two-face version
2014/ 04/02-23	Subotron Shop, Museumsquartier Vienna, Austria	V1.5		Easter Bunny Theme, see also Sec. 4.2
2014/ 10/10-12	FROG 2014, Vienna City Hall, Austria	V1.5		International politicians and other persons of interest
2015/ 09/10-15	IBC 2015, Amsterdam, The Netherlands	V2.0		International politicians and other persons of interest
2016/ 08/26-27	Museumsquartier Vienna, Austria	V2.1	None, just backgrounds	MasterCard ad campaign; smooth zoom/drag
2016/ 10/30	Oberbank Wels, Danube University Krems (2x), Austria	V2.2		Halloween; QR print-out; pseudo-alpha-blending; z-Skeleton filtering
2016/ 12/08	Welios Wels, Austria	V2.2		X-Mas Theme
2016/ 12/20	Danube University Krems, Austria	V2.2		X-Mas Theme
2017/ 04/15	Welios Wels, Austria	V2.2		Easter Bunny Theme; smooth zoom/drag
2017/ 10/09	Danube University Krems, Austria	V2.2		Halloween Theme

Creating Face Textures

The creation of high-quality face textures and meshes proved to be a major challenge. We initially thought that the Kinect V1 would only accept real-life faces, which would have made it hard to get e.g. Angela Merkel and then-US-president Obama's face textures. However, by conducting extensive tests we found that Kinect V1's face tracker relies mostly on color information and only uses depth information to ensure the correct size of the face w.r.t. distance. As far as we know there is no publication that describes the Kinect V1 face tracking algorithm but from our extensive observations we may assume it was a 2D/3D Active Appearance Model similar to the one described in (Cootes et al., 1998) with minor filtering by depth information, where the initial face position is taken from the head position of the estimated body pose.

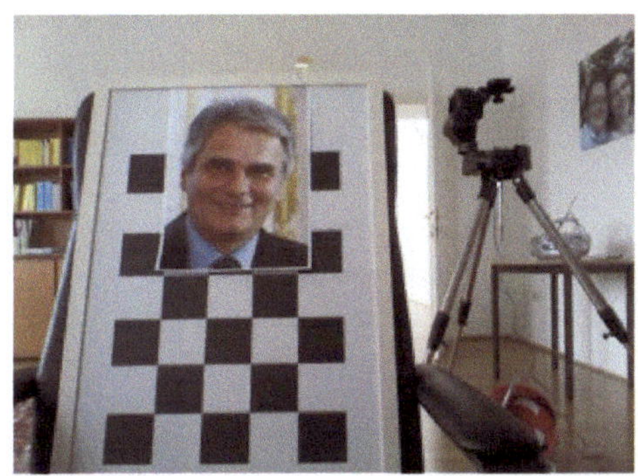
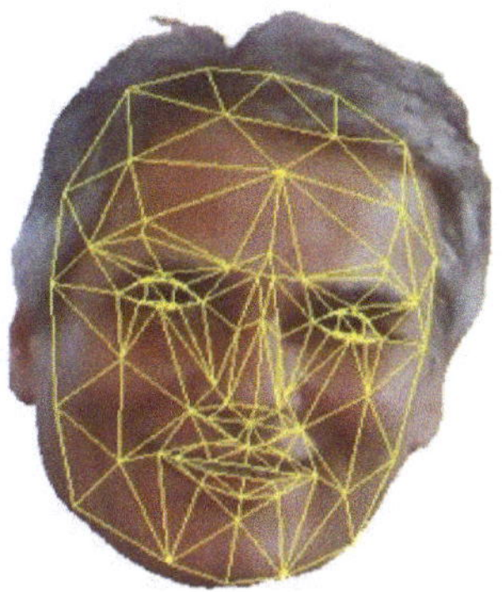

Figure 1: Face tracking from Kinect V1 image sample. Original image (left), Face texture w/ mesh (right, white=transparent)

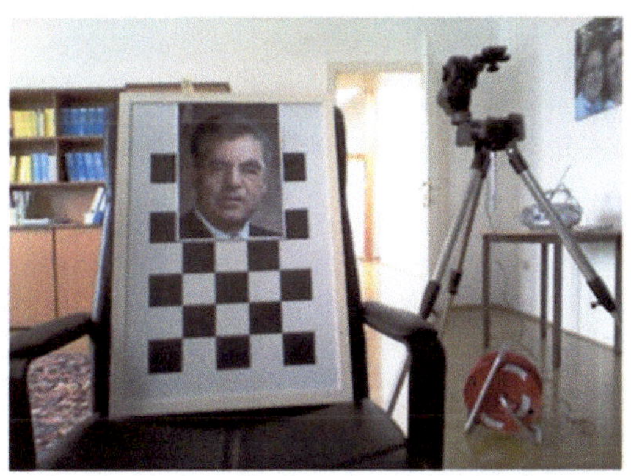
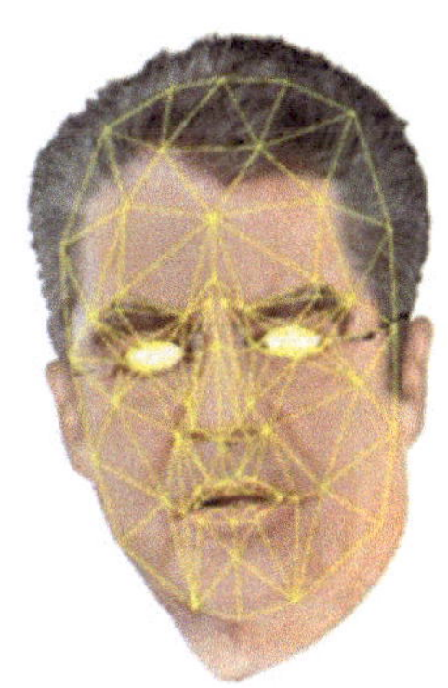

Figure 2: Face tracking with projection and high-quality face texture. Original image (left), Face texture w/ mesh (right)

So by printing out a 2D face image in approximately real size (face centered and scaled to an A4 page) and vertically positioning within in a sufficiently body-similar setting – we fixed the face image on a calibration rig with chessboard pattern and put it on a office chair (Fig. 1,2) – it was often possible to make the Kinect V1 detect it as a face by slowly turning the office chair left and right. In harder cases we would stand next to the office chair until our body and face was detected and then quickly move behind the chair, which in most cases was sufficient for our face mesh to be transferred to the printed face image. For the first version we simply used the image and the 2D triangle mesh[6] from the face tracker and projected each triangle to the corresponding triangle of the real face during usage of the system. However since the face could only be a small part of the image, and the Kinect V1 resolution was only 1,280x720 pixels, image quality and resolution were quite poor. Faces were at most 300x300 pixels large. Fig. 1 shows a sample image and the resulting face texture with the triangle mesh in yellow, showing distinct pixelated mesh lines with aliasing stemming from the low resolution.

By using a secondary camera (see later description of V1.5 system) we could improve this to about twice the size but it was still far less than the original face images which had about 1,000x1,000 pixel. Another issue was that lighting influenced the quality of the recorded image, leading to much worse dynamic range in the face textures versus the original image before printing.

The best solution for face mesh creation proved to be to project the 2D face triangles from the detected face onto the original face image by reverse projection. This was done by measuring the corners of the printed face image page at subpixel accuracy – yielding an irregular quadrangle – and projecting each 2D triangle corner point within the quadrangle back to the high-resolution face image. This yielded satisfactory results. Fig. 2 shows such a sample. In this case the resolution of the face texture may be arbitrarily high. The limitation is mainly the face tracker, which only outputs integer point values (i.e. does not track at subpixel resolution).

---

[6] The face tracker also provided a 3D triangle mesh but it was too noisy. However, we successfully used it to extend the mesh – more details see later in this section.

In some cases – e.g. the colorful Easter Bunny faces – synthetic faces were not sufficiently face-like to be detected. Minor modification were usually able to recover meshes from these faces as well, and the meshes could in most cases be applied to the original image with only minor modifications. Fig. 3 shows an example.

Except for the first mask set created in 2012, we have always improved the high-resolution face texture and meshes in four ways:

1. We removed lighting effects such as highlights and unequal brightness from the image as far as possible, yielding a good approximation of a ambient light source front-lighted face.[7]

2. We made the eyes about twice as large and then cut them out, yielding a mask where the user's eyes could be seen through just like a carnival mask. This increased self-identification and depth of immersion quite dramatically.

3. We built a face mesh editor and slightly modified the triangles around the mouth to make sure that it could be opened in a realistic manner. Due to the eye modifications, the mesh around the eyes sometimes also had to be changed slightly. If teeth were shown in the image, we replaced them with transparent background to make the user's teeth and mouth appear at their place.[8]

4. Lastly, we replaced all image parts not corresponding to the face with transparent background. This yielded our final high-resolution face masks which are similar to what is shown in Fig. 2 (right image).

---

[7] We later attempted to add lighting effects during rendering, but the 3D data from the Kinect V1 face tracker was of insufficient quality for a reasonable effect. We did not test the V2 face tracker, as due to it needing 3D faces there were only very few high-resolution face meshes available.

[8] For the rabbit face mesh we rendered rabbit teeth over the mouth area in an additional step.

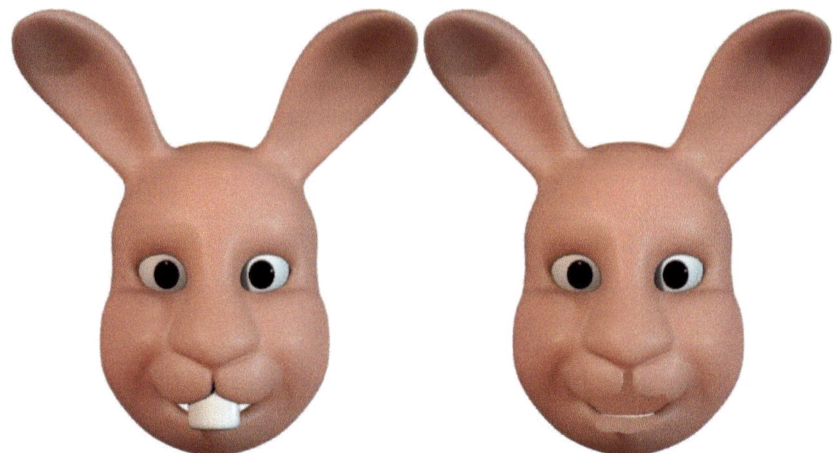

Figure 3: Initial rabbit face that was not tracked (left), changed face that was tracked (right).

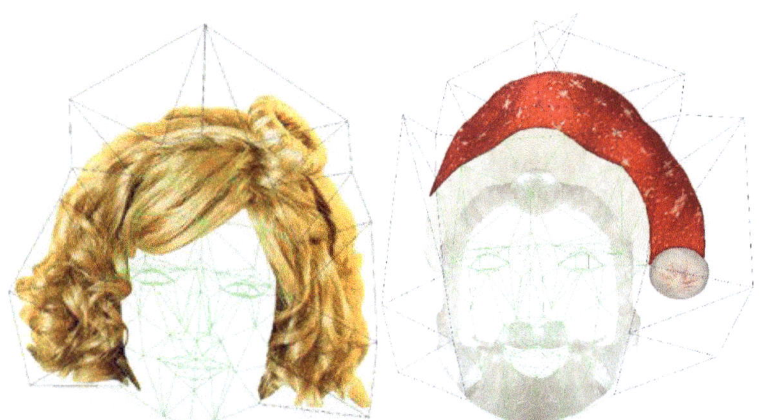

Figure 4: Two face samples with face mesh (green lines) and extended mesh (blue lines) that show masks with see-through face. Right mask is a 3D model mask from an earlier AR project, which was rendered to 2D.

Unfortunately, the Kinect V2 used a different face tracker described in Smolyanskiy et al. (2014) which could not be deceived in this way. In extensive experiments we could never make it recognize and track a flat 2D face print.[9] We did however

---

[9] It would still have been possible to make recordings of Madame Tussauds' wax figures.

manage to feed the color image data of Kinect V2 into the Kinect V1 face tracker and thus had slightly better and higher resolution tracking. This needed a PC with both frameworks installed as well as both Kinect V1 and V2 physically connected, so it was unfortunately quite cumbersome to use. Also, the new face tracker had about ten times the tracked points of the old face tracker, and these did not exactly correspond to points of the old face tracker.[10] We could still achieve satisfactory but not perfect results by mapping each point of the old face image mesh to a well-chosen point on the new face tracker mesh.[11]

Both the Kinect V1 and V2 face tracker only track the face itself and not the head, which means that parts outside the face – forehead, hair, ears, and beards – cannot be properly displayed on the rendered face. To also render these parts, we extended the outermost 3D face triangles by vector arithmetic, generating both new points and new triangles from the face texture mesh and the real-time face mesh, and applied the projection to these extended meshes. This method worked surprisingly well, and also enabled the use of extended masks which are transparent for most of the face area. Fig. 4 shows two examples. The right example is actually a 3D mask projected to 2D which was taken from an earlier unpublished Augmented Reality project. These were used for the X-Mas Theme version, see Fig. 5c.

---

[10] We did test recordings on two different machines using closely-placed Kinect V1 and V2 and doubly-redundant QR-Code timestamps at 15fps to align both V1 and V2 face meshes spatially and temporally for optimal alignment during head movements but this worked surprisingly badly, probably because the depth information of V1 is so noisy (data not shown). In the end we resorted to visual inspection, tested a few dozen sets of alignments and chose the one which looked best. We incidentially found out that the V1 timestamps from the API are much less reliable than the V2 timestamps and that the best set of aligned keypoints from both trackers strongly depends on head pose.

[11] We also tested if alignment could be improved by mapping to a linear combination of two points on the new tracker (data not shown). The main issue – as with the original alignment – was that depending on head pose, different sets of combined points and weights were obtained and there was no single set of points and weights with adequate results that could be automatically obtained that were independent of head pose.

Gesture Control

The gesture control was taken from our earlier unpublished project *Universal Remote* and contained three types of gestures: **left/right (one-handed slide), zoom in/out (two-handed),** and **one-handed drag**. We added another gesture, **two-handed-drag**, in 2016 exclusively for Magic Mirror. Table 2 shows all supported gestures. These could be dynamically assigned, e.g. zoom in/out could be assigned to making a screenshot or to resizing the background image smoothly and fluidly. The basis for this was the body pose tracking by Kinect V1 and V2 – thankfully very similar – described in Shotton et al. (2011).

The hand gesture recognition relied on the body pose estimated by Kinect V1 and V2 – namely on left/right hand and head positions. Table 3 lists all user-definable parameters. The minimum move distance is an absolute value. We could have normalized it to make it independent of body distance resp. size. However, since the left and right hand positions are quite noisy, especially in front of the body, this would have led to more spurious activations for far away bodies. Initially only the nearest body would be analyzed for gestures[12] – later all bodies would be analyzed. Most gestures refer only to the body itself and could be directly executed. In case of multiple parallel conflicting gestures, ties were abitrarily broken. Complete pseudocode is shown in Algorithm 1. For zooming, the multiplicative scale change factor was computed as $e^{\frac{currDist_i - lastDist_i}{200}}$. This function gave the most intuitive zooming behaviour according to feedback by our test users.[13] The two-handed-drag gesture was implemented by computing both scale and position for *display zoom*. The base position *lastX/Y* and the current position *currX/Y* was in this case the center position between both hands, i.e. $\frac{lHand + rHand}{2}$.

---

[12] This was the version which was used for our Pioneer Festival talk.
[13] The more obvious choice of *currDist* divided by *lastDist* performed very badly, scaling too fast with small movement and too slow with large movement – hence the switch to an exponential function.

Algorithm 1: Pseudocode algorithm for hand gesture recognition

---

for $\forall body_i$ **do**

  if $body_i$ has left hand, right hand and head positions **then**

    Compute $depth_{lHand}$, $depth_{rHand}$ and $depth_{head}$ for $body_i$

    if $depth_{lHand} < depth_{head} - DEPTH\_DIFF$ **or** $depth_{rHand} < depth_{head} - DEPTH\_DIFF$ **then**

      if $depth_{lHand} < depth_{head} - DEPTH\_DIFF$ **and** $depth_{rHand} < depth_{head} - DEPTH\_DIFF$ **then**

        if $lastDist_i > 0$ **then**

          $currDist_i \leftarrow |lHand - rHand|$

          if $time() - lastT_i > DELAY$ **and** $(\frac{currDist_i}{lastDist_i} > RATIO\_ZOOM$ **or** $\frac{lastDist_i}{currDist_i} > RATIO\_ZOOM)$ **then**

            | display zoom

          end if

        else

          | $lastX_i \leftarrow -1; lastDist_i \leftarrow |lHand - rHand|, lastT_i \leftarrow time();$

        end if

      else

        if $lastDist_i > 0$ **then** $lastDist_i \leftarrow -1; lastX_i \leftarrow -1;$

        $hand =$ **if** $depth_{lHand} < depth_{head} - DEPTH\_DIFF$ **then** lHand **else** rHand;

        if $lastX_i > 0$ **then**

          $currX_i \leftarrow hand_X; currY_i \leftarrow hand_Y;$

          if $|curr_i - last_i| > MOVE\_DIST$ **and** $time() - lastT_i > DELAY$ **then** display move;

        else

          | $lastX_i \leftarrow hand_X; lastY_i \leftarrow hand_Y; lastT_i \leftarrow time();$

        end if

      end if

    else

      if $lastDist_i > 0$ **and** $time() - lastT_i > DELAY$ **and** $(\frac{currDist_i}{lastDist_i} > RATIO\_ZOOM$ **or** $\frac{lastDist_i}{currDist_i} > RATIO\_ZOOM)$ **then**

        | display and finalize zoom

      else

        if $lastX_i > 0$ **and** $|curr_i - last_i| > MOVE\_DIST$ **and** $time() - lastT_i > DELAY$ **then**

          | display and finalize move

        else

          | $lastDist_i \leftarrow -1; lastX_i \leftarrow -1;$

        end if

      end if

    end if

  end if

end for

Table 2: Supported Hand Gestures

Name	Image	Description
move		Slide with your hand to the left or the right to activate left or right move gesture. Either hand will work, only the direction of movement is important.
zoom		Make a diagonal movement with both hands. Push both hands out to the front and move them away from each other (zoom in) or towards each other (zoom out), then retract them again.
one-handed-drag		Raise either hand to press the left mouse button. Afterwards push the other hand out to the front. This controls the mouse cursor. By moving the other (non-raised) hand you can drag the background image around just like normal drag-and-drop.
two-handed-drag		Push both hands out to the front. This controls the mouse cursor. By moving either or both hands, you can drag the background image around just like drag-and-drop. The center point between both hands is used for dragging, so using both hands will make the drag faster. By changing hand distance you can also zoom within the same gesture.

Kinect V1 (V1.0)

The first version for Kinect V1 only supported one face, but it was already possible to change backgrounds and faces by left/right hand move gestures. A snapshot could be taken using zoom in or out gesture. Fig. 5a shows a sample image. We used a z-filter with adjustable distance where all objects beyond a certain distance were replaced by background. This accounts for the presence of the chair and parts of the table in the sample image. Later – for Kinect V2 – we implemented z-Skeleton filtering which replaced all background except for recognized bodies (skeletons in Kinect terminology). We first demonstrated the system at the FROG 2012 conference.

The next version V1.1 in 2013 – demonstrated at the FROG 2013 conference – supported the maximum of two faces that was possible for Kinect V1 using the original Microsoft API.

Table 3: Parameters for gesture recognition

Parameter	Default	Description
DELAY / Minimum gesture duration (ms)	300	This is the minimum duration for gesture detection in milliseconds. Everything shorter than this is ignored completely. Increase if you gesticulate a lot and unintentionally activate gestures. Decrease if you want to be able to move/zoom faster.
MOVE_DIST / Minimum move distance (pixels)	40	This is the minimum distance for the move gesture. Everything smaller than this will be ignored. 40 pixels are about 1/8 of the depth image width of 320 pixels. Decrease if you are standing far away from the Kinect. Increase if you gesticulate a lot and unintentionally activate move gestures.
RATIO_ZOOM / Minimum zoom ratio	1.4	This is the minimum ratio at which the zoom gesture will activate. 1.4 means you must change the initial distance of both hands at least by a factor of 1.4 (either larger or smaller) for the gesture to be recognized. Decrease if you want to activate zoom gestures with less movement of your hands. Increase if you have very long arms or gesticulate a lot.
DEPTH_DIFF / Min. gesture zDepth difference (mm)	200	This defines how far you have to put your hands in front of your body center for them to be recognized. Up to this depth you can freely move your hands in front of your body without activating gestures.

We also replaced the local politicans with international politicans, the pope, Edward Snowden, and a Guy Fawkes mask. These masks already had see-through eyes and were fully optimized with all four steps mentioned earlier.

Improving Image Quality (V1.5)

Unfortunately the image quality of Kinect V1 was quite bad and image resolution was low, so we later combined it with a Hero GoPro 3, using its Mini-HDMI output port and a HDMI frame grabber card to generate a combined real-time video from the GoPro image data and Kinect depth data.[14] We treated the Kinect V1 and the Hero GoPro 3 as two cameras of a stereo-camera setting and computed intrinsic calibration matrices (K) for both using calibration rigs with a 5x8 chessboard pattern with size A2 and 61.5mm squares, followed by stereo calibration.[15] Eq. 1,2 show the standard calibration formulas for a single camera:

$$z_c \begin{bmatrix} u \\ v \\ 1 \end{bmatrix} = K[RT] \begin{bmatrix} x_w \\ y_w \\ z_w \\ 1 \end{bmatrix} \quad (1) \qquad K = \begin{bmatrix} \alpha_x & \gamma & u_0 & 0 \\ 0 & \alpha_y & v_0 & 0 \\ 0 & 0 & 1 & 0 \end{bmatrix} \quad (2)$$

---

[14] Initial experiments concerning feasibility were done with a Sony digital camcorder.
[15] All algorithms were from OpenCV V1.0.

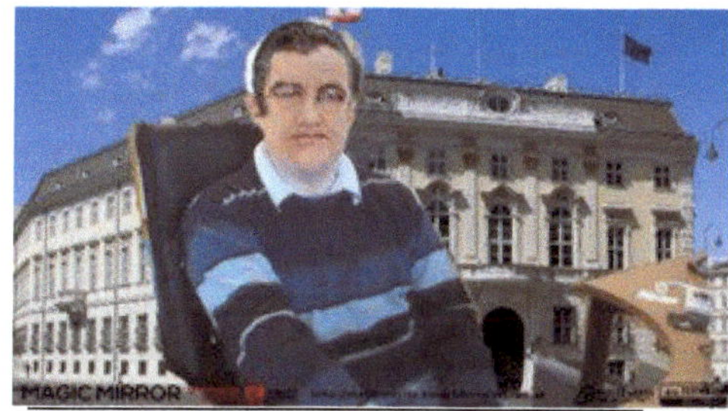
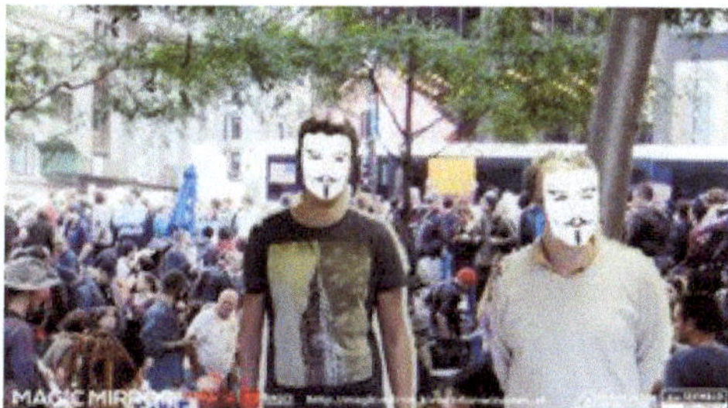
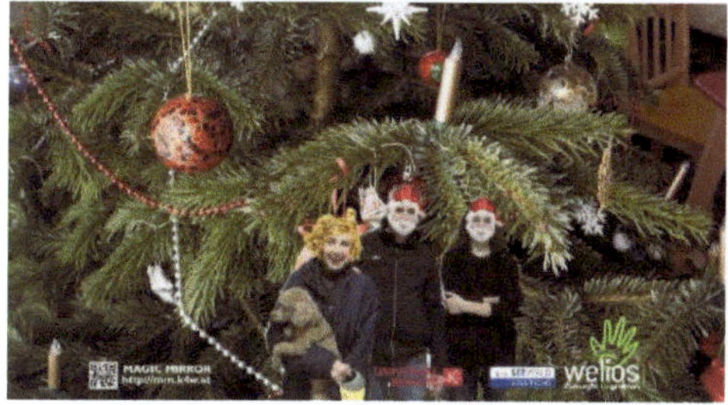
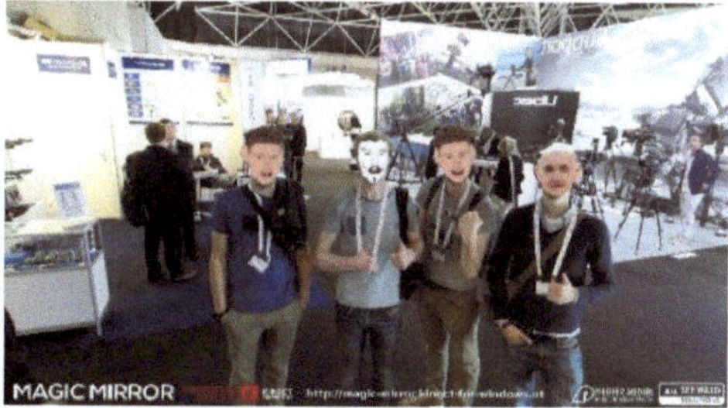

Figure 5: Sample images from various Magic Mirror installations: (a) Kinect V1, (b) Kinect V1 w/ Hero Gopro, (c) Kinect V2 w/ Xmas Thema, (d) Kinect V2

Stereo calibration returned the translation matrix T_{stero} and the rotation matrix R_{stereo}, which transform the world coordinate system of the Kinect into the one of the second camera. We generated a point cloud from Kinect V1's depth data using native API functions, transformed it by $R_{stereo}\,T_{stereo}$ to the second camera's view frame, and then projected it onto the second camera's focal plane using its intrinsic calibration matrices. This reproduces the almost perfect alignment between Kinect V1 color and depth images, so depth images can be filtered and combined with the color images very easily. We then optimized this mapping – including the initial native point cloud generating function – to a single matrix multiplication which proved sufficient for real-time rendering and yielded almost the same results. The 3D body part positions were transformed using the same matrix.

In 2014 we installed the final system for three weeks in a shopping window with Easter Bunny face textures and meshes – and showed that we could count in/outgoing people as well as compute a *window rating* for shopping window attractiveness and additionally a heatmap of gaze direction. More details can be found in Section *Tracking People*. For this system we evaluated putting a magnetic circular polarization filter on the camera. This did not help to improve recognition, but reflections from the shopping window were greatly reduced.

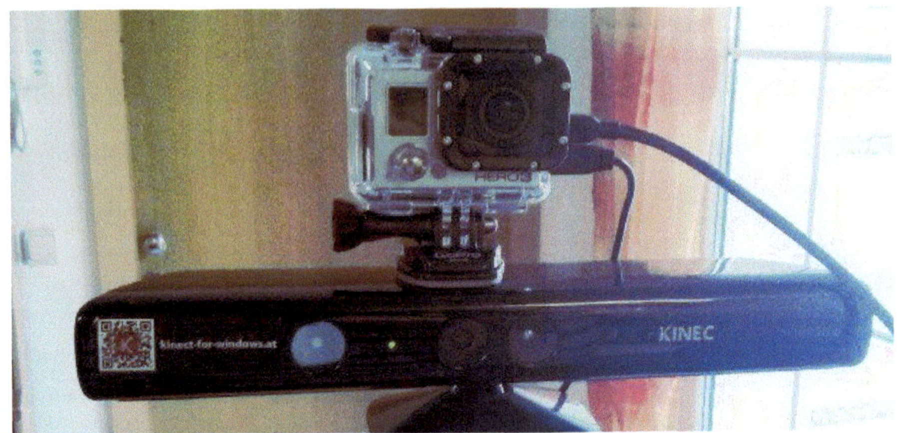

Figure 6: Kinect V1 w/ Hero GoPro.

This system was also demonstrated at the FROG 2014 conference using the international politicians face set. Fig. 6 shows the Kinect V1 with attached Hero GoPro camera and Fig. 5b shows a sample image from the system presented there.

Kinect V2 (V2.0)

In 2015 we ported the system to Kinect V2 as the Kinect V1 was no longer available. The API had completely changed, but by extensive use of C/C++ macros it was possible to keep changes to a minimum and still generate all V1 and V2 systems from the same source code project. This was important since we still needed the V1's facetracker to scan new faces. The Kinect V2 allowed up to six faces and had a newer, much more accurate facetracker, but it also had much higher hardware requirements since all color, depth, face and body pose streams were always sent at the highest possible resolution.[16] We demonstrated the

---

[16] Approximately 5GBit/s via USB 3.

system on our stand at the International Broadcasting Conference 2015 (IBC 2015). Fig 5d shows a sample image of the improved system taken at that conference.

In August 2016 we provided a Magic Mirror installation for an ad campaign by MasterCard Austria in the Museumsquartier Vienna.[17] For this we extended the system to use the zoom in and zoom out gestures – up to this time considered binary – to continuously zoom within a larger image, and also introduced the two-handed-drag gesture to position the zoomed image with less physical effort by removing the need to keep one hand raised. We also extended the system with an option to automatically print photo cards after each screenshot. This extended version was called V2.1. Running the system outdoors proved to be a challenge since the Kinect does not work in bright sunshine, so we used a pavillon to create shadow but had to reposition it every other hour. Getting a large screen which was visible in bright sunshine was on the other hand no problem at all.

In October 2016 we demonstrated a Halloween version of the Magic Mirror (using Halloween faces and background) at Oberbank Wels, and later a Christmas version at Welios Wels and Danube University Krems (both in Austria). We added an unique QR code on each printout which linked to the digital snapshot, thus integrating the visual printout and its digital twin. Before this change, people had often used their phones to make screen snapshots and share them. Now, it was possible to just scan the QR code on the photo card and get to a digital version of the same photo for easy sharing via social media as well as having a physical photo card to remember the event by. We also added rendering improvements such as pseudo alpha-blending (improves the appearance of the border between body and background) and z-skeleton filtering (prevents the need to set up the z-distance from which the background image is rendered, by simply rendering just the recognized body shapes – skeletons in Kinect terminology – on the background). This new extended version was called V2.2.

---

[17] The Museumsquartier is a wide plaza in Vienna, Austria with three large museums and several smaller spaces for modern art. It is open to the public.

In April 2017 we demonstrated an Easter Bunny version with zoomable background at Welios Wels in Austria, and printed photo cards, again with an unique QR-code that linked back to the image for easy sharing.

Planned Obsolescence

In 2017 Microsoft discontinued the Kinect V2, so from then on we only demonstrated the system for smaller informal private events as well as once yearly at our Future Media lecture at Danube University Krems, but have kept several systems for research purposes. From the beginning we had searched for alternatives and obtained several Asus XTION depth cameras which work similarily to the Kinect V1, and Google Tango depth cameras – however these cameras were discontinued even faster. Open source frameworks at that time only supported body pose recognition after striking a certain pose and were therefore not suitable for our purposes. Fortunately, in the meantime many other depth cameras have become available and most of the Augmented Reality functions of the Kinect can now – thanks to Deep Learning – be done with normal cameras.[18] Body pose tracking with normal RGB cameras has also been vastly improved and speeded up to the point that we can now track hundreds of people in real-time, but in most cases still only tracks 2D positions.

Uses of the System

Apart from its entertainment value, Magic Mirror can be used in several different ways either for analysis or to add new types of user interaction. Here, we note several ways the system was used in practice.

---

[18] Although the quality of the Kinect V2 face tracker remains unsurpassed, and hand gesture recognition works much better with reliable information about 3D body pose which is still best obtained with depth cameras or other active sensing technology.

Instant Whiteboard

One of the very first things we did with the Kinect in 2012 was a virtual whiteboard. Basically, the idea was to first point to the four corners of a monitor screen and then draw on it with your hand. This calibration is then reusable for anyone standing in front of the screen and valid as long as the relative position of Kinect, monitor and floor plane do not change (in the case of the monitor stand installation this is assured). We created a line between head position and hand position and computed the intersection point with the Kinect depth camera plane. We then used the four points obtained by consecutive pointing gestures and computed a homography, which we then applied to draw points on the screen. It was somewhat noisy but worked surprisingly well. We found out that the hand position is much better recognized against a far-away background, which means that hand positions in front of the body are much more noisy. So one should position oneself in front center of the screen and near enough so that all four corner positions are recorded against the background. A monitor with a minimum diagonal size of one meter (40 inches) seems to be necessary to get good results. We however did not follow up on this project and it is one of the few modules that has not been integrated into Magic Mirror.[19]

Tracking People

As we shortly mentioned before, in 2014 we put the V1.5 system behind a shopping window for 21 days with Easter Bunny faces and background at Museumsquartier Vienna (at the Subotron shop). The Museumsquartier is a wide open plaza in Vienna, Austria with three large museums and several smaller spaces for modern art. In front of this space there is a narrow very long building which most people cross to get into or out of the plaza and this is where we placed the system, perpendicular to this long building.[20] For this installation we added a magnetic polarization filter on the GoPro camera to reduce shopping window reflections. We used a 16:9 computer monitor with one

---

[19] Although with the benefit of hindsight it would seem that a one-handed pointing gesture is clearly missing in the list of supported gestures.
[20] It is also possible to enter and exit by the sides or at other positions of the narrow building, so we saw only a subset of the people crossing.

meter (40 inch) diagonal. While the system was mainly intended to provide entertainment, we were also able to track movements of people, determine how often they looked directly at the monitor, as well as compute aggregate approximate gaze direction into a heat map, without storing any kind of personal data.

Counting People Passing

We used the system to count people passing from left to right (*Enter*) and from right to left (*Exit* – both w.r.t the Museumsquartier Vienna) by tracking each bodyId (*bId*) separately and computing Pearson's correlation coefficient between time and the x position of body center for all body Ids with at least three tracked positions. For a correlation *corr* with *abs(corr)* > 0.9, we took the sign of the correlation to indicate either left or right directed linear movement. People where *abs(corr)* <= 0.9 were labeled *Neither*, since in this case no clear linear movement in one direction could be detected (see Eq. 3,4).

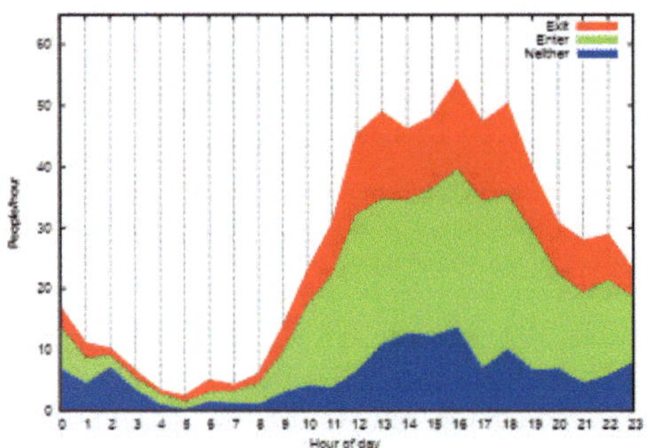

(a) *People going into / out of Museumsquartier Vienna by time of day, averaged over total timespan.*

(b) *Proportion of people looking at the screen (Facetracking success) by time of day, averaged over total timespan.*

Figure 7: Results from Sec. Tracking People and Sec. Counting People Passing

$$c_{bId} = \frac{n\sum t * x_{bId,t} - \sum t \sum x_{bId,t}}{\sqrt{n\sum t^2 - (\sum t)^2} - \sqrt{n\sum x_{bId,t}^2 - (\sum x_{bId,t})^2}} \qquad (3)$$

$$d_{bId} = \begin{cases} \text{Neither} & \text{if } |c_{bId}| \leq 0.9 \\ \text{Left} & \text{if } |c_{bId}| > 0.9 \text{ and } c_{bId} < 0 \\ \text{Right} & \text{if } |c_{bId}| > 0.9 \text{ and } c_{bId} \geq 0 \end{cases} \qquad (4)$$

Fig. 7a shows the number of people per hour who entered or exited within the given hour of the day. Computed values were averaged over the whole 21 days of the Easter 2014 installation and show a distinct daily pattern. Colored bands show additive values, e.g., for hour 15 there are on average 11.7 people exiting, 24.2 people entering, and 12.2 people neither entering nor exiting, yielding a total of 48.1 people counted at this hour (averaged over the whole time period). A total of 13,212 people were counted during this period. Note that due to signal attenuation by the shopping window, likely only a subset of people was counted – those who moved close enough to the shopping window (around 2.5m).

Shopping Window Rating

We also defined a shopping window rating to determine the attractiveness of the shopping window at different times. Here, the system tracked how long people watched the screen. For this we simply computed the proportion of tracked faces versus tracked bodies, since the API cannot return any tracked face without a corresponding body pose (see Eq. 5).

$$Rating_{hour} = \frac{1}{|hour|} \sum_{t \in hour} \frac{trackedFaces_t}{trackedBodies_t} \qquad (5)$$

Since the Kinect V1 face tracker reacts very strongly to front faces, very weakly to turned faces (up to 30°), and not at all to sidewise turned faces, this was sufficient to detect people looking directly at the screen. Once a face is tracked it can be turned ±30°

but only slowly, so these values might be slightly overestimated. On the other hand, such slow head movements are rarely observed in public.

Of all 13,212 people counted, 1,677 looked at the screen – on average for 15.5 seconds – which gives an overall rating of 12.69%. The system was watched for a total of 12,305 seconds (3.42 hours) 463 people (3.50%) watched for at least 15s, 205 people (1.55%) for at least 30 seconds, and 69 people (0.52%) for at least 60 seconds.

Depending on the hour of day – i.e. at peak hours – much higher ratings could be obtained, e.g. for hour 15 the rating was 22.51%. This means that of all people standing in front of the screen during this time period, almost a quarter looked at the screen. Rating estimates per hour are not smooth, partially due to small sampling size for some hours but also since people counts are not smooth. Fig. 7b shows the full results by hour, again averaged over all 21 days.

Gaze Direction Heatmap

We were also able to utilize the integrated face tracker to output rough estimates for head position and therefore approximate gaze direction, assuming the person looks straight to the front. To some extent this is quite likely since the face tracker initially only recognizes front faces and later fast movements to either side will make the face instantly lose tracking. We used this data to build a heatmap which was overlaid on an image of the actual shopping window. This shows what people tend to look at when viewing the shopping window and enhances the shopping window rating with very specific information on salient objects that is extremely hard to obtain using any other means. Fig. 8 shows the logarithmically scaled heatmap for the whole 21 days. As may have been expected, our installation was the most salient object.

Estimating Body Height

In 2016, we evaluated the use of Kinect V2 to determine people's height.[21] For this, we recorded several hours of body position data, yielding 129 people including 64 children. Body height was estimated as the distance from the floor plane in meters at the head position (corresponding to the center of the head plus the difference between head and shoulder vertical position, see Eq. 6-8).

$$plane_{floor} = a*x + b*y + c*z + d \tag{6}$$

$$dist_{part} = \frac{|a*part_x + b*part_y + c*part_z + d|}{\sqrt{a^2 + b^2 + c^2}} \tag{7}$$

$$height = dist_{head} + (dist_{head} - dist_{shoulderCenter}) \tag{8}$$

As we did not have ground truth data except for one person, we computed the standard deviation over all body positions with more than 25 consecutive frames, which was 3%. For the one person where ground truth height was available, the estimate from averaging all frames underestimated the true height by 4.3%. However, this may be a systematic error that is easy to correct. Even if not, the true height is within the 1.3fold confidence interval of the average and thus not significantly different at 95% confidence level, so a running average of body height should be sufficient to get reasonable height estimates within 1-2s (15-30 samples). We found it easy to distinguish between adults and children with a single threshold even when using just a single frame for each measurement.

---

[21] Initial experiments with Kinect V1 had been completely unsuccessful as height estimates depended on the elevation setting and were very unstable. Even an analysis of the depth image itself did not yield useful results (data not shown).

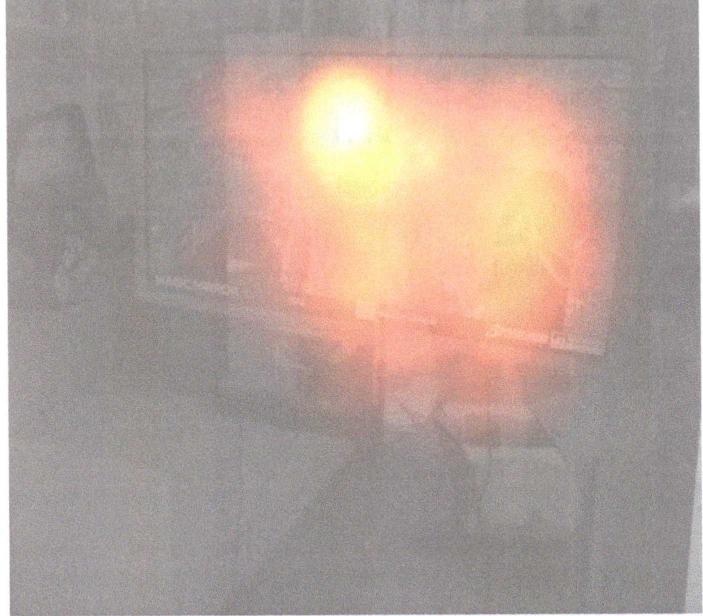

Figure 8: Heatmap for Museumsquartier Vienna Installation (approximate gaze points aggregated over total timespan). Brighter = more accumulated gazes at this point.

360° Move and Zoom

In 2016, we also implemented a 360° panorama prototype of Magic Mirror which allowed to smoothly move and zoom a given panorama with hand gestures. It used an appropriately projected equirectangular 360° image (a stitched image displaying 360° horizontally and 180° vertically), which replaced the normal 2D background image. We optimized it extensively down to a runtime of 70ms per frame on a single-threaded CPU, which was still too slow to be useful so it was not integrated into the main code at that time. In the meantime, a more powerful machine – or porting the code to GPU – should be able to run it sufficiently fast.

Ars Electronica 2019

We submitted a short video – see https://ars.k4w.at– demonstrating our system for Ars Electronica 2019. While we did not win any prizes, the submitted video gives a good overview of the capabilities of our system and contains video snippets for almost all different versions of Magic Mirror.

Discussion

It is quite sad that Kinect V1 and V2 were both discontinued after just a few years. The potential of their body pose and face tracking technology was quite high but seldom exploited in the research literature or in actual applications. Possible reasons could be that Kinect V1 was only available for three years, V2 for two years, the API had completely changed between V1 and V2, and that V2 required orders of magnitude faster machines to run similarily fast.[22]

Even now with pretrained systems for body pose estimation with 2D cameras (Osokin, 2018), we would be hard put to build a hand gesture recognition system that works as well as the one using the Kinect. The depth information is what makes gesture recognition extremely robust in a wide variety of settings, so any comparable system is likely to need depth cameras or other active sensors as well. Fortunately, there are now more manufacturers of depth cameras.

We did test a representative sample of depth cameras in 2019[23] to see whether they could see through window glass, but were disappointed. Standard active sensing time-of-flight depth cameras only barely see through one layered glass and not at all through multi-layered glass.[24]

---

[22] Although some of them are already laving the market again – for example, we bought an Intel Realsense D400 in module form a few years ago and tested it, but Intel has announced that they will leave this field, and now we seem to need to hurry to put it on one of our robots before they are gone forever.

[23] ZED mini, Orbbec Astra Mini, Intel Realsense D400 and Structure Core sensor.

[24] The original Kinect V1's method using a random dot pattern and an astigmatic lens performed much better, but there seem to be no available depth cameras using this method. It is however less robust against sunlight than Kinect V2.

Other depth cameras using deep-learning models were easily confused by minor reflections and did not return useful depth maps even when looking at natural scenes through window glass.

Magic Mirror was so compelling that we observed some instances of emergent behaviour when interacting with the system. For example, the original distance-based z-filtering where everything farther away than a user-configurable distance was replaced by background inspired users to create floating heads by moving just outside the cut-off distance and move their head slowly forward until it became visible. Another user would sometimes put the hand under this head, making it seem as if the head was on top of the hand. Simulated head bouncing was also observed. Similarily floating hands were created, sometimes by several people together. When we switched to skeleton-based z-filtering where all parts of detected body were always visible this was no longer possible, so in some cases we would deactivate it again to enable these kinds of interactions.

Conclusion and Future Work

Apart from qualitative results concerning the magic of Magic Mirror (see previous Section *Discussion*), we have additionally shown that with the Kinect V1 and V2 native API even relatively simple analytics return very useful results in challenging conditions for a variety of applications. The two main limitations were outdoor use – in bright sunshine no depth data was obtainable – and that the signal did not travel well through window glass.[25] Although the restriction to at most six people seems to be a limitation at first, it is actually tricky to position so many people in front of the Kinect without too much overlap, which is also not handled well.

---

[25] For one-layered window glass, directly mounting the Kinect V1 on the glass worked, but the V2 used a different ranging technology based on time-of-flight (now used by most other depth cameras) and was completely useless in this settings. With two-layered and three-layered glass results were very bad and only in very special circumstances could we observe a correct body pose or face tracker recognition.

One of our plans is to port Magic Mirror to a small platform such as Raspberry Pi 4 or – should it not be sufficiently powerful – small embedded PCs running Linux – and make it work with other depth cameras or perhaps even – one day – with normal 2D color cameras, using appropriate Deep Learning tracking systems at the same functionality level.

We would also like to enable high-quality tracking through window glass (without cutting a hole in it) and outside (without lugging a pavillon around and repositioning it every hour as we did for the Mastercard event). For this specially developed hardware is likely needed.

Every time we demonstrated Magic Mirror, we could count on smiling faces and happy people. So, since the ten-year anniversary of this project is in 2022, we also plan to take all our remaining Kinect sensors and build – as far as we can – all previous installations of Magic Mirror into a single room (just like a gallery), include free printout of photo cards, and make all of this available for at least several months of that year.

If you are interested in visiting, check https://mm.k4w.at for updates or send us an email.

Acknowledgements

This project was partially funded by the Austrian Research Promotion Agency (FFG) and by the Austrian Federal Ministry for Transport, Innovation and Technology (BMVIT) within the Talente internship research program 2013-2017, and by the Vienna Center for Innovation and Technology (ZIT) 2015. We would like to thank Max W., who edited all initial masks, wrote the Mesh-Manipulator single-handedly and contributed to this project in more ways we can count; character designer Emanuel A., who provided half of the Halloween masks as well as the Easter Rabbit masks; Jogi N., Brigitte R., Sonja S., Michael H., Julian F., Sonja F., Peter F., Mozart D. and all other people and students who contributed to the project over the years.

References

Caillois, R. (1958). Theorie des jeux. Revue de Metaphysique et de Morale, 63(1), 83–102.

Castro-Vargas, J. A., Zapata-Impata, B. S., Gil, P., Garcia-Rodriguez, J., Torres, F., et al.(2019). 3DCNN performance in hand gesture recognition applied to robot arm interaction.Caillois, R. (1961). Man, Play, and Games. Thames & Hudson.

Cootes, T. F., Edwards, G. J., & Taylor, C. J. (1998). Active appearance models. In European conference on computer vision (pp. 484–498).: Springer.

Ferrari, C., Berretti, S., Pala, P., & Del Bimbo, A. (2019). 3D Face Reconstruction from RGB- D Data by Morphable Model to Point Cloud Dense Fitting. In ICPRAM (pp. 728–735).

Gee, J. P. (2003). What video games have to teach us about learning and literacy. Computers in Entertainment (CIE), 1(1), 20–20.

Huizinga, J. (1938). Homo ludens: proeve fleener bepaling van het spel-element der cultuur. Haarlem: Tjeenk Willink.

Osokin, D. (2018). Real-time 2d multi-person pose estimation on CPU: Lightweight Open- Pose. arXiv preprint arXiv:1811.12004.

Seewald, A. K. & Pfeiffer, A. (2022). Magic Mirror: I and My Avatar - A Versatile Aug- mented Reality Installation Controlled by Hand Gestures. In Proceedings of the 14th International Conference on Agents and Artificial Intelligence (ICAART 2022), volume 3 (pp. 300–307).

Shotton, J., et al. (2011). Real-time human pose recognition in parts from single depth images. In CVPR 2011 (pp. 1297–1304)

Smolyanskiy, N., Huitema, C., Liang, L., & Anderson, S. E. (2014). Real-time 3D face tracking based on active appearance model constrained by depth data. Image and Vision Computing, 32(11), 860–869.

Stephenson, N. (1992). Snow Crash: A Novel. Bantam Books.

Garriot, R. (1995): Ultima IV: Quest of the Avatar

THE RITUAL – AN INTENTION BASED RANDOM NUMBER GENERATOR FOR GAMES

Frank Pourvoyeur

The random number generator (RNG) is a widely used concept in games to determine the outcome of an event. This randomness is needed to substitute for otherwise uncalculatable influences that determine the result. A special case of an event outcome in a game is the distribution of rewards to Players. Psychologically, random rewards are significant and trigger different emotions than when a reward is predictably earned (Chou 2013). Random rewards have been shown to trigger different emotional reactions in Players than when a reward is predictably earned. In games, however, the probability can be further manipulated by the Players themselves via adverse (buffs) or advantageous (perks) modifications. While a certain amount of randomness for events to happen is required and poses a necessary part in game design, pure randomness can lead to the unsatisfying occupation of the Player with busywork or grind that results in a negative experience. The Ritual is a concept inspired by real magickal practitioners and adapted for a better random number generator in video games, offering a more worthwhile and rewarding game experience. It is proposed that a mechanism be included in the game that makes the manifestation of otherwise pure random results more likely to occur when the Player puts effort and time into achieving that desired outcome. In a fully implemented installation, the Ritual is an intention-based luck modifier to make those events more likely to occur that the Player wants to happen by avoiding the grind and performing meaningful and interesting tasks instead.

Keywords: rng, random number generator, game design, intention

The necessity of randomness in games

Randomness is a simple substitute for the absence of creativity in machines that make calculation-based judgments with the goal of providing Players with novel and unpredictable outcomes. Games would be less gratifying and thrilling if they didn't contain a certain level of luck. Players want to be able to simply be lucky and be ecstatic about it. They even accept being unlucky for a long time, making the moment when they finally strike it richer.

The gambling industry as a whole is predicated on the human urge to be able to feel lucky while also giving some entertainment. However, in games, a totally predictable reward for completing a task makes the occupation feel more like work. As a result, in addition to the promised prize, most games include some unpredictability that affects the quality of the given reward. The quantity of gold obtained or the stats of a procedurally created weapon could be determined by this parameter. It is technically straightforward to implement, but it provides Players with an additional layer of success beyond what they have earned and expected, as well as motivation to anticipate and stay impelled while executing the activity.

In addition to its use for rewards, unpredictable gameplay is an important aspect in giving games high replayability. Unexpected challenges and unknown outcomes add excitement to games and keep them fresh. In genres such as "rogue likes" this is frequently employed in conjunction with procedurally generated worlds, where randomness serves as an initial seed in games such as *The Binding of Isaac (2011)*.

A reward feels like a compliment to the brain, generating Dopamine (Lembke, 2021) in the human body. It must be balanced and unpredictable to keep Players interested.

On the flip-side, these dynamics can lead to addiction, similar to gambling, where the pleasure and fun are replaced by a dependency. Even after threatening losses, the attempt to get lucky continues in order to keep the Dopamine thrill of being lucky flowing.

While randomness has its raison d'être in entertainment-oriented interactions, it can adulterate results. Randomness in competitive play devalues skill, converting an otherwise skill-based game into a gamble. As a result, games that place a large emphasis on random events are less ideal for competitive play. If luck plays a big factor in winning, Players will be less motivated to improve their skills when they are inevitably defeated by the RNG.

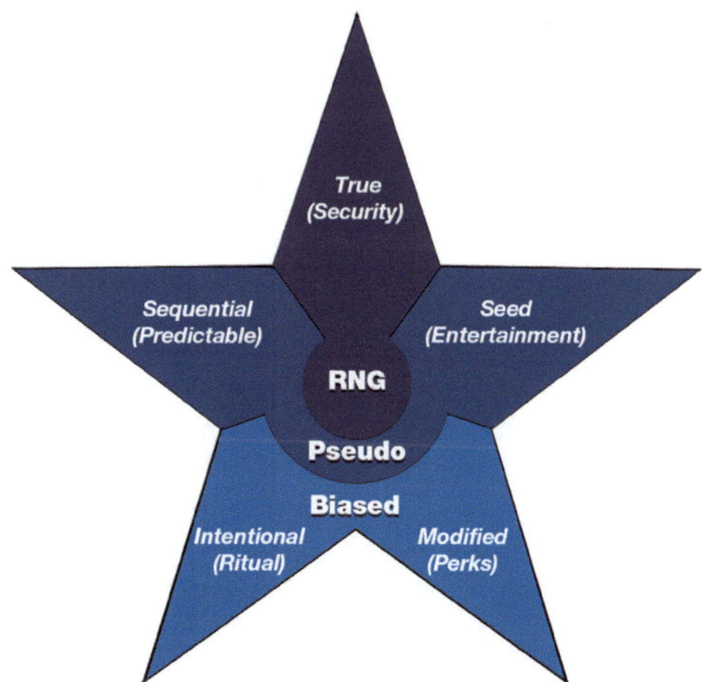

Figure 1: The layers of RNG Star Diagram

RNG – Random number generator in its purest form is true random

Seed – A pseudo random number initializes a function via a seed

Sequential – Results are predetermined by an algorithm

Modified – Modifiers contribute to a more desirable result

Intentional – Actions have an impact on the likelihood of a particular outcome.

Fundamentals of the RNG

In its core implementation, a RNG provides true random numbers. This is a technically challenging process based on physical properties with naturally occurring noise that can be measured and processed. Due to the lack of such sensors, this cannot be achieved on regular consumer devices. It is therefore only used in environments where predicting the outcome of a RNG would be a security hazard. True random number generators are mostly found in cryptography applications and commercial gambling enterprises where predictable randomness would be attacked by sophisticated algorithms.

Since humans are less receptive than machines to perceiving patterns in numbers, it is sufficient for most games and entertainment products in general to implement a simpler random number generator based on the system clock as a seed. These numbers with limited randomness are called "pseudo random" and are either based on a seed provided by the system clock that initializes a mathematical function or an algorithm that outputs pseudo random numbers based on a pre-determined input sequence. Due to the lack of a system clock, random events on classic consoles such as the Nintendo Gameboy were mostly sequential. And while the average Player might never have noticed this, a total understanding of its functioning enables them to manipulate the outcome of the RNG. Speedrunners nowadays use this weakness to take advantage of this exploit and manipulate the RNG, for example in Pokémon Red/Blue (1996) (Pokemonspeedruns.com, 2020) by playing behaviors to get specific items or avoid unwanted events altogether. This, however, is a very special use case not intended by the game design and requires a deep understanding of the internal programming of the game.

For developers, being able to produce random numbers with a foreseeable result provides a simple solution to calculate all possible outcomes in advance. Sequentially generated pseudo random numbers were useful in slot machines that were installed in unsupervised environments such as bars or gas stations where the manufacturer could make sure there would never be a win higher than the coins available in the machine to pay out the winnings.

The hereby introduced intention-based system is a special case of the pseudo RNG, which is essentially a "biased" RNG that favours certain outcomes. This means the game provides a mechanic for the Player to intentionally influence the outcomes of the RNG to a certain degree according to their desire. Modifiers, or perks, are an established concept in game design to actively manipulate the stats of a Players character that also include such attributes as luck. This leads to the concept of the Ritual, where the RNG is not solely influenced by items or character stats but the Players intention expressed by performing certain actions.

Intrinsic vs. Extrinsic Modifiers

Stats modifiers are a common part of RPG games to represent a character's development in a player-friendly and comprehensible way. The ability to create a character with stat progression is central to what is known as the role-playing genre. When the character stats can be modified by the Player by spending skill points or some representation of experience indicator, it is an intrinsic process. A modification of stats that are probability-founded basically alters the RNG to a more favourable outcome. Such stats might be even called "LUCK", as in *Phantasy Star 2* (1989), which represents the Player's chance of performing critical hits on opponents. Intrinsic modifiers may not be connected with actual skill points and might be based on previous actions and choices that would not otherwise have affected the stats of the character, such as membership in groups. All luck modifiers that are inseparably connected with the character are intrinsically connected with the character because they are only available to that certain character and are not transferable. Even though they can be potentially changed, stats resulting from alliances with factions or based on allegiances are defined as intrinsic as they stick with the character unless an altering process happens, as they can neither be transferred nor instantly dropped in the form of an inventory item.

When it is instantly possible to transfer the luck modifier from or to the possession of the character, it is an extrinsic modifier. This is usually an item that can be obtained, removed, or possibly shared with the whole party. For example, in *Divinity: Original Sin II (2017)*, there exists an item named "Lucky Charm" with the character stats "*+2 Lucky Charm*". According to its in-game description, the item "*increases the likelihood of finding extra treasure whenever loot is stashed*". Since this Lucky Charm is defined as an Amulet, the Player has to make the decision to use this character slot for the luck modification for the benefit of the whole party or spend this space with an Amulet with different perks.

While both intrinsic and extrinsic modifiers give Players a welcome instrument to have an influence on the randomness of future outcomes of events by taking advantage of their effects, there are traditionally no additional actions besides the quests given by the game available for Players to perform to intentionally modify the RNG in a specific way. It could be desirable for Players to perform certain actions to influence events beyond the predefined game story-line. This would not solely be based on tasks to obtain items ("*fetch quests*") or stats for intrinsic or extrinsic effects, but the performance of a task as a whole would influence the RNG, with little additional design effort for the game creator. As a result of such a mechanic, particular events, such as spawning a certain item or boss type, would occur more often in the game.

The Magic of Randomness

Every event happening in our physical reality is a sequel to a series of events that have happened before that led to this specific event outcome now. Objects generally lack a backstory when the origin is not explicitly told to the Players. In games, there is no internal process for the prehistory of items found or why events occur when it is not to be told to the Player to perceive the whereabouts. When in *Sea of Thieves (2018)* a Player finds a buried treasure, there is no prior occurrence of how the treasure was initially plundered by pirates, how much booty was made then, how much of the loot was spent otherwise, or the amount that was securely shipped to this certain location before it was finally buried there to be unearthed now.

In addition, the wooden chest was never a tree in the game that grew before it got processed into a chest. As there is no technical necessity for a prehistory of an item, it simply spawned from a pool of possible chest object variants that were put into the game. To hide from the fact that the treasure was actually just instantaneously created the moment it was uncovered by a Player, the treasure gets a back story tagged on. This could be a short note, giving the Players some hints to fuel their imaginations about who buried it here and why. Such additional information helps to let the Players frame the event as a generic random finding, although technically it was.

A certain degree of randomness assists in varying the content while staying strictly within a certain boundary of possible results. The obtaining of every reward has to be balanced in a way that makes the effort worthwhile but not too high so that the Player loses the necessity and desire to search for other treasures. Its property also has to match the expectations of the Player, be it a small random finding or a huge reward for a lengthy and difficult quest. So there are already variables that modify the content of the treasure. The intention of the Player finding something special is, however, only taken into account indirectly.

Generally, in games, all objects that are not uniquely hand-crafted ("unique item") but procedurally generated by an algorithm provided by an RNG have no pre-existence at all. As a result, creating such an object from RNG out of nothing and manifesting it into the game world is a process similar to how magic works in our realm of reality.

Randomness and probability in Chaos Magick

To distinguish between the fantasy representation and what is believed to be real sorcery by its followers, the term Magick is used to describe the practice of Chaos Magick as indicated by Peter J. Caroll (1992). Traditionally, Magick is understood to be used to change the probability of events occurring. Practicing Magickians attempt to make favorable events happen more likely while avoiding undesirable events from occurring. Despite the common understanding of how Magick works, it does rarely engage in making objects appear from nothing or try to make the impossible arise.

How games represent magic is very different from how modern practitioners understand their craft. Magick is not so much about manifesting, say, creating a fireball by the wizard, but using the mind to focus intention in the Magick act to increase its chance of happening by itself. In this approach, Magick is used to change the probability of events occurring by fueling them with mental power. In addition to focusing on a desired outcome, it is an essential part to consider where to leverage. As a simple example, when one wishes for great riches, it is highly unlikely for money to just appear in their pockets. It would be sufficient to capitalize on an already existing premise of a construct that would turn into richness when a seemingly unimportant conjuncture turns out to work differently all of a sudden, so that, through the magical act, the practitioner modifies the probability that the desired phenomena to happen by itself, as Carroll argues.

Utilizing such an approach with a suitable fulcrum gives a much higher success rate than aiming for the less probable direct approach. By identifying factors that can influence the success of a magickal act, Carroll (1992) developed a formula derived from probability theory to calculate the probability of a magickal effort being successful.

$$\Psi = G * L * (1-A) * (1-R)$$

$$P\Psi = P + (1 - P)\Psi 1/P$$

Ψ = Magick

$P\Psi$ = Magickal Probability

G = state of gnosis / altered state of consciousness

L = magical link (entanglement) practitioner has with phenomena

A = state of awareness

R = subconscious resistance

P = natural probability

To a certain probability, the desired outcome can happen by itself, and the authority of the Magick practitioner influences the likelihood of it actually happening in positive or negative directions. Consequentially, being the natural probability, other tasks and obtainable / craftable utensils to increase the possibility of a desired random event occurring. The attempt to influence an event with a 0 or close to 0 probability of occurring will not be successful and therefore most likely be fruitless. As performing magick will only slightly increase its probability, still making it practically impossible to achieve the desired outcome is represented in the formula. The formula accounts for partial influences of how much the Magick practitioner is entangled with his craft and its own resistance, which are practically hardly measurable. The additional usage of ritual objects or performing rituals that represent the purpose of the act might be used to further amplify the focus on the matter.

This formula shall be adapted so it can be used in the context of a more favourable RNG in games to give the intentional focus of the Player a computable purpose.

The Ritual to intentionally modify the RNG

To value the efforts of a Player, a game can appear to understand what the Player is intending to achieve by tuning the RNG more in their favor while keeping the desirable positive aspects of being able to feel lucky intact. This would be most beneficially perceived by Players as it gives the feeling that the game understands what the Player is trying to get achieved by its own intention and seemingly appears to react to that, making it appear thoughtfully created. This system, however, must be mechanical and easily implementable in existing game designs, even with completed story arches, without disrupting a previously thought-out balance of gains by the underlying game design. Such a mechanical system therefore requires an adequate amount of time, similar to brute force towards the desired outcome, but being more joyful in executing so.

Using the same metrics, the probability rises with each effort made toward achieving specific goals. While the formula structure remains unchanged in order to calculate a successful magical outcome, the variables are modified to be appropriately in a game design scenario:

$$\Psi = E * I * (1\text{-}A) * (1\text{-}T)$$

$$P\Psi = P + (1 - P)\Psi^{1/P}$$

Ψ = Ritual

$P\Psi$ = Ritual success probability

P = original occurrence of RNG

E = effort performed (ritual work) → dedication to task

I = possession of ritual relevant items → can be shared

N = penalty from contradicting character development, affinity / guild association

T = time penalty (shrinking)

The basis for the event to occur is the probability given by the RNG defined by the intended game design. Putting time and effort into certain tasks then further improves the probability of them becoming more and more likely. These tasks that are naturally possible to perform (collecting, hunting, discovering, etc.) in the game are expanded with attributes to contribute to internal scoring. Intrinsic factors that benefit this might be performing tasks in a certain environment, achieving certain character skills, or fighting a specific type of monster. A broader mix helps to steer away from blunt-grind busy work, which is repeating individual tasks to get a specific item. It offers the Player a wider array of endeavors to perform within the existing set of game mechanics. Additionally, the possession of extrinsic luck modifiers such as talismans or good luck charms can be collected and targeted for the desired outcome or potentially traded with other Players in a multiplayer environment. An example of this could be that equipping reptile armor makes it more likely to make a rare snake type boss spawn instead of the generic that has less desirable loot. The repeated attempts to make the random-based boss spawn are a lesser game experience than doing more entertaining tasks towards the Ritual. In this example, the time spent on obtaining the specific armor is rewarded towards brute forcing the random event appropriately. Certain clues can be interwoven with dialogues while letting the Players discover these secrets by themselves and share (presumably) discoveries in communities.

Valuing thoughtful progress by the Players actions requires a penalty from conflicting character development, affinity, or guild associations. While these factors are based on decisions in the past, they should not be irreversible, unlike the positive character stats, as it would potentially make the game permanently harder and consequently more frustrating for the Player. As a final benefit to counteract overly lengthy brute force attempts, the more often an attempt is made, the more likely the more beneficial event is going to occur. This creates a simple and elegant way to honor attempts to the outcome as gained soft experience for the Player.

Conclusion

The Ritual offers a concept recommended to be taken into account when designing the probability of events occurring triggered by a RNG. As in the Magick template, there are positive and negative factors that influence the event that is going to happen. Its mechanics can be added to already existing games with a minimum amount of effort. As a side effect, the Ritual adds an additional layer of secrets to discover in the game. The Ritual offers an additional optional layer in the game lore to give hints about possible Rituals that do not affect the previous design. By designing plenty of logic and semantic connections, what actions influence which parameters, even the most generic tasks perceive an additional layer of being awarded for, that makes them feel less like grinding and overall more beneficial and rewarding. At this time, the author is not aware of any game that supports the concept of "The Ritual".

References

Carroll, P.J.(1992).Liber Kaos. Boston: Weiser Books , 41–51

Chou.Y.(2013).The Six Contextual Types of Rewards in Gamification.
https://yukaichou.com/marketing-gamification/six-context-types-rewards-gamification/

Divinity: Original Sin II, Bandai Namco, Larian Studios (2017)

Lembke,A.(2021).Dopamine Nation: Finding Balance in the Age of Indulgence.New York : Dutton

Phantasy Star 2, Sega (1989)

Pokémon Red/Blue, Nintendo, Game Freak (1996)

Pokemonspeedruns.com.(2020).http://wiki.pokemonspeedruns.com/index.php?title=Pok%C3%A9mon_Red/Blue/RNG_Manipulation_FAQ

Sea of Thieves, Microsoft Studios, Rare (2018)

The Binding of Isaac, Edmund McMillen (2011)

Magics *of* Immersion and Transformation in GaMes

LIMINAL INTIMACY: ROLE-PLAYING GAMES AS CATALYSTS FOR INTERPERSONAL GROWTH AND RELATING

Josephine Baird

Sarah Lynne Bowman

Kjell Hedgard Hugaas

ole-playing games provide the ability to slip out of established social frames and explore identity, whether digital or analog. Thus, these role-playing groups can provide a transformational container: a space for growth within which players feel safe to explore new aspects of their identities within a liminal environment. If the group of players is supportive outside the game, players can feel validated in portraying a new social identity in their daily life and shape a more empowering narrative of their life story. Furthermore, role-playing games open new relationship frames connected to these identities and the fictions surrounding them. Previous work has addressed how players may experience such dynamics as erotic, confusing, or potentially detrimental to existing relationships, particularly as a result of bleed, when aspects spill over from character to player. Through co-creation, players can experience unprecedented intimacy, vulnerability, and connection, which can shake the foundations of players' self-concepts and understanding of relationships. Applying theoretical principles from object relations, psychodynamics, transactional analysis, and attachment theory to role-playing games, this paper explores intimacy within role-playing environments. These theories can help explain how role-playing games can hold space for players to catalyze new relationships, practice interpersonal skills such as flirting and sharing, and experience the magic of limerence through connection. Furthermore, players can transform intimacy in daily life, whether with specific people or within their understanding of their sexual and/or romantic identities, such as queer and polyamorous identities. This paper concludes with recommendations for exploring intimacy with an emphasis on integration, safety, consent, calibration, transparency, and trust.

Keywords: role-playing games, intimacy, relationships, bleed, transformation

Introduction

One of the most powerful aspects of role-playing games is the ability to slip out of established social frames (Goffman, 1986; Fine, 1983) and explore identity, whether digital (Bessière, Seay and Kiesler, 2007; Bowman & Shrier, 2018) or analog (Pohjola 2004; Bowman 2010). Players leave the frame of daily life and enter the magic circle of play (Huizinga, 1958; Salen and Zimmerman, 2003), within which the rules of social reality, self-presentation, and interaction temporarily change. When a role-playing group supports meaningful self-discovery, it can provide a *transformational container*: a space for growth within which players feel safe to explore new aspects of their identities within a liminal environment (Bowman and Hugaas, 2021; Diakolambrianou, 2021; Cazeneuve 2021). If the group of players is supportive off-game, players can feel validated in portraying a new social identity in their daily life (Stets & Serpe, 2013), as well as shaping a more empowering narrative of their life story (McAdams, 2011).

Furthermore, role-playing games open new relationship frames connected to these identities and the fictions surrounding them. Previous work has addressed the ways in which players may experience such dynamics as erotic (Brown & Stenros, 2018), confusing (Waern, 2010), or potentially detrimental to existing relationships, particularly as a result of *bleed*, when emotions, thoughts, physical states, and relationship dynamics spill over from character to player (Bowman, 2013; Harder, 2018; Hugaas, 2019). Role-playing is an inherently co-creative activity, where new modes of reality and, thus, *relating* are experienced, even if these dynamics are fictional. However, we posit that within those fictional systems, players can experience unprecedented intimacy, vulnerability, and connection, which can shake the foundations not only their self-concepts, but also their understanding of relationships.

Applying theoretical principles from object relations (Klein, 1975), psychodynamics (Freud, 1990; Jung, 1976; Assagioli, 1965), transactional analysis (Berne, 1996; Karpman, 2007), attachment theory (Levin & Heller, 2011), and other psychotherapeutic concepts, this paper will explore intimacy within role-playing game environments. Role-playing games can hold space for players to catalyze new relationships, practice interpersonal skills such as flirting and sharing, and experience the magic of limerence and *integration* through connection (Siegel, 2010). Furthermore, these containers can help players transform their understanding of intimacy in daily life, whether with specific people or with their own sexual and/or romantic identities, such as queer as polyamorous identities. This paper will conclude with recommendations for exploring intimacy with an emphasis on integration, safety, consent, calibration, transparency, and trust.

Role-playing Games and Relationship Dynamics

For the purposes of this paper, we are focusing primarily on analog role-playing games: tabletop, live action role-playing (larp), and hybrid forms, such as analog games played online on video conference platforms. We define role-playing games as co-creative experiences where participants immerse into fictional characters and realities for a bounded period of time through emergent playfulness (Bowman, 2022). The degree of playfulness varies in this case. Some role-playing experiences can be quite challenging, particularly those that explore difficult relationship dynamics that are painful to experience for the character, but also sometimes for the player, who is experiencing the character's emotions. When we use the term relationship, we include romantic and/or sexual relationships alongside other important dynamics, such as family, friends, coworkers, etc. The theoretical principles we discuss here can be extended to any significant relationship and are visible at a macro social level within intergroup dynamics. Thus, when we use the word *intimacy*, we refer to any significant experience of connection that involves the consensual revealing of vulnerable parts of oneself to another person or other people.

These parts may be specific to the player's personal identity or life experience, or they may be shared fictional moments that evoke closeness between not only characters, but sometimes also their players. As one role-playing game participant described in Bowman's (2010) ethnographic work, intense role-playing can lead to an accelerated off-game bonding process:

> "Especially with your more intense scenes, you can get an intimate connection with somebody. There is this woman I met in my last larp experience whom I've never met before, ever. And within five minutes, we both had to behave as if we were cousins, [spiritually-speaking]. And we did it, we pulled it off, and we role-played to each other like that for a couple of hours. And after that [...] how could I not feel close to somebody like that? I mean, [she was] able to go there with me, so quick, so fast. I don't even know her last name. I don't even know what her favorite color is, what her birthday is, and thus, I don't know her sign [...] I don't know anything about her [...] You don't know somebody so quickly outside of role-playing, I think." (Bowman, 2010, p. 78)

While many peak experiences can cause similar moments of instant bonding, role-playing games are unique in the way that players can spontaneously co-create fiction with one another. Play is protected by *alibi* (Montola, 2010; Deterding, 2017): the permission granted by the magic circle of the game to explore dynamics and behaviors that might otherwise be taboo.

To a certain degree, all role-playing games involve relationships of some sort. As human beings, we operate in relationship with ourselves, the people in our lives, and the world around us at all times. Because role-playing games involve many dimensions of interactions and require players to slip in and out of fictional characters and social realities, a player operates in relationship to many moving parts. At any given time, they may develop a relationship with:

✳   the designers and the game design;

✳   the role-playing community within which they play;

✳   the co-players within a particular game;

✳   the facilitators running the game; and/or

✳   the fictional world and story, including the metaplot and the unfolding emergent narrative

Relationships can also develop between:

✳   characters when contemplating, planning, or enacting the fiction;

✳   one's sense of self and one's own character;

✳   one's of self and another person's character;

✳   one's character and another person's character; and/or

✳   one's sense of self and another person's sense of self.

These relationships can sometimes be complex and multifaceted. For example, a designer might be playing their own game, which they created based on important aspects of their own lives, enacted within their regular gaming community. That person may additionally be enacting relationship dynamics within the story with a person with whom they have an interpersonal relationship outside of the game. This example illustrates how players experience a complex interwoven tapestry of psychological and social dynamics when engaging in an analog role-playing game.

Beyond the scope of the game, relationship dynamics explored through play might also remind players of patterns of behavior they experience outside of these contexts with other individuals, within social groups, or between different groups. Alternatively, these dynamics might recall ways in which the player relates with themselves intrapersonally. Some of these dynamics are more implicit and internal than others, e.g., one's relationship between their sense of self and their character's is likely more internal than one's enactment of relationship dynamics with others in the game. Thus, investigating dynamics within role-playing games is a vastly intricate process with many facets and layers to consider.

To narrow this scope, for the purposes of this paper, we will focus upon relationship:

1. between co-players;

2. between one's sense of self and one's own character;

3. between one's character and another person's character; and

4. with the fictional world and story, including the metaplot and the unfolding emergent narrative.

Additionally, while this paper will briefly touch upon game mechanics, unlike previous work on intimacy in role-playing games (Trammell and Waldron, 2015), our emphasis will be on narrative relationship dynamics rather than ways to simulate sexuality. Note that as our method focuses upon applying theory to existing games based on our design and play experiences, further research is needed to validate these theories, such as case studies, interviews, and quantitative measurements.

Theories of Intrapersonal and Interpersonal Relating

When considering relationship dynamics within and outside of games, we hold the opinion that role-playing game studies could benefit from deeper engagement with psychoanalytic theories related to psychodynamics, object relations, transactional analysis, and attachment. While extensive application of these concepts to games is beyond the scope of this paper, we will provide brief descriptions of these concepts and their implications.

Psychodynamic Theory

In psychodynamic theory, the human psyche is divided into parts. These parts are in relationship to one another, whether consciously or unconsciously. For example, in Freudian psychoanalysis, the psyche is subdivided into the *ego* (the conscious "I" self), the *id* (unconscious impulses toward sexuality, aggression, and death), and the *superego* (the unconscious "censor" who internalizes social norms and imposes them upon the ego) (Freud, 1990). In Jungian psychology, these parts have different names and connotations: the ego is made up of the *persona* (or front-facing social role) and other parts that are conscious; the *personal unconscious* includes repressed facets such as disowned aspects within the Shadow; and the *collective unconscious*, which contains universal archetypes and other symbols inherent to all humanity (Jung, 1976). These aspects become more complex in subsequent theories and practices such as Internal Family Systems, in which therapists guide individuals to engage in *parts work,* identifying and expressing dozens of facets of themselves that have unique forms of expression and needs (Riskin, 2013). Larp theorist and psychotherapist Elektra Diakolambrianou (2021) describes ego states as *configurations of self,* a concept described by psychologist Carl Rogers (1959).

Importantly, regardless of the theory, the ways in which these parts interrelate become central to therapeutic processes. In psychosynthesis developed by Roberto Assagioli (1965), individual parts represent archetypally-based subpersonalities that need to come into harmonious relationship with one another, forming a synthesis through the development of empathy. Some people experience these parts as distinct whole personalities who may or may be conscious of one another, may engage in intrapersonal strife, or may "take over" the body for periods of time through a process called *identity alteration* (Schnall & Steinberg, 2000). This experience is sometimes labeled as *Dissociative Identity Disorder (DID).* For people diagnosed with DID, therapeutic treatments either focus on creating an integrator personality who can manage these alter egos, or allowing each personality the chance to have their needs heard and come into harmonious relationship with the other selves - a more democratic form of integration. However, psychodynamic approaches sometimes view isolated parts or whole separate personalities not as evidence of "disorder," but rather as a function of the way consciousness operates at less conscious levels. An important aspect of self that is often engaged and cared for in therapeutic practice is the *Inner Child* (or Children), which each person is believed to have within them. This theory is used especially in processes of therapeutic healing for people who have experienced childhood trauma, such as illness, abuse, or neglect.

Therapist and neuroscientist Daniel Siegel (2010) has advocated for establishing a more integrated experience between the individual and their internal parts (intrapersonal); the people with whom they are in relationship (interpersonal); and their relationship with the external world in general. Siegel emphasizes the importance of this integration especially in regard to mental health and wellbeing. Along these lines, larp theorists have explored the way psychodynamic theories and practices are helpful in understanding larp, especially with regard to its similarities to psychodrama (Linnamäki, 2019), the need for psychological safety within leisure games (Burns, 2014), and its psychotherapeutic potential (Diakolambrianou, 2021).

Accepting that the psyche is psychodynamic has implications for the distinction between "player" and "character" in role-playing games. For example, if parts or personalities spontaneously emerge from our unconscious, role-playing can be a vehicle for such aspects to come to fruition and expression, even when constrained and bounded by fictional elements. Furthermore, some role-playing games are designed to externalize parts within the characters themselves. For example, Emily Care Boss' *Under My Skin* (2014), which is about relationships and the temptation to break agreements, involves other players enacting the inner voices of the Angel and Devil, attempting to convince the character to either resist or succumb to desire. This technique is called bird-in-ear, where an internal part becomes external and enacted by another player. Similarly, in the larp *Group Date* by Sara Williamson (2014), a group of 4-9 players enact different parts of a person's inner "committee," each representing a different desire. Thus, while only two characters are on a date, each player embodies an aspect of that player's inner world, including Lust, Optimism, Empathy, and Doubt. From a meta-cognitive perspective, these games allow the group the opportunity to represent and reflect upon the complex dynamics of intimate relationships, not only interpersonally, but also intrapersonally.

Transactional Analysis and The Drama Triangle

A related theoretical framework is transactional analysis, which views dysfunctional relationship dynamics between people through the lens of "games people play" (Berne, 1996). In this sense, the games do not refer to behavior within a magic circle of play, but rather the ways in which people engage in interpersonal conflict in order to "win strokes," meaning gain attention, power, and leverage over one another. Again, these games are usually unconscious, but certain patterns of behavior, or *transactions*, between people, are recognizable in relationships, whether romantic or otherwise. The implication of this terminology is that dysfunctional dynamics tend to involve individuals determined on "winning" interactions by engaging in transactions that place them at an advantage over others, but such "wins" are short-lived and often damage the relationship. Thus, the goal of transactional analysis is to be able to identify these games and find ways to interrelate more collaboratively, as well as win-win solutions for each person.

Within these dynamics, transactional analysis asserts that people shift between three distinct ego states throughout any given day and set of interactions (Harris, 2011):

The Parent, who often expresses traits similar to their primary caregivers during their upbringing. The Parent may express more *nurturing* behavior, which gives permission and security to others to express themselves, or more *criticizing* behavior, which focus upon restriction and punishment, i.e., a more authoritarian style of parenting.

The Adult, a fully conscious and aware ego state that is able to process information, make predictions about emotions, and operate accordingly. This ego state is the goal of transactional analysis, because the Adult has a more objective appraisal of reality and feels empowered within it.

The Child, who often expresses characteristics similar to their childhood personality, including emotional responses, spontaneity, playfulness, creativity and intimacy. This ego state may manifest as more *natural* or *free* as a result of a nurturing relationship with parental figures. Conversely, this Child state historically may have needed to *adapt* to the demands of the parent, including behaving in a rebellious manner or feeling pressure to perform the "Good Child" role.

Individuals inhabiting these ego states engage in transactions with each other. For example, two people in Parent ego states are likely to interact quite differently from one person as Parent with the other as Child. Indeed, certain relationship dynamics likely evoke unconsciously different ego states, e.g., in the workplace, a supervisor unconsciously embodying the Parent role, and the employee the Child. Associations embedded within these ego states based on early life experiences may have implications for transactions. For example, if the supervisor embodies the criticizing Parent, the employee may react as the Adapted Child, by rebelling, trying to please the Parent, or both. Transactional analysis focuses on establishing the experience of "being okay" within each person in the dynamic (Harris, 2011). In other words, if people do not feel that they or others are in a state of crisis that needs to be managed, they are more likely to interrelate in more healthy and empowered ways.

Applications of this model of ego states are too numerous to count, as role-playing games often invite players to assume roles of different ages, including enacting co-parents, children, and parent-child relationships. If we take into consideration the notion that we switch between these ego states consistently throughout any given day, we can understand why it might be easy for players to embody characters outside of their personal experience, e.g., a parent or a child when the player is a childless adult. Intriguing examples are found in *Vampire: the Masquerade* (Davis et al., White Wolf, 1991), in which the Camarilla faction establishes strict hierarchies, with the Prince of the city often acting as the criticizing Parent imposing punishments for transgressions and regularly making public displays of power. In addition, vampires are "sired" by other vampires in such a way that the sire is often expected to behave as a Parent to their "childe" regardless of their actual age difference, as most vampires are adults when "turned." This relationship becomes additionally complicated when these characters are also lovers, a fairly common occurrence despite the taboo. Alternatively, some characters were turned into vampires when they were children, which players may choose to express as an eternal state of child-like demeanor. Additionally, some players choose to enact child-like characters within the clan Malkavian, which allows for more socially unacceptable behavior due to "mental illness." This type of character may reflect a version of one's Inner Child, which Bowman (2010) has called the Repressed, or Regressive Self, i.e., regressing to an earlier state of personality and consciousness through play.

One of the most enduring and useful "games" emerging from transactional theory is the Drama Triangle, originated by Stephen Karpman (2007). The Drama Triangle describes dysfunctional relationship dynamics usually represented by three parties in recurrent conflict (but not always): the Persecutor, who persecutes the Victim, who the Rescuer tries to save (see Figure 1). Due to the ongoing nature of this dynamic, individuals tend to inhabit a "default" role in their interpersonal relationships, i.e., the Rescuer may unconsciously seek out perceived Victims to save, Victims unconsciously seek out Persecutors or Rescuers and vice versa, etc. Regardless of these default roles, it is important to note that the parties within these dynamics may switch roles at different times in the relationships and/or perceive themselves as inhabiting other default roles. For example, a Persecutor may impose their will upon others because they perceive themselves to be a disempowered Victim; the Rescuer may feel victimized by their consistently self-sacrificing behavior, occupying a role closer to the Victim part of the Triangle, the Martyr; etc. Importantly, each person within the triangle is trying to exert power in some way due to an inherent perception of disempowerment.

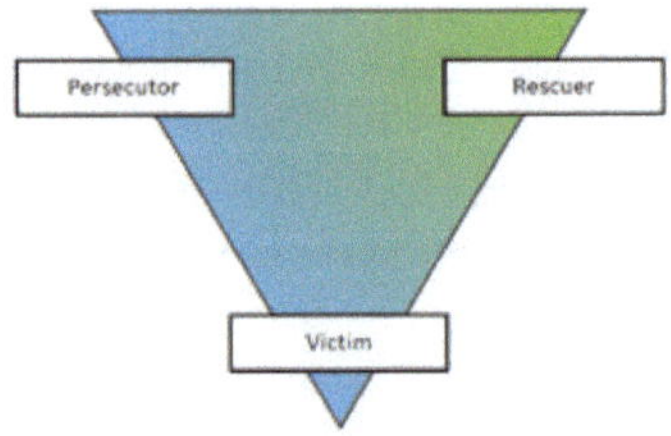

Figure 1. The Drama Triangle by Stephen Karpman. Image by 1000Faces on Wikimedia Commons. (CC BY-SA 4.0)

Many theories attempt to describe ways to step out of the dynamic of the Drama Triangle. Our preferred theory is The Empowerment Dynamic by David Emerald (2016), which emphasizes how these roles play out when individuals feel like they have agency in the world. In this model, the individuals shift from an anxious state to a passionate one: the Persecutor becomes the Challenger, the Rescuer becomes the Coach, and the Victim becomes the Creator.

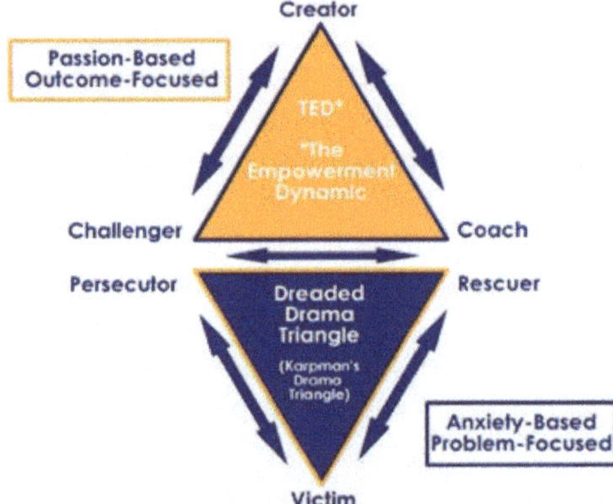

Figure 2. The Empowerment Dynamic. Image by Wiki-psyc on Wikimedia Commons. (CC BY-SA 3.0).

These theories have profound implications for understanding relationship design in role-playing games, as well as storytelling in popular culture in general. Indeed, many character relations embedded in larp design are likely rooted to some degree in the Drama Triangle as a source of conflict, whether the designers are conscious of it or not. Many Western narratives - as discussed in the *monomyth* by Joseph Campbell (1973) - emphasize a hero saving a victim in distress from a villain. Thus, the patterns embedded in many Western fairy tales, which impact romantic ideals people bring into relationships, and popular genres like fantasy, which have heavily influenced the development of RPGs like *Dungeons & Dragons* (1974), are inherently rooted in fundamentally dysfunctional and disempowering narratives.

An interesting design challenge involves taking these tropes and incentivizing players to help empower one another toward more autonomous states of being where boundaries are clear and respected. Bowman and therapist Dani Higgins' created an edu-larp called *Symbiosis* (2016, Golden Cobra) in an attempt to address such a challenge. The conceit of the setting is that adolescents on Saturn go to a retreat in which they learn how to identify their more "parasitic" traits that drain energy from others, and practice more "symbiotic" traits that enable them to grow in power harmoniously with others. In terms of character descriptions, players are given only a parasitic trait and a symbiotic trait, the latter of which they can teach to others. Characters play in dyads, triads, or quadrads, defined also in terms of their relationships with others. The Drama Triangle is the basis of one such triad:

Supernova (Persecutor): This character's Parasitic trait is to lash out or threaten to leave if they do not get their way. Their Symbiotic trait is to express how much someone means to them without expecting reciprocity.

Corona (Victim): This character's Parasitic trait is to get someone to do something for them that they could do on their own without asking directly. Their Symbiotic trait is to share their feelings while taking responsibility for them.

Eclipse (Rescuer): This character's Parasitic trait is to do something for someone else that they could do on their own. Their Symbiotic trait is to take full responsibility for their problematic behavior and apologize.

In *Symbiosis*, characters are allowed to leave the retreat once they have learned at least three Symbiotic traits. Their Parasitic traits never leave them, but this process is meant to mirror group therapy and other personal development processes of learning more empowering ways to interact with others.

Object-Relations and Attachment Theory

In addition to inner parts, psychodynamic theory also places strong emphasis on relationships with external parties, especially within the field of object-relations (Klein, 1975). For example, the relationship between client and therapist is central in psychotherapy and other counseling traditions as a trusting relationship within which clients can process emotions, practice interpersonal skills, and experience growth guided by a trained professional. Furthermore, psychoanalytic theories often focus upon the early relationships between parents and children as foundational to adult behavior, as seen with transactional analysis.

One of the most useful, enduring, and popular theories along these lines is attachment theory, which focuses upon the degree to which a child feels emotionally secure in their relationship with their caregiver. Mary Ainsworth and S.M. Bell's (1970) and John Bowlby's (1983) research in this field studied the ways in which toddlers reacted to their parents leaving the room while they are playing, i.e., a Strange Situation. For our purposes, we will focus on the ways in which attachment styles manifest in adult relationships, the kind most often embodied in role-playing games. Five main types of adult attachment have been established (Kirschner, 2020; Bockarova, 2019):

1. **Secure:** When a person tends to feel that their emotional needs will be met consistently by their partner

2. **Anxious Preoccupied:** When a person tends to fear abandonment and requires consistent reassurance

3. **Fearful Avoidant:** When a person tends to fear engulfment but also craves intimacy

4. **Dismissive Avoidant:** When a person tends to fear engulfment and convinces themselves they do not need love

5. **Disorganized:** When a person engages in a several of the styles, usually as a result of extreme trauma

Attachment styles can play out in basically any role-playing scenario where close relationships feature heavily. We most commonly consider attachment with regard to romantic relationships, but they also come into play in family dynamics, friendships, and other important connections. Since many role-playing games thrive on conflict, creating relationship dynamics between Anxious and Avoidant characters are simple ways to establish strife, as the two remain within each other's orbit, but each feel insecure in the relationship and are unsure if their needs will be met. In our view, however, since only roughly 50% of adults are securely attached (Levine & Heller, 2011), practicing secure attachment patterns within role-playing could bear fruit in terms of personal development and relationship success outside of the magic circle. Role-playing can allow players the opportunity to experience a lower-stakes way to practice relationship skills in a (hopefully) more accepting environment. In other words, while enacting explosive, dysfunctional relationship dynamics may be easy and emotionally stimulating to play; behavioral rehearsal through characters engaged in effective communication and reassurance in role-playing games can help us learn how to practice more secure relating practices with others in daily life. In addition, beyond the role, engaging in activities that feel safe can help people learn how to develop secure bonds within social groups or with individuals within a community. This safety can be especially important for people with histories of insecure attachment due to harm, neglect, or breaches of trust.

Identity, Bleed, and Transformational Containers

From our perspective, role-playing dynamics and insights drawn from them can impact daily life, including one's experience of social reality, one's own identity, one's relationships with others, and the stories one tells about one's life. We are particularly interested in the ways in which these role-playing experiences can help players experience personal and social transformation:

1.   Developing enhanced meta-awareness about their dynamics;

2.   Having breakthroughs in their understanding of the ways in which they relate to themselves and others;

3.   Distilling key insights through processing and reflection; and

4.   Integrating these insights into their daily lives in meaningful ways.

Thus, role-playing games become not only a playground for the imagination, but also a workshop within which players can intentionally express and explore ways of relating that they might otherwise find difficult to approach - such as harmful dynamics, or dynamics previously considered impossible for them - such as vulnerable emotional expression or experience of healthy, secure relationships. While many players may not intend to apply insights from role-playing experiences into their lives, we advocate for the conscious, intentional, consent-based play within which players support each other in such explorations. In this way, these insights can more easily transfer to a person's daily life with support from the group. Drawing from group dynamics theory, Bowman and Hugaas (2021) have adopted the term *transformational containers* (p. 76-79; Bion, 2013) for role-playing groups allowing for such growth. In these environments, participants feel securely supported enough to express authentic aspects of their inner world through play (Winnicott, 1960; 1971).

Such environments do not strictly bound play experiences within the magic circle (Huizinga, 1958; Salen & Zimmerman, 2003) by overly enforcing *alibi*. Alibi is the process by which players socially and psychologically agree that they are not personally responsible for occurrences within the fiction, nor should they be judged for them, i.e., "These feelings and actions were not mine; they were the character's" (Montola & Holopainen, 2012; Deterding, 2017). Instead, transformational containers support the creation of a safe(r) space for playing roles outside of societal norms by providing the alibi players need to escape the social policing to which they might ordinarily be subjected (Goffman, 1963; Deterding, 2017). From this perspective, the alibi is an essential component of the ritual that allows players to enter *liminality*: inhabiting another psychological and social space where social roles temporarily change within a group setting (Turner, 1969). Ritual space gives role-players the opportunity to experience the "magic" of engaging a different world that functions on a different set of principles and rules. Players are also able to shapeshift and inhabit "temporary autonomous identities" (Pohjola, 2004), experiencing another way of being and expressing themselves that is protected under the alibi of the "character."

Within this meta-cognitive framework, players can perceive the difference between their daily identities and those they enact in games. This space allows both for *role distance*, but also for *bleed*: when aspects of the player spill over to the character and vice versa (Montola, 2010). Theorists have discussed a variety of bleed effects, including:

* **Emotional bleed** (Montola, 2010; Bowman, 2013), involving the spillover of emotions and feelings;

* **Procedural bleed** (Hugaas, 2019), involving the spillover of physical actions or behaviors;

* **Memetic bleed** (Hugaas, 2019), involving the spillover of ideological concepts, paradigms, or other units of culture;

* **Ego bleed** (Beltrán, 2012; 2013), involving the spillover of conscious and unconscious personality traits and/or archetypal contents;

* **Emancipatory bleed** (Kemper, 2020), involving the spillover of liberatory thoughts and feelings for marginalized players;

✳ **Romantic bleed** (Waern, 2010; Bowman, 2013), involving the spillover of romantic and/or sexual feelings toward another person, whether tangible or imaginary, even after a game has concluded.

Each of these forms of bleed can have implications on role-players' identities, relationships, and even life trajectories. Consider romantic role-playing. While many players are able to engage with one another without experiencing bleed, in some situations, bleed can dramatically impact their lives. Players may feel the strong emotions of their character long after the game is done, e.g., feeling deeply in love, or *limerence*, toward a fictional character or with the player who enacted them. Sanne Harder (2018) describes how complicated such feelings can become, especially when the player experiencing the limerance is in another monogamous relationship and did not anticipate such feelings emerging. In situations such as these ones, players must learn how to navigate these intense and ongoing emotions, whether they are reciprocated by the other player in question or not. Some players never discuss such feelings and may conceal them out of shame. Other co-players may negotiate some sort of relationship off-game, be it a friendly, a romantic, or a sexual relationship. Such feelings may cause disruptions in previous relationships and/or require partners to renegotiate their relationship agreements. Many role-players report meeting long-time partners at these games, often due to playing a close relationship of some sort within which intimacy was explored and grew outside of the fictional context (Bowman, 2013).

Queerness, Polyamory, and Role-playing Games

Bleed experiences can destabilize temporarily or call into question a person's understanding of their self-concept and their ways of relating. Some examples include players identifying as heterosexual experiencing ongoing queer desires after a game, players identifying as monogamous experiencing romantic love for multiple people at once (Harder, 2018), or players discovering their authentic gender identity after exploring through play (Baird, 2021). As a result, role-playing games hold the potential to fundamentally shift a player's self-concept, e.g., a person previously doubting their off-game desirability feeling more empowered after successfully playing a romantic partner in a larp. Alternatively, some players do not report experiencing bleed per se, but still experience a shift in states of consciousness through role-playing. These shifts allow them to conceptualize another way of being, a different sort of relational system, and/or a more favorable pattern of interrelating that they can choose to adopt after play.

Thus, by allowing players to explore different versions of reality and ways of interacting within them, the liminal ritual space of the role-playing game provides an opportunity for self-discovery. A performative perspective on the social world suggests that we are at all times playing socially constructed roles (Butler, 1990; 1996), often within frames that we did not choose, much less consciously create (Goffman, 1959; 1986). Role-playing games allow us to intentionally engage with those social processes, which are often complex and obtuse in other aspects of our lives. Furthermore, they give us perspective to understand social processes as systems which adhere to a specific "logic" and set of rules. Consider the "logic" of hetero- and mononormativity within which people are expected to contain their behavior and perform their relationships in heterosexual, monogamous pairings. Within these intimate relationships, social pressure to remain within certain bounds of sexuality often exists, e.g., religious doctrine forbidding sex before marriage, expectations of normative sexual practices, etc. Role-playing games can provide new social structures with different social rules for relationships or opportunities to explore outside of existing norms: norms that we often unconsciously reproduce whether or not they bring us joy or fulfillment. Thus, some game designers seek to intentionally queer role-playing spaces in order to offer a glimpse into alternative ways of expressing gender and sexuality (Cazeneuve, 2018).

For example, the larp *Just a Little Lovin'* (2011-), explores dynamics between groups of lovers and friends within overlapping social circles within the context of the HIV/AIDS crisis in New York in the 1980s. Few relationships from these games are designed as heteronormative, and even mononormativity is challenged within the magic circle, which establishes a more permissive sexual container within which characters can explore alternative ways of relating (Groth, Grasmo, and Edland, 2021). Lovers can experience polyamorous dynamics, BDSM, and other modes of romantic and sexual expression. Friend groups that were previously focused on specific shared interests or lifestyle choices intermingle, resulting in a multiplicity of interconnected relationships in a complex web of entanglement (Bowman 2015). This web becomes extremely important within the context of the larp, as characters become sick or die of AIDS, and other characters provide support, comfort, and care, despite any differences they may have previously experienced.

Within tabletop role-playing games, Avery Alder's *Monsterhearts* (2012) and *Dream Askew* (2014) stand out as clear examples of queerness baked into the design of the game. In *Monsterhearts*, players inhabit characters in high school who each have an inner "monster," i.e., a witch, a werewolf, a vampire, etc. These characters consistently experience overwhelming attraction to one another despite social taboos, as a way to mimic both the teenage experience and as a metaphor for the queer experience. In *Dream Askew*, players enact characters who have been shunned by other groups and choose to live together in a post-apocalyptic enclave. These individuals have a variety of genders, including "goddess," "transgressing," "raven," and "dagger daddy," which lends to an inherently queer narrative. Additionally, the Belonging Outside Belonging theme evokes the idea of the "chosen family" so common in LGBTQIA+ communities. The mechanics of the game give tokens for behaviors that reveal vulnerabilities or create deeper intimacy between players, whereas tokens must be spent in order to engage in the sorts of power moves typical to role-playing games, such as enacting violence. Thus, *Dream Askew* rewards characters for establishing opportunities for connection, a refreshing subversion of the experience points and story rewards granted to characters for enacting violence in many role-playing games.

Within these frameworks, participants can explore the above-mentioned relationship dynamics through play through a queer and/or polyamorous lens. For example, within chosen family systems in games, characters may alternate embodying the ego states of Parent, Adult, and Child. For example, a grown adult within *Just a Little Lovin'* may shift into a Parent role when caring for a younger member of the community who has fallen ill, an Adult role when negotiating boundaries within their intimate polyamorous relationships, and a Child role when reacting rebelliously to an elder's advice-giving. Both players and characters may also enact attachment trauma through these games, particularly if they have experienced ruptures in their family of origin due to their gender and/or sexual identities. Within framework such as *Dream Askew*, within which characters have been rejected from the Society Intact, characters can explore insecure attachments and dysfunctional relationship dynamics such as the Drama Triangle. If they choose, they can also practice building secure attachments through their characters, working through key issues and developing communication skills similar to a psychotherapeutic process. However, regardless of what happens between characters, if participants consistently feel safe within their gaming group, they can practice building secure attachments through the play experience itself. In other words, whether or not characters within *Just a Little Lovin'* or *Dream Askew* resolve their attachment issues and dysfunctional relationship dynamics, the players themselves can feel more secure through self-expression and group acceptance outside of play.

These types of spaces can have profound impacts on the lives of players, allowing them to model, explore and move out of these established social frames. For example, for LGBTQIA+ people who have few socially-sanctioned opportunities in their everyday live to express their queer identities related to gender and sexualities, role-playing games can be a space to explore and embody them (Paisley, 2015; Stenros & Sihvonen, 2019; Diakolambrianou, Baird, Westborg, and Bowman, 2021). Upon reflection and within the support of the community holding this container, players may feel more confident expressing these aspects of themselves than in other contexts, such as changing their names, their gender performance, and other important identity markers (Moriarity, 2019; Stenros & Sihvonen, 2019; Baird, 2021).

Furthermore, role-playing games can provide spaces to explore complex relationship dynamics, such as interactions within flirting, cruising, dating, falling in love, sexuality, committed relationships, and breakups. While such interactions can lead to valuable insights in any context, they can become especially important for queer players, especially individuals who may have fewer opportunities to experience or unpack these sorts of dynamics in daily life. As Erik Winther Paisley (2016) writes about his experiences in *Just a Little Lovin'*, "the transformative part of the game is how it transplants players into a world where gay is the new normal. It was the best game I have ever played and I think that is true for a lot of other people, especially all the other queers" (p. 172).

Safety, Aftercare, and Integration

As discussed above, role-playing games can become transformational containers (Bowman and Hugaas, 2021), a catalyst for the magic of change to occur. Experiences within games may inspire a person to fundamentally alter their self-concept or their daily lives or may reinforce existing ways of being. Either way, role-playing allows people a taste of the experience of greater agency: they can see how social reality, systems, identities, and relationships are constructed and therefore can be *designed*. Such design thinking is prevalent in recent scholarship and self-development books, e.g., Mark A. Michaels' and Patricia Johnson's (2015) *Designer Relationships: A Guide to Happy Monogamy, Positive Polyamory, and Optimistic Open Relationships*. Through bleed, alibi, the magic circle, and safety structures, role-playing communities can become transformational containers: playgrounds for experience, exploration, and design of intimate life.

However, these sorts of experiences are best when players feel securely held, meaning that the community holds space for them to explore their emotions in- and off-game. Within this context, the social contract of the space should be made explicit by:

1.   the organizers, especially when the game features themes of love and intimacy; and

2. the players, especially when exploring content and dynamics that may expose vulnerabilities.

The perception of safety decreases mental vigilance, which can lead to greater risk taking and an experience of trust within gaming communities. Thus, communities can be structured to facilitate transformation by:

* establishing norms around vulnerability, acceptance, compassion, and care;

* demonstrating values of diversity, equity, and inclusion informing design and implementation of role-playing games; and

* acknowledging and honoring bleed, romantic (Waern, 2010; Harder, 2018) or otherwise.

Practices that can help cultivate safety are workshopping, debriefing, safety mechanics, codes of conduct, transparent safety protocols, consent negotiations, and calibration between players.

Additionally, groups should establish who is willing to give emotional care, when, and how to ask for it. Furthermore, groups playing with intimate dynamics may choose to establish a method of aftercare (Freidner, 2020), where co-players agree to support and give care to one another post-game. This support is especially important for players with marginalized gender identities, sexualities, or relationship styles, who may have experienced alienation, stereotyping, or microaggressions in previous role-playing groups (Paisley, 2016; Stenros & Sihvonen, 2019; Kemper, Saitta, & Koljonen, 2020). Supportive experiences can help such players feel like their gender and/or sexual identities are socially verified by others within the group (Stets & Serpe, 2013), especially for individuals who regularly have their identities rejected or unacknowledged by society at large.

Furthermore, players should engage in integration strategies (Bowman & Hugaas, 2019) that can help them reflect upon the game experience and process it. Integration practices can take many forms, including creative expression, intellectual analysis, emotional processing, strategies for transitioning to daily life, interpersonal processing, and community building. Additionally, players can work with a therapist or relationship coach to assist in their personal and social growth. Players can integrate the lessons distilled from their game narratives into their life stories, which can help shift their perception of their trajectories toward a more redemptive or empowering arc (Bowman and Hugaas, 2021).

Regardless of the method, the potential for alchemical potency in role-playing games with regard to exploration of identity and intimacy is undeniable and should be handled with care. In alchemy, magical processes occur within a crucible – a container that must be fortified in order to contain the often explosive and unstable interactions between components within it. Strengthening cultures of safety and care within role-playing communities can provide such a container, helping participants explore aspects of their relationships and identities that can lead to long-lasting personal and relational transformation.

References

Ainsworth, M. D. & Bell, S. M. (1970). Attachment, exploration, and separation: Illustrated by the behavior of one-year-olds in a strange situation. *Child Development, 41*, 49-67.

Alder, A. (2012). *Monsterhearts*. Buried Without Ceremony.

Alder, A. (2014). *Dream askew*. Buried Without Ceremony.

Assagioli, R. (1965). Psychosynthesis: Individual and social (some suggested lines of research). *Psychosynthesis Research Foundation: P.R.F. Issue, 16*.

Baird, J. (2021). Role-playing the self: Trans self-expression, exploration, and embodiment in (live action) role-playing games. *International Journal of Role-Playing, 11*, 94-113.

Beltrán, W. "Strix" (2012). Yearning for the hero within: Live action role-playing as engagement with mythical archetypes. In S. L. Bowman & A. Vanek Wyrd (Eds.), *Wyrd con companion book 2012* (pp. 89-96). Los Angeles, CA: Wyrd Con, 2012.

Beltrán, W. "Strix" (2013). Shadow work: A Jungian perspective on the underside of live action role-play in the United States. In S. L. Bowman & A. Vanek (Eds.) *Wyrd con companion book 2013* (pp. 94-101). Los Angeles, CA: Wyrd Con, 2013.

Bessière, K., Seay, A.F., & Kiesler, S. (2007). The ideal elf: Identity exploration in *World of Warcraft*. *CyberPsychology & Behavior, 10* (4), 530-535.

Berne, E. (1996). *Games people play: The basic handbook of transactional analysis*. New York, NY: Ballantine Books.

Bion, W. P. (2013). Attacks on linking. *The Psychoanalytic Quarterly, 82*(2), 285-300.

Bockarova, M. (2019, September 23). The forgotten attachment style: Disorganized attachment. *Psychology Today*.

Boss, E. C. (2014). *Under my skin: Who do you love?* Black and Green Games.

Bowlby, J. (1983). *Attachment: Attachment and loss, Volume one* (2nd ed.). New York, NY: Basic Books Classics.

Bowman, S. L. (2010). *The functions of role-playing games: How participants create community, solve problems, and explore identity.* Jefferson, NC: McFarland & Company, Inc.

Bowman, S. L. (2013). Social conflict in role-playing communities: An exploratory qualitative study. *International Journal of Role-Playing, 4*, 17-18.

Bowman, S. L. (2015). Love, sex, death, and liminality: Ritual in *Just a Little Lovin'*. In S. L. Bowman (Ed.) *The wyrd con companion book 2015* (pp. 8-19). Los Angeles, CA: Wyrd Con.

Bowman, S. L. (2022, January 5). *Introduction to transformative game design* [Video]. Transformative Play Initiative, YouTube.

Bowman, S. L. & Higgins, D. (2016). *Symbiosis*. Golden Cobra Challenge.

Bowman, S. L. & Schrier, K. (2018). Players and their characters in role-playing games. In J. P. Zagal & S. Deterding (Eds.) *Role-Playing Game Studies: Transmedia Foundations* (pp. 245-264). New York, NY: Routledge.

Bowman, S. L & Hugaas, K. H. (2019, December 10). Transformative role-play: Design, implementation, and integration. *Nordiclarp.org*.

Bowman, S. L. & Hugaas, K. H. (2021). Magic is real: How role-playing can transform our identities, our communities, and our lives. In K. K. Djukastein, M. Irgens, N. Lipsyc, & L. K. L. Sunde (Eds.) *Book of Magic: Vibrant Fragments of Larp Practices* (pp. 52-74). Oslo, Norway: Knutepunkt, 2021.

Brown, A. & Stenros, J. (2018). Sexuality and the erotic in role-play. In J. P. Zagal & S. Deterding (Eds) *Role-Playing Game Studies: Transmedia Foundations* (pp. 425-439). New York, NY: Routledge.

Burns, D. (2014). The therapy game: Nordic larp, psychotherapy, and player safety. In S. L. Bowman (Ed.) *The Wyrd Con Companion Book 2014* (pp. 28-41). Los Angeles, CA: Wyrd Con.

Butler, J. (1990). *Gender trouble: Feminism and the subversion of identity.* London, England & New York, NY: Routledge.

Butler, J. (1993). *Bodies that Matter: On the discursive limits of sex.* London, England & New York, NY: Routledge.

Campbell, J. (1973). *The hero with a thousand faces.* Princeton, NJ: Princeton University Press.

Cazeneuve, A. (2018). How to queer up a larp: A larpwright's guide to overthrowing gender binary. In R. Bienia & G. Schlickmann (Eds.) *LARP: Geschlechter(rollen): Aufsatzsammlung Zum Mittelpunkt, 2018.* Zauberfeder Verlag: Braunschweig, Germany.

Cazeneuve, A. (2021). Larp as magical practice: Finding the power-from-within. In K. K. Djukastein, M. Irgens, N. Lipsyc, & L. K. L. Sunde (Eds.) *Book of Magic: Vibrant Fragments of Larp Practices* (pp. 306-314). Oslo, Norway: Knutepunkt.

Davis, G., et al. (1992). *Vampire: the masquerade.* 2nd Ed. Stone Mountain, GA: White Wolf.

Deterding, S. (2017). Alibis for adult play: A Goffmanian Account of Escaping Embarrassment in Adult Play. *Games and Culture, 13*(3), 260-279.

Diakolambrianou, E. (2021). The psychotherapeutic magic of larp. In K. K. Djukastein, M. Irgens, N. Lipsyc, & L. K. L. Sunde (Eds.) *Book of Magic: Vibrant Fragments of Larp Practices* (pp. 95-113). Oslo, Norway: Knutepunkt.

Diakolambrianou, E., Baird, J., Westborg, J., & Bowman, S. L. (2021, May 28). The therapeutic potential of larp: cognitive considerations. Poster/video presented at *MET Conference: Neuroscience and Theater Therapy*, Bucharest, Romania.

Emerald, D. (2016). *The power of TED*: *The empowerment dynamic: 10th anniversary edition.* Edinburgh, Scotland: Polaris Publishing.

Fine, G. A. (1983). *Shared fantasy: Role-playing games as social worlds.* Chicago, IL: University of Chicago Press.

Freud, S. 1990. *New introductory lectures on psychoanalysis (The Standard Edition).* (J. Strachey Trans. & Ed.). New York, NY & London: W. W. Norton & Co. (Original work published 1933)

Friedner, A. (2020, April 15). Leaving the magic circle: Larp and aftercare. *Nordiclarp.org.* Retrieved from https://nordiclarp.org/2020/04/15/leaving-the-magic-circle-larp-and-aftercare/

Goffman, E. (1959). *The presentation of self in everyday life.* New York, NY: Anchor Books.

Goffman, E. (1963). *Stigma: Notes on the management of spoiled identity.* Englewood Cliffs, NJ: Prentice-Hall.

Goffman, E. (1986). *Frame analysis: An essay on the organization of experience.* Boston, MA: Northeastern University Press.

Harder, S. (2018, March 28). Larp crush: The what, when and how. *Nordiclarp.org.* Retrieved from https://nordiclarp.org/2018/03/28/larp-crush-the-what-when-and-how/

Harris,T. A. (2011). *I'm OK - you're OK.* New York, NY: Harper Perennial.

Hugaas, K. H. (2019, January 25). Investigating types of bleed in larp: Emotional, procedural, and memetic. *Nordiclarp.org.* Retrieved from https://nordiclarp.org/2019/01/25/investigating-types-of-bleed-in-larp-emotional-procedural-and-memetic/

Huizinga, J. (1958). *Homo ludens: A study of the play-element in culture.* Boston, MA: Beacon Press.

Jung, C. G. (1976). *The portable jung.* (J. Campbell, Ed., R.C.F. Hull, Trans.) New York, NY: Penguin Random House.

Karpman, S. B. (2007, August 11). The new drama triangles. Paper presented at the *USATAA/ITAA Conference*, San Francisco, CA.

Kemper, J. (2017, June 21). The battle of Primrose Park: Playing for emancipatory bleed in *Fortune & Felicity. Nordiclarp.org.* Retrieved from https://nordiclarp.org/2017/06/21/the-battle-of-primrose-park-playing-for-emancipatory-bleed-in-fortune-felicity/

Kemper, J. (2020).Wyrding the self. In E. Saitta, J. Särkijärvi, & J. Koljonen (Eds.) *What Do We Do When We Play?* (pp.). Helsinki, Finland: Solmukohta.

Kirschner, D. (2020, July 24). Overcoming attachment style fears to create lasting love. *Psychology Today.* Retrieved from https://www.psychologytoday.com/us/blog/finding-true-love/202007/overcoming-attachment-style-fears-create-lasting-love

Klein, M. (1975). Some theoretical conclusions regarding the emotional life of the infant. In M. Klein (Ed.)., *Envy and gratitude and other works 1946-1963* (pp. 61-93). New York, NY: The Free Press. (Original work published 1952)

Levine, A. & Heller, R. (2011). *Attached: The new science of adult attachment and how it can help you find - and keep - love.* New York, NY: Jeremy P. Tarcher/Penguin.

Linnamäki, J (Pitkänen). (2019). Formas o métodos para el cambio. ¿Cómo contribuyen al cambio el psicodrama, el sociodrama, el teatro playback y el role playing educativo de acción en vivo o EDULARP. *La Hoja de Psicodrama, 28*(71).

McAdams, D. P. (2011). Narrative Identity. In S. J. Schwartz, K. Luyckx, & V. L. Vignoles (Eds.) *Handbook of identity theory and research*. New York, NY: SpringerLink.

Michaels, M. A. & Johnson, P. (2015). *Designer relationships: A guide to happy monogamy, positive polyamory, and optimistic open relationships*. Jersey City, NJ: Cleis Press.

Montola, M. (2010). The positive negative experience in extreme role-playing. In *Proceedings of DiGRA Nordic 2010: Experiencing games: Games, play, and players*. Stockholm, Sweden. Retrieved from http://www.digra.org/wp-content/uploads/digital-library/10343.56524.pdf

Montola, M. & Holopainen, J. (2012). First person audience and painful role-playing. In E. Torner and W. J. White (Ed.) *Immersive gameplay: Essays on participatory media and role-playing* (pp. 13-30). Jefferson, NC: McFarland and Company Inc.

Moriarity, J. (2019, October 14). How my role-playing game character showed me I could be a woman. *Washington Post*. Retrieved from https://www.washingtonpost.com/outlook/how-my-role-playing-game-character-showed-me-i-could-be-a-woman/2019/10/18/a0200216-f109-11e9-b648-76bcf86eb67e_story.html

Paisley, E. W. (2015). Play the gay away: Confessions of a queer larper. In K. Kangas, M. Loponen & J. Särkijärvi (Ed.) *Larp politics: Systems, theory, and gender in action* (pp. 170-177). Helsinki, Finland: Solmukohta 2016, Ropecon ry.

Pohjola, M. (2004). Autonomous identities: Immersion as a tool for exploring, empowering, and emancipating identities. In M. Montola and J. Stenros (Eds.) *Beyond role and play* (pp. 81-96). Helsinki, Finland: Ropecon ry.

Rogers, Carl. 1959. "A Theory of Therapy, Personality, and Interpersonal Relationships, as Developed in the Client-Centred Framework." In The Carl Rogers Reader, ed. Howard Kirschenbaum and Valerie Henderson, 236 – 257. London: Constable.

Riskin, L. L. (2013). Managing inner and outer conflict: Selves, subpersonalities, and Internal Family Systems. *Harvard Negotiation Law Review 18*(1), 1-69.

Salen, K. & Zimmerman, E. (2003). *Rules of play: Game design fundamentals*. Cambridge, MA: MIT Press.

Schnall M., & Steinberg, M. (2000). *The stranger in the mirror: Dissociation, the hidden epidemic*. New York, NY: Cliff Street Books, HarperCollins

Siegel, D. J. (2010). *Mindsight: The new science of personal transformation*. London, England: Bantam.

Stenros, J. & Sihvonen, T. (2019). Queer while larping: Community, identity, and affective labor in Nordic live action role-playing. *Analog game studies: 2019 role-playing game summit* (Special Issue).

Stets, J. E., & Serpe, R.T. (2013). Chapter 2: Identity theory. In J. DeLamater & A. Ward (Eds.) *Handbook of social psychology* (pp. 31-60). New York, NY: SpringerLink.

Trammell, A. & Waldron, E.L. (2015). Playing for intimacy: Love, lust, and desire in the pursuit of embodied design. In M. Wysocki & E. W. Lauteria (Eds.) *Rated M for mature: Sex and sexuality in video dames* (pp. 177-194). London, England: Bloomsbury Academic.

Turner, V. (1969). Liminality and communitas. *The ritual process: Structure and anti-structure*. Piscataway, NJ: Transaction Publishers.

Waern, A. (2010). "I'm in love with someone that doesn't exist!!" Bleed in the context of a computer game. In *Proceedings of DiGRA Nordic 2010: Experiencing games: Games, play, and players*. Stockholm, Sweden.

Williamson, S. (2014). *Group date*. Golden Cobra Challenge.

Winnicott, D. W. (1960). The theory of the parent-infant relationship. *The International Journal of Psychoanalysis* 41, 585–595.

Winnicott, D. W. (1971). Transitional objects and transitional phenomena. *Playing & reality.* Tavistock, England: Tavistock Publications.

"BUT WITHOUT GAMES IT WOULD HAVE BEEN SOMEHOW EVEN GRAYER."

ABOUT COMPUTER GAMES, ADOLESCENTS, AND THE QUESTION OF OPPORTUNITIES FOR MAGIC IN THE COVID-19 CRISIS

Christin Reisenhofer

Andreas Gruber

Adolescents are considered to be especially affected by negative effects of the COVID-19 crisis. Multiple stressors and challenges associated with the pandemic can impact both the psychological and physical well-being of adolescents and young adults. Above all, the challenges that arose from the pandemic, such as limited social interactions and agency as well as severely restricted access to education and leisure activities, led to hardships for adolescents. However, it is interesting that initial findings of empirical studies suggest that adolescents' gaming increased during the pandemic. Digital gaming worlds provide a wide range of experiences and interactions, potentially substituting the lack of real-life access in a way. Agency, digital relationship building, and escapism may provide relief for players, especially in times of a pandemic. But to what extent can digital games counteract the challenges experienced in the COVID-19 period through their inherent immersion? And how can gaming provide opportunities to form and maintain relationships? How do adolescents experience computer gaming during this time – as magical or harrowing? This paper focuses on the initial findings of the qualitative-empirical study "Ich Zocke" (I play), in which a total of 15 gamers from Austria and Germany talk about their experience of the pandemic in terms of perceived stress, challenges, and their gaming behavior. The primary focus of the paper is on how these adolescents express and interpret their desire, ability, and necessity to immerse themselves in digital gaming worlds.

Keywords: adolescents, gaming, pandemic, immersion, gaming experience

Introduction

The first measures to tackle the COVID-19 pandemic in Austria and Germany were taken in the first quarter of 2020. These countermeasures to contain the spread of the virus included the switch to distance learning at schools, only offering childcare if absolutely necessary as well as strict restrictions for nearly all areas of life. Due to developmental reasons, children and adolescents are particularly affected by COVID-19 burdens, such as social distancing and distance learning (Kaman et al., 2021). As Carissa F. Etienne, director of the Pan American Health Organization (PAHO), points out: "The virus indirectly [and directly] has consequences and is hindering their growth and development, and [is] jeopardizing their chances at a bright future" (PAHO, 2021).

However, with the outbreak of the pandemic, increased computer game playing was also identified, especially among young people (YouGov, 2020). Columns and blogs online also turned their focus towards discussing questions and experiences about the correlation between gaming and the pandemic:

> "For some, gaming was a lifeline to normalcy while others used the medium as an escape when the world got too real. Whatever the case, gaming was a rock for many in 2020. It kept many of us sane in a rough year" (GiesonCacho, 2020).

To understand why this is the case, the authors conducted a survey at the research unit for psychoanalysis and education at the University of Vienna. The research focused on questions pertaining young people's experiences of the pandemic, whether they perceived this crisis period as merely burdensome, and to what extent digital games were able to counteract the challenges experienced in the COVID-19 period. The survey further intended to investigate how adolescents experienced computer gaming during this time – as magical or harrowing?

This paper aims to give insights into the research project "I play/Ich Zocke", which was started in spring 2021. Interviews with 15 participants took place between June and August, in which 15 adolescents were asked to share their experiences of the COVID-19 pandemic and related gaming experiences. The initial findings of our content analysis (Mayring, 2007) of the conducted interviews, each with narrative as well as semi-structured elements, are discussed with regard to the outlined research questions in this paper.

The pandemic's effect on adolescents

Studies on stress experiences, changes in quality of life and mental health, and changes in gaming behavior among young people and adolescents in the context of the pandemic are now extensive and differentiated.

In their research, Kapella et al. (2022) focus on the influence of digital technologies on the well-being of young people and, among other things, also address questions about subjective perceptions and useful or harmful influences of digital media on users or different user behavior in everyday life. Based on a social-constructivist and praxeological perspective, young people are considered to be active, autonomous and competent users, but at the same time seen as a group worth protecting, with different resources and competencies that (co-)shape their social relationships in and through digital media. The concept of 'doing family' serves as a social relationship construct that is redefined and reshaped daily by all participants; digital media and its tools, in turn, influence the family system and all its members. Methodologically, a systematic literature and data analysis of the state of research is followed by focus groups of children (5 to 10 years of age), family interviews and ethnographic case studies of children and families from four European countries with different social structures. The pandemic is explicitly considered mainly in terms of methodological complications such as difficulties in recruiting interview partners and data collection. According to the study findings, digital technologies are an integral part of young people's everyday lives, predominantly in the form of computer games, movies, music, and social media on a variety of devices. A significant factor in terms of media literacy and, accordingly, usage behavior is access to their own devices. With regard to the respective family system and in addition to the attitude of other family members toward digital media, the specific use and significance in everyday life is yet another meaningful factor. For example, digital media can serve as a means of communication within the family, as a tool for emotional balance, or as a stabilizing factor for the family system. Especially during the COVID-19 pandemic with distance learning and home office, digital media had positive or negative effects on the intra-family balance and well-being of individual family members, depending on the one hand on the frequency of media use. On the other hand, the attitudes and values of the family members towards digital technologies or the specific integration of digital media in everyday (family) life must be considered. The use of digital media can therefore have both positive and negative effects on mental health and/or social life within and outside the family, whereby teaching and support in the development of digital skills are decisive variables in addition to the everyday use of digital media itself. We conclude from the results that the earliest possible education in media literacy, the explicit parental supervision of the children's media use, and access to digital media and their own devices, thereby facilitating participation, are significant factors in ensuring positive effects, for example, with regard to general well-being and the prevention or reduction of vulnerabilities (Karpa et al., 2022). We note that parents serve as role models in this respect but it cannot be assumed that they also have the necessary media skills required to effectively supervise their children's media use, interaction with different kinds of media and help them not to be susceptible to mediatised influence. Nonetheless, they also postulate a kind of learning by doing, whereby all family members can learn with and from each other based on the respective media-related co-activity. Whether parents can and/or want to fulfil this role despite the corresponding recommendations, and accordingly also our conclusions, must be viewed critically.

Research that explicitly focuses on the comparison of the periods before and during the pandemic can subsequently be divided into two areas; on the one hand, the challenges during the COVID-19 pandemic and, on the other hand, in relation to changes in gaming behavior.

The COPSY study, first conducted mid-2020 (approx. end of the first COVID-10 wave), of the University Medical Center Hamburg-Eppendorf provides a useful example. Using online questionnaires, parents as well as children and adolescents were able to provide information about their experiences with stress. In the process, about 70% of participants between the age of 11 and 17 years stated they felt stressed by the pandemic and the associated changes. Distance learning and lack of contact with friends were cited as the main stressors. In addition, adolescents reported more frequent conflict situations within family systems, headaches, problems falling asleep, and a generally decreased quality of life (Ravens-Sieberer et al., 2020). Similar findings were published in other studies summarized and described by Walper et al. (2021). A deterioration in family climate from the first lockdown in April 2020, increased adolescent unease and anxiety regarding school, loneliness, and future prospects, and a distinct lack of social contact are commonly cited results.

With regard to changes in gaming behavior during and as a result of the COVID-19 pandemic, for example, the YouGov survey (2020) conducted by the Association of the German Games Industry should be mentioned. Results show that both the length of play and the type of games chosen have changed since the beginning of the pandemic, with 35% of participants stating that they played more frequently. Also important to note is that 28% of participants said computer games helped them to live through the pandemic better, while 27% played more often with family and friends (YouGov, 2020).

An online survey by Barr and Copeland-Stewart (2021) found a similar trend, with 71.3% reporting a change in gaming time and 63.1% reporting a change in preferred genres. In addition, positive effects of gaming on general well-being, mental health, and social contacts were found (Barr and Copeland-Stewart, 2021, 4). However, the increase in gaming time was not a constant trend of the pandemic, nor has it remained at the high levels of the initial pandemic period. According to Irpan et al. (2020), the peak of time engagement in gaming was around the mid-2020s, with a 41% increase over the previous year; since then, a trend toward normalization of gaming time to pre-pandemic (period) levels has been observed (Irpan et al., 2020, 8).

Experiencing the pandemic and the meaning of computer games

In contrast to these large-scale quantitative studies on the impact of the COVID-19 pandemic on the living circumstances and gaming behaviour of adolescents, there are hardly any qualitative surveys focusing on the subjective experience of young people thus far. In order to address this issue, the authors carried out a qualitative study with adolescents between the ages of 11 and 21, in which 15 interviews were conducted (9 of which via Discord or ZOOM) with approximately one-hour interview time. We distributed flyers via multipliers in schools and out-of-school settings (social workers, teachers, social pedagogues, etc.) and then asked interested adolescents to forward our digital flyers to their peers. Although the flyer was explicitly designed to be gender-neutral, hardly any girls or self-identified queer adolescents responded to our request, which results in a circumstance that could be critically considered in further research. The interviews opened with an open question ("Can you please tell me your life story in relation to computer games?") with the purpose of capturing the subjective experience of each participant. The narrative that followed was not interrupted until a deliberate end of response was detected. The first follow-up questions were oriented towards eliciting more detailed information on some of the interviewees' prior statements. To give an idea of this line of questioning, one follow-up question was: "You said that you got into computer games when you were 6 years old through playing Gameboy with your father. Could you tell me more about that?" However, to remain focused on this study's specific research interest, namely, the experience and meaning of gaming in the COVID-19 crisis, participants then entered an interview-phase in which they were asked questions addressing relevant research topics that may not have been addressed before, for instance: "Could you tell me about the pandemic, from the first time you heard about it until now?" This approach and the associated advantages and disadvantages of combining narrative and semi-structured interview techniques is also discussed by Scheibelhofer (2008). An initial evaluation was carried out following Mayring's (2007) concept of qualitative content analysis, taking into account the inductive category formation as a development of categories, which are identified in the material.

Among the 15 participants, a clear majority (n=13) identify as male and two consider themselves female. The survey sample consists of participants from a variety of educational backgrounds. At the time of data collection, seven participants between the ages of 11 and 15 attended middle school with each of the remaining eight participants stating to currently attend or complete an internship, special education centre classes, a bachelor's degree programme, community service, polytechnic secondary school, middle school, and middle school respectively. In addition, at least three of the interviewees mentioned precarious economic backgrounds and a conflict-ridden family life. These circumstances already existed pre-pandemic and became more severe or more acute particularly during the first lockdown. Two young participants who were placed in out-of-home care reportedly had less contact with their families of origin during the first period of the pandemic, and one adolescent recounted that internal family conflicts had increased noticeably for him during this time. All interviewees disclosed to play games on a daily basis with a discernible increase in gaming activity at least during the first week of the lockdown.

Playing through the pandemic: Gaming as a response to pandemic challenges

The evaluation of the interviews has shown an even distribution in terms of experience. Five participants said that their perception of the time was predominantly positive. Aspects such as fewer school obligations and more time for hobbies, especially (online) gaming (with their friends) were highlighted as particularly positive during this time. There are different explanations for this. In some cases, participants spoke of the time related to graduation from school and an associated sense of optimism. They referred to finishing school as a "high", a euphoria, which also helped them to overcome negative moods, as evident in the following statement:

> "This high of school finally off, that pretty much negated my negative mood (...) yeah and I have actually always been doing relatively well during that time" (B01, 391-393).

Four participants experienced the pandemic neutrally to ambivalently, from "completely okay" (B05, 407) to "almost depressive" (B05, 427) phases. Although, according to our analysis, in most cases the social environment of the adolescents (caregivers, peers) and their own competencies (e.g. adaptability) were available to a sufficient extent to get through the pandemic.

However, this does not apply to all interviewees as six participants described the period from the beginning of the pandemic to the time of the interviews as very demanding or stressful.

> "Because you just don't pay attention, nobody is interested somehow. You just game a lot with friends during the time and also in general, you stay up terribly late, sleep rhythm, everything is completely gone. (...) Somehow everyone is so depressed, and no one actually enjoyed gaming (...) Then you somehow noticed, yes it´s not getting better, it's not getting better. And you become more and more sad and depressed" (B11, 453-473).

With regard to changes in gaming behavior during the pandemic, the conclusion can be drawn that all but one interviewee played significantly more than before, at least during the initial period of the pandemic. For six interviewees, gaming time had increased and was still increasing by the time of the interview. For another six interviewees, gaming time initially increased but had returned to pre-pandemic levels by the time the interview took place. Two respondents reportedly played less than they did pre-pandemic at the time of the interview, despite an initial increase in gaming time (during the outbreak). For one respondent, gaming time has decreased due to not having access to computer games as he was living in a social pedagogical housing community at the time and the console remained in the parental household.

The collected results show a great variety of experiences, for a majority of the interviewees (online) gaming had a special significance, especially with regard to the social aspect.

> "Just playing with other people took a little bit of stress out of it, because I said, okay, at least that part of my free time activities didn´t change very much" (B04, 262-264).

Accordingly, gaming was considered a way to compensate for an experienced lack of social interaction in offline life. However, it was also mostly seen as a tool, with social interaction being the main motivation.

> "One has a large social environment now and if one is socially active, then one rather neglects gaming because to me it is primarily not about gaming, to me it is primarily about spending time with friends" (B11, 506-508).

These last quote leads to the conclusion that gaming can also have a strong social factor, and the changes in terms of gaming behavior are also due to a need or a longing, respectively, which is contact with other people, attachment, connectivity and sharing.

Opportunities for magic in the COVID-19 crisis

The analysis of the transcribed interviews not only allows conclusions on changed gaming behaviour or the interviewees' general experience of the pandemic. First inferences can also be made in regard to the question of whether there are opportunities for magic in the COVID-19 time. Following definitions of "magic" in common dictionaries, the term can be used

> "when you are referring to an event that is so wonderful, strange, or unexpected that it seems as if supernatural powers have caused it. You can also say that something happens as if by magic or like magic." (CollinsDictionary.com, 2022)

Magic understood in this sense and as understood in this paper, involves the possibility of experiencing moments of happiness, socially meaningful connections and agency through gaming and the immersion in games during this distressing period. During the interviews, we experienced such magical moments with many of our interviewees. Most notably when memories were shared that were experienced and described as particularly special. These moments were mostly related to playing together with friends, or when special in-game achievements, or very moving moments (e.g. sceneries, game design) were evoked. The interviewees then narrated with an expression of joy, amazement and delight, emotions which proved positively infectious. Since immersion emerged during analysis as a particularly significant criteria in relation to gaming during the pandemic, as will be subsequently illustrated, the framing of the term immersion will be outlined in the following section.

Wernbacher (2008) defines immersion as a construct which describes temporary mixing of real and virtual worlds, whereby the virtual environment is perceived as more real than the analogue environment. This leads to affective, emotional, and cognitive reactions of varying degrees in gamers. The quality depends on the game itself (e.g. auditory, visual presentation, credibility of what is presented) as well as on the readiness and constitution of the players, for example, their ability to concentrate or control of motor skills (Wernbacher, 2008).

According to Mittlböck (2020), switching back and forth between immersion and reflection is necessary so as not to perceive experienced feelings as overwhelming and that the devotion required for immersion in game worlds does not become self-destructive. It is, so to speak, also the task of the game to support the interruption of immersion in order to enable reflection; and finally, to promote deep learning (also in terms of personality development) (Mittlböck, 2020). Concerning the findings of the qualitative-empirical study "Ich Zocke" (I play) the question arises to what extent the verbal exchange during the game favors or hinders this interplay.

Following papers on immersion, several types of immersion can be identified. This paper focuses on social immersion, spatial immersion, ludic immersion, immersion and escapism, spatial immersion, and emotional immersion. This selection is related to the fact that those are the dimensions which emerged during the analysis of the transcribed interviews.

Social immersion and meaningful relationships

According to Reer and Krämer (2019), individuals can express social bonding and experience meaningful and lasting relationships through gaming, which can lead to (psychological) well-being and relaxation. Following Arbeau et al. (2020, 4) not only the combination of rewards and benefits in games lead to immersion, but particularly the social component of online gameplay. "In-game relationships helped participants feel more connected, not only to the people they were playing with, but also to the game itself, thus encouraging them to keep playing" (Arbeau et al., 2020, 4). Accordingly, online gaming carries the potential of a mutual interplay; the immersive nature of the game can strengthen in-game relationships and perceived attachment, but at the same time, this perceived attachment also strengthens the immersion. So, the first magic moment that can be identified is a kind of social immersion. Almost all participants explicitly mentioned the importance of friendship and the need to build or deepen relationships, especially during the first period of the pandemic, when they were unable to meet anyone outside, e.g. at school.

> "During Corona, it was also an opportunity to do things you normally would do with friends online and still have fun " (B01, 432-433).

The importance of (online) gaming is also reflected in the fact that all but one interviewee played significantly more than before, at least during the initial period of the pandemic. Very different motivations for playing computer games were mentioned, for instance, as a means against boredom or as a possibility to intensively pursue one's hobby. Particularly frequently mentioned motives were relaxation, getting away from everyday life, or simply to experience feelings as well as expressing or regulating emotions. For 12 of the 15 respondents, most social contacts shifted to the online space, with some having made considerable use of Discord as a social meeting place. In line with this shift, gaming was also used by a large number of respondents to compensate for a lack of social contacts in offline life.

> "If I just have free time, then I like to have at least two hours a day in which I can talk to someone, whether this is online or in real life, we have all realized that online [communication] can be a good substitute (...)" (B04, 221-224).

The quality of this alternative, that is online gaming versus contact in offline life, was perceived very differently. Social interactions in online games were either considered a full-fledged substitute for analogue communication or deemed as entertaining but hardly a substitute for real meetings, and everything in between. Negative experiences of gaming were also mentioned by some respondents, with reports on social exclusion in-game due to a lack of English skills or exclusion from conversations held in class because parents do not allow for a game to be discussed, to name a few. Loss of motivation to play the game was also mentioned because excessive use has resulted in a certain oversaturation; that is, too much playing over a certain period.

In summary, it can be concluded that gaming has a very diverse range of meanings in the perception of the gamers surveyed. Particularly the social aspect was emphasized by the respondents. Results of the interview analysis highlight that the experience of social presence of fellow players led to a higher degree of immersion, thus offline relationships and interactions could indeed be compensated to some extent in digital worlds.

> "Because it was like meeting each other, a little bit. Yeah, and it just helped a lot, in the Corona time. Yes, and otherwise, hm, yes otherwise it was also a cool pastime simply, as if one did not know what to do" (B15, 233-239).

It can be inferred that gaming can have a strong social factor, which led to the described changes in terms of gaming behavior, as they were a response to a need or a longing. Despite serving as a great substitute for some in the initial phase of the pandemic, gaming could not replace real life meetings equivalently and entirely over a long period of time.

Immersion and Escapism

Escaping into computer games, discussed in various papers (Hussain et al., 2021, Reer and Krämer, 2019; Bányai, Griffiths, Demetrovics, & Király, 2019; Blasi et al., 2019; Deleuze et al., 2019), can be considered fun, relaxing, joyful, or desirable. Reer and Krämer (2019) outline the dual mode of escapism, referring to two possibilities: escapism with negative outcomes, e.g. suppressing ones emotions or self-suppression, computer-gaming addiction, or depression, as well as escapism with positive outcomes, such as self-expansion, (psychological) well-being, stress-coping, recreation, satisfaction, expressing emotion, relaxation, and a more positive conceptualization of the meaning of life. For most of the participants, computer gaming has been a de-stressing, relieving, and reality escaping activity, especially during the first phase of the pandemic.

> „But without games it would have been somehow even grayer. Because (…) it somehow pulls you out a little bit, you forget it for once, you concentrate just on that for once and it is somehow also a nice distraction you can say, because it doesn't hurt anyone, yes" (B11, 506-508).

Computer games offer players the opportunity to escape from the reality shaped by COVID-19 and to immerse themselves in digital games, untouched by the crisis. The impression that everything feels much better in games can be evoked by experiencing agency, control, sociability, and flow.

> "And the Corona time was, I actually liked it a lot. I just played games and it was (sigh) it was not only a hobby, it was also something special" (B09, 422-425).

Thus, in the interviews conducted, adolescents sometimes describe plotlines, sceneries, and character constellations in great detail and with affection, suggesting a strong emotional connection to this digital world and how much their needs were met through gaming.

> "Just playing with other people has taken a little bit of stress
> out of it because I've said, okay, at least that part of what I do
> in my free time hasn't changed very much" (B04, 262-264).

This conclusion corresponds with the findings of Arbeau et al. (2020, 4), who describe online gaming as a tool for tension reduction, coping with stress, or taking a break from the challenges of everyday life. Regarding the crisis, the interviewees emphasised the relieving effects of gaming: "Without games through the Corona period? Then I would have freaked out" (B08, 273-276).

Spatial immersion

In the course of interview analysis, spatial immersion was identified as another magical aspect of games. According to Zhang, Perkis and Arndt (2017) spatial immersion is achieved by manipulating spatial aspects of the in-game virtual environment, such as swift zoom-in and zoom-out or the change of camera angles. Through this phenomenological experience, the players experience the virtual environment as if they could touch, feel, and walk it. When considering the rich and subjective experiences of the interviewees, engagement and involvement in and through games can also be explained by how spatial immersion is experienced as "entirely cut off from reality" (Brown, Cairns, 2004).

Some of the adolescents interviewed have used the virtual environment, especially Minecraft, for self-determined, creative and imaginative designing of virtual worlds according to their own imagination, needs and ideas.

> "Who listens to an 11–12-year-old? And somehow in Minecraft
> I was able to live that out. I could build whatever I wanted, I
> could build huge houses if I wanted, which I'm pretty sure did-
> n't look good, but whatever. I could also play with friends, we
> could fight against similar monsters, it's about surviving to-
> gether" (B10, 100-106).

This young person, who describes his position in the world as passive, unassuming and often overlooked, finds immersion and possibilities for alternative world designs in the digital environment. He can experience himself as actively and productively creating. Together with his friends, he confronts the hostile monsters (perhaps as a stand-in for the Corona virus) and experiences himself as victorious and successful in manipulating the spatial compositions and the digital environment itself.

Emotional Immersion

"Different emotional states have an impact on how individuals react to an environment", as Huang and Alessi (1999, 15) point out. Emotions are essential for how players experience gaming. Emotional immersion takes place, following findings of Zhang, Perkis and Arndt (2017), when players feel "emotionally aroused and absorbed by the narrative content of the story" (Zhang, Perkis, & Arndt, 2017, 4). This state of immersion allows identification and emphasizing with story characters or avatars in the digital world. Our findings suggest that emotional immersion not only occurs when players identify with an avatar in a predefined story, but when they place a more desired version of themselves in a self-created avatar in an online game.

> "Now I play quite often because I don't have any real friends, and playing gives me like... like I'm a different person; I'm always happy when I play with uh colleagues, it's fun, yeah, that's it. (...) I... I enjoy playing games ... I feel like ... like another person when I play" (B13, 100-106).

This statement, for instance, indicates that the young adolescent can try out alternative self-concepts via his avatar and his immersion in the digital world.

The interviewees also played games in which immersion was possible, to consciously feel emotions and therefore be able to cope with them.

Harrowing experiences & boundaries of magic

Not all experiences described in the interviews were valued as magical in the sense of experienced moments that were told in a particularly emotionally touching way or clearly positively connotated by the interviewees. There were also harrowing experiences, as some adolescents described that computer gaming was increasingly seen not as relieving and joyful, but as a burden and additional stressor.

> „However, after the summer it has become really annoying, really annoying (...) so it was in the end I got cabin fever, as much as I love gaming, I can't do it so many times in a row for so long. (...) I also played less and less CS:GO. Because CS:GO has become too much for me, I had played so much CS:GO that I uhh just all of a sudden the barrel was full, all of a sudden, I couldn't stand it any longer. And just the thought of it, made me sick. (...) Each day feels the same" (B12, 687-691).

Initially, this statement explains these gaming experiences as being perceived as a burden by the fact that with the removal of all other limitations of gaming (e.g. school, homework, meeting friends in non-virtual space, outdoor activities, etc.), gaming is hardly sufficient as the sole way of spending leisure time in a relieving manner. Gaming alone is not able to counterbalance offline relationships and activities for a long period of time. The substitution of computer games for all social relationships failed to work out for many interviewees.

> "Well, in the first lockdown it was somehow the worst because you couldn't meet outside. Somehow everyone was so depressed, nobody wanted to play anymore. Somehow, everything was completely neglected" (B11, 506-508).

Outlook

The research results presented are only initial findings that provide a first insight into whether adolescents perceive the COVID-19 crisis as merely burdensome, and to what extent digital games were able to counteract the challenges experienced in this period. Based on current study results on stress factors in the context of the pandemic, the qualitative study "Ich Zocke" (I play) could not only confirm but also differentiate initial findings. The COVID-19 crisis was not only burdensome so far, but also an opportunity for magical experiences, in the form of building friendships and bonding with friends as well as the experience of joy, relief, and happiness from gaming. Gaming in this respect can be described as a magical experience because it provides the interviewees with an element of joy in their lives, precious shared memories with peers, and a sense of belonging. These magical and positive gaming experiences have been described as particularly meaningful in COVID-19 times.

> "And above all, watch with glittering eyes the whole world around you because the greatest secrets are always hidden in the most unlikely places. Those who don't believe in magic will never find it." (Roald Dahl)

Gamers seemed to have found this magic described by Roald Dahl to some extent in their game worlds. Yet, with consideration of the established research findings, previously discussed, the findings of our qualitative study also indicate changed gaming behaviour, with a particularly high increase of gaming activity in the first COVID-19 period. Although some instances in which increased playing became a burden and playing time then decreased or nearly stopped entirely were found.

These findings correspond with research literature on the duality of immersion outcomes. Various forms of immersion led to relaxation, escapism, bonding with friends, and stress relaxation as immersion in gaming provided a counterbalance against a variety of individual stress experiences during the pandemic and different effects of (online) gaming, which had a positive effect on social interaction and general well-being. Further research, both continued qualitative interviews to increase sample size and to generate meaningful results as well as an extension of quantitative methods could provide additional insights and an expansion of the research field. Interviewing 15 adolescents only scratched the surface of what insights into gaming during the pandemic has to offer and opened the proverbial door to a room beyond which many more doors, or rather questions, lie; questions whose answers are waiting to be discovered.

Acknowledgments

Our sincerest thanks go to the participants who not only shared their experiences with us during one of the most challenging times of our and their lives, but who also graciously opened up and told us about their former gaming experiences in an authentic and fascinating way. Thank you for allowing us to learn so much from you and to share your experiences with others. In addition, we would like to thank Alexandra Autheried, whose proofreading gave our paper the final magic touch.

References

Arbeau, K., & et al. (2020). The meaning of the experience of being an online video game player. Computers in Human Behavior Reports, 2. DOI https://doi.org/10.1016/j.chbr.2020.100013

Bányai, F., Griffiths, M.D., Demetrovics, Z., & Király, O. (2019). The mediating effect of motivations between psychiatric distress and gaming disorder among esport gamers and recreational gamers. Comprehensive Psychiatry, 94, 117-152. DOI https://doi.org/10.1016/j.comppsych.2019.152117

Blasi, M.D., et al. (2019). Problematic video game use as an emotional coping strategy: Evidence from a sample of MMORPG gamers. Journal of Behavioral Addictions, 8, 1, 25-34. DOI https://doi.org/10.1556/2006.8.2019.02

Barr, M., Copeland-Stewart, A. (2021): Playing Video Games During the COVID-19 Pandemic and Effects on Players' Well-Being. Games and Culture. Retrieved from https://doi-org.uaccess.univie.ac.at/10.1177%2F15554120211017036

Brown, E., & Cairns, P. (2004). A grounded investigation of game immersion. CHI'04 extended abstracts on Human factors in computing systems, 1297-1300. DOI https://doi.org/10.1145/985921.986048

Deleuze, J., et al. (2019). Escaping reality through videogames is linked to an implicit preference for virtual over real-life stimuli. Journal of Affective Disorders, 245, 1024-1031. DOI https://doi.org/10.1016/j.jad.2018.11.078

Gieson, C. (2020). Top 10 video games of 2020: How coronavirus played heavy hand on choices. Retrieved from https://www.mercurynews.com/2020/12/23/coronavirus-plays-a-heavy-hand-in-our-10-favorite-video-games-of-2020/

Huang, M.P., & Alessi, N.E. (1999). Mental health implications for presence. CyberPsychology and Behavior, 2, 15–18.

Hussain, U., et al. (2021). The dual nature of escapism in video gaming: A meta-analytic approach. Computers in Human Behavior Reports, 3. DOI https://doi.org/10.1016/j.chbr.2021.100081

Irpan, E., TenBoer, N., Gohil, A., & Young, R. (2020): Covid-19's impact on the gaming industry: 19 takeaways. An examination of pandemic gaming behavior and game monetization. San Francisco: Unity Technologies

Kapella, O., Schmidt, E. M., & Vogl, S. (2022).Integration of digital technologies in families with children aged 5-10 years: A synthesis report of four European country case studies. DOI https://doi.org/10.5281/zenodo.6411126

Mayring, P. (2007). Qualitative Inhaltsanalyse. In U., Flick, E., von Kardoff, & I., Steinecke (Ed.). Qualitative Sozialforschung. Ein Handbuch. Hamburg: Rowohlt Taschenbuch Verlag

Mittlböck, K. (2020): Persönlichkeitsentwicklung und Digitales Rollenspiel. Gaming aus psychoanalytisch-pädagogischer Sicht. Gießen: Psychosozial-Verlag

PAHO. (2021). Children and adolescents deeply impacted by COVID-19 pandemic. Retrieved from https://www.paho.org/en/news/15-9-2021-children-and-adolescents-deeply-impacted-covid-19-pandemic-paho-director-asserts

Ravens-Sieberer, U., et al. (2020): Psychische Gesundheit und Lebensqualität von Kindern und Jugendlichen während der COVID-19-Pandemie – Ergebnisse der COPSY-Studie. Deutsches Ärzteblatt International, 117, 828-829. DOI https://doi.org/10.3238/arztebl.2020.0828

Reer, F. , & Krämer, N.C. .(2019). Are online role-playing games more social than multiplayer first-person shooters? Investigating how online gamers' motivations and playing habits are related to social capital acquisition and social support. Entertainment Computing, 29, 1-9. DOI https://doi.org/10.1016/j.entcom.2018.10.002

Scheibelhofer, E. (2008): Combining Narration-Based Interviews with Topical Interviews: Methodological Reflections on Research Practices. International Journal of Social Research Methodology, 11, 5, 403-416

YouGov. (2020). Gaming and Esports: The next generation. YouGov analysis of the global video games and esports landscape. Cologne: YouGove.com

Walper, S., Reim, J., Schunke, A., Berngruber, A., & Alt, P. (2021): Die Situation Jugendlicher in der Corona-Krise. Munich: Deutsches Jugendinstitut e.V

Wernbacher, T. (2008): Held für 30 Minuten : Aggressive Schemata, Spielerleben und Immersion in Computerspielen. Retrieved from https://unipub.uni-graz.at/obvugrhs/content/titleinfo/201260/full.pdf

Zhang, C., Perkis, A., & Arndt, S. (2017). Spatial Immersion versus Emotional Immersion, Which is More Immersive? DOI https://doi.org/10.1109/QoMEX.2017.7965655

ADOLESCENTS' USE AND PERCEPTION OF "FREE-TO-PLAY" GAMES IN AUSTRIA

Markus Meschik

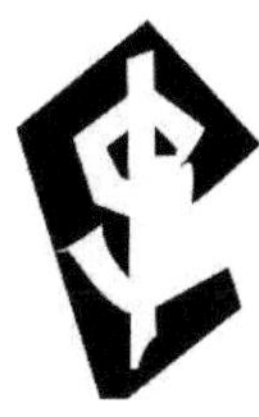

urrent financing models of digital games such as the "free-to-play" model are generating unprecedented revenues in the video game industry via in-game transactions. Many games seem to be tailored to and deliberately appeal to an adolescent target group, be it through their audiovisual design or by their easily accessible game mechanics. Other game series have been established for many years and added said financing models later. Due to structural similarities of these financing models with traditional gambling, this poses challenges for legislators as well as educators and gamers themselves. Some aspects, e.g. lootboxes, are perceived as particularly critical. However, lootboxes are just the tip of the iceberg when it comes to financing models. "Pay-to-win" mechanisms and other dark patterns receive much less international attention, but like lootboxes, they exploit cognitive dissonances in gamers. This contribution discusses the purchase motives of adolescents in Austria, how dark patterns in games can lead to increased spending, which cognitive distortions come into play in this process and how certain financing models take advantage of adolescent players. The contribution is based on the results of the author's dissertation, in which 30 adolescents between the ages of 12 and 17 were surveyed about their video game behavior using a qualitative approach. Results hint towards a strong social component of in-game transactions among predominantly male gamers which also has an influence beyond the game itself. Furthermore, dark patterns seem to exert a strong influence on young gamers and represent strong extrinsic facilitators for purchases.

Keywords: free-to-play, business models, Lootboxes, purchase motives, dark patterns

Introduction

Financing and marketing of digital games has changed dramatically in recent years. The idea that games are a commodity has been consistently abandoned in favor of the idea that games are a service. This means that game providers rely on new financing models to monetize their games. Many of these models involve making games available free of charge and offering opportunities to spend money within the game (in-game purchases). The games are therefore free to play, which is why the term free-to-play has become an established term. Within a short time, this model has turned out to be very lucrative for the manufacturing companies. Thus, in 2018, free-to-play games already accounted for a large part of the gaming industry's revenue (Wijman, 2018). This also drew the attention of researchers, who examined certain mechanics implemented in games, like lootboxes, for their similarity to classic gambling (Zendle et al., 2018; Drummond & Sauer, 2018, von Meduna et al., 2020). These mechanics are particularly prevalent in free-to-play mobile games, but many full-price titles also make efficient use of lootboxes and other dark patterns (see chapter *Dark Patterns*) to increase revenue.

In recent years, the interaction of gamers with these funding models has been researched primarily with a focus on conservative media education, mostly centering on the question of potential harmful effects of lootboxes, a particularly controversial form of funding. While the majority of research focuses on adult gamers (Lelonek-Kuleta/Bartczuk, 2021; Steinmetz et al., 2021), many free-to-play games are clearly targeted at and played by young gamers (MPFS, 2019; Forsa, 2019). Thus, there is a gap in research, as children and adolescents typically have lower impulse control developmentally (Holodynski & Oerter, 2002) and are a particularly vulnerable population. Nevertheless, children and adolescents appear to spend often large amounts of money in games (Parent Zone, 2019; RSPH 2019). Furthermore, there is a body of anecdotal evidence suggesting that at least some adolescent gamers invest significant amounts of money in various games (see (Gach, 2017; Thubron, 2016; Der Standard, 2020). However, it is not only unclear who invests how much money in digital games, there is also little research on the motives that lie behind this purchasing behavior and which facilitators favor these purchases.

State of research

In the following, the state of research on in-game purchases by children and adolescents will be described. On the one hand, the focus is on the prevalence of purchases by a young target group, on the other hand it is on the motives underlying these purchases. Finally, facilitators are mentioned that shape the game design of many free-to-play games and can lead to increased spending by children and adolescents.

Prevalences

While there are few representative figures on the actual extent of money spent on certain funding models, these figures mostly refer to adult gamers (von Meduna et al., 2020). There are only few figures on the spending behavior of minors.

In a representative survey of 1000 adolescents aged 12-17 in Germany, 28 percent of respondents who use computer games at least once a week reported spending money on extras such as cosmetic modifications, game items, or lootboxes in computer games in the last six months (Forsa, 2019). The number of people who spent money on these extras is significantly higher among male gamers (37 percent) than among female gamers (13 percent) (Forsa, 2019). From the participants of the survey 24 percent who held a high school diploma, but 38 percent held no diploma at all or an intermediate diploma, comparable to Hauptschulabschluss in Austria, spent money on extras in games (Forsa, 2019). This disparity could be indicative of a supporting socioeconomic component when it comes to paying for content in digital games. A survey in five European countries found that 36 percent of children between the ages of six and 15 surveyed spent money on extras in games (Gametrack, 2019). The fact that this figure is slightly higher than the figure in the German survey could also be related to the younger target group of this survey and an indication of increased in-game purchases at a younger age.

The purchase of particularly lootboxes was surveyed in some studies. In a survey by Zendle (et al., 2019) with a sample of 1020 adolescents between the ages of 16 and 18, a bit more than 40 percent of participants reported purchasing lootboxes in the past month. While the majority of respondents reported spending between 3 USD and 27 USD per month on lootboxes, there are also outliers who reported amounts over 2,000 USD (Zendle et al., 2019). These figures are only partially representative here, as the sample was approached via *Reddit* and the majority of respondents were male. In a recent survey in the United Kingdoms, 60 percent of 1001 children between the ages of 10 and 16 surveyed said they had heard of lootboxes, 40 percent of whom had purchased them (Parent Zone, 2019). Another survey from England, which polled 1025 people between the ages of 11 and 24, came up with a similar figure. Twenty-seven percent of young people between the ages of 11 and 14 had spent money on lootboxes in the previous week, compared to 16 percent of young adults over the age of 18 (RSPH, 2019).

Purchase motives

The desire to buy objects in digital games is expressed even more strongly among kids and adolescents, when especially in childhood the possession of objects (virtual or physical) takes on a meaningful aspect in self-definition (Böhnisch, 2018). However, the motives of adolescents to invest sometimes large amounts of money in free-to-play games have been little researched so far and represent a research desideratum (Steinmetz et al., 2021). Surveys cite aspects such as social interaction, undisturbed continued play or the economic weighing of the invested play time (Hamari et al., 2017) as reasons. However, the motives for purchasing further game content also differ depending on the type of game content, whereby a distinction must be made primarily between purchasable gameplay advantages (Steinmetz et al., 2021) and purely cosmetic content (Marder et al., 2019). A survey on the purchasing behavior of 1155 gamers aged 16 to 18 was able to establish six game motives: gameplay advantages, creating a specific collection, excitement and fun in opening the box itself, cosmetic reasons, to support the developers of the game, the perception that lootboxes are good value, time advantages and profit (Zendle et al., 2019). Interestingly, the ability to cash out on the content of lootboxes, also the depiction of "near misses" of lootboxes and the time-limited availability of certain lootboxes - all of which are external and non-intrinsical - were mentioned as motivational factors (Zendle et al., 2019).

In a more differentiated survey regarding the purchase of lootboxes in England (Close & Lloyd, 2020), 28 qualitative interviews were conducted with adult purchasers and their purchase motivations were collected. A division into six groups was undertaken:

* Opening experience: the sensation of excitement and audiovisual design of the opening process, value of content: i.e. the aesthetic, functional or financial value of the content of the lootbox

* Game related: paying to get a game advantage or to progress faster in the game

* Social influences: status gain and social pressure

* Emotive/Impulsive: out of escapist motives or boredom or inability to control desire to purchase

* Fear of missing out: concern about missing out on social aspects or time-limited offers

* Triggers/facilitators: incentives set by game providers to make purchases more likely to occur

The influence of game design or game providers was here captured in one item (Triggers/Facilitators) among the possible game motives. However, a look at the mechanics used to make purchases in games more attractive such as previous surveys (Zendle et al., 2019) also suggests that these facilitators play a large role in many of the other motivations as well.

Dark Patterns

When reading books on game design, one cannot avoid the term *ludic contract* (Schell, 2015; Swink, 2009). This represents an implicitly assumed form of collaboration between players and game developers, in which the former agree to invest time and possibly money in a game, and the developer agrees to provide the most enjoyable game experience possible in return (Schell, 2015). When the developer´s side breaks this contract and the game design has other objectives beyond making the game experience as pleasing as possible, we speak of dark patterns in game design:

> "A dark game design pattern is a pattern used intentionally by a game creator to cause negative experiences for players which are against their best interests and likely to happen without their consent." (Zagal et al., 2013).

These can take a variety of forms; some commonly used will be briefly discussed here. In doing so, I follow the observations and descriptions of Koubek (2020). The *Playing by Appointment* pattern is when it is not the players who determine the schedule and playing time of the game, but the game itself. This happens, for example, by scheduling special events at times when the game is less frequented to encourage players to play more. Another example is the possibility of losing game resources if other players can attack the base in the player's absence. *Daily Rewards* encourage players to open or play the game every day by promising additional resources or penalizing absences with resource withdrawals. These resources can be used to progress in the game. If this progress is seemingly unlimited, i.e. the game has no end state where little or no progress is possible, players find themselves in an *Infinite Treadmill*. In this case, the hunt for resources or rankings in high score lists can continue indefinitely. When developers release new game content, they sometimes make it more attractive by, for example, giving items better gameplay features than the previous ones. The deliberate acceptance by designers of the uselessness of older game items is called *Power Creep* (Magruder, 2022). Offerings in some games are also often limited in time or give the impression that the number of pieces is limited. The actual scarcity of digital game offerings is entirely at the discretion of the game developer, which is why this can be referred to as Artificial Scarcity. The *Endowment Effect* states that the value attributed to an item increases when the item is owned. Once you have made progress in a game, it is difficult to give it up because players have invested time and money on it. This effect is reinforced by the game design, for example by suggesting a higher value of the game state through more appealing graphical representations or animations.

While these are just a few of the many Dark Patterns found in digital games, they are also the ones that had the most obvious impact on interviewees during this survey.

Method

In order to find out about purchasing motives among adolescent gamers, qualitative interviews were used. These were conducted a part of a dissertation project. Hereby, 30 qualitative interviews were conducted with adolescents between 11 and 17 years and their educators, and this both in the context of traditional families and in stationary child and youth welfare, i.e., with adolescents who were taken out of their family system and placed in out-of-home care. The adolescents in the families were interviewed in the context of dyadic pair interviews (Lauer, 2011) together with one parent. The interview partners were recruited in the context of public lectures and events on digital games in education as well as through the offers of child and youth welfare services and participants received an expense allowance of 25 euros per interview. The fact that the young participants were exclusively male is due to the fact that only male young people and their parents reported back to us. This reinforces recent findings that in-game content buyers are primarily male (Close & Lloyd, 2020).

All interviews were pseudonymized, transcribed, and software-based analyzed using the software MAXQDA. Due to the limited prior knowledge and exploratory nature of the survey, the content structuring content analysis according to Kuckartz (2014) was chosen as evaluation method. The categories used for the evaluation were thus created both deductively from the results of previous work and inductively directly from the text material of the interviews. All interviews were originally conducted in German, thus quotes were translated into English.

Results

While spending money in digital games was described as a common practice among all adolescents surveyed, there are differences in the amounts of money invested according to the respondents. While some respondents only spend smaller amounts of money a few times a year, such as on the *Battlepass* in the game *Fortnite*, other young people describe themselves as indignant when making in-game purchases and proud when they can resist the temptation to do so. The latter also reported having invested more than 1000 euros in digital games. In terms of the amount of money spent, a tendency emerges according to which the adolescents interviewed in the context of child and youth welfare institutions, and thus representing the more vulnerable population, spent more money than the adolescents in traditional family systems. This could be related to increased monitoring of adolescents' financial situation in the family, but it could also be the result of socially desirable responses from adolescents who were interviewed together with their mothers. As described in previous research, there is a tendency in free-to-play games for a large portion of the games' revenue to be created by a small portion of the players - a tendency similar to the distribution of spending in traditional gambling (Fiedler et al., 2019). This raises the question, given this trend, of exactly who these few gamers are. If these gamers are part of a vulnerable population group such as adolescent residents of child welfare facilities, this results in a need for action in socio-educational practice. A clarification of the socio-demographic background of the gamers that spend more frequently and spend higher amounts in digital games would therefore be a research desideratum.

In addition to *Fortnite*, *FIFA* and *Grand Theft Auto 5*, mobile games such as Clash Royale were cited as the games in which most money was spent. Spending money is sometimes legitimized via other peers also spending money in the games:

"B: Yes, not just once, I must admit. Four, five hundred euros in total.

I: Four, five hundred euros?

B: Well, I'm not the only one in my class. All of them.

I: All of them?

B: All over 200, easily." (Beranek, age 11)

In-game content such as skins are described as aesthetically pleasing, but also serve as a status symbol when the game is played in the peer group.

> It is interesting to hear who owns what. Or since when he plays. (...) For example, I always compare myself with my friend, whether he has this skin and whether I have this skin. You can see which one I don't have and which one he does. (Alex, age 13)

It is described as particularly desirable to have exclusive game content that was either only available for a very short time or that players can only obtain by being lucky or having played for a long time. Child and youth welfare professionals also report how comparing cosmetic content (skins) acquired in games serves as a social ritual for some (male) adolescents when new adolescents arrive at the residential group. Thus, while cosmetic changes have no impact on what happens in the game or the game mechanics, they very much have an impact beyond the game itself.

Purchases in digital games also represent an investment for some participants, who expect a return on investment and sometimes a profit.

> And it should be more of a collection, because if I don't need Fortnite anymore, I can sell the account and get the money back. Because now it's actually worth twice of what I spent, a bit more. (Anton, age 14)

While selling game accounts is certainly possible, a profit on such a sale is very unlikely compared to the money invested. Statements like these or those of other young people who state that they can sell their accounts for a four-digit amount could thus be interpreted either as a wish on the part of the participant or as justification of the sums of money invested to adult interlocutors. The endowment effect becomes visible here.

Adolescents have every right to decide themselves how they spend their money, and this is not to be questioned here. This self-determination, however, becomes questionable when young people are led by certain Dark Patterns to make purchases in digital games that they regret afterwards. Some participants describe such feelings of regret. Here, a participant describes feelings of regret when reviewing the skins he purchased in the game *Fortnite*, for which he spent more than 1000 euros. Due to the constant updating of the game and the rapid availability of new content, players are encouraged to purchase the most recent skins - a mechanic that is similar and reminiscent of the Dark Pattern of *Power Creep*.

> F: And I regret it.
>
> I: You regret it?
>
> F: Yes, because you spend money thinking like that, but for what actually? At some point you don't play it anymore. (...)
>
> I: Where did you get the money from?
>
> F: From my grandfather. (...) Yes, because it's like that, the first day they're out, you think to yourself, Wow, they look really cool, I want to have them, I have to have them, and then at some point they're just useless. (Felix, age 13)

The fast pace and the associated requirement to constantly invest new money in the game is also criticized in other game titles. Many of the participants recognize and condemn predatory business models of their favorite games. Despite their sometimes clear condemnation of some financing models, however, almost all of the participants invest money in games. This discrepancy represents another distinctive feature. While most respondents condemn these financing models and even use derogatory terms such as *coiner* for those who invest money, almost all respondents stated that they regularly invest money in games. The term *coiner* is preserved for those players who win because they invested even more money. Winning in games and the associated status gain thus seem to outweigh the rejection of the purchase mechanic.

From the point of view that the game can also be a stressful medium for young people when it comes to keeping up with other players, it is understandable that some games offer functions that save players from constantly looking at their smartphones - for a corresponding fee.

> E: It simply brings in new content. You already know the old stuff, and when you get an offer like that and buy it, you get new content. Like, for example, if you buy the auto mode, it also works automatically and you don't have to stick to it permanently. So you can do other things as well.
>
> I: That means you spend money so that you don't have to play?
>
> E: No, I spend money, for example, so that (...) I get more support from this game. And in return I get things that other players don't get. (Emil, age 16)

When young people pay money for their games so that the game will automatically keep playing, this sounds somewhat counterintuitive, but it shows a successful implementation of Dark Patterns by the game developer. This leads to the reasons why adolescents make purchases in games.

The aforementioned aesthetics of purchasable content goes hand in hand with the social status enhancement associated with owning it. Closely related to the status gain is also the competitive advantage associated with making in-game purchases in games like *Clash of Clans* or *Brawl Stars*. Competitive advantage as a motive for purchases may be little surprising among male respondents, as masculine-stereotyped play activities may foster behaviors such as competition (Leaper & Friedman, 2007). In this context, adolescents outbid each other with purchases in digital games in order to remain competitive against each other.

The statements of some participants about their everyday gaming life sometimes seem exhausting and paint a picture of computer gaming behavior that is not only joyful, but also characterized by time pressure and stress, as can be seen in the following example. The influence of the Dark Pattern *Infinite Treadmill* can also be observed here, when a participant reports on his experiences in the game *Clash of Clans*.

> Well, you can't really stop it, because there is a new update almost every month and there is always something new to do. Now, for example, the June update comes with Master Hut 9, which is in Shadow Village, so there's already a second village now. And there I have to continue to expand and build up, continue to do all kinds of things. Right now I am on master hut 8, which is currently the maximum. (Ludwig, age 15)

Other participants state that the game is of great importance in their daily structure and also adapt their lives to possible actions and events in the game if this should be necessary. For example, one respondent states that he absolutely needs his smartphone at a certain time in the evening because there is an event in a game. This leads to the game manufacturer being granted power of disposal over young people's leisure time activities - the game is no longer played according to the player's desire; the game manufacturer has a say in player´s gaming behavior. Respondents report feelings of relief when they find time to catch up on events in certain games, and feelings of obligation to enter the game at certain times in order to receive in-game rewards as a result. Some players feel that participating in regular events within games is so important that during periods of game abstinence (imposed by educators), friends' devices were used to regularly open the game so as not to miss out on content. The concept of "Fear of Missing Out" (FoMO), which represents a fear of missing out on socially relevant events and therefore leads to increased consumption of social media (Roberts & David, 2019), could thus also be valid for video games in a similar form. Here, game designers specify certain game times in the form of offers and events, the missing of which can lead to disadvantages compared to other players. Thus, as long as the game is relevant in a peer group or is played in a team (e.g., a guild), social pressure among the players themselves as well as from the game design seems to be a major factor in microtransactions.

Conclusions

Spending money within games was shown to be a common social practice among the male participants as it fulfills various social needs and serves a purpose outside of the game itself as a means of gaining status or as an icebreaker for new friendships.

In the interviews conducted, an imbalance in the amount of money spent, which had already been assumed by previous research (Fiedler et al., 2019), was reproduced, with respondents in child and youth welfare tending to spend higher amounts and emphasize the topic more strongly. Here, a further quantitative survey would be a research desideratum.

Different purchasing motives of the respondents also emerged. On the one hand, these included aspects attributable to the respondents' character and social situation (e.g., gaining social status). On the other hand, the major role of game developers and game design is emphasized by the analysis of the qualitative interviews. Certain Dark Patterns designed to entice players to make purchases in games serve their purpose and represent facilitators for players to make purchases. This, in turn, raises a question of game developer´s responsibility and player protection. From both a pedagogical and a player protection point of view, it seems questionable if game developers can integrate unregulated mechanics into games that entice a young, vulnerable gaming population, whose impulse control is not yet fully developed, to make more purchases and determine their daily schedules. In this respect, further research should not only investigate personal and psychological aspects of people who spend large amounts of money in digital games, but should focus more on the role of game design and thus of game developers. It also remains unclear to what extent the extensively researched motives for buying lootboxes in particular differ from the largely unexplored motives for making in-game purchases. In addition, some participants mentioned influencers and streamers who make in-game purchases in their streams, thus encouraging players to do the same. The role of influencers in making in-game purchases is also a research topic worth exploring.

References

Borhart, H. M., & Terrell, H. K. (2014). Perceptions of aggression are colored by gender roles. The Psychological Record, 64(3), 441–445.

Böhnisch, L. (2018). Sozialpädagogik der Lebensalter. Eine Einführung. Weinheim, München: Beltz Juventa.

Close, J., & Lloyd, J. (2020). Lifting the Lid on Loot-Boxes. Chance-Based Purchases in Video Games and the Convergence of Gaming and Gambling. Gamble Aware.

https://www.begambleaware.org/sites/default/files/2021-03/Gaming_and_Gambling_Report_Final.pdf

Der Standard (2020). Söhne von Ex-NBA-Star verprassten 15.000 Euro bei "Fortnite". https://www. derstandard.at/story/2000116740207/soehne-von-ex-nba-starverprassten-15-000-euro-bei (23.09.2021).

Drummond A., & Sauer, J. (2018). Video game loot boxes are psychologically akin to gambling. Nature Human Behavior, 2, 530-532.

Fiedler, I., Lennart, A., & Steinmetz, F. (2019). Die Konvergenz von Gaming und Gambling. Eine angebotsseitige Marktanalyse mit rechtspolitischen Empfehlungen. Wiesbaden: Springer.

Forsa (2019). Geld für Games - wenn Computerspiel zum Glücksspiel wird. Ergebnisse einer repräsentativen Befragung von Kindern und Jugendlichen im Alter von 12 bis 17 Jahren für die DAK-Gesundheit. https://www.dak.de/dak/ download/computerspielsucht2103404.pdf (19.09.2021).

Gach, E. (2017). Meet The 19-Year-Old Who Spent Over $17,000 On Microtransactions. https://www. kotaku.com.au/2017/11/meet-the-19-year-old-who-spent-over17000-on-microtransactions/

Gametrack (2019). Europe: In-Game Spending Study. https://www.isfe.eu/wpcontent/uploads/2019/12/ GameTrack-In-Game-Spending-2019.pdf (20.09.2021)

Holodynski, M. & Oerter, R. (2002). Motivation, Emotion und Handlungssteuerung. In R. Oerter & L. Montada (Hrsg.), Entwicklungspsychologie (S. 551-589). Beltz.

Koubek, J. (2020). Monetarisierung von Computerspielen. Baden-Baden: Nomos.

Kuckartz, U. (2014). Qualitative Inhaltsanalyse. Methoden, Praxis, Computerunterstützung. Weinheim, Basel: Beltz Juventa.

Lauer, N. (2011). Das Paarinterview als Erhebungsinstrument in der sozialpädagogischen (Familien-) Forschung. In G. Oelerich, & H. Otto (Hrsg.), Empirische Forschung und Soziale Arbeit. Ein Studienbuch (293 – 301). Wiesbaden: VS Verlag für Sozialwissenschaften.

Leaper, C., & Friedman, C. K. (2007). Socialization of gender. In J. E. Grusec, & P. D. Hastings (Eds.), Handbook of socialization: Theory and research (pp. 561-587). New York: Guilford.

Lelonek-Kuleta, B., Bartczuk, R., & Wiechetek, M. (2021). Pay for play–behavioural patterns of pay-to-win gaming. Computers in Human Behavior, 115, 1-10. doi: 10.1016/j.chb.2020.106592

Lloyd, J, Nicklin, L., Spicer, S., Fullwood, C., Uther, M., Hinton, S., Parke, J., Lloyd, H., & Close, J. (2021). Development and Validation of the RAFFLE. A Measure of Reasons and Facilitators for Loot Box Engagement. Journal of Clinical Medicine, 10. Doi: 10.3390/jcm10245949

Hamari, J., Alha, K., Järvelä, S., Kivikangas, M., Koivisto, J., & Paavilainen, J. (2017). Why do players buy in-game content? An empirical study on concrete purchase motivations. Computers in Human Behavior, 68, 538- 546. doi: 10.1016/j.chb.2016.11.045

Magruder, D. (2022). A Conservative Metric of Power creep. Games and Culture, 1-31. DOI: 10.1177/15554120211050812

Marder, B., Gattig, D., Collins, E., Pitt, L., Kietzmann, J., & Erz, A. (2019). The Avatar´s new clothes. Understanding why players purchase non-functional items in free-to-play games. Computers in Human Behavior, 91, 72 – 83. Doi: 10.1016/j.chb.2018.09.006

MPFS - Medienpädagogischer Forschungsverbund Südwest (2019). JIM-Studie 2019. Jugend, Information, Medien. Basisuntersuchung zum Medienumgang 12- bis 19- Jähriger. https://www.mpfs.de/fileadmin/files/Studien/ JIM/2019/JIM_2019.pdf

Roberts, D., & David, M. (2019). The Social Media Party: Fear of Missing Out (FoMO), Social Media Intensity, Connection, and Well-Being. International Journal of Human– Computer Interaction, 36(4),386 – 392. doi: 10.1080/10447318.2019.1646517.

RSPH (2019). Skins in the Game. A high-stakes relationship between gambling and young people´s health and wellbeing? https://www.rsph.org.uk/static/uploaded/be3b9ba8-ea4d-403c-a1cee2ec75dcefe7.pdf (19.09.2021)

Parent Zone (2019). The Rip-Off Games. How the new business model of online gaming exploits children. Online unter: https://parentzone.org.uk/system/files/attachments/The%20Ripoff%20Games%20-%20Parent%20Zone%20report.pdf

Schell, J. (2015). The Art Of Game Design. A Book Of Lenses. CRC Press/Taylor and Francis

Steinmetz, F., Fiedler, I., von Meduna, M. & Ante, L. (2021). Pay-to-Win Gaming and its Interrelation with Gambling: Findings from a Representative Population Sample. Gambling Studies. doi: 10.1007/s10899-021-10042-1

Swink, S. (2009). Game Feel. A Game Designer´s Guide To Virtual Sensation. Amsterdam, Burlington: Elsevier

Thubron, R. (2016). Teenager spends almost $8,000 on microtransactions without father's knowledge. https://www.techspot.com/news/63454-teenager-spends-almost8000-microtransactions-without-father-knowledge.html (23.09.2021).

von Meduna, M., Steinmetz, F., Ante, L., Reynolds, J., & Fiedler, I. (2020). Loot Boxes Are Gambling-Like Elements in Video Games with Harmful Potential. Results from a Large-Scale Population Survey. Technology in Society, 63, 1-12. doi: 10.1016/j.techsoc.2020.101395

Wardle, H. (2019). The Same or Different? Convergence of Skin Gambling and Other Gambling Among Children. Journal of Gambling Studies, 35(4), 1109 – 1125. doi: 10.1007/s10899-019-09840-5.

Wijman, T. (2018). Mobile Revenues Account for More Than 50% of the Global Games Market as It Reaches $137.9 Billion in 2018. https://newzoo.com/insights/articles/global-games-market-reaches-137-9-billion-in-2018- mobile-games-take-half/

Zagal, J., Björk, S., & Lewis, C. (2019). Dark Patterns in the Design of Games. Society of the Science of Digital Games (Hrsg). Foundations of Digital Games in 2013. http://www.diva-portal.org/smash/get/diva2:1043332/FULLTEXT01

Zendle, D., & Cairns, P. (2018). Video game loot boxes are linked to problem. Results of a large-scale survey. PLOS ONE, 13(11). doi: https://doi.org/10.1371/journal.pone.0214167

Zendle, D., Meyer, R. & Over, H. (2019). Adolescents and loot boxes: links with problem gambling and motivations for purchase. Royal Society Open Science, 6. doi:c10.1098/rsos.190049

THE MAGIC OF GAMES FOR LEARNING

Sonja Gabriel

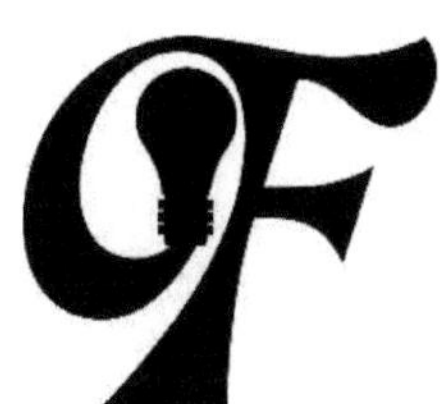airy tales have a long tradition and probably developed along with mankind. Apart from the well-known classic fairy tales of Brothers Grimm, there are also modern fairy tales as well as new multimedia productions of fairy tales leaving the genre of books and being adapted for movies, drama, or videogames. Even if a story is not based on an actual fairy tale, quite often motifs or characters can be found in modern versions. When talking about the genre of fairy tales, there are certain elements that keep occurring, like a certain structure (going on a quest, fighting the evil or developing into a powerful person, there is nearly always a happy ending) or stereotypical characters (the heroes and the villains, the helpers, the magical creatures). Finally, a common characteristic of most fairy tales is that they want to teach a moral lesson. In formal education, these stories have been used in different ways – of course for teaching children how (not) to behave but also for creative writing, foreign language teaching or mathematics fairy tales are used. As digital games are also used for learning and teaching, the step towards using fairy tales in educational games seems to be a small one. However, there are huge differences between the way fairy tale elements are used in educational games. The contribution will discuss some examples and show that some learning games use fairy tale elements only to make the game more appealing to the players, others integrate the elements in their game-designs and in some cases the learning game might become a fairy tale itself.

Keywords: games for learning, fairy tales, serious games, education, fantasy

Introduction

The history of fairy tales reaches back quite a long time although we do not know when and where exactly the first fairy tales were told. As Zipes (2012) suggests, people might have even told each other stories before speech was developed – using sign language. Moreover, fairy tales can be found in every human culture (White, 2017). Ever since, these narrations involving fantastic creatures, magic and wonders have been important to mankind. Although the term fairy tale was only coined in the late 17th century as a translation from French, such oral and written narratives have been around in every culture and at any point of time. As per Greenhill & Matrix (2011) the characteristics of classic fairy tales (folk-tales) include the use of human and nonhuman protagonists. Although the characters of the stories differ from culture to culture, they usually include magic and the belief in the supernatural. Another characteristic is that fairy tales usually cannot be traced back to an original version:

> "Each traditional fairy tale telling forms a copy for which there is no original. Every version offers a snapshot - a view of that story in time and space that refers to its sources and predecessors - but fidelity to an original is profoundly beside the point." (Greenhill & Matrix, 2011, p. 10)

Fairy tales have always included moral messages and have been used as way of transferring knowledge and models for behavior throughout the centuries. Although there are different sub-categories for fairy tales to be found in the literature, it is hard to tell them apart because they share lots of elements and motifs (Drews, 2017). Zipes (1979) lists characteristics of folklore vs. literary fairy tales but admits that the lines are blurry, and the distinction might in some cases really hard to find.

Although fairy tales are often linked to titles like *Little Red Riding Hood, Cinderella, Jack and the Beanstalk,* there are modern fairy tales as well. The most popular one of the last decades is the *Harry Potter* narration by *J. K. Rowling* which can be regarded as a modern version of fairy tales. Havirova (2005) points out that the hero's lack of something and the circular structure as well as the use of magic and magical creatures, the opposition of good and evil and the use of magical objects are typical elements that quite often can be found in fairy tales as well.

Elements of Fairy Tales and Fantasy Stories

Fairy tales differ depending on the culture in which they were originate. However, there are some elements that can be considered as typical features of this kind of narrative. When having a look especially at traditional fairy tales from Europe, the following elements can be found[1]:

Stereotypical characters

Many fairy tales use a hero or heroine who is innocent, honest, humble, believes in magic and miracles and is sometimes even naïve (for example Snow White who believes the old woman offering her an apple). Opposed to these good characters are the villainous ones. Quite often they are powerful, hungry for power and wealth and able to either do magic or use magical objects or creatures with which to fight, control, exploit or destroy others. They even often trick others by pretending to be a good person (like Snow White's stepmother who lured her father into marrying her or the wolf in Little Red Riding Hood pretending to care for the girl's grandmother). And finally, there is one or more friend/s helping the hero or heroine. These friends are usually magical or mysterious creatures or characters (like a fairy or talking animals) and help by giving gifts (often magical ones). Quite often, fairy tales use opposites when introducing the main characters – there are rich kings and queens and poor men and women, there are the beautiful and the ugly ones, the ones that work hard and the others that are lazy and so on. The characters often do not have names but are referred to by their jobs (the miller), their status (the princess, the queen) or their role/character/appearance (the witch, the dwarf, the giant).

---

[1] In this contribution, only some typical elements will be described in detail. Apart from the ones mentioned here, there are many more like the use of magic numbers (three and seven), fixed phrases (for example: Once upon a time) or the importance of colors (golden hair, golden objects).

"The typical character of the European fairy-tale is a poor, brave and resourceful hero or heroine, who come into wealth and well-being after many risky trials." (Andersone, 2009, p. 112)

Especially, when looking at classic fairy tales (like for example those of Brothers Grimm), the good characters start out at being quite young, sometimes poor and/or unhappy. At the end of the fairy tale their fate has changed completely, and they have found happiness, love, wealth and power.

Structure of the story

Basically, the structure of a fairy tale is rather predictive: In the beginning of the story, the setting and the hero/heroine are described. There is a situation present that leads to a problem or conflict and there are obstacles the main character has to overcome (there might be three quests or riddles to solve). The hero/heroine might have to go on a journey – either travelling places or become stronger and/or wiser to resolve the conflict. As (Zipes, 1979) puts it "[...] each narrative begins with a seemingly hopeless situation and that the narrative perspective is sympathetic to the exploited protagonist of the tale." (Zipes, 1979, p. 9) Many fairy tales provide a happy ending, even if the details of the story might change (according to the oral or written version looked at) (Brewer, 2006). Although there are so many different fairy tales around, the structure can basically always be reduced to some elements:

"Therefore, the focus of fairy tales, whether oral, written, or cinematic, has always been on finding magical instruments, extraordinary technologies, or powerful people and animals that will enable protagonists to transform themselves along with their environment, making it more suitable for living in peace and contentment. (Zipes, 2012, p. 2)"

Teaching a moral lesson

As Lewin (2020) states, folk stories got a didactic intent only from the middle of the 18th century on as the genre of children's literature was emerging. Therefore, fairy tales should warn of dangers (for example: Don't take anything from strangers! Don't walk alone into the forest!) and show children that virtue is rewarded, and bad behaviour punished.

> "Ultimately, these punishments that lead to a clear moral of the tale show the destructive outcomes of disobedience, selfishness, laziness, and the importance of valuing the structure of the family above the needs of the individual. In essence, fairy tales usually show that good is rewarded, whereas villains are almost always punished." (Herrero Ruiz, 2017, p. 120)

Herrero Ruiz (2017) shows in her work that many metaphors that are essential in fairy tales are still used in linguistic expressions in everyday language. For example, beauty and health are considered being important for wealth, whereas immoral characters are often described as ugly. Moreover, the pairs good vs. evil are often referred to as light vs. darkness, white vs. black, clean vs. dirty.

> ""Mother Holle" is a story in which the beautiful stepdaughter in Mother Holle's house is industrious in the house and helps the overdone bread just before getting burnt and the over-burdened apple tree; whereas the ugly, evil daughter is characterised by a selfish lack of charity towards the bread and the tree, besides being lazy at home. The beautiful girl is rewarded by a shower of gold which sticks to her, making her more beautiful, and the ugly one is punished by a shower of pitch that sticks to her till the end of her life. In this tale, both girls were already characterised at the beginning by their external aspects, but the morality metaphor is further applied with the punishments. In fact, as pitch is black and gold is bright, we have the MORALITY IS LIGHT metaphor (which may be found in linguistic expression such as *His actions were obscure, She has a dark side,* etc.). Moreover, the good girl is rewarded via the MORALITY IS WEALTH metaphor, with gold being the reward." (Herrero Ruiz, 2017, p. 122)

It is especially this kind of moralizing that has been criticized about fairy tales. As Lester (2007) points out children are confronted with a world in which dominantly white heterosexual people act, pretending that the ultimate goal in life is the happily ever after.

Fairy Tales and Their Elements in Popular Media

Since the evolution of television, fairy tales moved to this new medium as well. Children and adults no longer depended on reading books or being told stories about fairies, giants, dragons and brave knights, but can watch the characters moving on the screen. On the one hand, classic fairy tales (like the ones from Brothers Grimm) were adapted for TV being either quite close to the original or changing them to modern times, putting them in different settings or clothes. As Short) (2015) claims, many of the current films in cinema or TV take their narratives, motifs and plot features from fairy tales. On the other hand, in many films, series or shows elements of fairy tales are used. By using the example of the fairy tale *Hansel and Gretel,* (Greenhill, 2014) shows several television shows that base on the original fairy tale. Although certain details have been changed, the parallels are striking:

> "No longer do children need fear cannibalistic witches in gingerbread houses; they now must deal with pedophiles, serial killers, and child abductors. Like their fairy-tale counterparts, they often show considerable pluck and capability [...]" (Greenhill, 2014, p. 66)

Many of the films by *Disney* are based on classic fairy tales – the older ones stick quite close to the originals (like for example *Snow White and the Seven Dwarfs* (1937), *Cinderella* (1950) or *Sleeping Beauty* (1959)). Disney does not only rely on fairy tales well known in Western Europe like the ones by *Brothers Grimm* or *Hans Christian Andersen,* but also takes account on Chinese folktales (*Mulan,* 1998) or the Arabic world (*Aladdin,* 1992). Some of the modern films are interpretations of the original fairy tales by adding certain characters or plots (Tangled (2010) or Frozen (2013)). Greenhill & Matrix) 2011) list many films that borrow motifs, characters and stories from fairy tales, not only for children's films but especially for adults[2].

---

[2] In their earliest versions many of the classic fairy tales we now regard as children's literature were addressed at adults containing sex and violence. It was especially for the Western European area that Brothers Grimm collected fairy tales and wrote them down in a style that was more appropriate for children.

"Nonetheless, we can often recognise a 'Cinderella' or 'Bluebeard' plot, partly because these are some of the earliest stories we hear, but also because we have grown accustomed to seeing fairy tale motifs redeployed in popular culture. Not only are they regularly referenced in music, advertisements and literary rewrites, they have served as the inspiration for a clutch of contemporary TV series such as Grimm (NBC, 2011–), Once Upon a Time (ABC, 2011–), Sleepy Hollow (Fox, 2013–) and Beauty and the Beast (CW, 2012–) – many of which rely on our familiarity with conventional tropes, as well as occasionally testing underlying assumptions." (Short, 2015, p. 2)

Of course, there are also fairy tale elements in videogames. Some games are – like shown before with films – based entirely or partly on fairy tales, others just use some elements. As Gabelica (2017) points out it is important to distinguish between videogames which use fairy tales only paratextual (for example by using motifs and themes), those relying on a specific fairy tale and those "that build a new narrative but according to fairy tale conventions" (p. 267). One characteristic that videogames in general quite often share with fairy tales is the notion of good vs. evil. Characters often fulfil – in both genres – a certain function and can be divided in seven broad character types which are hero, dispatcher, helper, donor, villain, false hero, princess (Gabelica, 2017). Robertsen (2012) shows some more similarities between videogames and fairy tales by referring to Holbek (1989) and stating:

"These six traits are easily applied to the realm of the video game: highly skilled specialists are responsible for the narrative design and code; video games have been met with mixed reception by critics unsure of their aesthetic value; they are often marketed to adults (especially the more violent titles); they are usually targeted specifically to male or female players (although the stereotype that the majority of gamers are male has thankfully begun to erode); the games strive to create an in-world level of veracity to sustain the player's suspension of disbelief; and, in many cases, the protagonist of the game can be understood as an avatar of the player, so that the gamer's "I" becomes directly identifiable with the character." (Robertsen, 2012, p. 1)

Although there are not so many videogames that are a fairy tale adaptation (compared to films where often dozens different versions of the same fairy tale can be found – like for example Cinderella or Little Red Riding Hood), there are many videogames that draw upon elements of fairy tales (Antoniazzi, 2013).

Fairy Tales and Education

Apart from teaching children moral lessons, fairy tales have played an important role in formal education for quite some time. Thorne-Thomsen (1903) discussed the significance of good stories for children already at the beginning of the 20th century. The author does not see the moral of fairy tales as useful for education when she writes "It is not for literature to assume the power to teach moral laws." (Thorne-Thomsen, 1903, p. 164) The strength of fairy tales is more seen in assisting in teaching science, inspire children or showing them different life phases. As children look for role-models and take them often from media, fairy tale characters can inspire them and offer orientation for their own lives (Götz, 2019).

Especially in the foreign language classroom, fairy tales have found a fixed place in teaching: beginners as learners are mostly familiar with the story, the language used is quite simple and the introduction of vocabulary in a communicative context is easy (Bertrand, 2022; Lee, 2003). Andersone (2009) discusses in her work the importance of fairy tales for mathematics as there are often measures and their measurements, numbers, quantities, directions, sequences, geometrical places, and so on are included. Thus, children can acquire

> "mathematical notions about surrounding world, its variety and glory. Fairy-tales not only develop children's imagination but also develop their skills to use mathematical connections and basic notions in a simple understandable language in primary and preschools matehematics education, at the same time putting stress on these connections and so paving the way to further serious acquisition of the systemic course of mathematics." (Andersone, 2009, p. 117)

Apart from language learning and mathematics, there are also approaches to use fairy tales for example for teaching geography (Scoffham & Jewson, 1993), science (Starfish Education, 2022), creative writing (Taufiq, 2021) or culture (Walter, 2011).

Fairy Tale and Fantasy Elements in Learning Games

As has already been shown, fairy tales and education / teaching can be combined well. Therefore, it is not surprising that also learning games use fairy tales or fairy tale elements.

Geometric Forms as Characters: Dragonbox Elements Geometry Proofs

Dragonbox Elements Geometry Proofs (MobyGames, 2014) is a mathematics learning game based on the work *Elements* by Euclid, a Greek mathematician. These books are seen as foundation of geometry and being referred to for more than 23 centuries. Targeted at players at the age 9 upwards, Dragonbox Elements Geometry Proofs teaches the most important of Euclid's axioms by exploration. Instead of presenting the axioms and explaining how they work, the game wants learners to discover them themselves (We Want to Know, 2022).

The story behind the game reminds on a fairy tale: The player has to fight an evil dragon called Osgard. The shapes (triangles, circles, quadrilaterals) need to be rescued and will then fight with the player against the dragon. The levels are organized in seven chapters and in each chapter the player gets new power (which basically are new mathematical rules: for example, that the interior angles of a triangle always total 180° or that an equilateral triangle has three equal sides). Each figure in the game symbolizes a geometric form and they all look like little fantasy warriors.

So apart from the narration that puts the player in a fairy tale like environment, the players themselves can (and need to) perform magic to play the game. They need to solve different puzzles which are similar to being on a quest (like many heroines and heroes in fairy tales). The longer the journey of the player takes (the more puzzles she/he has solved), the more experience is gathered which means the power of magic grows. *Dragonbox Elements Geometry Proofs* includes a lot of important mathematical theories but presents them in a way that learners feel more like the protagonists of an adventure fairy tale. This game combines fairy tale elements with learning in a motivating way to engage learners. Learning by doing (Dewey, 1938) has been seen as a good way of learning in various contexts for many years. This positive view of the game is also confirmed in a study by Cates (2018).

On a magic journey through Great Britain: Wizadora

Wizadora (Planet Schule, 2019) has especially been developed for pupils who have only recently began to learn English (primary school, but also secondary school) and teaches vocabulary, basic sentence structures as well as facts about Great Britain. Players are students at a magic school (which is the starting point for all activities, songs, and videos). The spell book is an interactive vocabulary book with pictures including all the words the learners have already come across in the game. The setting of the game– apart from the magic school – resembles modern Great Britain but there are some non-playable fairy tale characters: The teacher, *Wizadora,* is a magician, her assistant Phoebe is a telephone, the butler is a coat hanger and there are other characters like talking socks, a very old talking fish as well as a scarecrow living in the garden. Apart from the magic creatures, there are the two neighbor children Tom and Katie who do not have any magic power but are the ones that go on adventures. The player is not represented by any avatar but can take (limited) decisions for Tom and Katie.

Within the single exercises the player sometimes sees *Wizadora* as a teacher (explaining an exercise for example) or a magic wand (for example when baking a cake to put the cake magically into the oven or take it out again). Decision taking for the player is very limited and the player cannot do any magic. Mini-games are only accessible when all the language exercises have been completed.

To sum up, *Wizadora* only uses some elements of fairy tales (like magic objects or magic characters) but only to set the scene and to make learning more engaging for players. All the exercises present learning content without any possibility to skip one or to take meaningful decisions within the game. Exercises or videos that are used within the game do not support the narrative of being a pupil at a magic school which results in learners not becoming fully immersed in the story. Magic here is just the sugar coating that shall loosely connect various language exercises and videos about Great Britain. Compared to *Dragonbox Elements*, this game is very teacher centered and refers to magic and fairy tales only very superficially.

Helping others with magic: The Language Magician

The Language Magician (Ovos, 2018) is not a learning game per se but rather a game for assessing pupils' language skills. Feedback and assessment are regarded as very important for the learning process – no matter which skill or age we are talking about (The Teachers Toolbox, 2012). However, for teachers it is often difficult to get information about their pupils' learning processes and their current skills. This is where The Language Magician wants to help by providing a game that sends learners on an adventure where they have to solve puzzles (involving the target language) without the feeling that they are tested about their language competence.

The description of the story out of the handbook for the game already reads like a fairy tale:

> "The pupils in your class play the game as individuals; each one takes on the role of a young magician, living on a farm and developing magical skills; at the start of the game they choose the appearance of their avatar. With lots of animal friends on the farm, life is good, until, one day an evil magician living nearby in a dark tower decides that he needs company and kidnaps the animals. The young magician now has to try and get them back by overcoming the challenges of the dark tower. The main story is told on screen in the language of schooling/ mother tongue which you select (English, German, Italian or Spanish); only the language challenges are in the foreign language. As the evil magician has cast his spells in a different

language to imprison the animals, the player must use language skills to overcome them. The player is just a young magician with a lot to learn, but everybody knows that the evil magician's power is concentrated in his hat. " (Goethe-Institut London, 2018, p. 7)

Many of the elements in this game are taken from fairy tales: There is the heroine/hero who sets out on an adventure to rescue those who are helpless (the animals) because of an evil power (Winivil, the evil magician who lives in a magic tower) that threatens the peaceful life. Apart from magic objects and magic creatures, the players themselves use magic to free the animals by casting spells (certain movements with their wands) which gives them the illusion of being a young magician.

All the challenges of the game (which include listening, reading, and writing) are embedded in the game. One of the assessment game design principles the project team agreed upon was that the game should be fun for the learners (Schlueter, 2016) and this can only be done if players are fully immersed in the game and the narration. Compared to *Wizadora*, *The Language Magician* succeeds in keeping the learners in the fairy tale.

Fight against monster diseases - Outbreak Squad

Outbreak Squad (Innovative Media Research & Extension, 2019) deals with the topic of health outbreaks and how to fight them from the point of view of food safety. The game was designed for learners in grade five and above. The game is based on the fight of the good (the Squad) versus the evil (diseases). The Squad consists of four different characters: The Enforcer who makes sure that producers, shops and restaurants stick to food safety laws, the Researcher who tries to find new and effective ways of preventing outbreaks as well as treatments, the Educator who spread knowledge about prevention, and finally, the Healthcare Professional who takes care of people suffering from the consequences of an outbreak. These characters stand for different approaches that can be taken when there is a food disease outbreak and thus come with a unique set of superpowers. The villains consist of six different diseases based on actual outbreaks of food diseases. The aim of the game is to show that only a combination of different superpowers i.e. different approaches is successful when it comes to tackle such diseases. Therefore, players need to find a strategy which differs depending on which villain needs to be fought.

> "Throughout the game, players must also evaluate their actions against policy events that could occur during an outbreak, such as a lack of faith in treatment options or a flood of emergency funding. A key learning goal of the game is to recognize that some policy decisions bolster (or impair) action in an outbreak." (Newbury, 2020, p. 4)

When comparing the game to a fairy tale, the fight good vs. evil is put in the foreground. This time, there are four helpers with magical power to defeat the villains. The players themselves do not have any superpower but they need to find a strategy which power is most successful in a fight – by having 10 points which can be used for different activities. After having decided on a strategy each superhero steps forward and does their magic. Then the disease attacks. The characters are designed in a modern way but still remind of magicians and fairies, partly using crystal balls or elixirs to do their magic. Some of the figures (especially the Enforcer) resemble more a character from science fiction – wearing a futuristic glove and helmet and sitting in a futuristic wheelchair.

The use of magic here might also be counterproductive as players might think that tackling a disease outbreak is just about casting spells. Like in some other games, magic and fairy tale elements here do not support the topic of the game but cater for a superficial layer that does not really match the topic. Fancy characters that can perform magic seem to be used to make the game more enjoyable but they do not help to engage players more as there is no change in between rounds.

A Fairy Tale of its own: Epistory Typing Chronicles

The game *Epistory Typing Chronicles* (Fishing Cactus, 2016) immerses the player into a fantasy world made of origami objects. The protagonist is a girl who is an author's muse riding on a giant three-tailed fox and fighting enemies that want to destroy the world. This fighting is done by typing words that appear above the heads of the attacking insects. If you are not fast enough at typing, you stand no chance to advance in the game. However, the game adapts itself to the skills of the player – if you type faster, the words will get more difficult.

Although this game does neither refer to a specific fairy tale nor use popular story motifs, it includes various elements of a fairy tale. For instance, it creates an atmosphere that reminds instantly on a fairy tale: the beautiful country is threatened with destruction by an evil power and only the heroine can stop this. By progressing in the game, the player gets to know more of the story which is narrated in the style of fairy tales using expressions that remind on old folk tales.. The words to be typed always relate to the item on which the player is working on. There are some puzzles integrated as well reminding on the quests protagonists of fairy tales often have to manage. The quests in videogames, as (Gabelica, 2017) puts it, often lead to emancipation of the player and help her/him overcome problems or inner conflicts. By getting to know more about the protagonist of the game, the player experiences a journey telling about somebody experiencing writer's block. From the character's point of view of fairy tales, the player is more of the helper than the heroine herself. However, there is a kind of magic plot twist at the end.

> "Like any good adventure, Epistory's journey is not just seeing about strange lands or surviving unexpected perils. It is about character, identity, and discovery. For the greatest adventures lie within, rather than without." (VirginRedemption, 2016, p. 11)

To sum up, *Epistory* relies on fairy tales in certain elements: There is magic to be performed by the player, a narrator tells a story which is placed in a fantastic island. The whole game is one big fairy tale of its own.

Conclusion

As the examples discussed in this paper show, fairy tale elements are quite frequently used in games for learning. The reason might be that fairy tales have been around us for a long time and children still grow up with fairy tales and are usually fascinated by them. Thus, emotions are created, the contents presented can be linked to experiences with fairy tales which might make remembering easier for learners. Moreover, fairy tales left oral and written stories a long time ago and conquered other media like film, and videogames. Finally, fairy tales have already been used in formal (and informal) education, especially for younger children.

The videogames discussed show different approaches of how fairy tale elements can be used in educational games. There are examples where characters or certain elements are used to make the game more enjoyable, but the elements do not combine well with the topic the game is about. This is the case with *Wizadora* and *Outbreak Squad* – in both games there are no real connections between the tasks players have to do and the fairy tale elements which means immersion and remembering learning content might be harder for learners. When it comes to learning, however, the game design should match the teaching objective in order not to become chocolate-covered broccoli (Behnke, 2018). Games like *Dragonbox Elements Geometry Proofs* and *The Language Magician* integrate the fairy tale elements in their game design. Tasks given within the game cannot be seen without the story being told, the objective of the game and the teaching objective are well put together in the game design so that the game is kind of an interactive fairy tale that supports learning or assessment. Finally, there is *Epistory Typing Chronicles* which enables the players to create their own fairy tale while playing (and while improving typing skills).

In conclusion, fairy tale elements are important to many learning games but not all of them integrate the elements the same way. As Rathle (2019) puts it, fairy tales can be easily adapted and they are versatile. However, especially when the game is designed to teach its players – especially in the education sector – it is really important not only to take some elements of fairy tales and mix them together with learning content but to think carefully about the role the fairy tale elements can help learners to understand and finally learn. An educational game using fairy tale motifs, figures or stories will only be successful when the game can enchant players – like fairy tales have been able to for many generations. The learning content has to be married to the fairy tale and the elements of the game design (no matter if talking about mechanic, narrative or aesthetics) need to form a coherent game system with the purpose of the game. As Mitgutsch & Alvarada (2012) put it: "[...] the purpose of the game needs to be coherently reflected throughout the formal conceptual design of the game, otherwise the system is conflicting and not cohesive" (p. 127)

References

Andersone, R. (2009). Through Fairy-Tales to Math in the Lessons. Acta Didactica Napocensia, 2(2), 111-118.

Antoniazzi, A. (2013). Storytelling and Videogames. An interdisciplinary approach to interactive multimedia models for children. Studi Sulla Formazione(1), 67–76.

Behnke, D. (2018). Chocolate-Covered Broccoli - Wenn Lerninhalte und Spielelemente NICHT zusammenpassen - digital | spielend – lernen. Retrieved from https://digital-spielend-lernen.de/chocolate-covered-broccoli-wenn-lerninhalte-und-spielelemente-nicht-zusammenpassen

Bertrand, J. (2022, April 7). Fairy Tales. British Council. Retrieved from https://www.teachingenglish.org.uk/article/fairy-tales

Brewer, D. (2006). The Interpretation of Fairy Tales. In H. R. E. Davidson & A. Chaudhri (Eds.), A companion to the fairy tale (pp. 15–37). Brewer.

Cates, M. (2018). The Effect of Using Dragonbox on the Mathematics Teaching Efficacy of Preservice Middle Grade Teacher [Dissertation]. Georgia State University.

Dewey, J. (1938). Experience and education (First free press edition 2015). The Kappa Delta Pi Lecture Series. Free Press; Simon & Schuster Inc.

Drews, I. (2017). Disney als heimlicher Erzieher [, (:none)]. DataCite.

Fishing Cactus. (2016). Epistory - Typing Chronicles [Computer software].

Gabelica, M. (2017). Videogames - New Forms of Fairy Tale? In P. Drummond (Ed.), The London Film & Media Reader 5: Questions of Cultural Value (pp. 265–275). The London Symposium.

Goethe-Institut London (Ed.). (2018). Manual for THE LANGUAGE MAGICIAN. Retrieved from https://www.thelanguagemagician.net/de/ressourcen/

Götz, M. (2019). Die Medienheld_innen der Kindheit. TV-Figuren und ihre Rolle in der Identitätsarbeit. Communicatio Socialis, 52(3), 317–328. https://doi.org/10.5771/0010-3497-2019-3-317

Greenhill, P. (2014). Channeling Wonder: Fairy Tales on Television. Series in Fairy-Tale Studies. Wayne State University Press. Retrieved from https://ebookcentral.proquest.com/lib/kxp/detail.action?docID=3446595

Greenhill, P., & Matrix, S. E. (Eds.). (2011). Fairy tale films: Visions of ambiguity. Utah State University Press. Retrieved from https://search.ebscohost.com/login.aspx?direct=true&scope=site&db=nlebk&db=nlabk&AN=344719

Havirova, T. (2005). Fairy tale elements in JRR Tolkien's The Lord of the Rings and JK Rowling's Harry Potter stories [Dissertation, Masary University, Brno]. RIS. Retrieved from https://is.muni.cz/th/74471/ff_b/b.a.pdf

Herrero Ruiz, J. (2017). AT THE CROSSROADS BETWEEN LITERATURE, CULTURE, LINGUISTICS, AND COGNITION: PUNISHMENT AND MORAL METAPHORS IN FAIRY TALES. ODISEA. Revista De Estudios Ingleses. Advance online publication. https://doi.org/10.25115/odisea.v0i9.151

Holbek, B. (1989). The Language of Fairy Tales. In R. Kvideland (Ed.), Folklore studies in translation. Nordic folklore: Recent studies (pp. 40–62). Indiana Univ. Press.

Innovative Media Research & Extension. (2019). Outbreak Squad [Computer software].

Lee, C. (2003). The uses of enchantment: Fairy tales as instructional materials to facilitate primary English language education. Journal of National Taipei Teachers College, 16(1), 29–48. Retrieved from https://academic.ntue.edu.tw/ezfiles/7/1007/img/41/16-1-2.pdf

Lester, N. A. (2007). (Un)Happily Ever After: Fairy Tale Morals, Moralities, and Heterosexism in Children's Texts. Journal of Gay & Lesbian Issues in Education, 4(2), 55–74. https://doi.org/10.1300/J367v04n02_05

Lewin, D. (2020). Between horror and boredom: fairy tales and moral education. Ethics and Education, 15(2), 213–231. https://doi.org/10.1080/17449642.2020.1731107

Mitgutsch, K. & Alvarado N. (2012). Purposeful by design? A serious game design assessment framework. In Proceedings of the International Conference on the Foundations of Digital Games (pp. 121-128). ACM.

MobyGames. (2014). DragonBox: Elements - Geometry Proofs [Computer software].

Newbury, E. M. H. (2020). Exploring the Complexity of Pandemics Through Play. Retrieved from https://www.wilsoncenter.org/blog-post/exploring-complexity-pandemics-through-play

Ovos. (2018). The Language Magician [Computer software].

Planet Schule. (2019). Wizadora [Computer software].

Rathle, S. (2019). Fairy Tales in Video Games: Ancient and Modern Media Together. Retrieved from https://medium.com/@shanerathle/fairy-tales-in-video-games-8fc27e6fa84f

Robertsen, A. (2012). The New Tale: Locating the Fairy Tale in New Media Narrative. Retrieved from https://ojs.library.dal.ca/verso/article/viewfile/515/522

Schlueter, N. (2016). Standards and principles for the design of THE LANGUAGE MAGICIAN tool - The Language Magician. Retrieved from https://www.thelanguagemagician.net/standards-and-principles-for-the-design-of-the-language-magician-tool/

Scoffham, S., & Jewson, T. (1993). Geography through fairy tales. Primary Geographer. Retrieved from https://repository.canterbury.ac.uk/item/8630v/geography-through-fairy-tales

Short, S. (2015). Introduction: Fairy Tale Films, Old Tales with a New Spin. In S. Short (Ed.), Fairy tale and film: Old tales with a new spin (pp. 1–20). Palgrave Macmillan. https://doi.org/10.1057/9781137020178_1

Starfish Education. (2022, April 10). Teaching STEM through Fairy Tales Archives – Starfish Education. Retrieved from https://starfisheducation.com/category/fairy-tales/

Taufiq, W. (2021). The Local Fairy Tales for Teaching Writing. In Advances in Social Science, Education and Humanities Research, Proceedings of the 1st Annual International Conference on Natural and Social Science Education (ICNSSE 2020). Atlantis PressParis, France. https://doi.org/10.2991/assehr.k.210430.054

The Teachers Toolbox. (2012). Professor John Hattie's Table of Effect Sizes - The Teachers Toolbox. Retrieved from https://www.teacherstoolbox.co.uk/effect-sizes/

Thorne-Thomsen, G. (1903). The Educational Value of Fairy-Stories and Myths. The Elementary School Teacher, 4(3), 161–167.

VirginRedemption. (2016). We're not going to tell you Epistory's secret. Retrieved from https://www.moddb.com/games/epistory/news/were-not-going-to-tell-you-epistorys-secret

Walter, C. C. (2011). Teaching Culture through Reading Fairy-Tales. Retrieved from https://ufdc.ufl.edu/UFE0042718/00001

We Want to Know (Ed.). (2022, April 10). Information for Teachers: The math behind DragonBox Elements - explore the elements of geometry. Retrieved from https://dragonbox.com/educators

White, R. S. (2017). Fire in the Dragon and Other Psychoanalytic Essays on Folklore, An Introduction to the Psychology of Fairy Tales and The Uses of Enchantment: The Meaning and Importance of Fairy Tales. Journal of the American Psychoanalytic Association, 65(4), 705–728. https://doi.org/10.1177/0003065117728074

Zipes, J. (1979). Breaking the magic spell: Radical theories of folk and fairy tales [Nachdr.]. Univ. Press of Kentucky.

Zipes, J. (2012). The Irresistible Fairy Tale: The Cultural and Social History of a Genre. Princeton University Press. https://doi.org/10.1515/9781400841820

Magic Circles
in the
GaMes Discourse

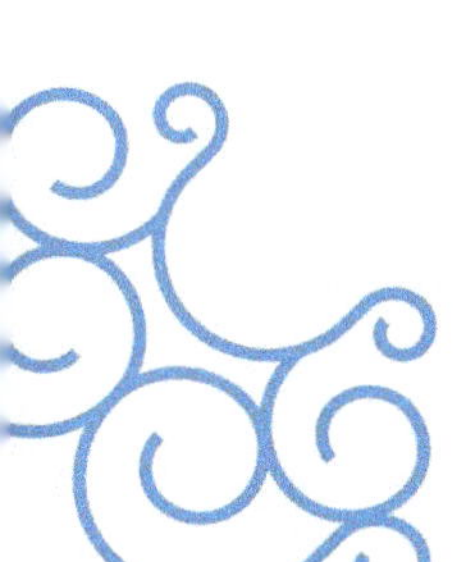

THE MAGIC OF VIDEOGAME ART CURATION: REMEDIATION OF VIDEOGAMES TO PHYSICAL EXHIBITIONS

Alexis Ibarra Ibarra

 ideogame aesthetics have much to do with magic. At times, the experience of gaming can be so intense that the player feels completely immersed in the work, developing strong emotional and cognitive responses. Videogames are complex works that are configured by a highly interdependent network of elements. Videogame aesthetics are equally complex. Here, eight important exhibitions that utilize different curatorial approaches for exhibiting videogames as artworks in physical spaces were analyzed. Two other examples were studied since they are thought-provoking cases of remediation of videogames to physical spaces despite their purpose being for entertainment only. In this paper, some strategies on how to translate the aesthetics, haptics, and significant properties of videogames into a physical art exhibition, as well as how to design an exhibition that allows the audience to comprehensively (re)experience the aesthetics of videogames and (re)create or (re)enact the magic people experience when gaming are analyzed. There are several ways to design a videogame exhibition, but remediation and participatory design seem to be the best ways to approximate a comprehensive display and understanding of Videogame aesthetics. In this paper, only some existing strategies are delineated, and a few others are offered. The curator's imagination should develop innovative ways of transmitting the marvel of gaming as the job of the curator is not only to organize, display and preserve the works but to design a meaningful experience that allows the participants to enjoy the emotions of gaming: The job of the curator is to recreate and create magic.

Keywords: Videogames, Art, Curation, Exhibition, Remediation

The Magic of Videogame Art: An Introduction

Videogame aesthetics have much to do with magic. At times, the experience of gaming can be so intense that the player feels completely immersed in the work, developing strong emotional and cognitive responses. The player's senses are heightened and overstimulated to the point of losing track of time and the perception of the world outside of the game world. Videogame art curation is an exciting field where curators need to use their creativity to recreate that state of engagement with the works.

Videogames are complex creations that are configured by a highly interdependent network of elements. The audiovisual elements are tied to the mechanical aspects, and both are inexorably tangled with the analog systems that allow the players to experience the software. However, without the players' performance, the aesthetics of the game are meaningless, as, just like any other interactive work (Seevinck, 2017, p.6), videogames are unfinished by nature. However, the players do not exist in a vacuum: They are part of heterogeneous socio-cultural contexts that influence their very personal, sensorial, emotional, and cognitive experience of the work, as well as their interpretation of it (Gee, 2016; Goethe, 2019; Niedenthal 2009). Moreover, game creators are also influenced by their own contexts, which tend to be large groups of people in the case of videogames.

All of those elements are part of the aesthetics of the work, so it is extremely challenging to find a way to portray and convey the videogame aesthetics comprehensibly (McDonough et al., 2010, p.14; Sharp, 2015; Swalwell, 2009, p.276). Videogame art curation also entails the difficulty of depicting the entertaining nature of videogames without leaving behind the encouragement for critical thinking. Contrary to digitization, which consists of remediating a physical object into digital media (Wiencek, 2018; Wiencek, 2021), in this paper, the author tries to elucidate how to translate the aesthetics, haptics, and significant properties of videogames into a physical art exhibition, how to design an exhibition that allows the audience to comprehensively (re)experience the aesthetics of videogames, and finally, what strategies can be used to (re)create or (re)enact the magic people experience when gaming. Accordingly, the objectives of this paper are: 1) to analyze the way different Videogame art exhibitions translate the aesthetics, haptics, and significant properties of videogames into physical exhibitions; 2) to analyze different approaches to design exhibitions that allow the audience to comprehensively re(experience) the aesthetics of videogames; 3) to identify and propose strategies to (re)create or (re)enact the magic people experience when gaming. There are several ways to design a videogame exhibition with no fixed formula, but remediation, "the representation of one medium into another," (Bolter & Grusin, 1999, p.45) and participatory design, that seeks the active participation of the audience, (Simon, 2000) seem to be the best way to approximate a comprehensive display and understanding of Videogame aesthetics.

The Enchanting Spells of Videogame Aesthetics

For this paper, a videogame is defined as "a game which we play thanks to an audiovisual apparatus, and which can be based on a story" (Esposito, 2005). Videogames are complex creations that involve a wide variety of elements like audio, visual, and haptic design, narrative and story, gameworld and gameplay, mechanical aspects, analog and digital components, interactivity, participation, experience, immersion, among many others. Covering all these aspects can become a titanic task for a videogame exhibition, and sometimes, it is unnecessary to highlight or show all of them. It is the curator's job to decide which elements are pertinent to the exhibition's topic and identify the *significant properties* of the works, properties that make a videogame "look and feel" like that specific videogame (Swalwell, 2009, p.276). Conveying the cultural context in which the videogame was created, developed, and received is also essential (McDonough et al., 2010, p.14).

Videogame aesthetics are more than the addition of the material elements, the analog, and the digital content; they also involve complex sensorial, emotional, cognitive, psychological, and physiological processes. For Niedenthal (2009), "Game aesthetics refers to the sensory phenomena that the player encounters in the game (visual, aural, haptic, embodied) [...] Where hands, senses, bodies and the tangible qualities of games meet, the aesthetic meaning of games emerges". Therefore, to truly appreciate the aesthetics, it is necessary to interact with the work. Consequently, participatory design and remediation seem to be pertinent and valuable for designing a meaningful, engaging, and even immersive videogame art exhibition.

Magic Lenses and Recipes: Methodology and Tools

This paper consists of an exploratory qualitative analysis of some of the most relevant videogame art exhibitions in the international arena. The eight cases selected were considered of special interest, as they utilize different curatorial approaches for exhibiting videogames as artworks in physical spaces. Additionally, two other examples were studied, since they are thought-provoking cases of remediation of videogames to physical spaces despite their purpose being for entertainment only.

The cases analyzed were:

1. *Into the Pixel: An Art Exhibition into the Art of Video Games* by The Academy of Interactive Arts & Sciences and Entertainment Software Association (USA, 2004).

2. *The Art of Videogames* by The Smithsonian (USA, 2012).

3. *Game Masters: The Exhibition* by the Australian Centre for the Moving Image (Australia, 2012).

4. *Videogames: Design/Play/Disrupt* by Victoria and Albert Museum V&A (UK, 2019).

5. *Virtual Realms: Videogames Transformed* by ArtScience Museum (Singapore, 2021).

6.   *Homo Ludens: Videojuegos para entender el presente* by Caixa Forum (Spain, 2021).

7.   *Game On* & *Game On 2.0* International by Barbican Centre and The Museum of Scotland (UK, ongoing since 2002).

8.   *Computerspielemuseum* (Germany).

The two cases from the entertainment industry analyzed were:

1.   *Final Fantasy XR Ride* by Visual Works, Square Enix, and Universal Studios Japan (Japan, 2018).

2.   *Super Nintendo World* by Nintendo and Universal Studios Japan (Japan, 2020).

For each case, the author identified the topic(s), intention, and organization of the exhibition; the main remediation strategies used, their novelty, and their purpose; the levels of interactivity and participation; the architecture, space, and pathway design; the form of providing and displaying context; the presence of symbols, icons, and elements that belong to the gaming imaginary. The results were organized according to the type of approach: traditional or participatory. In the participatory category, the results were structured according to the curatorial or remediation strategies identified in the exhibitions. In the discussion, additional strategies and information are offered by the author.

The primary sources utilized were information and data regarding each example and were obtained from online documentation by the responsible institution and published interviews with institutional representatives. The secondary sources used were academic papers, press releases, wikis, reviews, and blogs that included photographs and videos.

Results

The topics, intentions, and organization of the analyzed exhibitions were various, which shows the versatility of curators to approach the medium and the artworks. However, a popular way of organizing works was through a timeline, which could be considered a more traditional approach to the objects and subjects. It is noteworthy that symbols and icons of the videogaming imaginary are present in almost every exhibition. The most utilized symbols were coins, and the allegories were arcade machines. The most alluded eras were the 80s and the cyberfuture.

Old Tricks: Traditional Approaches

Timeline organization of the works was a popular way of organizing and displaying the works. *The Art of Videogames* (2012), *Game On* (ongoing since 2002), and the *Computerspielemuseum* utilized that structure. Moreover, it is not a surprise that two of the oldest cases analyzed, *Into the Pixel: An Art Exhibition into the Art of Video Games* (2004) and *The Art of Videogames* (2012), were the ones that followed the most traditional ways of curating exhibitions. However, even if their strategies fall into minimal levels of interactivity and participation, and their content does not encompass the totality of the aesthetics of videogames, the novelty of presenting videogames as art may have been more than enough to spark some feeling of magic in the audience back then.

Into the Pixel, now an annual videogame art exhibition, utilized and still utilizes traditional ways of curation and approaching videogames as artworks, being this exhibit the one with the lowest level of interactivity of the whole set of cases. Although the mere fact of exhibiting videogames as artworks could already be considered heterodox, the exhibition does not seem to encourage participation beyond the act of contemplation. The works displayed consist of concept art illustrations and sculptures in the latest editions. The illustrations are over walls, following a straightforward path. While concept art and illustrations are a substantial part of videogame aesthetics and deserve to be praised, selecting concept art, illustrations, and sculptures as the exhibition's objects may contribute to the generalized idea that only the audiovisual elements of games deserve to be considered art.

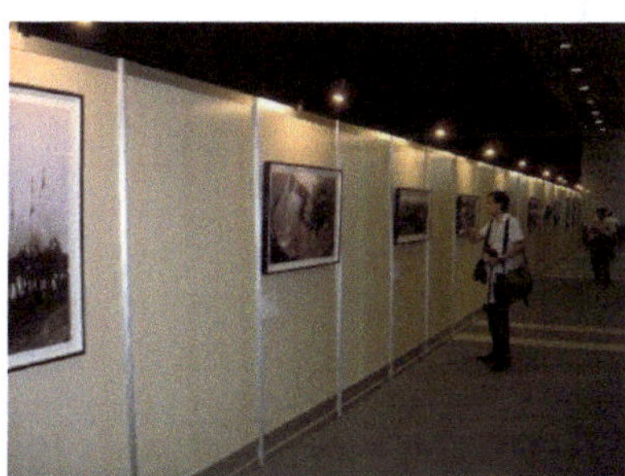

Figure 1. "Into the Pixel: An Art Exhibition into the Art of Video Games" presented illustrations and followed a traditional design (Caron, 2008).

Despite allowing the interaction with some works using an original controller design and a projected screen, the Smithsonian's exhibit *The Art of Videogames* could also be considered a traditional approach to these types of works. The most adventurous strategy was remediating *Pacman* (1980) and a few other works to be playable outside of an arcade machine or its respective console. *Pacman* became the exhibition's main feature as the public, particularly kids, felt compelled to play it. Notwithstanding, *Pacman* is available in multiple emulators and versions, so probably the magic of the display fell more into the social participation and appreciation of the wonder of kids approaching the work for the first time. As for the rest of the exhibition, most of it consisted of video footages and still images, so it is not a surprise that the media criticized this lack of interactivity (Gitlin, 2012; Suderman, 2012). The importance of this exhibition does not fall into the exhibition itself, but in its contribution to the legitimization of the medium as art, being the Smithsonian an established and respected institution.

New Spells: Contemporary and Participatory Approaches

First-Hand Experience

The most direct approach to encompass the whole aesthetics of videogames was also one of the most popular: Displaying the original software in the original hardware. *Game On, Game Masters: The Exhibition* (2012), and the *Computerspielemuseum* allow the audience to play with the original hardware and software. This strategy comes with the challenge of preserving the works. During big events, the hardware and software can deteriorate rapidly due to their usage. This is particularly alarming with pieces of historical value. First-hand experience is a valid and valuable approach but can only be successful if the organization and the rest of the exhibit design open spaces for discussion, social participation, and co-creation of meanings.

Creation of an Environment Through Architecture and Space Design

Remediating videogames to physical spaces naturally implies using architecture and space design. Creating an environment can enhance the experience, give context and meaning to the works, and facilitate interactivity and social participation. *Videogames: Design/Play/Disrupt* and *Game On* Madrid (2019) are two of the best examples of how vital architecture and space design are. The first one presented a space "conceived as a grey box render," alluding to one of the basic stages of the visual design development. The designers created a navigable space that borrowed techniques and elements from videogame design (Pernilla Ohrstedt Studio, 2021; Wood, 2019). *Game On* took place in a former underground cistern, and the designers used more than 150 LED neon arches to immerse the audience into the 1980s, the Golden Age of videogame design. The LED simulated the "first experiments in design with vector graphics, with the creation of 3D environments". The critics considered that the juxtaposition of the industrial archaeology of the underground space with the 80s vectorial LED environment created an impressive setting, "an enchanted place" (Bürklein, 2020). (Hahn 2020).

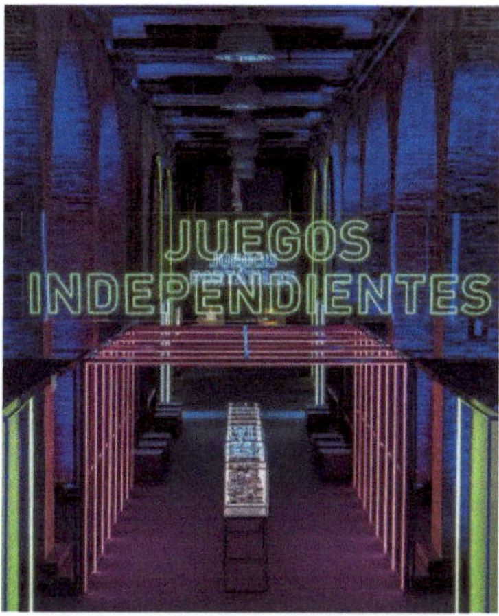

Figure 2. The award-winning architectural design of Game On Madrid was praised by the critics and the public (Hahn, 2020b).

Immersive Context-Giving Installations

A way to provide context through immersion is by recreating the space where the games were originally played or designed. For example, in the special exhibition: *Serve Games. How digital games entered our lives*, the *Computerspielemuseum* (2022b) decided to recreate some spaces like 80s arcades and living rooms and bedrooms from different decades. This approach allowed the audience to experience for the first time or reexperience the feeling of playing a game in the original context. Furthermore, these installations allowed both the first-timers and the knowledgeable to share a retro experience and their perspectives.

These installations can also show hidden social problematics, generating a more substantial impact. In *Homo Ludens*, an art installation of a mannequin sitting in front of a computer raised awareness of the problem of *Gold Farmers*, which are Chinese players that large corporations overexploit. These players "farm" gold and items by killing monsters in online games to sell the prizes to other players. The computer screen displays a notepad where the mannequin representing a gold farmer writes how exhausted, exploited, and lonely he feels.

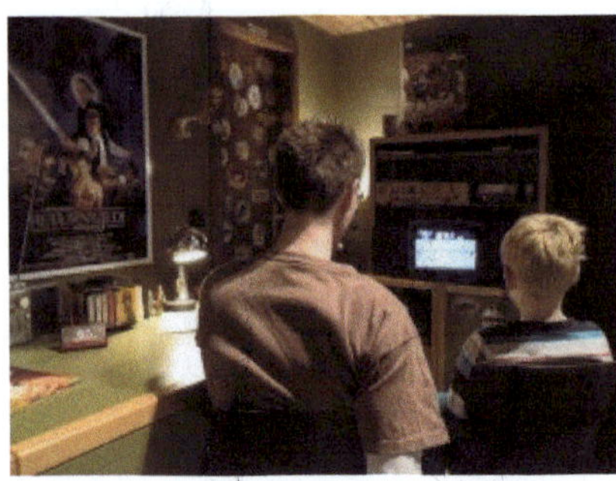

Figure 3. Father sharing a (re)experience of the intimate context of gaming in the 90s (Computerspielemuseum, 2022d).

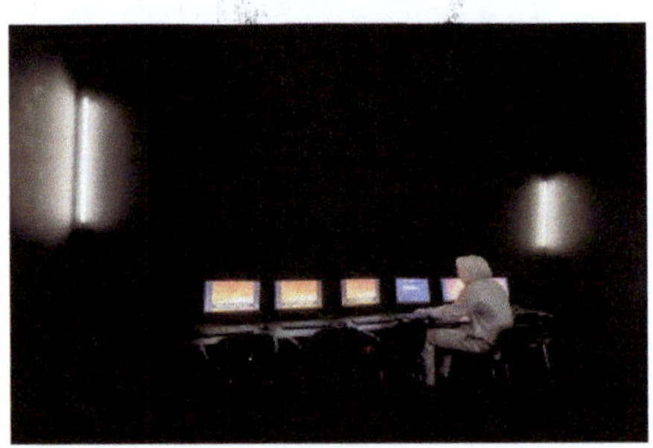

Figure 4. The impactful installation Gold Farmer in Homo Ludens (Hernández, 2021).

Extreme Dissection of the Videogame as Art Medium

Virtual Realms approached the Videogame, as an art medium, from a different perspective. The ArtScience Museum (Singapore), in collaboration with the Singapore and Melbourne Museum, commissioned six videogame developers, which partnered with six media art studios (Kojima Productions-Rhizomatiks; Enhance-FIELD.IO; thatgamecompany-The Mill; Tequila Works-Marshmallow Laser Feast; Media Molecule- onedotzero; David O'Reilly-The Workers), to create six interactive, immersive installations that explained different abstract aspects of the medium: *Synesthesia, Unity, Play, Connection, Narrative,* and *Everything.* The installations were not concerned with specific videogames, but with the structure and possibilities of the medium, videogame experience, and art in videogames. For example, the *Unity* room consisted of a light installation that would react to the movement of groups of people while the *Narrative* room allowed to interact with a story that would change according to the choices made by each of the group members interacting with the work.

Gamification in Videogame Exhibitions

In *Homo Ludens*, the public would be given a big, black coin at the entrance, a token used to personalize an avatar according to their demographics and perspectives. The participants had to answer a few questions before going into a themed room and leaving the area by placing the coin on a sensor labeled with their answer; the token retained the information. In the final room, the participants had to place the coin on a sensor that revealed their avatar and some information about their perspective of videogames according to their answers. To end the experience, the participants had to place the coin into a box that resembled an arcade machine (Sesé, 2021), leaving the exhibition and entering the "real world" as the *Homo Ludens* they are.

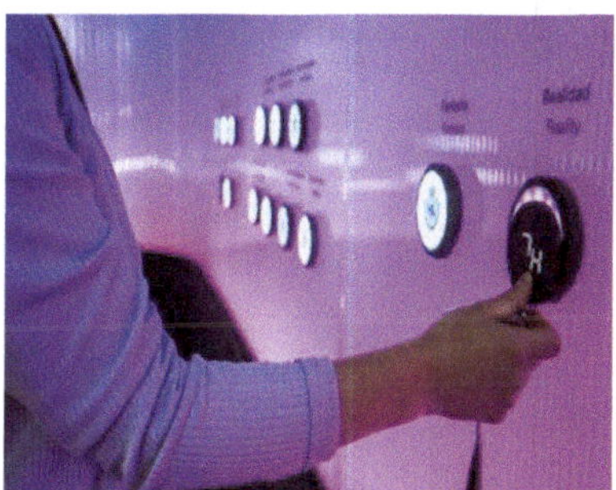

Figure 5. The symbolic and practical use of the coin/token to create an avatar and interact with the space was an effective gamification strategy for Homo Ludens (Moreno, 2022).

Ludic Hardware Mannerism

The *Computerspielemuseum* designed giant controllers to play classic games, honest to the original design. This is an exciting way to spark the magic of fun while highlighting the importance of the hardware.

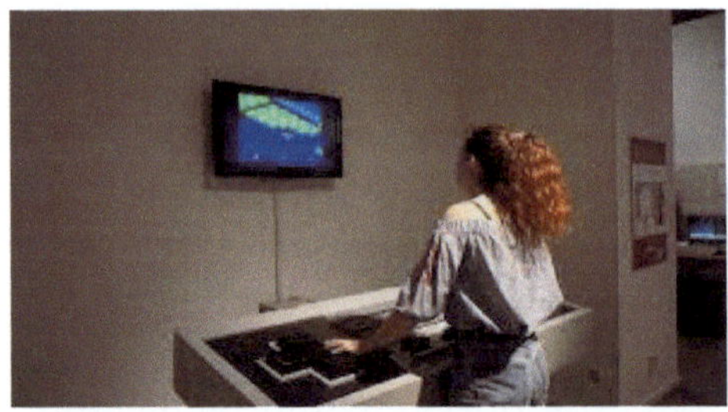

Figure 6. Giant controller that allows the participants to play with the original software (Computerspielemuseum, 2021 e).

3D Screening of 2D Videogames

The *Computerspielemuseum* also modified videogames from the first 3D videogame consoles to be compatible with 3D lenses and visuals. This way, the participant could recreate the excitement felt when playing with the innovative technology back in the 90s.

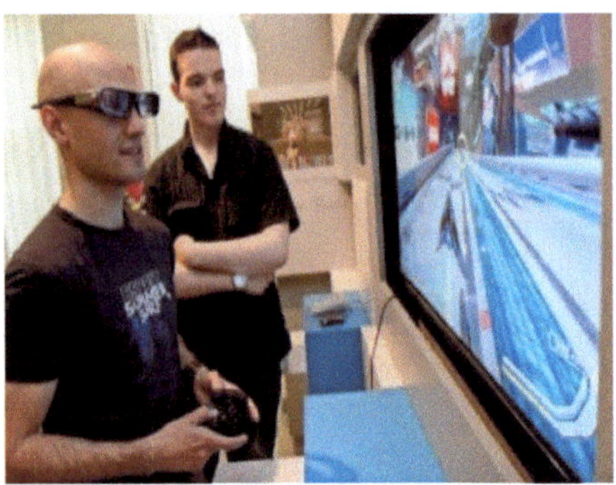

Figure 7. Man playing a 90s videogame remediated to be played on a 3D TV (Computerspielemuseum, 2022c).

Interactive Digital Panoramas

In *Virtual Realms*, the *Narrative* room would combine the 18th Century immersive technique of panoramas with digital screens. Moreover, the participants were able to make individual decisions that would add to the decisions taken by the other participants to manipulate the story.

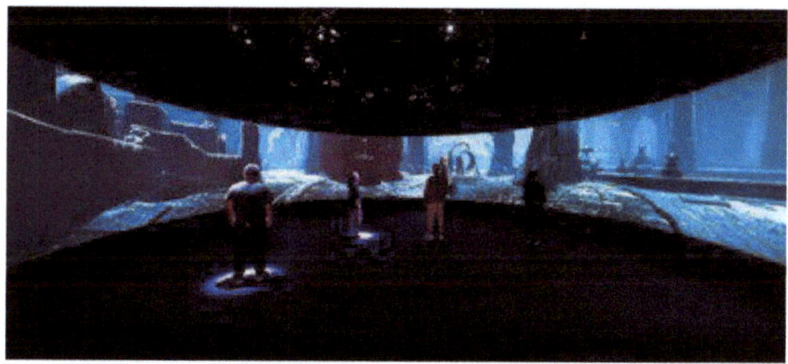

Figure 8. Interactive Narrative on a 360° Digital Panorama in Virtual Realms: Videogames Transformed (ArtScience Museum, 2021b).

Virtual Reality

Although VR devices were identified in the images and documentation in *Game Masters*, *Game On*, and *Computerspielemuseum*, there was no information about their use. Most probably, the VR devices were used to display VR videogames; however, as the *Final Fantasy XR Ride* exemplifies, VR remains a powerful tool for the remediation of the digital content of videogames, augmenting the sense of immersion in the game world.

A Mix of Physical and Virtual Realities

In *Virtual Realms*, the *Play* room utilized big, soft, shaped objects and tracked helmets to mix physical and virtual elements. The experience was intended to be performative, joyful, and silly, immersing the participants in the playing world. The participants would use the objects to interact and move around colorful digital balls on a wall screen. In the *Final Fantasy XR Ride* (2018), the public rode a rollercoaster while wearing VR visors that displayed a video of a Final Fantasy mission specially designed for the ride (Final Fantasy Wiki, 2022). The combination of VR technology and the movement of the mechanical ride provided a sense of full immersion into the world of the work.

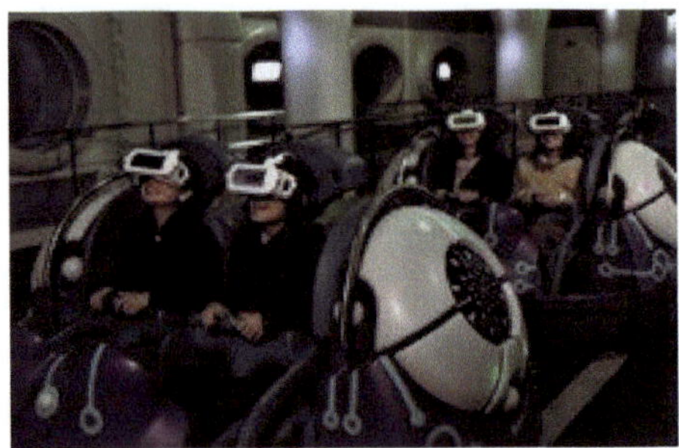

Figure 9. The Final Fantasy XR Ride combines VR and rollercoasters to achieve full immersion (ArtStation, 2018).

Remediation of the Game World or Universe

Super Nintendo World (2020) is probably one of the most successful spaces at igniting the inner childish wonder of the public. Universal Studios and Nintendo designed and built the area dedicated to the world of Mario. This extensive installation that houses several themed rides and attractions remediates the significant properties of an entire game world. Each attraction represents a different videogame of the series, so it could be said that the installation represents not only a game world but a game universe. Evidently, this type of installation could only be possible with a substantial financial investment, but rooms of different sizes, depending on budget, could be adapted for exhibitions. The challenge for this approach is to incorporate content effectively that could induce critical thinking and co-creation of meanings by the participants.

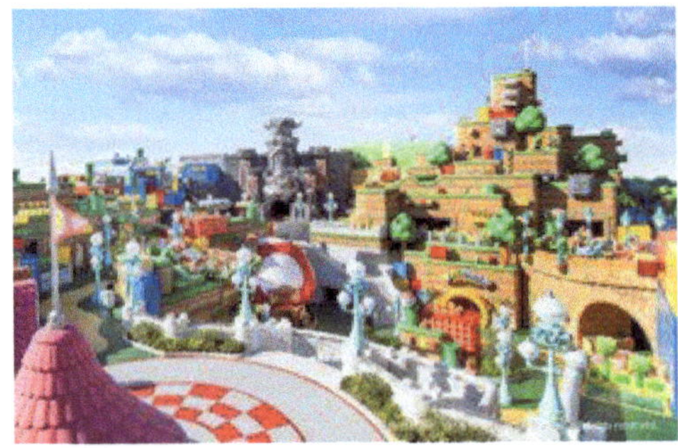

Figure 10. Super Mario World is an extraordinary example of game world remediation to the physical world (@USJ_Official, 2020).

Chants and Incantations: Discussion

The remediation of videogames to physical art exhibitions requires both immediacy and hypermediacy to represent the analog, the digital, and the aesthetic experience in the most convenient way for exhibition's purposes. While immediacy implies the transparency of the medium to achieve immersion and the sensation of directly experiencing the content and aesthetics, hypermediacy combines several media in a heterogeneous space of fragmented representations with randomized access and a multiplicity of layered meanings. (Bolter & Grusin 1999; Moutat 2016, p. 405; Ramey 2014; Wiencek 2021). It is important to notice that if the exhibition of a videogame focuses only on the digital content and fails to show the link with the analog, the public may believe that it can be played on any device, which would be dishonest to the materiality and aesthetic of the artwork. Similarly, if the exhibition focuses too much on the analog, the digital content may be diminished, pushing the exhibition to the category of science and technology instead of art. (Dekker, 2013; Paul, 2008; Sharp, 2015).

A direct and literal approach that could be taken, particularly with videogames produced for a specific platform, would be allowing the audience to interact and play with the works using the original analog devices like controllers, consoles, platforms, and screens. Notwithstanding, part of the job of a curator is to preserve them. This task adds a layer of complexity because the fragility of the components of the analog systems and the industry's market, structured under the model of perpetual innovation capitalism that promotes an artificially accelerated and programmed obsolescence (Kline, 2003, p.67; Newman, 2012, p.23; Todd, 2019, p. 7), make videogames hard to conserve. Paradoxically, as stated in *Preserving Virtual Worlds Final Report*, the most important guide for videogame conservators, a videogame has to remain playable to be considered truly preserved. This is due to the importance of interactivity and the player's performance (McDonough et al., 2010, p.14; Todd, 2019, p.6).

In most cases, remediation is the only way to display videogames without damaging the analog systems, mainly if the exhibition is intended for a larger public. However, if this is the desired way of display, the perceivable design of the devices could be replicated (i.e., retro consoles like Nintendo Classic Editions) or, if the hardware wants to be accentuated, could be adapted or even modified in a mannerist way. It is true that, since the processors are faster than the previous generations, the content, mainly the gameplay, will be slightly different as it would become faster too. Notwithstanding, even if that is not resolved, as long as the significant properties are present, the work should be honest enough to be displayed this way.

Architecture and space design are fundamental parts of the overall experience. The space could be adapted to immerse the audience in the socio-historical context in which the videogame was released (i.e., the living room experience or the simulation of old arcades) or in a bigger theme or symbolic narrative (i.e., the impact of videogames on science, economics, and cities, or the historical progress to a cybersociety). The space can also be used to enable the discussion between and among works, contents, technologies, and times through a predetermined path or movement flow (i.e., to exemplify the advancements of the medium by strategically positioning an early work next or in front of a new prototype). Special rooms and open spaces could be used to encourage social interaction (Vosmeer, Ferri, Schouten, & Rank, 2016). Some good options to enhance the experience of the space are using sound ambiance, Augmented Reality (AR), and appropriate gamification strategies to interact with the environment and the critical content. The use of symbols and icons from the videogaming imaginary in the space also contributes to contextualizing the works and exhibits.

Currently, only exclusives are released for particular platforms (i.e., Nintendo's classic sagas like *Super Mario* and *The Legend of Zelda*). As a result, most videogames in the present-day market, from big and small studios, can be played on different platforms and devices, diminishing the high dependency between digital content and the specificity of analog devices characteristic of earlier works. However, despite their portability, the experience of interacting with a 2D screen remains, becoming a defining trait of their materiality. This is naturally distinct from Virtual Reality videogames, where the VR device tricks the player by creating the illusion of 3D, which can be achieved in 2D screens, and the illusion of the body being inside of the simulated 3D space.

If the purpose of the exhibition is to highlight the digital content, by invoking immediacy and immersion in the world, the curator needs other kinds of displaying designs and mediums. Using VR is tempting, and many exhibitions dedicate at least one room to this kind of media. The benefits of VR are that it does not require a big space, and it can recreate the sense of immersion achieved while gaming. However, VR devices may not be sufficient for the number of participants, so the exposure to the work could be fragmented and limited. A solution to this problem may be allowing spectators to see the live reactions of the active participants and the content being displayed to them (Romualdo, 2018).

Nevertheless, VR is not the only medium that can recreate the magic of immersion: the physical space can act as a medium too. Something as simple as creating installations through "3D printing" or sculpting the characters, scenarios, or even the entirety of the game world accompanied by sound and music ambiance can bring even more excitement to the public and could be appreciated by many participants at once. A clear example of this is the extremely positive reception of *Super Nintendo World* in the Universal Studios Japan. This kind of installation allows any person, independently of their background in gaming and level of skill, to get immersed into the videogame's world, interact with characters, and (re)experience the sense of wonder provided by gaming.

The attempt to replicate full fictional worlds is certainly not new: amusement and theme parks, festivals, and events have been doing this for a long time now, but, just like *Super Nintendo World*, they were usually intended for entertainment. Still, there are theme parks, festivals, and events that try to recreate ways of living to educate the public about other times and places. Moreover, natural history and science museums have often utilized 3D installations to replicate historic or hypothetical scenes, characters, or beings, illustrate processes, and immerse the audience into different contexts and habitats.

The main challenge of this strategy applied to videogames is to find the right balance between entertainment, which is part of the aesthetic of the majority of the videogames, and the critical engagement with the work. Gamification strategies to interact with the objects and the environment, artistic interventions, and performances, as well as individual or group dynamics that resemble the gameplay or allow to exploring the world freely or purposely, could help to promote discussion and the development and co-creation of new meanings and interpretations in concert with the participants. Some events like renaissance fairs or cosplay conventions that utilize performance, the personification of characters, and the fulfillment of roles could serve as a guide to design pertinent dynamics. Group dynamics could also simulate the experience of multi-player and online videogames. Physical devices or AR features could also accompany this approach to palliate the possible disconnection with the analog.

Another aspect to consider is the participants' level of skill and knowledge. The curator may develop more complex ideas that involve the display and interaction with gameplay and mechanics or tackle specific problematics that may seem foreign to the general public. Romualdo (2018) proposed the division of halls, rooms, or spaces between levels of skill or knowledge. According to the self-assessment of the public, the participants would be able to start from different rooms or engage in different types of experiences.

It is important to remember that the strategies or paths mentioned are not mutually exclusive, and a mix of them could bring a more meaningful experience through hypermediacy. Furthermore, by offering fragmented representations that highlight different aspects and perspectives, hypermediacy could help with the analysis and synthesis of the elements of the work, as well as with the deconstruction of meaning systems and the construction of new ones with the help of the audience (Baumgärtel et al., 2008; Romualdo, 2018).

Creating Magic: Conclusion

One of the limitations of this paper is that the formal documentation of the exhibitions found online does not describe in detail some of the exhibitions' designs. Furthermore, the informal documentation, essential to understand the audience and evaluate the effectiveness of the design of the experience to transmit the magic of gaming, is also limited. Therefore, it is essential to develop further participant observation, ethnography on-site, and reception studies.

Moreover, for future research, it is necessary to analyze other already existing and upcoming videogame art exhibitions in various regions and other types of events or places that try to remediate and exhibit videogames in physical spaces independently of their purpose. Considering full digitization of videogames and curatorial practices in contemporary art and other types of institutions dedicated to science, natural history, and social sciences, among others, is also necessary as some of those strategies can be integrated into the exhibitions. Creating immersive environments is becoming the norm for new institutions and a tactic that established and traditional ones are taking to renovate themselves, so keeping an eye on their curatorial and remediation practices is of utmost importance.

The implications of this paper for videogame and new media art curators are various. First, this paper shows how different remediation forms can enrich exhibitions and should be considered crucial strategies for exhibiting videogames. Second, bringing these works to physical exhibitions placed in institutions like museums and galleries will contribute to the legitimization of the Videogame as an art medium, a debate that has not been settled within some art circles. This paper shows that legitimizing the medium does not imply using strict and old methods, as the aesthetics of videogames need a different treatment than other types of works. Creating new spaces that let the videogame aesthetics shine can contribute more to its legitimization than following more traditional patterns.

Third, this paper seeks to encourage curators to embrace their creativity and innovate in favor of the works, artists, and the public. Although there is no right formula, the author strongly recommends contemplating remediation, participation, and open spaces for co-creation of meanings with the audience during the exhibition design process, which should be focused on providing a magical experience to the public. It is highly recommended that videogame art curators look into what other institutions are proposing and developing, establish interdisciplinary groups of experts to look for the best ways to present the works according to the exhibit's purpose, and extensively and systematically document the exhibitions.

Curators need to build bridges and collaborate with the creators, artists, and industry to ensure proper documentation and preservation of the works, learn from their remediation practices, include their ideas in the exhibition, and face copyright and financial challenges. Prompting creators to keep documentation about their process and prototypes is a challenge. On the one hand, small studios lack of knowledge around its importance, face shortage of staff and specialized professionals, and have budget and space restrictions. On the other hand, although bigger studios and publishers are becoming more aware about the importance of videogame conservation, they do it selectively and usually keep the information for themselves. Analogously, creators, artists, and the industry could benefit from the experience, not only financially, but by visualizing and designing remediation practices, they can also find stimulation for their innovations in the medium.

For Academia, understanding the curatorial practices around videogames is crucial as it is a socio-cultural context that interprets videogames through different lenses. One of the biggest research lines inside the field of Game Studies is videogame aesthetics, being curatorial practice and remediation essential parts of it, so this paper contributes to engrossing the available literature. Moreover, the analysis of exhibitions and remediation strategies and the fragmentation through hypermediacy and immediacy of the content can offer fresh perspectives and interpretations and, in consequence, open new lines of research.

Remediation of videogames to physical art exhibitions is a fascinating field full of possibilities. In this paper, the author only delineated some existing strategies and offered a few others, but the curator's imagination can and should develop innovative ways of transmitting the marvel of playing a videogame. In contemporary curatorial practice, the curator is no longer transparent (Hansen et al., 2019), as it has become an artist, a fairy-tale being that must use its creativity to enchant the audience, to seduce and induce them to immerse themselves into the emotion, the magic that arises from the experience of gaming because the job of the curator is not only to preserve, document, and display videogames: The job of the curator is to recreate and create magic.

References

ArtScience Museum. (2021). Virtual Realism: Videogames Transformed. [Exhibition]. https://www.marinabaysands.com/museum/exhibitions/virtual-realms.html.

ArtScience Museum. (2021b). *Virtual Realism: Videogames Transformed* [Photograph]. https://www.marinabaysands.com/museum/exhibitions/virtual-realms.html.

ArtStation. (2018). *Final Fantasy XR Ride* [Photograph]. https://www.artstation.com/artwork/DxxkLy.

Australian Centre for the Moving Image. (2012). *Game Masters: The Exhibition.* https://www.acmi.net.au/about/touring-exhibitions/game-masters-touring/.

Barbican. (2021), *Game On & Game On 2.0* International. https://www.barbican.org.uk/hire/exhibition-hire-bie/game-on-game-on-2-0.

Baumgärtel, T., Christ, H. D., & Dressler, I. (2008). games: Computerspiele von KünstlerInnen (games: Computer games by artists). In C. Paul (Ed.), *New Media in the White Cube and Beyond: Curatorial Models for Digital Art* (pp. 233-250). Berkeley and Los Angeles, CA: University of California Press, 233-250.

Brown, E., and Cairns, P. (2004). "A grounded investigation of game immersion," in *Proceedings of the CHI'04 Extended Abstracts on Human Factors in Computing Systems* (Vienna: ACM), 1297–1300. Doi: 10.1145/985921.986048.

Bürklein, C. (2020). Architecture and video games, *Game On* exhibition in Madrid. Floor Nature Architecture & Surfaces. https://www.floornature.com/blog/architecture-and-video-games-game-exhibition-madrid-15552/.

Caixa Forum. (2021). *"Homo Ludens: Videojuegos para entender el presente."* [Exhibition]. https://caixaforum.org/es/madrid/p/homo-ludens-videojuegos-para-entender-el-presente_a12678239.

Caron, F. (2008). *Into the Pixel* [Photograph]. Ars Technica. https://arstechnica.com/gaming/2008/07/into-the-pixel-high-art-and-expensive-champagne-meet-gaming/.

Collins, K. (2008). *Game Sound. An Introduction to the History, Theory, and Practice of Videogame Music and Sound Design.* MA, USA: MIT Press.

Computerspielemuseum. (2022). Highlights des *Computerspielemuseums.* https://www.*Computerspielemuseum.*de/1215_Highlights_des_*Computerspielemuseums.*htm.

Computerspielemuseum (2022b). Sonderausstellung.
https://www.Computerspielemuseum.de/1299_Sonderausstellung.htm.

Computerspielemuseum (2022c). *3D TV* [Photograph]. Computerspielemuseum Archive.
https://www.computerspielemuseum.de/mediabase/img/cache/173_280x500.jpg.

Computerspielemuseum. (2022d). *Serve Games* [Photograph]. Computerspielemuseum Archive.
https://www.computerspielemuseum.de/1299_Sonderausstellung.htm

Csikszentmihalyi, M. (1975). *Beyond Boredom and Anxiety: Experiencing Flow in Work and Play*. San Francisco, CA: Jossey Bass.

Dekker, Annet. *Methodologies of Multimedial Documentation and Archiving. Preserving and Exhibiting Media Art: Challenges and Perspectives.* Netherlands: Amsterdam University Press, 2013, p. 168.

Drabble, B. (2003). "Fw: March Theme." *New-Media-Curating Discussion List*, 25 March.

Esposito, N. (2005). A Short and Simple Definition of What a Videogame Is. *Proceedings of DiGRA 2005 Conference: Changing Views - Worlds in Play.*
https://www.utc.fr/~nesposit/publications/esposito2005definition.pdf.

Final Fantasy Wiki. (2022). Final Fantasy XR Ride. *Fandom.*
https://finalfantasy.fandom.com/wiki/Final_Fantasy_XR_Ride?oldid=3615231.

Gee, J. P. (2016). Video Games, Design, and Aesthetic Experience. *Rivista di estetica*, 63.
http://journals.openedition.org/estetica/1312; DOI: https://doi.org/10.4000/estetica.1312

Gitlin, J. M. (2012). Ars at the Museum: The Art of Video Games at the Smithsonian. *Ars Technica.* https://arstechnica.com/gaming/2012/04/ars-at-the-museum-the-art-of-video-games-at-the-smithsonian/

Goethe, O. (2019). *Visual Aesthetics in Games and Gamification.* Springer Link.

Graham, B., Cook, S. & Dietz, S. (2010). *Rethinking Curating: Art after New Media Art.* MIT Press.

Hahn, J. (2020). *Game On*'s neon-filled exhibition design pays homage to 80s video games. *Dezeen.* https://www.dezeen.com/2020/10/23/game-on-smart-green-design-exhibition-fundacion-canal/#.

Hahn, J. (2020b). *Game on Madrid* [Photograph]. Dezeen.
https://www.dezeen.com/2020/10/23/game-on-smart-green-design-exhibition-fundacion-canal/#.

Hakuville. (2019). *Woman Playing with big NES controller* [Photograph]. Wordpress.
https://hakuville.wordpress.com/2019/06/14/computerspiele-museum/.

Hansen, M. V., Henningsen, A. F. & Gregersen, A. (2019). *Curatorial Challenges: Interdisciplinary Perspectives on Contemporary Curating.* Routledge.

Into the Pixel. (2004). Into the Pixel: An Exhibition into the Art of Video Games. [Exhibition].
https://www.intothepixel.com/.

Hernández, J. (2021). *Instalación Gold Farmer* [Photograph]. Ars Magazine.
https://arsmagazine.com/homo-ludens-y-el-universo-del-videojuego-en-caixaforum-madrid/.

Into the Pixel. (2004). *Into the Pixel: An Exhibition into the Art of Video Games.* [Exhibition].
https://www.intothepixel.com/.

Jenkins, H. (2008). Convergence culture. NY, USA: NYU Press.

Jennett, C., Cox, A. L., Cairns, P., Dhoparee, S., Epps, A., Tijs, T., et al. (2008). Measuring and defining the experience of immersion in games. *Int. J. Hum. Comp. Stud.* 66, 641–661. Doi: 10.1016/j.ijhcs.2008.04.004.

Kline, S., Dyer-Witheford, N., & de Peuter, G. (2003). *Digital Play: The Interaction of Technology, Culture, and Marketing.* Montreal & Kingston: McGill-Queen's University Press.

Lanham, R. (1993). *The Electronic World: Democracy, Technology, and the Arts.* University of Chicago Press.

Marks, A. (2002). *The Complete Guide to Game Audio: For Composers, Musicians, Sound Designers, and Game Developers.* Kansas: CMP Books.

Mäyra, F. (2008). *An Introduction to Game Studies.* Cornwall, UK: Sage Publications, 2008.

McDonough, J., Olendorf, R., Kirschenbaum, M., Kraus, K., Reside, D., Donahue, R., Phelps, A., Egert, C., Lowood, H., & Rojo, S. (2010). *Preserving Virtual Worlds Final Report.* http://hdl.handle.net/2142/17097.

McGonigal, J. (2011). *Reality is Broken.* USA: Penguin Books.

McLuhan, M. (1964). *Understanding Media: The Extensions of Man.* Timer Mirror.

Michailidis, L., Balaguer-Ballester, E., He, X. (2018). *Flow and Immersion in Video Games: The Aftermath of a Conceptual Challenge Front.* Psychol. https://doi.org/10.3389/fpsyg.2018.01682.

Moreno, H. (2022). Exposición *Homo Ludens* [Photograph]. Barcelona Secreta. https://barcelonasecreta.com/homo-ludens-gamers/.

Moutat, A. *Digital art: when mediacy becomes remediation.* http://afsemio.fr/wp-content/uploads/Sens-et-m%C3%A9diation.-A.-Moutat.pdf.

Moreno, H. (2022). *Exposición Homo Ludens* [Photograph]. Barcelona Secreta. https://barcelonasecreta.com/homo-ludens-gamers/.

Newman, J. (2012). *Best before: Videogames, supersession and obsolescence.* Retrieved from https://ebookcentral-proquestcom.proxy01.its.virginia.edu/lib/uva/reader.action?docID=1016029.

Niedenthal, S. (2009). What We Talk About When We Talk About Game Aesthetics. *DiGRA.* http://www.digra.org/wp-content/uploads/digital-library/09287.17350.pdf

Nintendo. (2020). Super Nintendo World. [Amusement Park]. Universal Studios Japan. https://super-nintendo-world.usj.co.jp/en/us/about.

Paul. C. (2018). *Challenges for a Ubiquitous Museum. New Media in the White Cube and Beyond.* University of California Press.

Pernilla Ohrstedt Studio. (2021). *V&A Videogames.* http://pernilla-ohrstedt.com/category/va-videogames.

Ramey, L. (2014). Immediacy, Hypermediacy, and New Media in The Secret of Kells (Moore 2009). *Medieval Perspectives*, 29: 109-120.

Romualdo, S. (2018). Curating The Arcade: Strategies For The Exhibition Of Videogames. *International Journal Of Film And Media Arts*, 1, 2.

SAAM. (2012). *The Art of Video Games.* [Exhibition]. https://americanart.si.edu/exhibitions/games.

Salen, K. y Zimmerman E. (2003). *Rules of Play.* Boston: MIT Press.

Seevink, J. (2017). *Emergence in Interactive Art.* Springer Series on Cultural Computer. Springer, Cham.

Sesé, T. (2021). *Todos somos jugadores de un gran videojuego.* La Vanguardia. https://www.lavanguardia.com/cultura/20211202/7903057/todos-jugadores-gran-videojuego.html.

Sharp, John. *Works of Game: On the Aesthetics of Games and Art.* MA: The MIT Press, 2015, p. 33.

Sicart, M. (2008). "Defining Game Mechanics." *Game Studies*, 8.

Simon, N. (2010). *The Participatory Museum. Museum 2.0.*

Smithsonian American Art Museum. (2012). "*The Art of Videogames.*" https://americanart.si.edu/exhibitions/games.

Suderman, P. (2012). *Gamers' letdown: Smithsonian's videogame exhibit scores low on interactivity.* Washington Post. https://www.washingtontimes.com/news/2012/mar/29/gamers-letdown-smithsonians-video-game-exhibit-sco/.

Swalwell, M. (2009). *Towards the preservation of local computer game software. Convergence: The International Journal of Research into New Media Technologies.* Vol 15(3): 263- 279. Retrieved from https://journals-sagepubcom.proxy01.its.virginia.edu/doi/pdf/10.1177/1354856509105107.

Todd, B. (2019). *Preserving Video Game Significance: A Practical Guide for Video Game Preservation, Exhibition, and their Significant Properties.* John Hopkins University. https://jscholarship.library.jhu.edu/bitstream/handle/1774.2/62117/Todd,%20Benjamin%20C.pdf?sequence=1.

Vermeeren A.P.O.S. et al. (2018). Future Museum Experience Design: Crowds, Ecosystems and Novel Technologies. In: Vermeeren A., Calvi L., Sabiescu A. (eds) *Museum Experience Design.* Springer Series on Cultural Computing. Springer, Cham. https://doi.org/10.1007/978-3-319-58550-5_1.

Visual Works. (2018). Final Fantasy XR Ride. [VR Rollercoaster].

V&A. (2022). *Videogames: Design/Play/Disrupt.* [Exhibition]. https://www.vam.ac.uk/exhibitions/videogames.

Wardip-Fruin, N. & Harrigan P. (2014), *First Person: New Media as Story, Performance, and Game.* MIT Press.

Wiencek, F. (2018). *Digital Mediation of Art and Culture. A Database Approach. Department of Social Sciences & Humanities.* Jacobs University.

Wiencek, F. (2021). Lecture in Donau Universität Krems. Austria.

Wood, K. (2019). Videogames: Design/Play/Disrupt. CAA. Reviews. https://10.3202/caa.reviews.2019.71.

THE GENESIS OF XYZZY – THE FIRST MAGIC WORD IN VIDEO GAMES

Damiano Gerli

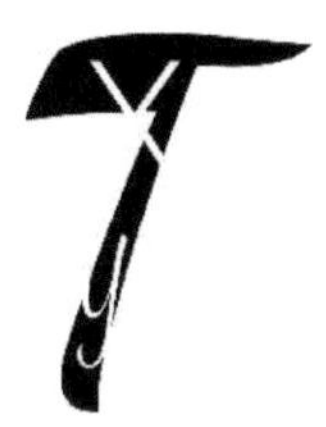

This paper analyzes the origin of the first magic word to be used in video games, Xyzzy, and its connection to the notion of "cheating". Despite its origin being shrouded in mystery, there have been several theories on the origin of the magic word, used as a cheat for the player to skip an entire section of the game. Despite not being the first in the genre, Adventure ended up being incredibly influential in shaping the future genre of adventure games. Xyzzy would become one of the first video game references to be recognized by players all over the world, surviving, well beyond the 70s, up to the present. The paper also looks at the later Atari 2600 conversion of the original Adventure and how it also, somehow, ended up influencing mystery and magic in games, having the first - recognized as such - Easter egg. In the 80s and 90s, cheating still had a layer of magic, with many devices, sold to kids, which could be connected to consoles to allow inputting codes. Many of these devices' names and marketing were connected also to magic and mystery.

Keywords: adventure, Atari, cheat, history, parser

The Original Adventure

Playing video games in the 70s was not all about the arcades. Still, with home computers being quite far on the horizon, for most of the decade being able to play games outside of Pong was reserved only to people who could have access to a mainframe computer. These were mainly used in places like universities, big

279

companies and science labs, so playing games was mostly an activity that would still take place, for the most part, outside of one's own home. Later, from 1977 on, home computers became much more accessible, even though still quite expensive, with the rise in popularity of the so called "1977 trio": the TRS-80, the Commodore PET and the Apple II. Subsequently, from the following decade, home computers became a staple in many households, with prices dropping significantly and interfaces becoming simpler to use. Still, the mainframe is where games first found a small audience and began exploring genres outside of the realm of simple arcade gameplay. It is also where magic first appeared in the realms of gaming, in the guise of one mysterious word: Xyzzy.

Adventure (or *Colossal Cave Adventure* as it was more widely known when it was later commercially released) is recognized today by many to be one of the first adventure games ever released. While the honor of being the first would go to Peter Langston's *Castle* from 1974, *Adventure* by Will Crowther, developed in 1975 and released in 1976, is still the most culturally significant out of the two. Crowther, along with his wife Patricia, was a fan of cave exploration. The two would have lengthy trips together and had especially explored the Mammoth Caves in Kentucky. But in 1975 the two had grown quite distant and had separated, with Patricia living in another state with their two daughters (Smith 2019). So, as a way to also reconnect with his children, Crowther started developing a textual adventure game that they could play together, featuring a whole system of caves to explore. For inspiration, he naturally went to the source, the very same caves he had come to know by heart: the Mammoth caves (Smith 2019). But he did not want to just develop a simple adventure where the player explored caves with nothing much else to do. As a lover of RPG and D&D aficionado, he started inserting fantasy elements into the gameplay: treasures, dwarves and magic. The goal in *Adventure* is not that of simply completing the narrative, since there is really no story to speak of, but instead that of collecting as much treasure as possible. By interacting with a simple text parser with one or two words, the player is able to move between places, collect and use items in order to solve puzzles.

```
PAUSE   INIT DONE statement executed
To resume execution, type go.  Other input will terminate the job.
go
Execution resumes after PAUSE.
 WELCOME TO ADVENTURE!!  WOULD YOU LIKE INSTRUCTIONS?


y

 SOMEWHERE NEARBY IS COLOSSAL CAVE, WHERE OTHERS HAVE FOUND
 FORTUNES IN TREASURE AND GOLD, THOUGH IT IS RUMORED
 THAT SOME WHO ENTER ARE NEVER SEEN AGAIN. MAGIC IS SAID
 TO WORK IN THE CAVE.  I WILL BE YOUR EYES AND HANDS. DIRECT
 ME WITH COMMANDS OF 1 OR 2 WORDS.
 (ERRORS, SUGGESTIONS, COMPLAINTS TO CROWTHER)
 (IF STUCK TYPE HELP FOR SOME HINTS)


 YOU ARE STANDING AT THE END OF A ROAD BEFORE A SMALL BRICK
 BUILDING . AROUND YOU IS A FOREST. A SMALL
 STREAM FLOWS OUT OF THE BUILDING AND DOWN A GULLY.
```

Figure 1. Adventure

But there are also enemies dwelling around, so that the player is supposed to bring the treasures back to the house without running into the evil dwarves. Since exploring the cave will require having to memorize the whole map as much as possible, the main strategy consists in trying to find the shortest route between the treasures and the house. Still, the game was being developed especially with a young audience in mind, so Crowther wanted players to also be able to complete it or, at least, have an easier time. In one instance in the game, scribbled on a wall, the narrator informs the player that there is a word: "Xyzzy" (which is pronounced as "zizzy" as Don Woods recalled in a post on Usenet[1]). Using the magic word as a command, at the right spot, will automatically teleport the player much closer to the house, thus saving quite a lot of time in trekking around. If, instead, used in any other place, the game would respond with "nothing happens". Despite the magic word not being the only one in the game (there are also Plugh and Plover), it was the first one that many players would encounter. To this day, it remains the one thing about the original 1975 game that still manages to be

---

[1] Woods, Don Subject: Re: XYZZY - Usenet post (February 27, 1997)

recognized by many gamers everywhere (Adams 2005). Indeed, along with its status as the first magic word in gaming, Xyzzy can also be recognized as, probably, the first cheat code ever.

The success of Adventure and its Colossal variant

The first version of *Adventure* published on mainframe by Will Crowther was quite a short game, with a simplified system of caves and only a few items. Still, it definitely got attention by many players and, among them, also a young programmer, Don Woods. He liked the idea so much that he decided to improve upon it (Lessard 2013). Woods went so far as developing an entirely new version of the game, while designing new rooms, new objects and overall expanding on the original idea. That second version would indeed be the one that started circulating on many computer mainframes around the United States and, in the end, proved to be revolutionary both for the industry and for many future adventure developers. In many offices and universities, the release of the game meant that work temporarily came to a halt as everyone was busy trying to finish it. Among many influences, the success of *Adventure* inspired Scott Adams to create his company Adventure International (Herzog 1988), which was the first company to release adventure games on personal computers. *Adventure* would also inspire a few college students at the MIT to create Infocom and release *Zork* in 1977, another classic mainframe textual adventure. While much less serious than Crowther's original vision, the references to the seminal adventure game in *Zork* were indeed many. A couple of years since its original debut on mainframe, Adventure began to be sold commercially, under the more easily distinguishable name *Colossal Cave Adventure*. But it also came out under the title *Microsoft Adventure* as one of the very first software programs originally available for the IBM personal computer.

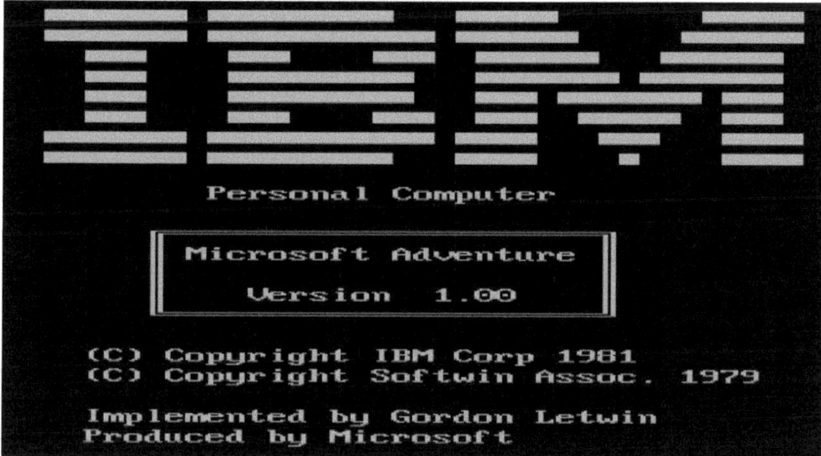

Figure 2. Microsoft Adventure

In more than one way, *Adventure* changed the course of gaming and the industry (The Digital Antiquarian 2012). Will Crowther, and subsequently Don Woods, had developed a text adventure that would allow the player to explore a place where they could not go in reality, at least not without danger or fear of getting lost. It pushed the boundaries of what a simple line of text on a screen could do, while at the same time referencing the fantasy scenarios that many kids were familiar with. It was also not about simple exploration, but featured puzzles to solve and interactive choices that would influence the outcome of the game itself.

A peculiar case: Adventure on Atari 2600

After the success of the original, many companies started noticing the potential of making their own version of *Adventure*. Among them, there was Atari, which chose it as the first textual adventure game that should receive a full-on conversion on their 8-bit console, the VCS. The conversion was handled by programmer Warren Robinett, his original intentions were to develop something that felt much closer to the original, having all the different gameplay features intact, but with a different interface. But he ended up clashing with the company, as those were not the intentions of Atari: the company wanted him instead to program a full-on adventure game with entirely different gameplay features to accomodate for the fact that, obviously, the console did not come with a keyboard that one could use to interact with a text parser.

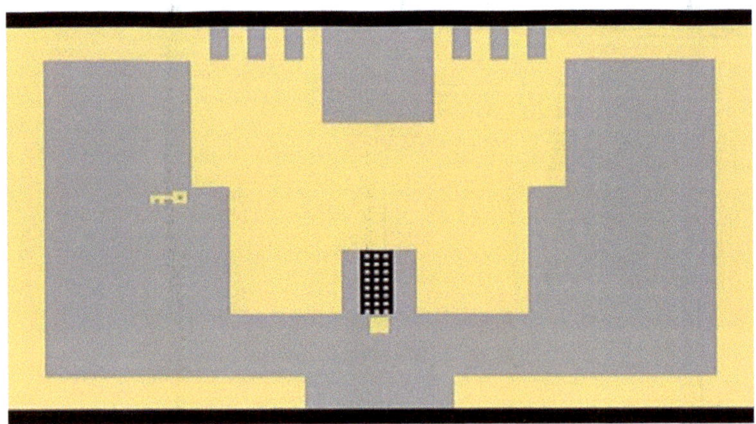

Figure 3. Adventure on the Atari VCS

Adventure on the Atari VCS can be recognized as one of the very first action/adventure games to ever be published (Merrill 1998). The final objective in the game is not that of collecting treasures and returning to the house but, instead, recovering a single golden chalice, in order to bring it back to the Golden Castle, while trying to avoid roaming enemies like dragons and bats. Because of conflicts with Atari and having to deal with the limitations of the hardware, development took more than a year, with the game coming out only in 1977.

Adventure on Atari 2600 still retained several magical elements, in one way or another. In particular, Robinett's original intentions were to make all rooms in the game to be connected bidirectionally, but a few programming bugs made several rooms just connected in a single direction. These bugs are, indeed, quickly explained in the game's manual as being "bad magic". So, while *Adventure* on Atari does not feature a magic cheat code with a single word that can be typed in, for obvious reasons, it still does feature something quite unique. Because of the conflicts with the company and Atari's notorious habit of prohibiting developers to feature credits in the games (supposedly to avoid them being poached by other companies), Robinett would program what is commonly referred to as the first Easter Egg in the history of video games.

A "Easter Egg" in games is mostly defined as "a trick or a hidden part of the game which features a little secret for the player to discover" (Connelly 2003). In *Adventure* for the Atari 2600, the easter egg is a hidden room which features a line of vertical text with the original credit: "created by Warren Robinett". Despite the common reference to the on in *Adventure* as the first Easter Egg in gaming, there were secret rooms and hidden items in games before 1980. Truthfully, the term was coined because Robinett purposefully hid it so that no one would find it in a short time, thus his job would have no negative repercussions. In the end, the hidden room was found within a year after the original release (Yarwood 2016). By then, Robinett had already left Atari, but the company still had the same policy of not crediting developers in place. But because the costs of reprogramming and republishing the game on a new batch of cartridges were quite high, in the end Atari decided to keep the Easter Egg. Secret rooms actually became a staple of all their future games, thus enticing the players to keep playing as to find various secrets.

The multiple roles of Xyzzy

Beyond its status as a magic word, Xyzzy can be recognized as probably the first ever cheat code in the history of gaming. It was not simply a hack that was found analyzing the program or a trick found while playing, but an actual way provided by the developer himself to allow the player to skip quite a big section of the game. The origins of the word are shrouded in mystery, as Crowther himself reported having just made it up out of the blue (Adams 2005). But it was later discovered that it is a mnemonic mathematical trick to remember the definition of the cross product. There is also a passage from *The Wonderful Wizard of Oz* by L. Frank Baum, which features Dorothy saying to the flying monkeys the magic words: "Ziz-zy, zuz-zy, zik!".

The word was kept in most other versions of adventure released in the following years after 1976 and, as early as 1978, it had already become something of an immediate cultural reference for many players. Since many future developers also started their career playing *Adventure* at quite a young age, the cultural significance of the word in both games and applications is still very much present. The first game to strongly feature the word would be another seminal textual adventure from the time: *Zork*. Developed by Scott Adams, which - as mentioned - was influenced by the work of Will Crowther himself, the adventure was a quite more humorous take on the genre, despite having a similar background. If a player tried to use the word Xyzzy in *Zork*, along with several of its sequels, the parser would usually respond "A hollow voice cries out: you fool!" as in belittling the player for trying to use a cheat from another game.

Zork started a bit of a trend in the genre of textual adventures featuring a parser that would respond to the player trying to use Xyzzy in various humorous ways. It came to the point that anyone developing a textual adventure, was almost forced to feature a sort of custom reply to Xyzzy in the parser. There are also websites that compile all of the games that feature a specific reply to the magic word (Welbourn 2009). The influence was so felt over the genre that the annual interactive fiction award is still called after the magic cheat word[2]. But the influence of the word does not stop with interactive fiction, since even early versions of the popular 'minesweeper' game under Microsoft Windows had a cheat mode triggered by the command xyzzy. Even beyond games, several operating systems featuring the word as an easter egg, even Gmail via IMAP still features the Easter Egg. Xyzzy has indeed, magically, managed to transcend time.

Xyzzy and the early cheat code

While cheat codes have been a reality of the gaming industry for decades, they surely were not a common thing in the 70s. For the most part, until the early 80s, games just had to be completed the hard way by finding out the right technique, memorizing the levels or the enemies pattern. In the case of *Adventure*, it was mostly a case of having down the pattern for the quickest way to collect all the treasures and bring them back to the house. Later

---

[2] https://xyzzyawards.org/

adventure games featuring a story to be completed could not easily feature a cheat code, since that would have meant randomly jumping towards a future point in time or removing entire parts of the game. Adventure was a very peculiar case in this regard, sitting somewhere between an arcade title and a classic adventure one, so its debut of a cheat code definitely made sense.

While Xyzzy can be easily recognized as one of the earliest cases of an intended cheat code in video games there are several other interesting examples. One in particular would be ZX Spectrum classic platformer *Manic Miner* (1981) where the number 6031769 could be written to activate cheats (Smith 2007). The code actually came from developer Matthew Miner's driver license. One much more relevant example, that has now also become part of the common pop culture, even beyond the world of video games, would be the Konami code which, from 1986, would activate cheat codes on several titles developed by the Japanese software house on the Nintendo Entertainment System.

Before cheat codes became prominent, several early games on the Commodore 64 could be hacked into in a rather simple manner. By using the STOP key on the computer, some games would be interrupted and the Commodore would show a prompt command. The user could, then, interact with the game - still in memory - via POKE commands and experiment to try and find a way to make completing the game easier or, perhaps, even see the ending screen. In that same era, many cracked/pirated games came with trainers: hacks developed by the "pirates" which allowed the player to have an easier time with the game. Many times they would allow the player to have a level selection, invincibility, endless lives and several other useful cheats.

```
READY.
LIST

100 DATA 000,000,000,000,000,000
110 DATA 000,000,000,000,000,000
120 DATA 000,000,000,000,000,000
130 DATA 000,000,000,000,000,000
140 DATA 000,000,000,000,000,000
150 DATA 000,000,000,000,000,000
160 DATA 000,000,000,000,000,000
170 DATA 000,000,000,000,000,000
180 DATA 000,000,000,000,000,000
190 DATA 000,000,000,000,000,000
200 DATA 000,000,000,000,000,000
60000 PRINT"DELETE BASIC LINES...  FROM B
ASIC":PRINT:GOSUB 60160:PRINTCHR$(147)
60005 PRINT CHR$(19)"          "CHR$(19);L
1
60010 PRINT"L1=";L1;":S1=";S1;":L2=";L2;
":AD=";AD;":GOTO 60020"
60015 POKE 631,19:POKE632,13:POKE633,13:
POKE198,3:END
BREAK
READY.
```

Figure 4. Poke Commands on the Commodore 64

The influence of magic on the world of cheating

While it might be a bit of a stretch to consider *Adventure* as influential on the world of cheat codes, it is still notable how, as late as the 80s and 90s, cheat codes were being considered very similar to a magic trick. For reference, several of the available solutions that would allow the player to use cheat codes where the game itself did not really provide anything, were often called with names that would recall supernatural beings.

Most famous is the Game Genie, which debuted in 1990 for NES, produced by Codemasters. The player could be allowed to interact directly with the game's code by inserting in the cartridge slot an accessory. Turning on the machine, with the Game Genie inserted, prompted a text input screen where the player could insert words and check what happened. The included manual would make direct references to some of the cheats available for the most widely available games. While most of them were useful, some of them could even end up making the game harder. Some cheats even went as far as allowing access to unreachable areas or features that were left off the "normal" gameplay. In a way, they did function in a similar way to a genie's three wishes, especially because it was difficult to predict the final outcome of typing some of the codes.

The magic world of *Adventure* is now distant in time and the adventure genre as a whole has evolved tremendously since 1975. But, still, that one cave exploration game stands as a strong influence for many developers and on the industry as a whole. Along with establishing many tropes and rules for the interactive fiction genre, it also influenced the way developers decided to tell a story through an interactive medium. Among these many important stepping stones, its touch of magic, Xyzzy, shall also always remain, beyond a timeless gaming reference, that first magical cheat word that helped players overcome difficulties.

Acknowledgments

Those who supported and believed in my research and work as a gaming historian, among them Konstantinos Dimopoulos, Richard Cobbett and Alexander Chatziioannou. Thanks to Viola too.

References

Adams, R. (2005) Everything you ever wanted to know about Xyzzy Retrieved from URL

Lessard, J. (2013). "Adventure before adventure games: a new look at Crowther and Woods's seminal program". Concordia University Montreal

Connelly, J. (2003) Of Dragons and Easter Eggs: A Chat With Warren Robinett. Retrieved from URL: http://tjg.joeysit.com/of-dragons-and-easter-eggs-a-chat-with-warren-robinett/

Electronic Games Issue 1 (Winter 1981). Reese Publishing Company, Inc.

Interview with Matthew Smith (1997). Retro Gamer Magazine Issue 48. Future Publishing.

Herzog, M. (1988). Neil Harris. Comics Interview. No. 54. Fictioneer Books.

Merrill, A. (1998). Warren Robinett Interview: A. Merrill's Talks to the Programmer of "Adventure" for the Atari 2600. Retrieved from URL: https://web.archive.org/web/20101122075921/http://arthurshall.com/x_adventure.shtml

Smith, A. (2019). They Create Worlds: The Story of the People and Companies That Shaped the Video Game Industry Volume 1, 1971-1982. CRC Press.

The Digital Antiquarian (2012) The Roots of Infocom Retrieved from URL: https://www.filfre.net/2012/01/the-roots-of-infocom/

Welbourn, D. (2009) Assorted responses to Xyzzy Retrieved from URL: http://www.plover.net/~davidw/sol/xyzzy.html

Woods, D. (1997). Subject: Re: XYZZY - Usenet post.

Yarwood, J. (2016) Easter Eggs: The Hidden Secrets of Videogames Retrieved from URL: http://www.pastemagazine.com/articles/2016/03/easter-eggs-the-hidden-secrets-of-videogames.html

"PLAYERISM"

Ivo Antunic

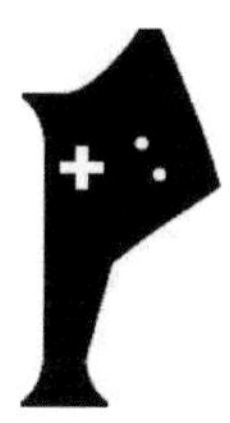lay and religion may be natural enemies, and a culture of not wanting to grow up may be destructive in its own unique style. These are the basic observations as a result of both a personal journey about the discovery of a board game that had almost gotten lost to this world, and an academic journey about taking the long way from architecture towards Game Studies. Sometime growing up I felt I had to escape a life that I grew up in, revolving only around games in order to look for "the real world" outside of society's rule book within the Caribbean jungle. It was, however, not the field of anthropology but architecture that ultimately made me see reoccurring patterns in the real world, in the form of "physical magic circles" like theatres or stadiums. The magic circle as a blurry border between the ordinary world was what led me to Homo Ludens (Johan Huizinga, 1938) and the further exploration of this concept during my research about ancient board games. After I had crowdfunded a board game simply called "World Control" (imago.im, 2017) on the day a Game-show-host was elected US-president, I wanted to carve a modern archetype of a game of power, as a publisher. World Control had already been pieced together by Michael Lee Cregger in the US in 1992, right after the collapse of the Soviet Union, but had remained unpublished. It can be roughly described as a mashup of the board game classics "Risk" and "Monopoly" with added control and agency and serves as a playbook for a multipolar world of disorder, when only the mechanics of money and power are at play. The journey was a quest to find my medium for artistic and political expression, of a cultural observation I had vaguely called "Playerism" and it is now the perfect time to tell of it, since the game was originally created 30 years ago, and it also marks the 10th anniversary of the death of my father, whose poem of peace I featured on the cover of the game. As I am writing this, Europe also finds

itself confronted with the first war of aggression in generations.

Keywords: Culture, Magic, Politics

————

Introduction

"In the future all governments have failed & a billionaire elite with private armies now play WorldControl.": with these words, the game's original author, Michael Lee Cregger, would initiate every game. In its rudimentary form, World Control[1] is a mix of the board game classics Monopoly (Parker Brothers, 1935) and Risk (Parker Brothers, 1959), to model a connection of monetary and military power. Whenever I repeat the short narrative to start the game about a billionaire elite with private armies playing World Control, the most common response I get is: "Isn't that the real world?"

The inception of World Control

The times in which Michael conceived World Control cannot be understated. Right after the final collapse of the Soviet Union and the establishment of the United States as global hegemon and its permanent military presence in the Middle East, the free market was now to be the dominating global game. With the birth of the World Wide Web, global interconnectivity and outsourcing labour started "to make the world flat again", as economist Thomas Friedman would write later (Friedman, 2004), which is of course entirely unrelated to the flat-earthers movement that believes in the actual physical world being flat.

Friedman's observation that no country who had McDonald's ever declared war on each other was rosier than picturing the future as being dominated by multinational corporations, as Michael did in typical 90s pop-cultural fashion for World Control.

————

[1] http://www.world-contro.net

Nation states would cease power to major global cities, which would house most of the world's population and wealth, and the future of global power was pictured as a multipolar world of disorder. We can observe our world heading into this multipolar disorder of armed conflict, however coming from nation states and not corporations, once again. Of course, the artistic freedom of designing narratives is a given, and most likely much better abstracted as faceless corporations than fuelling a narrative of culture wars. Either way this narrative was significantly darker than real estate competition like Monopoly and did not place war in the distant past or interstellar future, but the current times and its major cities. Multiple board game agents had rejected the game, as it was expected from board games to be family friendly with very simple mechanics, while different dices from Dungeons & Dragons and the concept of control cards added more options and complexity to the game. On the other hand, indie developers would not want to see yet another Monopoly spin-off. World Control was sitting between two worlds and remained within the elite circle of family and friends, to which I was introduced when I spent a high-school year abroad and found a loving home within the Cregger family.

It was, however, precisely the familiar layout of Monopoly that made the game so easily accessible and the global narrative so exciting for an adolescent, while the global war on terror was emerging. World Control also had a visual pull effect that set it apart from other board games. Even though rudimentary, Michael's prototype had a submerged dice-rolling arena built in, that set the scene and gave it the extra third dimension. Without knowing the gameplay, I was ready to spend a long night even if it was just going to be a differently styled Monopoly with all its internal unfairness and lack of agency. Simply rolling dice to gamble for the world and feel like a global supervillain of iconic blockbuster movie format would be role-play enough. Its sophisticated mechanics, however, would get me hooked. The option to declare war instead of paying gave players agency and the ability to turn the game around by risking one's own ability to grow, and the way to invest in control cards gave players control over the chance to achieve fixed outcomes of dice rolls. It was an archetypical game of power, and it was hypnotizing to learn its ways.

Playerism

The interplay between wealth and military force is a recurring theme throughout the ages, which the evolution of public institutions, creating ever more complex control systems of checks and balances, seeks to tame. These control systems though have not prevented that this recurring theme remains popular among the broad spectrum of society and politics and can periodically mobilize populist movements. It was therefore hardly a coincidence that, in times where the borders of fiction and fact are widely discussed, World Control was crowdfunded on the day a billionaire game-show host was elected to the highest office of the world's most powerful armed forces. Indeed, the game seemed to get real, and the design process was accompanied by the campaign trail and first year in office of Donald Trump. Apart from breaking with all conventions of common decency, I thought the distinct feature of the Trump-phenomenon was that it went past the ordinary necessity of needing to win an election in order to gain legitimacy to push an agenda. The agenda itself was now simply "winning". Winning does not necessarily imply to gain profit, but to defeat the opponent, and winning was what mattered for the ordinary world now. A constant need for entertainment, and a childish urge for revenge, majority policy. It is a populist style spearheaded by former Italian prime minister and media-mogul Silvio Berlusconi and it did not stop with Donald Trump. Among the many explanations for this growing phenomenon, I kept wondering: "Could this broad cultural phenomenon be a result of a generation that plays like never before?"

Within this generation, the gaming industry had, seemingly overnight, grown bigger than the music and movie industry combined, while mobile devices now provide such a broad ability to enter magic circles anytime, anyplace. The exciting principles of risk and return of the stock market have become more broadly accepted, compared to the ordinary economic principles of supply and demand. Tribalism has become an issue, where supporting a public representative would feel more like supporting a sports team than a policy or ideology. And lastly, even common human communication was turned into a game with points of gratification on social media. I felt generational questions arise to me: "Can we not separate the ordinary from the play-world anymore, or has it always been like this?" "What if we simply don't want to separate those worlds? Isn't it more fun anyway to enter the play-world and break the magic circle behind us? #YOLO".

Lacking an answer, I had simply called this cultural force "Playerism". Playerism as a style of populism. Playerism as the total breach of the play-world into the ordinary world. It was clear to me that to express this, the correct medium must therefore come in the form of a game, and World Control had been waiting in the dark for too long.

Games as an artistic medium

My design process of World Control started when an Oxfam study suggested that 62 of the wealthiest individuals were as wealthy as the bottom half of the global population (Oxfam, 2016). With the thought that it was maybe a matter of a decade until the game of World Control, with its maximum of 6 players, could roughly represent global power, I contacted Michael to suggest it was time for World Control to be published. With his permission to alter the rules and publish the game, I started to design the game in my spare time. When, a couple months later, a self-proclaimed billionaire, Game-Show-host and Casino-owner announced his candidacy for the office of President of the United States and Commander-in-Chief of the world's most powerful armed forces, the game seemed to become real way too quickly.

Since the rules of the game already existed, I had thought of my work as a game designer as someone like a stage designer of a theatre. I would set the scene and the narrative, so that players can act out themselves. As a student of architecture, I always wanted to design an epic physical magic circle that captures the modern play-world, something so robust that even if archaeologists would find it thousands of years in the future on a possible desert planet earth, they could figure out what had happened to society in present times. I began to design and carve a heavy physical magic circle for this board game, and the Trump-phenomenon felt like a train rolling directly through it while I was shaping it. To mark the game's mechanics of a contorted reality,

Immanuel Kant's moral guideline was twisted and featured on the header of the rules as: "Human dignity is irrelevant". After all, since most of politics had become so heavily gamified, my main driving force was that games had to become openly political. Being an Austrian publisher, I felt that a possible World War 3 simply had to come from the same country that sparked the first two, but to ban it into the play-world this time around.

With a rough prototype, minimal preparation and no marketing-budget a Crowdfunding-campaign was launched, and World Control funded on the day that Donald Trump won the 2016 US presidential elections. [2] To link the board game to social media, the Twitter-Bot @MinisterVlatin - modelled as Vladimir Putin sitting on the Lincoln memorial - was conceived, that allowed players to write their own #fakenewz event cards for the game. After the election it had become clear that Russian trolls had influenced the US election. As if the age of Playerism had now begun, a chilling magic accompanied the design process, that felt as if the ordinary world and the game were in a deep struggle with each other. All I wanted was to capture this force adequately and finally put its cover on.

The profound way of experiencing a different and dark sides of us, and how systems of rules generate certain outcomes and interactions between players, is a major part of the magic that is the natural safe space of the play world. To draw a line - no matter how blurry it may be – to the ordinary world in order to apply these learning experiences and to never forget that the ordinary world has an array of completely different value systems and irregularities, has become important to me. Especially since the learning experience of World Control has been that a multipolar (or multiplayer) world, based on a competitive, zero-sum framework, can lead to very bad outcomes for the majority involved. For these reasons, I came to see an understanding and appreciation for the magic circle concept as highly beneficial, and felt that it was becoming even more necessary, especially for a gamified generation, to draw a line between both worlds, if only artistically. I therefore featured a simple multilingual poem for peace on the cover of the box. It was created by my father, who

---

[2]   https://www.kickstarter.com/projects/avocadovic/worldcontrol-boardgame-perfection

had been the founder of the international poetry school in Vienna[3], days before he died, which was of course a deep personal touch, but also meant to symbolically mark the thin veneer of diverse and complex human behaviour that makes a colourful world full of differences possible. When this cover is lifted and the game's magic circle entered, the mechanics of raw power are put into play.

The poem is utterly simple, and is represented by the phonetic symbol [ʃ]. It came after his long obsession with collecting short video clips of native speakers saying the word "peace" in their native language. Ultimately, he was working on turning it into a song solely consisting of these words but did not want to raise any language above any other for the chorus of the song. Thus, he wanted to find a universally acceptable word or sound, and it was shortly before he died that he realized that the sound "sh" [ʃ] is done by every mother on earth to pacify her child, mimicking the sound of gently crashing waves as a universally soothing sound. By additionally framing the globe, depicted on the cover, with the unique translations for "peace" in the 50 most spoken languages and their respective fonts, I sought to represent our world as the diverse mix of different understanding. For my publishing venture it served as a silent reminder that the world is not a game, but World Control is.

---

[3] https://sfd.at

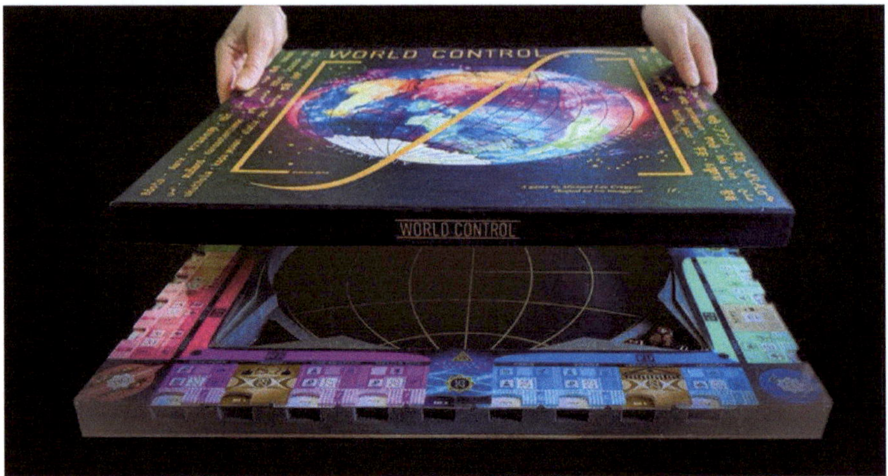

Figure 1. World Control - Elite Edition. Photo: imago.im, 2021

The expectation that games deserve to be recognised as an artistic medium that is valued for its freedom of form and expression, like it is reserved for the world of literature, music or film, and not pure entertainment or commercial scalability, defined the struggle of making these heavy, material-intensive game boards. It was to capture my archetype of Playerism and give the play-world its proper frame within the real world. And it was preluded by a long journey.

Leaving the play world

While the boomer generation has experienced a huge development in the artistic use of audio-visual mediums like recorded music and film, like many among my generation I have spent most of my conscious life growing up actively playing (video) games, besides the passive media consumption of music and films. From playing Pac-Man (Namco, 1980) on Atari, Donkey Kong (Nintendo, 1981) on Tric-o-Tronics, upgrading through the family of Nintendo consoles to playing every kind of game on the PC. As I grew up, so did the world of gaming. From being a couple of pixels to 3D-rendered virtual reality the visual modelling of games had gone a long way very quickly, but the fading abstraction and approaching ability to model the real world, made video games lose its thrill for me. My excitement turned to escape the Matrix (WB, 1999) in search for the actual "real world". The travel bug had gotten hold of me, but the virtual world offered me access to the adult's game of trading stocks online in high hopes of quick returns to finance my travels. But upon my arrival in New York City on September 30th in 2008, it just so happened to be the exact day a complete meltdown of the stock market started to unravel. "Game Over" was flashing all over my personal plans, and upon a visit to the Cregger family, World Control was the last game I played for a long time, as I made the radical decision, only a 21-year-old is capable of: To leave the play-world and society absolutely.

The Jumanji archetype

This voluntary decision to leave comfort and safety led me into the jungle of a Caribbean Island and was guided by the mysterious thrill for adventure as portrayed by the drumbeats in the iconic movie Jumanji (Sony, 1995). The movie is about a couple of kids discovering an ancient board game within a highly civilised and boring American suburb. By starting to play the game, the laws of the jungle are unleashed and start to alter the ordinary world in brutal ways.

Watching the movie from the point of view of a student of Game Studies to observe the game mechanics, Jumanji must have received the poorest reviews possible. Players simply take turns, rolling the dice in order to move a figure along a path to the end, while the players' agency is virtually inexistent. Even though imaginary, Jumanji represents an archetype of a game that is purely built on the immersive factor and the initial excitement to enter this magic circle into a different world. The players are so deeply immersed to the point that the character displayed by Robin Williams has been sucked into the game at a young age and spends most of his life within it. He only gets a chance to return to ordinary life when the game is finally finished, and throughout the movie, the players are not seen having fun but are in constant fear for survival. To win the game is simply to survive together.

When the game is finally closed and its magic circle has evaporated, what will bleed into ordinary life will be a deep appreciation of the safe and boring environment of civilisation and a deep bond between the former players remaining. Society as the ongoing cooperation of surviving together, while the laws of the jungle are best left to the play world. For my personal journey this turned out to be true. With a hunger for interaction with people my re-entry into society continued with a passion for the physical world and the study of architecture.

The Nero archetype

My academic journey started with a passion for ancient Greek architecture. Besides its temple architecture, it was the emphasis on public forums, courts and theatres, that had a clear form of creating culture. It seemed that physical manifestations of magic circles were its fundamental characteristic in building lasting public institutions.

The Hellenic world is credited in originating theatre which most likely developed out of ritual play for the divinity of Dionysus. (Hildy, 2022). and its designated building, like many cultural aspects of Hellenic origin, they have been adapted and further developed by the growing Roman republic. As the Roman republic grew and incorporated more foreign slaves, ever grander arenas were built, and games turned ever more spectacular and brutal. Leading to the end of the republic and the rise of the Roman empire, warlords would stage ever greater games to harness the support of the people and to consolidate power into fewer hands. "Bread and games" would ultimately become the Empire's to provide a social fabric, that glued a diverse population together for centuries.

Its crescendo can be portrayed by the popular image of emperor Nero. Although recent historic research paints a different picture, the iconic enfant terrible remains. Living for the games completely, Nero himself took the stage to engage in acting and racing - normally reserved for slaves - of ever more spectacular games. For this behaviour he gained popularity by soldiers and the general public, while being despised by the political elite for the disrespect for the high office. The whole empire and known world as a spoiled child's game. A populist archetype for later populist figures like former Italian prime minister Silvio Berlusconi or the 45th president of the United States, Donald Trump. The rumours that Nero himself was responsible for the great fires in Rome, while blaming the early Christians, who had gained great popularity among the poor and disenfranchised, only to make space for a golden house, prevail to this day. Whether this image of Nero is historically accurate or simply a construct of later Christian propaganda has not been settled. What we do know is that Tertullian, who would ultimately become known as the father of Latin Christianity and the inventor of the concept of hell, had widely condemned theatre and games as sinful behaviour in his writings "De Spectaculis" in the late 2nd century AD (Tertullian, 1988).

Religion kills play

Gatherings that moved emotions were attributed to the pagan ways of life, unworthy of God-fearing Christians, and the Roman ways of exhibiting status, wealth and splendour had become part of the seven deadly sins. Just like early Christians vandalised the library of Alexandria to tear out generations of European knowledge, the play element was tossed out of the accepted cultural sphere. Ultimately, the Olympic games were stopped in the 5th century AD, the last definite record of a theatre performance in Rome was in 533, and in the Eastern Roman capital of Constantinople, the church passed a resolution forbidding all mimes, theatres, and other spectacles in 692 (Hildy, 2022). The magic circles of ancient theatres had been ripped of their magic and were turned into military facilities, housing, or simply used for building materials for which production the knowledge had been lost. At least in public, Play was dead, and Europe did not see architectural manifestations of physical magic circles like theatres or stadiums for more than a millennium until the Renaissance would once again flood the European continent with intellect and creativity.

Medieval religious drama only arose centuries later out of the church's desire to educate its largely illiterate flock, using dramatizations of the New Testament as a dynamic teaching method (Hildy, 2022). Passion plays would then be held in closed parts of churches or in the streets, and from the 6th to the 14th century CE, many complaints are recorded about women taking part in <u>licentious</u> public performances on festive occasions. Indeed, many jugglers, acrobats, dancers, singers, and musicians of the dark ages were women (Hildy, 2022), while for the honour of an insulted knight, arenas for jousting were set up, and losing this game most likely meant death. The attention of masses within a great circle during those times was mostly focused on a variety of execution methods, and we know how authoritarian regimes or religious extremists use stadiums for the same purpose of focused attention to this day. Physical circles may survive, but not necessarily their magic.

Games are bigger than God

I had begun to perceive how these magic circles are manifested physically in "the real world" as possibly providing a measure on how much games and play are valued within a society. It provided a new dimension for me to understand history and the strength of civilisations, apart from military success, economic factors, religion, politics or diplomacy, but by how much a culture provides space for play. The more conflict, competition and the laws of the jungle, so deeply rooted in our human condition, are pushed into the play world, the more innovative and prosperous a society would become. It dawned on me that this was not a chicken and egg situation but that the play-element truly seems to be the chicken that gives birth to innovation and civil progress, as Huizinga suggested (Huizinga, 1938, p.5).

With my research into the ancient world of play intensifying, the realisation arose that almost every high culture has invented some form of board games. Men's Morris as one of the oldest surviving games, can be dated back to pharaonic Egypt and has been played globally throughout the aeons. (Grunfeld, 1975, p.59) Even earlier, Egyptian royals played Senet, and Tutankhamun himself was buried with 4 game boards, and before that Sumerians knew the royal game of Ur. (Livingstone, 2019, p.24) The Chinese developed Weiqi, commonly known as Go, the abstract strategy game, probably closest to perfection. Ethiopian culture grew Mancala, of which many variants are played all over

Africa and, by now, internationally. Interestingly, both Aztecs and Indians played similar cross-shaped games named Patolli or Pachisi. (Livingstone, 2019, p.32) It remains unsettled whether Backgammon was invented in Persia, the Middle East or the Roman Empire, which had developed numerous board games (Livingstone, 2019, p.31).

As my research went along, I would stumble across a familiar pattern, namely that it is next to impossible to find a truly authentic Buddhist, Jewish, Christian or Islamic game. Quite to the contrary, a common trait for religious teachings worldwide is that playing games distracts from one's duty of labour and prayer. As early as 500BC, Buddha taught principles of a devout life and wrote of a list of games in the Digha Nikaya, that he would not play, which coincidentally is also the earliest known list of games. (Murray, 1913) Among them dice games or games on grids, on which he was quite specific with quoting games of rows of 8 or 10 (Livingstone, 2019, p.31). Despite these religious rules, a game with a grid of 8 would originate in India a millennium later that grew widely popular. In the 6th century AD, it was known by the name of "Chaturanga" and was soon adapted by the Arab conquests, who changed the figures of elephants and horses into abstract pieces, since depictions of deities were forbidden. It became widely popular among the Muslim elite as "Shah" in Baghdad during the golden age of Islam, with writings about game strategies and a system of evaluating a player's strength appearing. However, the Islamic clergy already declared playing games as being Haram – forbidden – as early as the 8th century AD. Declared a waste of time, the struggle on legal rulings continues to this day with the game having been outlawed by the Iranian revolution in 1979 (even though this was reversed later) and being banned by Saudi Arabia as recently as 2019.[4] The game became known in the western world as "chess" and had entered Europe as early as the 10th century via the Muslim world. It also survived a struggle with Christian clergy in the 15th century, having been banned by the Russian orthodoxy as well as in England before (Murray, 1913). Today chess is, of course, the most popular board game globally, and grand masters are heralded for their superior intellect. According to its history,

---

[4] https://www.theguardian.com/world/2016/jan/21/chess-forbidden-in-islam-rules-saudi-arabia-grand-mufti

though, perhaps chess could also become known as the game that has already beaten three gods.

The battle between play and religion is a profound one. Religion being a make-believe-world with agreed upon rules has many characteristics of the play world. As early board games suggest, chance also had a strong connection to the divine, and a lucky roll of dice that beats all odds can truly feel like the gods are on one's side. But religious doctrines cannot deal with chance, since above all god has a universal plan and will, an instance that even quantum physicist Niels Bohr would famously discuss with Albert Einstein, as the notion that "god does not roll dice". However, as it later turned out with ever more complex quantum-mechanics experiments, God does.[5] The observation that games of chance and gambling could also lead to addictive behaviour and people wagering livelihoods of hard work on easy returns could be seen as a big danger to social cohesion and what is considered fair, and religion usually has a strong urge to keep order within society. However, as demonstrated with chess, religion can't deal with games of strategy either. Perhaps only God can have a plan and ultimate agency. Just like the magic circles of theatre-play are not widely accepted, regions under extremist Islamic rule not even accept music to this day. Regardless of the level of extremes, as a general pattern religion seems to be the biggest killer of the play element, and for all the joy that is missing in life, God is here with a purpose, always. Voluntary action for no purpose at all does not play well with the concept of religion.

If all culture, art, science, law and order is indeed rooted within the play world (Huizinga, 1938, p.5) the rules of a ritualistic play-world have stuck and became deadly serious for the ordinary world in the form of religion. If religion can be seen as a make-believe play-world, it has no end and has no limit in space. Its rules apply all the time, anywhere, even after death. Therefore, there can be no magic circle to be entered or left anymore, as one is locked inside this play-world forever. There is no difference between the play world and the ordinary, which it demands to rule. And while no one should expect laws to be fun in order to enforce social cohesion, it may just be religion's overarching claim

---

[5] https://plus.maths.org/content/why-god-plays-dice

to rule both the ordinary as well as the play-world that makes it so addictive to totalitarian behaviour. If Huizinga observes that in play the cheater is treated kindlier than the spoilsport (Homo Ludens, p. 11), we can easily draw the line to the play-world of religion, where being blamed a hypocrite has been not nearly as dangerous as denouncing god. Religion does not accept any other play-worlds besides itself and takes its own play-world incredibly seriously, with spoilsports of a religious play-world having been prosecuted with utmost brutality throughout history. After all, the magic circle may be one of the strongest concepts to promote well-being within secular societies.

No play, no culture

As it turns out, cultures who would deal with the demands of the ordinary world most efficiently were the ones who gave the play-element ample space. That the ludic character is seen even more clearly in Chinese civilization than in the Hellenic world (Huizinga, 1938, p.55) can also be observed with China's long history of gambling and developing games (McKenzie, 2004). The abstract strategy game of Weiqi, or Go, remains the oldest continuously played board game in the world. It's simple grid, a set of identical black and white stones and essentially only 2 rules, has an emergent variety of options that exceeds the number of atoms in the universe, which is why it famously took 20 years longer to develop the AI AlphaGo to beat the then world champion, Ke Jie, in 2017, then it took to develop a chess AI, when Deep Blue beat Garry Kasparov in 1997. [6] Chinese has the same word for playing cards as it does for playing tiles, like Mah-jong, and having already invented paper in the 6th century AD, Chinese culture had the first card games developed as early as 868 CE, when Yezi Ge (the Leaf Game) was mentioned (Livingstone, 2019, p.56). It also created the classic deck of 4 types of cards, which originally had 32 cards, before the Arab world later extended it to 52 (McKenzie, 2004).

Around the same time chess entered Europe around the 10th century via the Muslim influence on the Iberian Peninsula,

---

[6] https://www.deepmind.com/research/highlighted-research/alphago

continental Europe had been introduced to the Nordic board game variations of Tafl after the Viking invasions. The book of games (Libro de Juegos, Alfonso X.) commissioned in 1283 by Alfonso X., is the first European written document about games, featuring variations of 3 games: Chess, dice games and table games like backgammon. The writings feature many strategic chess problems and long mathematical calculations of different possibilities of dice rolls, however evading moral connotations and framing it under astronomical research. The origin of the tile game Domino is not certain, but it was most likely brought from China to Europe by Marco Polo in 1295 (McKenzie, 2004). Playing cards were brought from the Muslim world by traders, and in 1365, playing cards were first mentioned in Italian documents, after which their popularity rapidly spread across Europe. (Livingstone, 2019, p. 59)

Theatre groups of religious passion and mystery plays had mushroomed in popularity since the early 15th century, but only after the catholic church started to crumble in a power struggle with the rising reformists in the 16th century did theatre stage its big comeback. Professional acting groups from an emerging civil society were now emancipating themselves from religious liturgy or entertaining the royal courts. The Confrérie de la Passion, which had performed mystery plays for almost 150 years, is said to have opened the first European purpose-built public theatre since Roman times in 1548, within the hotel de Bourgogne. The first true Renaissance theatre and oldest existing theatre in Europe, the Teatro Olimpico, built by Andrea Palladio, opened in Vicenza in 1585. And in London the big wooden Globe Theatre was built in 1599, where Shakespeare's plays were first performed (Hildy, 2022).

In short, the European renaissance was accompanied by an influx of games, and the play-world once again started to act freely and permanently manifest its physical magic circles within the public space after more than a Millenia of suppression.

The western power of games

It may be another coincidence of history that the initial spark for the French revolution in 1789 happened within a ballroom, where members of the Third Estate pledged the Tennis Court Oath. Ballrooms had been built for playing new sportive games like squash or tennis and had become very popular among a growing civil elite. Playing these games, where one could meet on an equal footing in fair competition, was not only fun but could also provide access to nobility and political power. A broader civil society not only wanted to be part of the game, but also to simply watch a competitive game of sports. In 1804, the first European stadium built since antiquity was the Lord's cricket stadium in London. Watching sports became so popular that, in the decades to come, stadium building spread greatly all over the rapidly expanding European empires around the globe to India, Australia and the Americas. Despite oppressive British colonisation, the large, occupied public of India gladly accepted the imported magic circles of the Anglican world and builds the most massive Cricket-stadiums to date. 1896 would see the Olympic games take place in Athens for the first time in about 1500 years, and almost no superpower today values little things more than showing off their strength at this global spectacle. By far the biggest growth in stadium building happened in the United States, which as a newly independent, colonial offspring, started to build baseball stadiums on a large scale with the latest steel-technology. With almost any American high school or college today featuring a small to large stadium for football or baseball, these magic circles are an integral part of modern American culture.

Even Japan constructed a baseball stadium near the point of the nuclear bomb drop of Hiroshima in 1957 shortly after the peace memorial was completed in 1952, being absolutely in love with the game. As for the Indian love for cricket and not even a nuclear bomb being able to spoil the Japanese love for baseball, I would wonder: "Why would cultures adapt and celebrate the games of other cultures that have caused so much pain to them?" Instead of a definite answer for the human power of forgiveness or the possible need to beat the humiliator at their own game, I was simply struck by a familiar feeling how games can be perceived as "bigger than life". Even though games do not always bring out the best in people, it has stood the test of being highly beneficial in binding society together by providing an extraordinarily safe space for competitive traits. Games and Play are truly creators of a common culture, and Japan would become a leader in the video game industry and a close ally of the United States.

In addition to offering masses of people access into stadiums, board game prints would appear on kitchen tables in the 20th century. Besides the easily reproduceable games to be played with some seeds and drawn grids like Mancala, Men's Morris or Go, board games have historically been among the most elite products of craftsmanship that only the highest elites could afford. Now they could be enjoyed by the average family, and it is ironic that the most popular board game in history would eventually be about something so incredibly ordinary like real estate. Invented by the Quaker woman Lizzy Maggie as "The Landlord's Game" to teach about mechanics of inequality, it featured two gameplays: A cooperative mode and a competitive mode to become the monopolist. (Pilon, 2015) Ultimately, it was the monopolist's gameplay that excited the masses after her idea had been blatantly copied and published as "Monopoly". It showed that the thrill of being in a position of power would be more exotic and engaging to the ordinary family player, but also that a major demand on games is to provide an inherent learning experience about something of great importance to any given society. The way to the afterlife was the major concern of Egyptian Senet, war or conquest is the general theme of most games, and now the struggle to pay rent or own real estate was on top of the list.

As the theme of inequality remains relevant in the cultural and political world, owning hotels Monopoly-style seems to be almost cute in these times. With the Trump phenomenon, an unhinged play-element rose from being a hotel-owner to commander in chief of the world's most powerful armed forces. This was a different game. This was World Control style. To remember how this play of power works but to ban it into the play-world was the main idea behind its publication, so that the playful and liberal culture, that the rest of the world has aspired to copy for generations now, can continue. After all, we have many more games to play.

Final thoughts on the age of Playerism

"In play we may move below the level of the serious, as the child does; but we can also move above it – in the realm of the beautiful and the sacred." (Huizinga, 1938, p.19)

Being convinced that the more a society values the play-element within itself, the more it prospers, a lot of access to play and games can greatly inspire creativity and innovation, create social cohesion or simply lets people blow off some steam within a safe environment.

The suppression of the play-element stems from a deeply illiberal mindset that usually claims total ownership over the realm of the beautiful and sacred, like religion has attempted to for Millenia, in order to control the ordinary world. While it is safe to assume that large parts of the world will not follow Saudi Arabia's example of banning chess, the trend to limit game-time can already be seen under the authoritarian regime of the people's republic of China.

The amount of time we spend playing games can't be ignored, and we might want to consider the risks of not wanting to leave the play-world at all, as well. To stay below the serious forever, with an urge to win at all times is completely cynical and can suffer all the consequences of an enfant terrible in control.

Just like getting sucked into Jumanji, the essential magic of a game - being fun - fades when it continues indefinitely. It becomes addiction, and it is most likely to happen when playing alone. The kid who must get drawn away from the screen or console, kicking and screaming, or the slot machine addict who doesn't even get the slightest reaction from a winning roll anymore, but still can't stop while all their time and money is slowly eaten away. When unhinged and not contained to a certain time or space, the play-element can become hard to snap out of, hypnotic and fanatic, and I believe it is not unreasonable to assume that when a large part of society does so at the same time, societies can be led back to the law of jungle, as unhinged Playerism can treat its own peers as mere competitors or total enemies.

As we progress deeper into the age of Playerism, the value of the magic circle concept may significantly improve in relevance, as well as an understanding how ludic mechanics can shape human interactions. After all, we only have a limited time on this limited space called Earth, and it is probably wise to make it as fun and peaceful as possible.

References

World Control [Board game]. (2017). Imago.im

Monopoly [Board game]. (1935). Parker Brothers

Risk [Board game]. (1959). Parker Brothers.

Pac-Man [Video game]. (1980). Namco.

Donkey Kong [Video game]. (1981). Nintendo.

Johnston, J. (Director). (1995). Jumanji [Film]. Sony.

Wachowski, L. & L. (Director). (1999). The Matrix [Film]. Warner Brothers.

Huizinga, J. (1938). Homo Ludens. Random House.

Grunfeld, F.V. (1975). Games of the world. Holt, Rinehart and Winston.

Murray, H.J.R. (1913). History of Chess. Skyhorse.

McKenzie, C. & Irving, L.F. (2004) Asian Games: The Art of Contest, Asia Society (NY).

Friedman, T. L. (2004) The world is flat. Farrar, Straus and Giroux.

Grunfeld, F.V. (1975). Games of the world. Holt, Rinehart and Winston.

Livingstone, I.L. (2019). Board games in 100 moves – 8000 years of play. DK.

Pilon, M. (2015). The monopolist. Bloomsbury.

Tertullian, De Spectaculis. (1988). „Über die Spiele: Lat./Dt.". Reclam

Oxfam. (2016). An economy for the 1%. Retrieved from https://www-cdn.oxfam.org/s3fs-public/file_attachments/bp210-economy-one-percent-tax-havens-180116-en_0.pdf

Hildy, F.J. (2022). Theater Building. Retrieved from https://www.britannica.com/art/theater-building/ (last updated Jul 30, 2022)

Alfonso X. (1283). Libro de Juegos, Retrieved from http://jnsilva.ludicum.org/HJT2012/BookofGames.pdf

THE HIDDEN MAGIC OF MAGIC CIRCLES

ON THE LUDIC, CULTURAL, AND POLITICAL SIGNIFICANCE OF HUIZINGA'S METAPHOR

Nikolaus Koenig

Gabrielle Trépanier-Jobin

In this paper, we argue that Salen and Zimmerman's take on the magical circle concept does not fully do justice to Huizinga's original one, partly because it reduces it to a pragmatic tool for game designers rather than a statement aimed at deepening our understanding of play and games, but also because it neglects the term "magic" in favor of the term "circle" that connotes separation. Discussing the appropriation of Huizinga's ideas in today's game studies discourse and relating them to other relevant contributions to the theory of play – most notably the work of the French philosopher Jacques Henriot – we show that there are different levels on which "magic" can fuel discussions of play; the "highest" of these levels being the idea of play as a creative force akin to magic. We argue that this is Huizinga's underlying conception of play, as well as the foundation of his argument on play as the root of culture that was intended as a political stance against totalitarianism and fascism.

Keywords: magic circle, Huizinga, play, creativity, law of nations, Homo Ludens

Introduction

The magic circle concept is generally attributed to the Dutch historian Johan Huizinga. In his book *Homo Ludens* (1938), the expression "magic circle" features in his list of "play-grounds" alongside the arena, the card-table, the temple, the court of

311

justice, "within which special rules obtain" and which "are temporary worlds within the ordinary world, dedicated to the performance of an act apart." (p. 10) Today's use of the term in game studies is, however, strongly influenced by its appropriation by Salen and Zimmerman who, in their book *Rules of Play* (2004), single out the expression "magic circle" and use it as a short-cut for the idea of a "special place in time and space created by a game." (p. 95) This idea of games as being separated from "real life" – supposedly expressed by the magic circle metaphor – has proven controversial and has led to heated but often productive debates.

In this paper, we argue that Salen and Zimmerman's take on the concept does not fully do justice to the original one, partly because it reduces it to a pragmatic tool for game designers rather than a statement revealing deeper truths about the nature of play and games, but also because it neglects the term "magic" in favor of the term "circle" that connotes separation. Drawing on Michael J. Apter's, Jacques Henriot's and Johan Huizinga's own theoretical considerations, we show that there are different levels on which "magic" can fuel discussions of play; the "highest" of these levels being the idea of play as a creative force akin to magic. We argue that this idea is the key to understanding Huizinga's conception of play, as well as to fully appreciate his argument on the play-roots of culture as a political stance against totalitarianism and fascism.

The magic circle in game studies

Many game scholars criticize the spatiotemporal separation between games and ordinary life that has become almost synonymous with the "magic circle" metaphor.

Copier (2005), for instance, argues that the "closed magic circle" is a problematic utopia, since the play-space is always negotiated between players and producers as well as among players. Similarly, Taylor (2007) believes that the magic circle rhetoric is misleading because it implies that games are closed systems that allow players to operate outside everyday life, while, in fact, players constantly push against their boundaries. Even though Consalvo (2009) admits that the idea of a boundary marking game space from the outside world can be useful, she specifies that this boundary is constantly breached, since everyday rules apply in game environments and compete with rules that are specific to a game, a player community or a gaming context. For example, "real" money is often involved during gameplay, and cheaters judge their gaming practices according to their real-life moral values. Similarly, Lehdonvirta (2010) claims that the inaccurate dichotomy between the "real" world and the "virtual" world is rooted in the magic circle concept and ignores that social norms and laws influence how people interpret games' rules; that relationships between players can be as genuine as face-to-face relationships; that players' geographic locations impact their possible alliances with other players; that avatars and players' identities are intertwined, etc.

For all these reasons and many others, several game scholars suggest replacing the expression "magic circle" with more accurate metaphors. Lehdonvirta (2010), for instance, recommends using Strauss' concept of "social world" instead, which refers to a universe of discourses and a sphere of effective communication rather than territorial or formal borders. Consalvo (2010), for her part, suggests "Turner's (1969) conception of liminal spaces" (p. 410), which refers to a change of attitude that one adopts while remaining in the same geographical space, as it is the case in the context of a carnival, for instance. In reference to Goffman's idea of "frames" (perceptual organizing principles), she also suggests "conceptualizing gamer activity as movements between frames" (p. 414) as a possible alternative. Juul (2008) proposes the puzzle metaphor, which better reflects that the boundaries between games and daily life are constantly negotiated by players, and that a game must be part of a context to be experienced as something separate from that context. Arsenault and Perron (2009) propose the expression "magic cycle" (p. 113) which better illustrates that playing a game is a "continuous loop between the player's input and the game's output" (ibid.) and that the temporal dimension of gameplay prevails on its spatial dimension.

Even though most criticisms of the magic circle's strict separation in time and space are justified, we will see that they rely on a narrow interpretation of Huizinga's original concept.

Into the bottle, genie!

Almost a decade after *Rules of Play*, Eric Zimmerman (2012) prominently engaged in the debate once again with his essay "Jerked Around by the Magic Circle: Clearing the Air Ten Years Later." Identifying a tendency in game studies to evoke a strict interpretation of the magic circle, only to be able to tear it down, he sets out "to clarify where this magic circle idea came from, what it was intended to mean, and to stop the energy being wasted by chasing the ghost of the magic circle jerk - a ghost that simply doesn't exist" (ibid.). While the essay can be read as an ardent plea for open-minded and multi-perspective approaches in interdisciplinary research[1], it is also an attempt to put the magic circle genie back in its bottle. To do so, Zimmerman follows two lines of argumentation.

On the one hand, he aims to defuse the criticisms by pointing out that an "orthodox, narrow view of the magic circle" (ibid.) is merely "a fiction that people project onto Homo Ludens and Rules of Play" (ibid.). Regarding Huizinga, he states that:

> [...] he never takes the full-blown magic circle point of view that games are ultimately separate from everything else in life or that rules are the sole fundamental unit of games. In fact, Huizinga's thesis is much more ambivalent on these issues and he actually closes his seminal book with a passionate argument against a strict separation between life and games. (ibid.)

Zimmerman even gets Huizinga out of the discursive line of fire by laying claim on the concept himself:

> The magic circle is not something that comes wholly from Huizinga. To be perfectly honest, Katie and I more or less invented the concept, inheriting its use from my work with Frank [Lantz], cobbling together ideas from Huizinga and Caillois, clarifying key elements that were important for our book, and reframing it in terms of semiotics and design – two disciplines

---

[1] Zimmerman urges us to apply "different cognitive frames to knowledge at different moments" and reminds us that "Concepts and ideas should be understood within the framework of their originating discipline." (2012)

that certainly lie outside the realm of Huizinga's own scholarly work. But that is what scholarship often is – sampling and remixing ideas in order to come to a new synthesis. (ibid.)

While Zimmerman clearly refuses the idea that he might be the "ignoramus that holds these strange and narrow ideas about games" (ibid.), he does not invoke the passage in *Rules of Play* that might absolve him and Salen from this allegation. In this passage, they ask to what extent the boundary between the real world and the artificial world of the game delimited by the magic circle is permeable.[2]

His second line of argument takes quite another direction: "Rules of Play is a book about game design. Every concept between its covers was conceived as something useful for designers struggling with the process of creating games" (ibid.). The concepts presented in the book (including the magic circle) are merely "tools that can be used to understand, construct, and modify games" (ibid.). After laying an arguably justified claim to the contemporary version of the magic circle concept and making the (maybe less justified) suggestion that the magic circle was merely an arbitrary example Huizinga used among many others, he finally backs down on the concept's relevance by saying it was never intended as more than a pragmatic tool.

This conclusion is hard to accept. Even if the concept promoted in *Rules of Play* had indeed been devised as a pragmatic tool for game designers rather than a statement revealing deeper truths about the nature of play and games, this understanding might not be everything that the magic circle metaphor has to offer.

What is it all about, Johan?

No matter what one thinks about the debate itself, the whole story revolves around the magic circle as a delineated play-space. However, this is not what the magic circle is really about. As

---

[2] Approaching games as systems, and thereby already taking a specific perspective within the games and play discourse, they state that "the answer to the question of whether games are open or closed systems depends on which schema is used to understand them: whether games are framed as RULES, as PLAY, or as CULTURE." (Salen & Zimmerman 2004, p. 96)

Arsenault and Perron (2009) point out, Huizinga's magic circle cannot be reduced to spatial aspects, but rather "illustrates the fact that we see and behave in games differently than in our ordinary-life psychological frame." (p. 111) This is what Huizinga meant at the end of his famous attempt to define core aspects of play:

> Play is a voluntary activity or occupation executed within certain fixed limits of time and place, according to rules freely accepted but absolutely binding, having its aim in itself and accompanied by a feeling of tension, joy and the consciousness that it is "different" from "ordinary life." (Huizinga 1938, p. 28)

From that perspective, the idea of a separation between play/games and real life is a good starting point for psychological, cultural, or even metaphysical investigations of play and games. The question is, however, if this idea should be tied to Huizinga's initial mention of the magic circle, or if his use of the term points to another aspect that might be equally or even more significant.

We are aware that a thorough discussion of what Huizinga intended with the magic circle metaphor might seem to miss the point, as he never elaborates on what he "means" with the term. However, there is an argument to be made (and we will attempt to make it) that the term does (i) reveal more about Huizinga's concept of play than what is apparent at first glance, and that (ii) this concept of play is more relevant for today's discourse than it is usually credited for. Trying to uncover this initial meaning, which may have been "overpainted" with Salen and Zimmerman's conception and the ensuing debate, should probably start at its textual origin: Huizinga's list of "play-grounds".

Et cetera?

When Huizinga lists "the arena, the card-table, the magic circle, the temple, the stage, the screen, the tennis court, the court of justice, etc." (1938, p. 10) as manifestations of play-grounds, we tend to accept this assemblage simply as a list of arbitrary examples that all reflect what play is. After all, Huizinga ends his list with an *et cetera*. In that case, the magic circle might just be "another example of a ritual space" as Zimmerman (2012) states.

However, there is also the possibility that Huizinga's examples are (deliberately or intuitively chosen) illustrations of the various aspects of play; the *et cetera* meaning that there are numerous other examples for every one of these aspects.

Indeed, the arena is the emblematic example of a dedicated space which can be entered and left, and where play takes place within, not without. The card table is the only example which showcases an actual gaming activity. The temple highlights the sacred earnest with which we perform our ritualistic play. The stage illustrates the idea of taking on roles that transcend our everyday identity. The screen refers to the experience of illusions and to our willing suspension of disbelief. The tennis court is the only example for engaging in an artificial conflict. As for the court of justice, it shows how the outcome of our play (within the playing field of the courtroom) is often seen as binding for the world outside of the game.

In this understanding, each of Huizinga's examples highlights another feature of what he thinks play entails. While they "are all in form and function play-grounds", each feature is also distinct from any others, and none can be omitted if one wants to understand play. If this is the case, it would make little sense to take the magic circle as a reference to the seclusion of the play-space, because that would already be covered by the "arena". What aspect of play would the magic circle example serve to highlight instead? Perhaps it is time to ask what is so magical about the magic circle?

Magic & Play

It is quite striking that the contemporary understanding and ensuing criticisms of the magic circle concept tend to insist on the term "circle" and ignore the term "magic". It does, however, make sense in the context of *Rules of Play*, which is, after all, "a book about game design" (Zimmerman 2012), and as such prone to pragmatic ideas like circling off the game-space to foster meaningful play experiences. "Magic" is no such pragmatic concept.

Yet, in Huizinga's list of play-grounds, from which Salen and Zimmerman borrowed the expression "magic circle", the two words actually refer to a ritual magic circle. Indeed, Huizinga was trying to highlight the similarities between sacred rituals and play to demonstrate that playgrounds such as the "[t]he turf, the tennis-court, the chessboard and pavement-hopscotch cannot formally be distinguished from the temple or the magic circle" (1938, p. 20).

If we switch for a moment from the magic circle concept we have gotten used to in the game studies discourse and take a closer look at the ancient idea of the ritual magic circle instead, it seems that the often-marginalized aspect of magic may in fact be what makes the concept so relevant. In ritual magic, a "magic circle" is a sacred space marked out physically with salt, flour, chalk, or only visualized, by a ritual magician. Magic circles are believed to contain energy or to provide a protective barrier between the practitioner of ritual magic and what they summon (Stratton-Kent 2010, p. 46). This protective barrier is believed to be fragile, so that leaving or passing through the circle would weaken, dispel, or break it (Buckland 2002, p. 224).

While the fragility of the ritual magic circle hints at an awareness that it stands against the physical world, which exists *independently of our actions or beliefs*, the ritual magic circle is at the same time a manifestation of great power; a power which is *dependent on our actions and beliefs*, and therefore seizes to exist the moment our faith falters.

Huizinga's mention of magic circles suggests a certain connection of magic and play that is overlooked by game scholars. The extent to which the idea of magic can be illuminating for the study of play is by no means straightforward, as magic can relate to play in different ways and on different levels: as a *delusion*, as a *transmutation*, as a *defiance of pragmatism*, as an *oscillation of player identities* or – most significantly – as a *creative force*.

Play as a delusion that makes us believe in magic

On a most basic level, one might think of magic as something that only exists in our fantasy, and of play as a delusive state that makes us (falsely) belief in such fantasies. This corresponds to Apter's idea that:

> In the play-state you experience a protective frame which stands between you and the 'real' world and its problems, creating an enchanted zone in which, in the end, you are confident that no harm can come. Although this frame is psychological, interestingly it often has a perceptible physical representation. (1989, p. 15)

As a psychologist, Apter clearly focuses on the psychological dimensions of play, pointing to the mentally created protective frame of the play-space as well as its instillment of confidence. Apter's enchanted zone is not truly a safe space but is only experienced as such. In other words, the enchantment is merely psychological, as we simply enter a state of mind in which things appear different than they are.

While Apter's protective frame is reminiscent of ritual magic circles, the psychologically framed understanding of the play experience does not equate play with magic: the "enchanted zone" is not actually enchanted. Apter's definition of the play-state is therefore representative of the prevalent view of play as a counterfactual delusion, as something that may be given different degrees of reality status by its participants, but which is nonetheless in competition with a superior reality outside of the play-space.

As a psychological perspective, it bears an almost clinical distance, as it presupposes a certainty about the precise line between fantasy and reality that only an outside observer can claim, but that a player will almost always lack. Depending on the viewpoint, this opposition between play and "reality" can be useful; it does, however, seem rather pragmatic. Within the game studies discourse, it focuses on what game designers want to pay particular attention to: creating games intended to draw players out of reality into a play-state. It is therefore no coincidence that Salen and Zimmerman quote Apter's passage in Rules of Play (2004, p. 94).

This approach to play as a mental state accommodates the prevalent understanding of the magic circle metaphor as a separation between an inside and an outside – and there is hardly anything magical about it. On the contrary, from this point of view, magic could never even exist, except when a delusional state (such as play) makes us falsely believe it is real.

Magical transmutation as an aspect of play

But does the idea of play as a delusion even hold up? French philosopher Jacques Henriot takes a more differentiated stance on the matter, and interestingly, magic plays a crucial part in his perception of play as a subjective experience.

For Henriot (1989) the play experience involves a ludic attitude characterized by three moments. Magic (or irrealism) is the first moment which implies a magical transmutation of the objects and situations that take on new meanings. During this moment, the player loses touch with reality to enter the fictional world. Lucidity (or realism) is the second moment when the player takes a step back and becomes aware that it is a game and not a hallucination. But neither magic (the attribution of new meaning to objects and situations) nor lucidity (the awareness that the objects and situations have not really changed) suffices for an experience of play. Such an experience requires a third moment, which marks a balance between the first and second moment. Henriot calls this moment illusion (or surrealism), and it occurs only when the player allows herself to be enchanted without losing contact with reality (Perron, 2013). She does not really believe in the fiction but pretends to believe in it in order to keep having fun.

Henriot gives the experience of play a turn that cannot be underestimated: instead of being either aware or unaware that the experience is fictional, players are both at the same time, and even more: it is the apparent contradiction itself that defines the play experience.

Play and magic as the defiance of pragmatism

The notion of simultaneous awareness and unawareness leads us to the notion of ambivalence, which is a recurring motive in the theoretical discourse on play. As Claus Pias (2007) pointed out, the idea of play as something "that can join contradictions together into a common productiveness rather than dissolving them" (p. 262, authors' translation) can be traced back as far as Schiller's considerations on the aesthetic education of man (ibid. 262f). What makes Henriot's remarks especially interesting, however, is the way he introduces the notion of magic into play: not as a metaphor for play itself, but as one of two elements the player needs to reconcile. While magic stands in for the part of the experience that transcends reality, the play experience requires an awareness of this unreality at the same time. Magic, therefore, is not a result of the (deceptive) play experience, but a problematic element that requires our belief in order to emerge. At the same time, play demands that we do not fully believe in order to appreciate it without being consumed by it in psychosis.[3]

Coming back full circle to Huizinga, this idea that belief and disbelief are not necessarily opposites is also central in Homo Ludens:

> To describe the phenomena we have to use the term "play" over and over again. What is more, the unity and indivisibility of belief and unbelief, the indissoluble connection between sacred earnest and "make-believe" or "fun", are best understood in the concept of play itself. (Huizinga 1938, p. 24)

While the opposition between play and non-play seems central to understanding play at first glance, a closer look suggests to regard it as a more dialogic principle and also reveals that this position has long had its place in the play discourse. While the coexistence of opposing principles that are usually regarded as mutually exclusive (such as play and non-play, reality and fantasy, truth and delusion) is not necessarily magical *per se*, it

---

3 By pointing to the experience of play as being at the same time immersed into and distanced from the fiction, Henriot's model can be compared to Coleridge's (1817) willing suspension of disbelief, or to the concept of near-belief as it has been formulated by Price (1969, p. 307), who suspects that some people, when reading a novel or watching a stage-play, "do not quite believe" in the narrated events, but neither "refrain from disbelieving it." (Price 1969, p. 307f.) While Coleridge and Price focus on the reception of fictional accounts rather than play, their concepts resonate with Henriot's inextricable connection between magic and lucidity.

marks the same defiance against a pragmatic, positivist world view as magic does: play as well as magic dissolve the pragmatic clarity that things are either true or false, and that two opposing ideas cannot exist simultaneously.

The somewhat magical experience of oscillating player identities

The play experience, however, is insufficiently explained with the reference to the mere cognitive awareness of contradictions and their resolution, because play does not only change how we think about the issues at play, but also how we experience ourselves while playfully negotiating these issues. In order to fully account for this playful awareness of the self, we must, once again, pick up (and pick on) the idea of a separated play-space. As we have already shown, the idea that the magic circle metaphor must imply some kind of separation has remained widely uncontested, regardless of the different and often opposing positions within this debate. However, as the opposition between play and non-play, belief and disbelief, or irrealism and realism dissolves, we are drawn closer to another conclusion: the sometimes useful idea of separation as a defining element of play might obstruct the view on other crucial aspects of play – for instance, the positioning of players as being inside and outside of play simultaneously.

Again, it is Henriot who hints at this playful self-positioning: in the following paragraph, in which he explains how the tension between the first and second moment (magic and lucidity) results in the moment of illusion, Henriot points at a complex relation between the inside and outside of the magic circle by highlighting the position of the player:

> A game in which one does not enter, in which one does not let oneself caught up, is not a game. The game forms an enchanting circle around the player: you have to be inside to play. If you stay outside, you are not playing – you may not understand what the game is about, or even if it is a game. But if you enter the game to the point where you forget that you are playing, then you are alienated: you are no longer playing. Whoever does not enter does not play; whoever allows himself to be caught up does not play anymore. (Henriot 1983, p. 94,

authors' translation)

Henriot's remark opens up an alternate understanding of the magic circle by shifting the attention from the "circle" as a border, a delineation, a separate space, to the enchantment created by this circle which allows to enter without being caught up in the play-state. Play, therefore, constitutes the experience of being inside and outside of the play space at the same time, in what can best be described as an oscillation between two states. This oscillation still presupposes a certain separation, but the separation itself becomes trivial, while the simultaneity of the two processes gains significance.

This experience of oscillating between two states, between being inside and outside, between existing in reality and in a fantasy changes our perception of self in a way that allows us not only to experience both fantasy and reality, but also to distance ourselves from each by clinging to the other. In doing so, it allows us to face real life from a safe position, because we are oscillating between the safety of the play world and the menaces of the "real" world.[4]

This is why Henriot (1969) argues that to be able to posit oneself as a player involves taking sufficient distance from oneself: "Play relies on the interval which separates the subject from himself" (p. 95).

This experience is still not *akin to magic* in the sense of affecting a change in the world around us. But it can very well be regarded as a *somewhat magical* experience, as it playfully entangles us from the necessities and constraints of our daily lives, without the need to deny their reality. It thereby empowers us to approach reality from a new position, one that we have created ourselves. However, this creation did not occur by means of a magic spell or an incantation, but through play. This newly created position

---

[4] Gregory Bateson (1973) has famously described this ability to create abstract versions of real phenomena that borrow some, but not all of their features as the precondition not only for play, but also for psychotherapy, in which we often manage to confront insufferable problems by creating a more tolerable fantasy version of them (p. 211).

might only exist for the duration of play, but it might help us to uncover new truths about ourselves and our reality that might well prevail long after our play has ended.

Play as a creative force akin to magic

So far, we have gradually moved away from the magic circle as a synonym for a separation of some kind. We now want to suggest that what makes the magic circle a strong metaphor for play is not the fact that this circle circumscribes a physical, mental, or symbolic realm, but the ability, implied with the term magic, to imagine something that can become real through play. In other words, the key feature of the magic circle is not separation, but creation. It is not far-fetched to ascribe this interpretation to Huizinga himself, as it resonates with the very beginning of his argument, where he introduces various practices through which "man creates a second, poetic world alongside the world of nature." (Huizinga 1938, p. 4)

The first practice is language, which allows us "to distinguish, to establish, to state things; in short, to name them and by naming them to raise them into the domain of the spirit." (ibid.) Language is a creative doubling of the natural world we find ourselves thrown into, but it is not just a passive reproduction of our experiences: it gives us an abstract means to label our perceptions, to form concepts, and to express and negotiate our ideas to enable a shared experience of the world. Bateson's famous example "the word, 'cat', has no fur and cannot scratch" (1973, p. 183) also brings to the point how words are not the same as, but reference the things they describe.

The second practice to which Huizinga refers is myth, which goes a step further, as we not only give names to the things we experience, but also imagine stories that enable us to make sense of arbitrary phenomena that we cannot otherwise account for. Myths help us to imagine meaningful causes, relations and explanations, as much as they can naturalize or legitimize events that lack inherent justifications.

The third and most prominent practice in which play is the most tangible and to which Huizinga comes back to again and again is ritual. In rituals, we do not only form abstract meanings, as in language, or exchange meaningful stories, as in myth, we actually perform meaning through our actions by conforming to rules that we (as a culture, not necessarily as individuals) have agreed to in advance. This performative element makes ritual special, as it means that there is a tangible element of agency to it, and with it the possibility to either perform well or not so well. This variation of conduct enables different possible outcomes, which is significant because it means that in ritual, as in play, "[t]here is something at stake" (Huizinga 1938, p. 49).

Hence, apart from showing most clearly how Huizinga conceives the relation between play and the human ability to "create a second world alongside the world of nature", this third practice of ritual also holds the key to understanding how play can be perceived as something that is a creative force akin to magic.

This creative power does not lie in the creation of these second worlds (these are still no more than fictitious imaginations, after all). But ritual (and play) is not content with imagining a fictional world, it also urges us to act as if this world was real and this is when the imaginary play-world begins to impact the world outside the play-space. In other words, what began as a fantasy becomes a reality as soon as we start acting as if it was real.

This is especially significant when we consider that, for Huizinga, play is rarely a solitary practice, and almost always a social activity. In play, players relate to an outside world, but more importantly, they relate to this world together, turning a solitary practice into a social activity that does not solely exists in someone's minds, but that actually takes place in the real world.

The political relevance of the magic circle

The field's lack of interest in its own history (see Tobias Unterhuber's contribution to this volume) might explain why Huizinga's text is often read as if it was primarily motivated by a purely academic interest in phenomena of play and games. In game studies (and, it seems, only in game studies), we tend to overlook that Huizinga was not a scholar of play and games, nor was his assessment of play simply an output of his work as a historian.

Indeed, Homo Ludens was part of his political activism, his involvement in the League of Nations and his efforts to promote the Law of Nations as a guarantee for peaceful cooperation between countries. These ideas flare up in Homo Ludens' closing remarks[5] - especially in its criticism of Carl Schmitt and his idealization of war as the full realization rather than the complete failure of international politics (p. 209). But Huizinga expresses his political convictions even more explicitly in his earlier book In the Shadow of Tomorrow (1936), where he states that "[t]he world can no longer bear modern war. It can only be mutilated by it" (p. 191), and where he depicts the image of "a boat in which the nations are crowded together, to live or to sink together" (ibid., p. 193), suggesting that cooperation (in the form of international law) is necessary to humankind's survival.

With the growing authoritarian and totalitarian tendencies in 1930's Europe, ideas of international law as an antidote to martial conflict and the ill-fated dominance of the strong over the weak comes increasingly under attack. Fascists and especially national socialists portray such ideas as imaginary and whimsical fantasies of a few unworldly intellectuals and contrast them with the authority of the facts and the incontestability of the "real world". It's just a piece of paper, the Nazis say when others point to the Versailles Peace Treaty, we'll just tear it to shreds, and who's going to stop us? Huizinga's Homo Ludens can be read as a refutation of this ruthless "might makes right" rhetoric. In his eyes, we cannot simply give in to the harsh realities of life: This is not who we are, because there is an "imperishable need of man to live in beauty" (Huizinga 1938 p. 63), and "[t]here is no satisfying this need save in play." (ibid.) The world may seem unforgiving and cruel, but as humans, we do not have to submit to the world as it is.

As humans (and this is what makes us human), we have this special ability, almost akin to magic, to not just see the world as

---

[5] Thanks to Tobias Unterhuber for pointing this out.

it is and accept that the ruthless and the strong will always have the upper hand. Instead, we can imagine a better world, we can "create a second, poetic world alongside the world of nature" (ibid., p. 4) and imagine rules that would make such a world work. Most importantly, we can all decide to act according to the rules we have made up together.

This is the sacred obligation of play Huizinga insists on: "pacta sunt servanda"[6] (ibid., p. 208). In this sense, culture itself can be understood as a magic spell: as long as we keep believing in it and act accordingly, the spell holds, and we are safe from the evil spirits of egotism, violence, totalitarianism and fascism. However, when the spell breaks, the whole house of cards tumbles down. Just as Huizinga has pointed out (ibid., p. 8), we know that this belief will just hold until we let ourselves overcome with doubt (the spoil-sport is working hard to achieve this). This is precisely why it is so important to play the game with sacred earnest; we know that the possibility of a better world depends on it.

Indeed, acting based on imagined rules has the power to create a world that is potentially better for all of us, and if we do not spoil the sport (ibid., p. 11f.) and work together by engaging in this performance (ibid., p. 23f.) we can create something that is different and maybe better than the world we find ourselves thrown into. Huizinga's idea of culture is rooted in the creative power that emerges from our upholding the illusion of the game in order to create a better world.

> We have gradually become convinced that civilization is rooted in noble play and that, if it is to unfold in full dignity and style, it cannot afford to neglect the play-element. The observance of play-rules is nowhere more imperative than in the relations between countries and States. Once they are broken, society falls into barbarism and chaos. (ibid., p. 210)

This is the closest we can ever get to the creative power of magic as a force that begins in our minds but ends with affecting a

---

[6] "agreements must be kept"

change in the real world – at least if we do not want to succumb to actual superstition.

Conclusion: magic matters

In this paper, we have suggested that the magic circle metaphor, even though it was only used in passing by Huizinga himself, reveals more about Huizinga's concept of play than what is apparent at first glance. It implies an understanding of play as the human ability to imagine counter-factual realities, to believe them to be real in spite of knowing they are just imaginations, to act as if they were real and, in consequence, to affect change in the "real" world; an ability that Huizinga believes to be the root of all culture, and that can be seen as a creative force akin to magic. We have also implied that such an understanding of Huizinga's play concept might be especially relevant for today's game studies discourse, which is usually aware of, but often not very interested in this political dimension.

Wherever play is to be used as a metaphor, a concept, or a lens to approach the ways in which humans deal with, engage in or try to settle conflicts and attempt to find ways of coexistence (i.e., politics), it might be useful to consciously employ the magic circle metaphor with an emphasis on its magical aspects. Not only because it hints at Huizinga's deep-seated conviction that imagining something and committing to this imagination can change the world, but also because insisting on the power of the counter-factual can itself be a defensive stance against the spoil-sports of civilization.

Whenever the seemingly strong and powerful lay their authoritarian claims, create facts, resort to brute force, violent oppression and ruthless destruction, we can be sure that there is no creative might and no true empowerment. In a hopeless zero-sum game, the only freedom that can be gained is the freedom taken from others, and the only thing created is the re-creation of the oldest and dullest of all ideas: the victory of the temporarily strong over the momentarily weak and the displacement of today's victims by today's victors, who now wait to be displaced by the next usurper.

There is little strength in constantly re-creating what has already been a fact. True power (akin to magic) lies in the creation of counterfactual realities, in making real what did not exist before. In defiance of all the horrors humans bring to the world, this is the beauty of humankind. This is the spell that can keep the evil spirits at bay.

References

Apter, M. J. (1989). Reversal theory: Motivation, emotion and personality. Routledge.

Apter, M. J., & Kerr, J. H. (1991). Adult play: A reversal theory approach. Swets & Zeitlinger.

Arsenault, D., & Perron, B. (2009). In the frame of the magic cycle: The circle (s) of gameplay. In The video game theory reader 2 (pp. 131–154). Routledge.

Bateson, G. (1973). Steps to an Ecology of Mind. The Western Political Quarterly, 26(2), 345. https://doi.org/10.2307/446833

Buckland, R. (2002). Buckland's complete book of witchcraft. Llewellyn Worldwide.

Coleridge, S.T., (1884). Biographia Literaria; or, Biographical Sketches of my literary life and opinions; and Two Lay Sermons [1817]. George Bell and Sons, London.

Consalvo, M. (2009). There is no magic circle. Games and Culture, 4(4), 408–417.

Henriot, J. (1969) Le Jeu - Initiation philosophique. Presses Universitaires de France, Paris.

Henriot, J. (1989). Sous couleur de jouer. José Corti, Paris.

Huizinga, J. (1936). In the shadow of tomorrow. Norton & Company.

Huizinga, J. (2002 [1938]). Homo Ludens - A Study of the Play-Element in Culture. Routledge.

Juul, J. (2009). The magic circle and the puzzle piece. In S. Guenzel, J. Juul, & D. Mersch (Eds.), Conference Proceedings of The Philosophy of Computer Games 2008 (pp. 56–67).

Lehdonvirta, V. (2010). Virtual worlds don't exist: Questioning the dichotomous approach in MMO studies. Game Studies, 10(1).

Perron, B. (2013). L'attitude ludique de Jacques Henriot. Sciences Du Jeu, 1.

Pias, C. (2007). Wirklich problematisch. Lernen von "frivolen Gegenständen." In C. Holtorf & C. Pias (Eds.), Escape! Computerspiele als Kulturtechnik (pp. 255–269). Boehlau.

Price, H. H. (1969). Belief: The Gifford Lectures delivered at the University of Aberdeen in 1960 by HH Price. George Allen and Unwin Ltd./Humanities Press.

Salen, K., & Zimmerman, E. (2003). Rules of play: Game design fundamentals. MIT press.

Stratton-Kent, J. (2010). Geosophia: The argo of magic: From the greeks to the grimoires. Scarlet Imprint/Bibliothèque Rouge.

Zimmerman, E. (2012). Jerked around by the magic circle-clearing the air ten years later. Gamasutra - The Art & Business of Making Games. https://www.gamasutra.com/view/feature/6696/jerked_around_by_the_magic_circle_.php

A MAGIC DWELLS IN EACH BEGINNING?

GAME STUDIES, ITS RHETORIC RITUALS AND THE MYTH OF BEING A YOUNG FIELD

Tobias Unterhuber

Looking at game studies publications at large researchers frame themselves and their studies often very similarly: 1) game studies is a young field and a young discipline. 2) The research topic is young as well and underappreciated. 3) This research is the first of its kind. 4) We 'happy few' are the only ones interested in researching games. This rhetorical positioning might have been appropriate in 2001, when Espen Aarseth declared the Year One of game studies (even though there was already a lot of research before). However, it seems rather strange to still uphold these sentiments 20 years later. Especially if you look at the amount of game studies publications which can make the entrance into the field a rather daring endeavour. These declarations might originate in the structure of game studies itself. Game studies is caught in a paradoxical situation. It is a prolific field, but still lacks the appropriate institutionalization and embedding in academic structures. Therefore, the interest in the study of the history of game studies itself is rather underdeveloped, as researchers seem to have to prove their worth repeatedly. Because of this lack of interest, the field lacks a central technique of self-reflexivity and self-evaluation. However, beside these structural problems, there might be a third reason. Keeping the myth of a young field and of being the first in a field alive immunizes research against certain critiques and creates exclusivity and thus game studies' own magic circle.

Keywords: Game Studies, Subject History, Myth, Magic Circle, Discourse

Forever Young?

> *Forever young*
> *I want to be forever young*
>
> - Alphaville

The search for research gaps is understandable. To find something nobody has focussed on before can be exhilarating, offers a specific kind of freedom and has the potential to be a fundamental contribution to a field. It seems that the drive to search for new aspects might be universal for academia in general. But game studies has a particular relation to this eagerness to find something new: It wants to be new itself. As anecdotal evidence, I heard a student say only recently during their thesis defense that video games and game studies are still young and that games research is still in its fledgling stage. These are statements we can hear and read in game studies almost every day. (Raessens, 2006, p. 56; Järvinen, 2008, p. 15; Mäyrä, 2008, p. 4; Egenfeldt-Nielsen et. al., 2013, p. 4; Quant et. al, 2015; Mukherjee & Lundedal Hammar, 2018, p. 1; Nguyen, 2021) I want to elaborate why we repeat these statements time and time again.

But first I have to note that this is not a way to oust colleagues. What I want to describe and talk about is something we all – as game scholars – do or at least have done. We position ourselves and our research as well as games research in general as some kind of pioneer work. It is an insight Magdalena Leichter formulated in an essay where she describes how it feels to start out as a young games researcher today:[1]

> Although it is often emphasized that it is a young discipline, my early involvement with game studies oscillated between challenge and curiosity, between the impression of being able to contribute ideas and the realization that much that was supposedly new had already been explored and formulated

---

[1] All translations from German texts are my own.

more precisely than in my own imagination. As a student / junior researcher, a subject does not feel very young at first either, when you can look back on a solid twenty years of relevant inter- and multidisciplinary research. (Leichter, 2021)

And she is right. There is a prevalent way of framing research on games that follows along the following lines:

* Game studies is a young field and a young discipline.

* The research topic is young as well as underappreciated.

* This research is the first of its kind.

* We 'happy few' are the only ones interested in researching games.

But as Magdalena Leichter points out: Can we really say that game studies is a young discipline?[2] Twenty years ago, Espen Aarseth declared the year one of game studies. He states:

> 2001 can be seen as the Year One of Computer Game Studies as an emerging, viable, international, academic field. This year has seen the first international scholarly conference on computer games, in Copenhagen in March, and several others will follow. 01-02 may also be the academic year when regular graduate programs in computer game studies are offered for the first time in universities. And it might be the first time scholars and academics take computer games seriously, as a cultural field whose value is hard to overestimate. (Aarseth, 2001)

The rhetoric is clear. Year one, first conference, the first graduate program, the first time games are taken seriously. The whole point of Aarseth's text is to establish a field by declaring it (Unterhuber, 2022). It is a performative and formative act, or to be more specific: it is a perlocutionary gesture. By declaring it, Aarseth creates the "New Discipline" (2001). Understanding this

---

[2] Compared to established and 'older' disciplines with institutional legitimacy (e.g. literature, history, etc.) game studies are indeed quite young. This chapter, however, focuses on the self-image of game studies and its consequences, not on the actual age of the discipline.

declaration in its rhetorical dimension helps to recognise that it is actual an empty gesture (Žižek, 2013, p. 23) and not founded in facts. The only thing new about it is the declaration and the naming of the discipline. There has been games research way before 2001, for instance Janet Murray's *Hamlet on the Holodeck* (1997), but there are even earlier examples such as Mary-Ann Buckle's dissertation on *Adventure* from 1985. Aarseth ignores all that in the name of his rhetorical play. As he claims, "they", meaning researchers from other disciplines, "did have thirty years in which they did nothing" (Aarseth, 2001). That he makes the contribution of others, especially women, invisible is of note here. Janet Murray states that this might have been the groundwork for the exclusion of feminist games criticism in broader games culture as well (2017, p. 193).

Hence, even in 2001, the "newness" of games research is heavily debatable. So, why do we still use this rhetoric as of today? I argue that the framing of game studies as a young field can be understood in two directions:

1. A rhetoric ritual and part of the discipline of the field

2. A myth(os) of game studies

The Game of Discipline

The statement in question can be understood as a rhetoric ritual and thus as a part of game studies' discipline. Discipline is a central term in Michel Foucault's early discourse analysis and part of the procedure of controlling and delimiting discourses.[3] While the production of discourses deploys different procedures, most of them are concerned with who can say what about what in what way. (Foucault 1981, p. 52). Discipline is one of the principles of this limitation. Foucault states:

> [A] discipline is defined by a domain of objects, a set of meth-
> ods, a corpus of propositions considered to be true, a play of

---

[3] While Foucault later used the term discipline to describe a new form of power "that radically differs from 'sovereign power'" (Havis, 2014, p. 111), I use the term the way it is used in his inaugural lecture *The Order of Discourse*.

> rules and definitions, of techniques and instruments: all this constitutes a sort of anonymous system at the disposal of anyone who wants to or is able to use it. (ibid, p. 59)

Foucault goes on, that this plethora of components, as varying as they may be, are all "requisites for the construction of new statements. For there to be a discourse, there must be the possibility of formulating new propositions, ad infinitum". (ibid.) Thus, you have to comply with the discipline to be part of a discourse. Therefore, the utterance must not necessarily be true. It does not even have to adhere to "some principle of coherence or systematicity." (ibid, p. 59f.). It only must comply with the rules in play.

> In short, a proposition must fulfil complex and heavy requirements to be able to belong to the grouping of a discipline; before it can be called true or false, it must be 'in the true', as Cunguilhem would say. (ibid, p. 60)

If we follow this approach, the framing of 'youngness' and 'newness' is not a statement that actually describes games research. It has become an entrance ritual for any utterance to count as part of game studies. It has become a rule, which one has to follow to be part of the game studies discourse. Or, to phrase it more cautiously: It helps propositions and thus researchers to be counted as part of the discourse, to be part of the game.

This might be an explanation for how this framing became ritualized, but it does not explain why. It seems rather contingent at first. Every field, every discourse might have such rituals – may they be implicit or explicit – but why do game studies follow exactly this framing? As often, I see the reason in the structure of game studies itself, in its rather paradoxical situation:

1. Game studies is a prolific field, but it still lacks the appropriate institutionalization and embedding in academic structures.

2. There is also lacking interest in the history of game studies, in the sense of subject history (*Fachgeschichte*), within the field itself (Hennig & Krah, 2021).

Ad 1) Even though Aarseth said that the first study programs started in 2001, game studies study programs are still rather few and far between (even more so for bachelor programs than master programs).[4] The same is true for departments and institutes. In German-speaking countries, the situation looks especially dire (Matuszkiewicz, 2021). Additionally, funding of research projects is also quite difficult. The situation might have improved a little over the last twenty years, but the dream Aarseth had in 2001 remains unrealized. He admits so himself when he states that one of the main goals of the journal *Game Studies* to this day is "to make the field visible and appear established" (Aarseth, 2021). Not being acknowledged as its own discipline on an institutional level might not always be bad, as games research fits rather well in a broader media culture studies (*medienkulturwissenschaftlichen*) approach. However, this unacknowledged status still informs the positioning of the research itself by forcing researchers to repeatedly prove and justify the worth of games research. More often than not, the question is still not how or what to research about games, but whether to research them at all. Emphasizing the pioneering one could supposedly do in the field thus can be a way to address these concerns or turn them into their opposite. Furthermore, it also follows the market logic of research funding, which prioritises research described as excellent and ground-breaking, albeit with mixed results, as projects on games are often deemed to be "on the fringe". This focus on newness has other consequences as well.

Ad 2) Except for the spectre of the ludology versus narratology debate (Unterhuber, 2022) we seldom talk about or study our own discipline's history. Even if we use 'older' sources, we rarely contextualize them in the broader study of games and play, whether it be analogue or digital, and what is more we don't contextualize games research in the development of academia and research in general. Thus, game studies lacks one of the central techniques of self-reflexivity and self-evaluation of academic

---

[4] It has to be noted that this does not apply to Game Design and Game Development programs, which seem to thrive in recent years.

disciplines. Subject history is imperative as it allows to observe connections, traditions and divergences over time or to make them even observable in the first place.[5] Thinking of games research as being without history renders it impossible to see what research already happened and to contextualize our own research. It removes diachronicity and preserves everything in a vague synchronicity. It also isolates games research from its material, institutional, discoursive, disciplinary and historical premises, thus decontextualizing the field in its entirety. Therefore, it gets harder to recognize that the structural problems of game studies are connected to the development of academia in general. We are, in fact, not an island. For instance, game studies are not the first or only field, which faced or faces delegitimization For example, the emergence of film studies had similar problems as films were not counted as high culture artefacts and thus worthy of academic study (Quendler, 2011). Or, to present more recent examples: To this day, or even especially today, gender studies and critical race theory face delegitimization out of ideological reasons even through legislation in Hungary (Kováts, 2020, p. 76) and the United States (Schwartz, 2022).

So much for the statement "game studies is a young field" as a rhetoric ritual and as part of the discipline of the field. However, the statement can also be interpreted differently: As a myth of and about the field.

Mythic Youth

Game studies is a young field. At first glance, it might look like this statement meant nothing more than that, compared to other fields like literary studies or even media studies, game studies only have a rather short history. However, there is more to it, especially as we have been repeating this statement for more than twenty years. Roland Barthes' concept of mythos or myth might help us here.

---

[5] As much as the debate about the constant crisis of literary and especially German studies might seem problematic or even as a form of self-chastisement, it is an example how the self-critical perspective of a discipline can be a productive way to reevaluate and reinvigorate a discipline (Jahraus, 2004, p. 13).

Barthes writes: "[M]yth is a system of communication, that it is a message." (1991, p. 107) Based on Ferdinand de Saussure's theory of signs, Barthes proposes that mythic speech attaches itself to existing signs.

> But myth is a peculiar system, in that it is constructed from a semiological chain which existed before it: it is a second-order semiological system. That which is a sign (namely the associative total of a concept and an image) in the first system, becomes a mere signifier in the second. (ibid, p. 113)

Thus, the sign "game studies is a young field" can be the signifier for something different which erases the signified of the original sign. It becomes an empty sign but through its ritualized and repeated use, another meaning seems to shine through. Without getting further into the specifics of Barthes' semiology, we can already see how myths "corrupt" or at least occupy speech. What seems important here is the intention of speech:

> We now know that myth is a type of speech defined by its intention [...] much more than by its literal sense [...]; and that in spite of this, its intention is somehow frozen, purified, eternalized, made absent by this literal sense [...] This constituent ambiguity of mythical speech has two consequences for the signification, which henceforth appears both like a notification and like a statement of fact. (ibid, p. 122f.)

The mythic speech thus makes itself ahistorical and its intention, its motive turns into something else:

> We reach here the very principle of myth: it transforms history into nature. We now understand why, in the eyes of the myth-consumer, the intention, the adhomination of the concept can remain manifest without however appearing to have an interest in the matter: what causes mythical speech to be uttered is perfectly explicit, but it is immediately frozen into something natural; it is not read as a motive, but as a reason. (ibid, p. 128)

To declare something natural instead of historically and socially constructed is the opposite of the cultural studies paradigm (Culler, 2001, p. 4f.) most of game studies adheres to.

But this opposition does not seem to extend to its self-conception where we have created an omnipresent blind spot (Jahraus, 2001, p. 321). Because if we come back to the exemplary statement at hand, what does its myth actually say? Game studies stays a young field. The study of games is eternally connected to youth and newness, and it has no history. Thus, the sentence is true in 2001 and in 2021 and, if we do not change the game, it will be true in 2041. It works more like a magical spell than a statement. This is the power of ritualized myth. It is the power of sociocultural construction on repeat. Production and reproduction. If we don't change the discipline of our field, if we don't stop to repeat the phrase ad infinitum, we enclose game studies in its very own Peter Pan syndrome. The best countermeasure is a united effort towards subject history, or even broader: the historicization of games research. Otherwise, we not only endanger games research, but ourselves, too, because the situation is even more calamitous if we connect the statement to its producers: us as game researchers. We claim to be the perpetual first and thus immunize our research against certain critiques; because if we are the first and the field is young, who could be able to criticize us? We as a field are still at our beginning; problems are thus natural and not really our fault. Of course, this stands diametrically opposed to the desired recognition game studies seeks and leads to an outside perception of games researchers as an extension of game culture (Vossen, 2018, p. 214) rather than an academic discipline (Gekker, 2020). In fact, this self-conception harmonizes quite well with the discoursive rules and practices of games culture which also favours newness above all else (Unterhuber, 2020). Moreover – and as stated before –, it makes all the work that has been done before invisible or marginalizes it. This leads to another consequence: game studies' self-image as a separated and exclusive field.

Magic Circles

The myth of the pioneers creates exclusivity. Combined with the *us versus them* rhetoric that games research is underappreciated and nobody else is interested in it (something which might have been partially true 20 years ago, but certainly not today), this exclusivity contributes to game studies closing itself off[6]. The happy few as pioneers in a young field is the self-proclaimed image of game studies. Ironically, games research already has a concept to describe such a constellation: Johan Huizinga's magic circle. Huizinga describes that play is not only limited on a temporal level, even "[m]ore striking [...] is the limitation [...] to space. All play moves and has its being within a playground marked off beforehand either materially or ideally, deliberately or as a matter of course." (1949, p. 20) Here, Huizinga again describes play and ritual as indistinguishable because "the 'consecrated spot' cannot be formally distinguished from the play-ground". (ibid.) Whatever form spaces of ritual or play take:

> All are temporary worlds within the ordinary world, dedicated to the performance of an act apart. Formally speaking, there is no distinction whatever between marking out a space for a sacred purpose and marking it out for purposes of sheer play. The turf, the tennis-court, the chess-board and pavement-hopscotch cannot formally be distinguished from the temple or the magic circle. (ibid.)

This spatiality of games and play secludes them from the rest of the world, but as Huizinga points out, it also constitutes order:

> Inside the play-ground an absolute and peculiar order reigns. Here we come across another, very positive feature of play: it creates order, is order. Into an imperfect world and into the confusion of life it brings a temporary, a limited perfection. (ibid, p. 10)

This order has to be accepted just like the discipline of a discourse. It is not a coincidence that Foucault writes that "discourse is no more than a play" (1981, p. 66) and that to adhere

---

[6] Unfortunately, the growing acceptance of games research cannot prevent that, due to the lack of institutionalization of game studies, scholars are often spread across many disciplines and thus quickly feel isolated within their home institutions. Consequently, they are interested in finding places and groups outside the institutional structures of their universities that share their interests and offer them a sense of belonging. Although this motivation is more than understandable, it nevertheless brings with it the negative consequences described here.

to discipline means "to join the game" (Degeling, 2017, p. 109)[7] or to be part of a "provisional theatre" (Foucault, 1981, p. 52; Degeling, 2017, p. 107). For Huizinga, the order play creates makes it necessary to focus on the players who do not comply with it. Thus, he differentiates between the spoil-sport and the cheat:

> The player who trespasses against the rules or ignores them is a "spoil-sport". The spoil-sport is not the same as the false player, the cheat; for the latter pretends to be playing the game and, on the face of it, still acknowledges the magic circle. It is curious to note how much more lenient society is to the cheat than to the spoil-sport. This is because the spoil-sport shatters the play-world itself. (Huizinga, 1949, p. 11)

Therefore, as long as you accept that the rules of play exist even though you break them, you are part of the magic circle. However, if you question the rules of play or play itself, you endanger it and thus become excluded. Thus, Huizinga shows that the magic circle has not just an inside but also an outside. He clarifies that the magic circle with its inclusion/exclusion-difference, forms communities:

> A play-community generally tends to become permanent even after the game is over. Of course, not every game of marbles or every bridge-party leads to the founding of a club. But the feeling of being "apart together" in an exceptional situation, of sharing something important, of mutually withdrawing from the rest of the world and rejecting the usual norms, retains its magic beyond the duration of the individual game. The club pertains to play as the hat to the head. (ibid, p. 12)

This is what the myth of researchers as pioneers does. It creates a community through ritual, discipline and myth. However, this community is dependent on exclusion: All the researchers who came before, all who do not ascribe to the same self-image of game studies and all the people, especially students and young researchers, who are interested in games research but who are

---

[7] The central but often overlooked position of play and game in Foucault's writing (Degeling, 2017, p. 103), might not be a coincidence. Knut Ebeling (2014) showed how Huizinga's ideas were widely distributed in France by Georges Bataille, who might have influenced Foucault.

not part of the in-group. Through this lens, the ludology versus narratology debate (Philipps, 2020) as well as all the problems and failed attempts to stabilize the structures of games research appear in a new light. How can game studies hope to change or become institutionalized if it shuts itself off like this, if it denies or forgets its own history and with it the people who built the foundation we stand upon? In addition, how can we shape game studies into an open and diverse field if exclusion is one of its central characteristics?

This brings me to the end and my conclusion: the self-ascribed youngness and newness of game studies has dire consequences. On the one hand, it contributes to its structural problems, making it difficult to establish game studies as a discipline. On the other hand, and at the expense of marginalized researchers, it creates exclusivity and thus game studies' own magic circle, or if I may: magic circle jerk.

References

Aarseth, E. (2001). Computer Game Studies, Year One. Game Studies 1 (1). http://gamestudies.org/0101/editorial.html.

Aarseth, E. (2021). Two Decades of Game Studies. Game Studies 21 (1). http://gamestudies.org/2101/articles/aarseth_anniversary.

Barthes, R. (1991). Mythologies. New York: The Noonday Press.

Buckles, M. A. (1985). Interactive Fiction: The Computer Storygame "Adventure" [Doctoral Dissertation, University of San Diego]. https://archive.org/details/maryannbuckles.

Culler, J. (2001). Literary Theory. A Very Short Introduction. Oxford: Oxford University Press.

Degeling, J. (2017). Über die Rhetorik des Spiels bei Michel Foucault. In A. Deuber-Mankowsky & R. Görling (Eds.). Denkweisen des Spiels. Medienphilosophische Annäherungen (103-118). Wien, Berlin: Verlag Turia + Kant.

Ebeling, K. (2014). Nachwort. In K. Ebeling (Ed.). Johan Huizinga. Das Spielelement der Kultur. Spieltheorien nach Johan Huizinga von Georges Bataille, Roge Caillois und Eric Voegelin (pp. 112-152). Berlin: Matthes & Seitz.

Egenfeldt-Nielsen, S. et. al. (2013). Understanding Video Games. The Essential Introduction. New York & London: Routledge.

Foucault, M. (1981). The Order of Discourse. In: R. Young (Ed.), Untying the Text. A Post-Structuralist Reader (pp. 51-78). Boston: Routledge & Kegan Paul.

Gekker, A. (2020). Against Game Studies. Media and Communication, 9 (1), pp. 73-83, https://doi.org/10.17645/mac.v9i1.3315.

Havis, N. (2014). Discipline. In L. Lawlor & J. Nale (Eds.), The Cambridge Foucault Lexicon (pp. 110-119). Cambridge: Cambridge University Press. doi:10.1017/CBO9781139022309.023.

Hennig, M. & Krah, H. (2021). Spielzeichen – eine Bilanz. PAIDIA – Zeitschrift für Computerspielforschung. https://www.paidia.de/spielzeichen-eine-bilanz/.

Huizinga, J. (1949). Homo Ludens. A Study of the Play-Element in Culture. London: Routledge & Kegan Paul.

Järvinen, A. (2008). Games without Frontiers. Theories and Methods for Game Studies and Design. [Doctoral Dissertation, University of Tampere]. https://trepo.tuni.fi/bitstream/handle/10024/67820/978-951-44-7252-7.pdf.

Jahraus, O. (2001). Zur Systemtheorie Niklas Luhmanns. In O. Jahraus (Ed.). Niklas Luhmann: Reden und Aufsätze (pp. 299-334). Stuttgart: Reclam.

Jahraus, O. (2004). Literaturtheorie. Theoretische und methodische Grundlagen der Literaturwissenschaft. Tübingen, Basel: A. Francke.

Kováts, E. (2020). Post-Socialist Conditions and the Orbán Government's Gender Politics between 2010 and 2019 in Hungary. In G. Dietze & J. Roth (Eds.). Right-Wing Populism and Gender. European Perspectives and Beyond (pp. 75-99). Bielefeld: transcript.

Leichter, M. (2021). Später ins Spiel kommen. Oder: Eine Perspektive auf ca. drei Jahre Game Studies. PAIDIA – Zeitschrift für Computerspielforschung. https://www.paidia.de/spaeter-ins-spiel-kommen-oder-eine-perspektive-auf-ca-drei-jahre-game-studies/.

Matuszkiewicz, K. (2021). 10 Years Later – Beobachtungen zur Entwicklung der Game Studies als Fach in Deutschland. PAIDIA – Zeitschrift für Computerspielforschung. https://www.paidia.de/10-years-later-beobachtungen-zur-entwicklung-der-game-studies-als-fach-in-deutschland/.

Mäyrä, F. (2008). An Introduction to Game Studies. Games in Culture. London et. al.: Sage.

Mukherjee, S. & Lundedal Hammar, E. (2018). Introduction to the Special Issue on Postcolonial Perspectives in Game Studies. Open Library of Humanities 4(2), pp. 1-13. https://doi.org/10.16995/olh.309.

Murray, J. (1997). Hamlet on the Holodeck. The Future of Narrative in Cyberspace. Cambridge, MA: MIT Press.

Murray, J. (2017). Hamlet on the Holodeck. The Future of Narrative in Cyberspace. Cambridge, MA, London: MIT Press.

Nguyen, A. (2021). Ein ‚Gamer' an der Universität und in der Wissenschaft: Vom Studium zur Videospielforschung. PAIDIA – Zeitschrift für Computerspielforschung. https://www.paidia.de/ein-gamer-an-der-universitaet-und-in-der-wissenschaft-vom-studium-zur-videospielforschung/.

Phillips, A. (2020). Negg(at)ing the Game Studies Subject: An Affective History of the Field, Feminist Media Histories 6 (1), pp. 12–36, https://doi.org/10.1525/fmh.2020.6.1.12.

Quant, T. et. al. (2015). Digital Games Research: A Survey Study on an Emerging Field and Its Prevalent Debates. Journal of Communication 65 (6), 975-996. https://doi.org/10.1111/jcom.12182.

Quendler, C. (2011). Musing by Numbers: Couting the Arts in the Age of Film. In P. Bianchi, G. Bursi & S. Venturini (Eds.), il canone cinematografico/ the film canon (pp. 117-123). Udine: FilmForum.

Raessens, J. (2006). Playful Identities, or the Ludification of Culture. Games and Culture 1 (1), 52-57. https://doi.org/10.1177/1555412005281779.

Schwartz, S. (2022). Map: Where Critical Race Theory Is Under Attack. Education Week. https://www.edweek.org/policy-politics/map-where-critical-race-theory-is-under-attack/2021/06.

Unterhuber, T (2022). Of Parents and Siblings, Disciplines and Debates – Game Studies as Media Culture Studies and the Possibility of Schools of Thoughts. In C. Mejeur, A. Karabinus, C. Kocurek & E. Vossen (Eds.), Historiographies of Game Studies: What it Has Been, What it Could Be. Santa Barbara: Punctum Books (in preperation).

Unterhuber, T. (2020). Mit Kanones auf Spiele schießen? – Die (Un)Möglichkeit eines Computerspielkanons und die Rolle der Game Studies. PAIDIA – Zeitschrift für Computerspielforschung. https://www.paidia.de/mit-kanones-auf-spiele-schiessen-die-unmoeglichkeit-eines-computerspielkanons-und-die-rolle-der-game-studies/.

Vossen, E. (2018). On the Cultural Inaccessibility of Gaming: Invading, Creating, and Reclaiming the Cultural Clubhouse. [Doctoral Dissertation, University of Waterloo]. https://uwspace.uwaterloo.ca/handle/10012/13649.

Žižek, S. (2013). Lacan – Eine Einführung. Frankfurt a. M.: Fischer.

authors

IVO ANTUNIC has a Bachelor's degree in architecture and is a student of Game Studies since 2021. He has crowdfunded the board game "World Control" in 2016 and has released it as an independent publisher in 2017. He is currently a Serious Game Designer at the logistics-company RailCargo.

https://www.world-control.net

JOSEPHINE BAIRD is a Lecturer at Uppsala University's Department of Game Design and a Ph.D. candidate at the University of Vienna. She is a game designer and game design consultant, as well as a writer and visual artist. Her work often relates the intersection between games, identity, gender, and sexualities. She is also an actor, public speaker, and co-host of the podcast It Is Complicated.

https://www.josephinebaird.com

SARAH LYNNE BOWMAN is a scholar, game designer, and event organizer. She is an Associate Professor for the Department of Game Design at Uppsala University Campus Gotland and the Coordinator for Peace & Conflict Studies at Austin Community College. McFarland Press published her dissertation as The Functions of Role-playing Games: How Participants Create Community, Solve Problems, and Explore Identity (2010). Bowman has edited for The Wyrd Con Companion Book (2012-2015), the International Journal of Role-playing (2016-), and Nordiclarp.org (2015-). She helped organize the Living Games Conference (2014, 2016, 2018) and Role-playing and Simulation in Education Conference (2016, 2018).

http://www.sarahlynnebowman.com

NATALIE DENK has Master's degrees in Educational Science and Game Studies. Her research focuses on Game-based Education, Educational Game Design, and the gender dimension of digital gaming culture. Since 2014 she has been involved in several national and international research projects at University of Krems' Center for Applied Game Studies, acting as Head of Center since July 2019.

Twitter: @Natalie_Denk

SONJA GABRIEL has been working at University Teacher College Vienna/Krems (Austria) since 2011, in 2017 she was appointed professor for media literacy. She teaches, researches and publishes on topics like digital game-based learning and gamification as well as using digital media for learning and teaching, information literacy, social presence in online environments and the consequences of Covid-19 measures at universities on teaching and learning. She has already been involved in national and international projects.

DAMIANO GERLI is a gaming historian and journalist and has a Laurea Magistralis in Negotiation Sciences. His research focuses on software houses from all over the world, with a particular focus on researching cancelled projects and lesser known games. Since 2019 he has been involved in documenting the history of the Italian gaming industry through the years and publishing articles and essays on the subject.

Twitter: @damgentemp

ANDREAS GRUBER studied educational science at the University of Vienna and worked in a social pedagogical community with children and teenagers for the last years. Meanwhile he works in a crisis center of the city of Vienna. He had his first gaming experiences in elementary school with Gameboy and Nintendo alongside Super Mario. In the meantime, he plays first-person shooters like Rainbow Six Siege as well as action-adventure and smaller indie titles on the PS5. His favorite games of the last few years include Death Stranding, TLOU2, RDR2 or Ghost of Tsushima.

Instagram: @last_petrus

BENJAMIN HANUSSEK is a researcher, lecturer and developer in game studies and design. He has worked in and with different institutions, including Teachers College at Columbia University and the University of Klagenfurt. He is currently pursuing the roles of lecturer and research advisor at the Polish-Japanese Academy of Information Technology in Warsaw, Poland. When writing this paper he was working as a teaching assistant at the Klagenfurt Critical Game Lab.

https://bhanussek.com

KJELL HEDGARD HUGAAS is a Northern Norwegian game designer, organizer, writer, theorist, and trained actor. He has engaged in the Nordic larp community for about two decades. Hugaas has theorized how ideas impact players through the process of memetic bleed, and how the physicality of play does the same through the process of procedural bleed. Lately he has, in close collaboration with Sarah Lynne Bowman, explored the transformative potential of games, and proposed specific game design practices that facilitate transformative effects. He currently works as a Research Assistant at Uppsala University, where he is getting his MA in Game Design.

ALEXIS IBARRA IBARRA holds a BA in International Relations by the Mexico's Autonomous Institute of Technology. She holds a MA in Communication oriented to New Media and Global Processes by the National Autonomous University of Mexico, where she specialized in videogames and hermeneutics. Currently, she is a student at the Erasmus Mundus Joint Master's Degree in Media Arts Cultures Programme and is preparing to become a videogame curator. This year, she assisted ZKM | Zentrum für Kunst und Medien Karlsruhe's curatorial team with the reopening of the videogame exhibition "gameplay. the next level". Alexis is also an artist and writer.

NIKOLAUS KOENIG is a game and media scholar with a background in communication studies and constructivist theory. He currently works as a researcher and lecturer at the University of Krems' Center for Applied Game Studies, where he is concerned with games and play theory, media ethics, and serious game design. His research interests revolve around the recursive construction of cultural ideas and mediated meaning, on the relation between interactive media experiences and the systemic nature of human cognition and its effects on social discourse and democracy, as well as mediated human experience in all its forms.

ATEFE NAJJAR MANSOOR has a bachelor's degree in English Language Translation. She is an independent researcher, and her research focuses on videogames and ideology.

Twitter: @AtefeNJ95

KATARZYNA MARAK is an Associate Professor in the Department of Cultural Studies at Nicolaus Copernicus University in Torun, Poland; she is the author of Japanese and American Horror: A Comparative Study of Film, Fiction, Graphic Novels and Video Games and the co-author of the monograph Gameplay, Emotions and Narrative: Independent Games Experienced, as well as a number of papers and chapters about independent games, game mechanics, player experience, the storytelling aspects of games. Her research interests concern game studies, with particular emphasis on independent game texts, and horror fiction.

Email: kmarak@umk.pl

MIŁOSZ MARKOCKI is an Associate Professor in the Institute of Social Communication and Media at Kazimierz Wielki University in Bydgoszcz, Poland; whose expertise and research concerns fantasy fiction and online gaming (especially massively multiplayer online role-playing games), as well as the related communities. He is the co-author of the monograph Gameplay, Emotions and Narrative: Independent Games Experienced, as well as several peer-reviewed journal articles about online gaming and machinima videos. He is also the author of book chapters concerning game mechanics, storytelling, and various aspects of gameworld design (including cultural framework features), as well as online player communities and related culture.

Email: markocki@ukw.edu.pl

MARKUS MESCHIK holds a doctorate in social pedagogy. His research interests include the use of digital media by adolescents and the associated youth cultures. He is a lecturer at the Universities of Graz and Klagenfurt as well as at the University of Applied Sciences Linz. With the counseling center enter in Graz, he accompanies and advises parents and their children on the topic of problematic media use.

https://www.fachstelle-enter.at

HOSSEIN MOHAMMADZADE has a master's degree in English Language and Literature. He is currently an independent researcher, and he studies television and videogames. His main area of interest is the relationship between ideology, narrative, and videogames.

*Twitter: @H_Mohammadzade_*

CLIO MONTREY is a musician, writer, and gamedev who weaves imaginary worlds out of words and sound. Her genre-defying creative works blur the borders between folk, classical, electronica, and science fiction.

ALEXANDER PFEIFFER is currently working as a senior researcher at the center for applied game studies at Donau-Universität Krems, Austria. He is a recipient of a Max Kade Fellowship awarded by the Austrian Academy of Science to work at the MIT Education Arcade, USA from 2019-2021.

https://www.alexpfeiffer.at

ANDREW "ANDY" PHELPS is an artist, designer, and professor at the Human Interface Technology Laboratory NZ, and the Programme Manager of the Digital Screen Campus, at the University of Canterbury in Christchurch, New Zealand. He is also a professor in the School of Communication, holds a joint appointment in Computer Science, and is the director of the AU

Game Center at American University in Washington DC, USA. His latest games are The Witch's Way (Itch.io, 2021) and Fragile Equilibrium (XBOX, Steam, Itch.io 2019), and he maintains a website of his publications, popular writing, artwork, curriculum development, and more at andyworld.io.

Social: @andymphelps

FRANK POURVOYEUR is an independent game developer and artist. His research interest is in games that are beneficial for the individual consciousness of players and the positive aspects of cooperative experiences. His research aims to make gaming more enjoyable while also allowing for deeper revelations about one's personal awareness. He graduated from the Danube University in Krems in 2020 with a degree in game studies.

CHRISTIN REISENHOFER is a university assistant (prae doc) at the unit of Psychoanalysis and Education at the department of Education (University of Vienna). Her focus is on early childhood, young child observation as a research method and game studies from an educational and psychoanalytic perspective. She is a psychoanalytic-pedagogical educational consultant (APP Vienna) and child's assistant in court proceedings. Her favorite games are Child of Light and The Legend of Zelda: Ocarina of Time.

Facebook: @christin.rei.1

DORIS C. RUSCH is a professor of game design at Uppsala University. Her work focuses on transformative play to facilitate personal insight and development in self-directed and un-coerced ways. She is the author of "Making Deep Games - Designing Games with Meaning and Purpose" and various publications together with Andy Phelps on the existential transformative game design framework. Her award-winning games have been shown in juried festivals and showcases from Tokyo Game Show to Meaningful Play, FDG, Indiecade and the Smithsonian.

ALEXANDER SEEWALD has been working in the research area of Machine Learning and Artificial Intelligence since 2000, and in the area of Image Analysis/ Pattern Recognition since 2004. He has processed various data using self-developed or modified learning algorithms, e.g. spam e-mails, handwritten numbers, biological research papers, EEG data, binary TCP/IP data packets, image, audio and video data and depth sensor data.

https://www.seewald.at

GABRIELLE TRÉPANIER-JOBIN is a Professor in Game Studies at the School of Media of Université du Québec à Montréal and the Co-Director of the research group Homo Ludens. She holds a PhD in Communication Studies from Université du Québec à Montréal. Her PhD thesis explores the possibility of using parodies as playful means to denaturalize gender stereotypes. During her postdoctoral fellowship at MIT Comparative Media Studies | Writing, she pursued her work on gender parody in the field of game studies. She is currently conducting research on player immersion, on equality, diversity and inclusion in the video game industry, as well as on the potential of video and board games to raise awareness about social and environmental issues.

TOM TUCEK is currently graduating with a Master's degree in Game Studies and Engineering from the University of Klagenfurt. With a background in both computer science and Japanese studies, he tries to bridge the gap between sciences and humanities through videogames. His current research topics are instrumentalized morality in videogames, affective game design, and microtransactions.

Social: @Yen_Rye

TOBIAS UNTERHUBER studied modern German literature, comparative literature and study of religion at LMU Munich and at the University of California, Berkeley. In 2018, he earned his PhD with his thesis on the works of Swiss author Christian Kracht. He is a post-doc for literature and media studies at the Leopold-Franzens University Innsbruck. Research interests: pop literature, literary theory, discourse analysis, literature & economics, gender studies, media history, video game research in the field of cultural studies. He is an editor of the game studies journal PAIDIA and the Zeitschrift für Fantastikforschung.

Twitter: @letobili

THOMAS WERNBACHER is a media psychologist and works at the University of Krems' Center for Applied Game Studies. In his work, he investigates the use and effects of game-based approaches in the context of mobility, education, and health. His expertise includes concepts of behavior theory in the form of gamification and nudging with a special focus on incentive models. The current focus of his research activities is on the communication and mediation of sustainable development goals in conjunction with emergent technologies.